Some noteworthy comments about THE SOUL AFIRE:

"No one is likely to become a mystic merely by reading this collection . . . but we hope our readers will come to an awareness of the beauty and loftiness of the narrow and steep path, and feel stimulated to make some of these texts their favorite contemplative reading."

H. A. Reinhold

"The present volume is not a discussion of mysticism but an anthology of selections (in length, from detached sentences to passages of three or four pages) from the writings of persons who may be called mystics, or, in a few cases, of those who report the mystics' accounts of their own experiences or an observer's description. For the student of mysticism, whether credulous or critical, this is an invaluable source book."

Christian Century

"The best compilation available of mystical writings. [Reinhold] starts with the pre-Christian Greeks, giving with them one excerpt from Indian literature, and then covers the whole range of Christian mystical writing admirably."

Liturgical Arts

"This will appeal not only to mystics, but to all seeking souls, Catholic and Protestant."

Virginia Kirkus Service

"The editor has done an excellent piece of work. It is the best book of its kind in English."

Catholic World

THE SOUL AFIRE
Revelations of the Mystics

EDITED BY H. A. REINHOLD

IMAGE BOOKS
A Division of Doubleday & Company, Inc.
Garden City, New York

Image Books edition 1973
by special arrangement with Pantheon Books
Image Books edition published February 1973

Dedicated to

JACQUES MARITAIN

CONTENTS

II

ALL THINGS ARE BUT LOSS

DETACHMENT

A BROKEN HEART THOU WILT NOT DESPISE

THE FLESH, ERROR AND SIN

III
APPREHENDED BY JESUS CHRIST

THE MYSTICAL BODY

THE NEW CREATION: OUR CONVERSATION IS IN HEAVEN

THE TWO WAYS: MARTHA AND MARY

EUCHARISTIA

IV

THE CLOUD OF UNKNOWING

THE WOUNDED HEART

THE BRIDE

ECSTASIS: WORDS NO MAN CAN UTTER

SOBRIA EBRIETAS: THE GREAT SILENCE

THE LOVING GAZE

CONCLUSION

INTO PARADISE

THE EXCELLENCE OF THE KNOWLEDGE OF OUR LORD

THE CHANGING OF OUR VILE BODY

*The version used for quotations from the New Testament
is the Knox translation from the Vulgate. Various versions
have been used for the Old Testament quotations.*

INTRODUCTION

This book is not, as might be expected, a mere collection of mystical texts, an anthology. A number of texts in it are not mystical in the strict sense. Nor does the book follow the customary pattern of mystic progress through the three stages of purification, illumination and union. Those who desire a learned and correct treatise in the ways and methods of mysticism will have to turn to the scholarly works of experts such as Poulain, Underhill, von Hügel and Brémond, or better yet, to the sources themselves. The drawback of these works, however, is that they are either too esoteric or too abstract to make our contemporaries stop and listen. And of the few excellent anthologies of mysticism, none gives us mysticism as the result of a development—as the end of a long road which we have not yet traveled. For the most part they take us in one large leap across the tedious and laborious approaches into the very middle of the sanctuary, where we are blinded by such intensity of light that we are unable to see any connection between this realm and the life of common men and women; we become uneasy, we are no longer at home.

To keep clear of these difficulties in the approach to mystical thought and experience we have included in this collection a number of texts which, while not in themselves mystical, help to prepare the mind for truly mystical writings. So, for instance, neither prayer nor poetry is in itself mystical, but if degrees are at all accept-

able to us, we have to admit that the poems of Gerard
Manley Hopkins are a better approach to the understanding of Augustine's or Teresa's message than some compe-
tent treatise taken from a theological textbook. Correct
theology is of course the basis of orthodox mysticism, and
a mystic whose life is a contradiction to the law of the
Church will be regarded as a fraud, yet scholarly discussion of these problems has not as much to do with
mystical experience as Francis' canticle to Brother Sun,
even if it does not treat of God's attributes and moral
perfection, but of created and visible things, like the sun,
the water, the birds. However, we must keep in mind that
all Christian mystic experience rises above the purely
natural mysticism, which begins with an experience of
elation in nature, and that its aim and content are not self
or nature, but God; which, in turn, does not mean that a
most heartfelt poem on God, a genuine expression of faith,
represents true mysticism. Mysticism is more: it is something which defies words. All mystics have groped in the
dark in their effort to describe what they experienced
when they felt God. At best they took refuge in symbols,
allegories and analogies taken, as in poetry, from natural
and visible things. The *Canticle of Canticles* with its
oriental lushness of imagery, its surface sensuality, its
chaste candor, has served as an inspiration to one group
writing of their own experiences. Others have taken
refuge in an allegorical explanation of Holy Writ. Others
again, continuing along a line established by Plato,
Plotinus and the Prophets, drown us in a "glossolalic"*
flood of stammering words of awe, reverence and darkness. Birth and death, embrace and fulfillment, caresses
and kisses, light and darkness, heat and cold, flight and
surrender, sight and blindness, sweetness and bitterness,

---

* Glossolalic, glossolaly: speaking in tongues, described by
St. Paul, repeatedly, especially in I Cor. 14. Although the
phenomenon here described is not decidedly identified as the
same which made the early Christian pronounce strange sounds,
both seem to witness things that are unutterable.

desolation and bliss—these are the analogical terms which are common coin to all lovers of God once they have been admitted to a communion of being which is so strong that it bursts through the rational approaches to God. There is a great distance between the enamored ragings of Maddalena de' Pazzi and the inspired rivers of thought flowing endlessly from Meister Eckhart; Augustine's quiet and noble taciturnity is in sharp contrast with Bernard's verbose and tender effusions. We can scarcely recognize the identical reality in the almost pedestrian pedantry of the late mystic writers as in the hymnic and soaring rapture of the sacramental mysticism of the liturgy and of the early Fathers. And yet, all have the same message about that very thing which no soul can utter; the immediate experience of God.

There are many among whom strange notions of mysticism are current, ranging from black magic and spiritualism to hysteria and its various phenomena. In one of her books, Evelyn Underhill distinguishes mysticism from magic by a clear and simple definition: "Magical are all forms of self-seeking transcendentalism." Perhaps it would be better to enlarge this definition and say that all magical pseudo-mysticism is based on an assumption that God, angels, superior powers and demons can be forced, by repetition of formulas and weird irrational practices, by sheer human effort to rise above itself through a kind of self-intensification, to do whatever one wants them to do. When this is not demonism pure and simple, it remains within the boundaries of nature, although within the subconscious or unconscious. Natural forces as yet unprobed like telepathy and suggestion or hypnosis are neither mystical nor supernatural. In all these sometimes preposterous, sometimes evil incantations and forcings of what is falsely deemed the supernatural, the principal agent, singly or collectively, is man.

Mystics have nothing in common with such irrational and evil or silly doings. No person seeking after extraordinary phenomena—mystical symptoms rather than cause—can claim to have understood the true nature of mysticism. The texts in this book will show that the greatest of all mystics are those who rise to union with God and leave behind that aspect of mysticism which intrigues the world. Just as mysticism takes different forms in all its initiates, so it varies often from age to age, from mind to mind, from men to women, and even from nation to nation. The mystics are people who—while their personality not only suffers no diminution, but is expanded to an exhilarating richness—become so perfectly an instrument of God that in their highest activities they are completely passive to Him, humbly allowing Him to do what He wills with them in the outpouring of His love. It is in such circumstances that our great mystics resort to the symbolic language of bridal relations. In a word, orthodox mysticism is nothing but the experience intensely lived of the mystery of grace and freedom—which is the crucial point of all theology.

Our collection opens with quotations from Plato and neo-Platonic metaphysical speculation. It is easy to see that these highly academic writings have nothing of magic, since magic is essentially practical and empirical. These and other ancients are witness to the longing of man's heart after God, and also to the fact that mysticism is not basically irrational, but rather suprarational; the intellect is fully active, and strives disinterestedly for awareness, instead of being drowned out, as in the case of pseudo-mysticism, by bodily sensations, weird rumblings of the subconscious, or frank solicitings of occult phenomena. Only if the speculations of the unaided natural mind assume the haughty air of finality, as does agnosticism, are they fatal to genuine mysticism. "The only final thing is personal experience—the personal and costly exploration of the exalted and truth-loving soul."*

Passages from the Bible have been inserted throughout the book, though they are not mystical in the modern

* Evelyn Underhill, *Mysticism,* page 72, E. P. Dutton, New York, 1930.

sense; their object is to make clear that the God who revealed Himself to Abraham, Moses and Isaias is the very God of the mystics.

As a final note, it must be said that a collection of mystical writings like this book may mislead some readers into the belief or self-deception that they themselves are mystics after having read or pondered samples of mystical writings. This collection is not intended to be a school of mysticism, nor does it surreptitiously suggest some scale of perfection, according to which Plotinus, Silesius, St. Catherine of Genoa and St. John of the Cross represent so many rungs of a ladder leading up into the ineffable mysteries of mysticism. No one is likely to become a mystic merely by reading this collection, but by contrast and affinity, by similitude and witness, we hope our readers will come to an awareness of the beauty and loftiness of the narrow and steep path, and feel stimulated to make some of these texts their favorite contemplative reading. Some pure and simple soul may even recognize a strange resemblance to landmarks unwittingly passed before, and then take up reading the mystics in their great works, not as scholar or as curious observer of phenomena, but as apprentice.

H. A. REINHOLD.

FIRST PART

Thou hast made us for Thee

THE EROS OF THE INTELLECT

LOGOS SPERMATIKOS

Even in the time before Christ there were among people those who belonged to the spiritual Jerusalem and lived according to God and were pleasing unto Him. The ancients also knew what is now called the Christian religion, and this existed from the very beginning until Christ appeared in the flesh. From then on, the name Christian was given to the true religion.

Saint Augustine

THE ASCENT FROM THE UNDERGROUND DEN

The release of the prisoners from chains, and their translation from the shadows to images and light, and their ascent from the underground den to the sun, while in his presence they vainly try to look on animals and plants and the light of the sun, but are able to perceive even with their weak eyes the images in the water (which are divine), and are the shadows of true existence (not shadows of images cast by a light of fire which, compared with the sun, are only images)—this power of elevating the highest principle in the soul to the contemplation of that which is best in existence, with which we may compare the raising of that faculty which is the very light of the body to the sight of that which is brightest in the material and visible world—this power is given, as I was saying, by all that study and pursuit of the arts which has been described.

Plato

THE WINGED SOUL

If man had eyes to see the true beauty—the divine beauty, I mean, pure, and clear and unalloyed, not clogged with the pollutions of mortality and all the colours and vanities of human life—thither looking, and holding converse with the true beauty simple and divine? Remember how in that communion only, beholding beauty with the eye of the mind, he will be enabled to bring forth, not images of beauty, but realities (for he had hold not of an image but of a reality), and bringing forth and nourishing true virtue to become the friend of God and be immortal, if mortal man may.

Plato

THE TRUE EROS

He who would proceed aright in this matter should begin in youth to visit beautiful forms; and first, if he be guided by his instructor aright, to love one such form only —out of that he should create fair thoughts; and soon he will of himself perceive that the beauty of one form is akin to the beauty of another; and then if beauty of form in general is his pursuit, how foolish would he be not to recognise that the beauty in every form is one and the same! And when he perceives this he will abate his violent love of the one, which he will despise and deem a small thing, and will become a lover of all beautiful forms; in the next stage he will consider that the beauty of the mind is more honourable than the beauty of the outward form. So that if a virtuous soul have but a little comeliness, he will be content to love and tend him, and will search out and bring to the birth thoughts which may improve the young, until he is compelled to contemplate and see the beauty of institutions and laws, and to understand that the beauty of them all is of one family, and that personal beauty is a trifle; and after laws and institutions he will go on to the sciences, that he may see their beauty, being not like a servant in love with the beauty of one youth or man or institution, himself a slave, mean and narrow-minded, but drawing towards and contemplating the vast sea of beauty, he will create many fair and noble thoughts and notions in boundless love of wisdom; until on that shore he grows and waxes strong, and at last the vision is revealed to him of a single science, which is the science of beauty everywhere.

Plato

OUR KINDRED ARE IN HEAVEN

And we should consider that God gave the sovereign part of the human soul to be the divinity of each one, being that part which, as we say, dwells at the top of the body, and inasmuch as we are a plant not of an earthly but of a heavenly growth, raises us from earth to our kindred who are in heaven, for the divine power suspended the head and root of us from that place where the generation of the soul first began, and thus made the whole body upright. When a man is always occupied with the cravings of desire and ambition, and is eagerly striving to satisfy them, all his thoughts must be mortal, and, as far as it is possible altogether for him to become such, he must be mortal every whit, because he has cherished his mortal part. But he who has been earnest in the love of knowledge and of true wisdom, and has exercised his intellect more than any other part of him, must have thoughts immortal and divine, if he attain truth, and in so far as human nature is capable of sharing in immortality, he must altogether be immortal; and since he is ever cherishing the divine power, and has the divinity within him in perfect order, he will be perfectly happy. Now there is only one way of taking care of things, and this is to give to each the food and motion which are natural to it. And the motions which are naturally akin to the divine principle within us are the thoughts and revolutions of the universe. These each man should follow, and correct the courses of the head which were corrupted at our birth, and by learning the harmonies and revolutions of the universe, should assimilate the thinking being to the thought, renewing his original nature, and having assimilated them should attain to that perfect life which the gods have set before mankind, both for the present and the future.

Plato

THE UNKNOWING KNOWING OF THE SUPREME GOOD

When a man enters a house rich in beauty he might gaze about and admire the varied splendour before the master appears; but, face to face with that great person— no thing of ornament but calling for the truest attention— he would ignore everything else and look only at the master. In this state of absorbed contemplation there is no longer question of holding an object: the vision is continuous so that seeing and seen are one thing; object and act of vision have become identical; of all that until then filled the eye no memory remains. And our comparison would be closer if instead of a man appearing to the visitor who has been admiring the house it were a god, and not a god manifesting to the eyes but one filling the soul.

As for the soul, it attains that vision by—so to speak— confounding and annulling the Intellectual Principle within it; or rather that Principle immanent in the soul sees first and thence the vision penetrates to the soul and the two visions become one.

The Good spreading out above them and adapting itself to that union which it hastens to confirm is present to them as giver of a blessed sense and sight; so high it lifts them that they are no longer in space or in that realm of difference where everything is rooted in some other thing; for the Good is not in place but is the container of the Intellectual place; the Good is nothing but itself.

The soul now knows no movement, since the Supreme knows none; it is now not even soul since the Supreme is not in life but above life; it is no longer Intellectual Principle for the Supreme has Intellection and the likeness must be perfect; this grasping is not even by Intellection for the Supreme is not known intellectively.

Plotinus

STRIPPED TO NAKEDNESS

Since it is the author of all that exists, and since the multiplicity in each thing is converted into a self-sufficing existence by this presence of the One, so that even the particular itself becomes self-sufficing, then clearly this principle, author at once of Being and of self-sufficingness, is not itself a Being, but is above Being and above even self-sufficing.

May we stop content with that? No: the soul is yet, and even more, in pain. Is she ripe, perhaps, to bring forth, now that in her pangs she has come so close to what she seeks? No: we must call upon yet another spell if anywhere the assuagement is to be found. All the need is met by a contact purely intellectual. At the moment of touch there is no power whatever to make any affirmation; there is no leisure; reasoning upon the vision is for afterwards. We may know we have had the vision when the soul has suddenly taken light. This light is from the Supreme and is the Supreme; we may believe in the Presence when, like that other God on the call of a certain man, He comes bringing light: the light is the proof of the advent. Thus, the soul unlit remains without that vision; lit, it possesses what it sought. And this is the true end set before the soul, to take that light, to see the Supreme by the Supreme and not by the light of any other principle—to see the Supreme which is also the means to the vision, for that which illumines the soul is that which it is to see just as it is by the sun's own light that we see the sun.

But how is this to be accomplished?

Cut away everything.

Plotinus

FLIGHT OF THE ALONE TO THE ALONE

Our self-seeing there is a communion with the self restored to its purity. No doubt we should not speak of seeing, but instead of seen and seer speak boldly of a simple unity. For in this seeing we neither see nor distinguish, nor are there two. The man is changed, no longer himself nor self-belonging; he is merged with the Supreme, sunken into It, one with It; only in separation is there duality. This is why a vision baffles telling; for how could a man bring back tidings of the Supreme as detached when he has seen It as one with himself? It is not to be told, not to be revealed to any that has not himself had the happiness to see It. Since beholder was one with beheld, and it was not a vision compassed but a unity apprehended, the man formed by this mingling with the Supreme would, if he but remembered, carry Its image impressed upon him; he is become the Unity, having no diversity either in relation to himself or anything else; no movement now, no passion, no outlooking desire, once this ascent is achieved; reason is in abeyance and intellection and even the very self; caught away, God-possessed, in perfect stillness, the entire being calmed, he turns neither to this side nor to that, nor even inwards to himself; utterly resting, he has become rest itself. He has risen beyond Beauty, the choir of the virtues overpassed; like one who, having penetrated the inner sanctuary, leaves the temple images behind; for there his converse is not with image, nor with trace, but with the Deity Himself, in view of whom all the rest is but of secondary concern. This is the only seeing reserved for the sanctuary; look otherwise and there is nothing there.

Things here are but signs that show to the wise how the Supreme God is known; the enlightened priest reading the sign may enter the holy place and make the vision real. This Term, attained only by those that have overpassed all, is the All-Transcending. There is thus a converse in virtue of which the essential man outgrows Being, becomes identical with the Transcendent of Being. He that knows himself to be one with This has in himself the likeness of the Supreme; if from that heightened self he can pass higher still—image to archetype—he has won the term of all his journeying.

This is the life of gods and of godlike and blessed men—liberation from the alien that besets us here, a life taking no pleasure in the things of earth—a flight of the alone to the Alone.

Plotinus

UNREDEEMED NATURALISM GRASPING FOR TRUTH

Many times it has happened: lifted out of the body into myself; becoming external to all other things; beholding a marvellous beauty; then, more than ever, assured of community with the loftiest order; living the noblest life, acquiring identity with the Divine; poised above whatsoever is less than the Supreme. Yet there comes the moment of descent, and after that sojourn in the Divine I ask myself how it happens that I can now be descending, and how did the soul ever enter my body, the soul which, even within the body, is the high thing it has shown itself to be.

Heraclitus, who urges the examination of this matter, tells of compulsory alternation from contrary to contrary, speaks of ascent and descent and says that change reposes; Empedocles says that it is the law for faulty souls to descend to this sphere and that he himself was here because he turned deserter and wandered from God.

The Divine Plato who uttered many noble sayings about the soul everywhere expresses contempt for all that is of the senses, blames the commerce of the soul with body as an enchantment, an entombment, and upholds the saying of the Mysteries that the soul is here a prisoner. In the Cavern of Plato and the Cave of Empedocles I discern this universe, where the breaking of the fetters and the ascent from the depths are figures of the wayfaring of the soul towards the Intellectual Realm. In the *Phaedrus*, Plato makes a failing of the wings the cause of entry to this world; there are judgments, fates, and necessities driving other souls down to this order.

In all these explanations he finds guilt in the arrival of the soul into the body. But treating in the *Timaeus* of our universe he exalts it and calls it a blessed god and holds that a soul was given it by the goodness of the Creator to the end that the totality of things might be possessed of intellect, for thus it cannot be except through the soul. In the same way, the soul of each of us is sent that the universe may be complete.

Plotinus

NONE BUT GOD'S PRESENCE

Time after time I came to your gate
with raised hands, asking for more and
yet more.

    You gave and gave, now in slow
measure, now in sudden excess.

I took some, and some things I let
drop; some lay heavy on my hands;
some I made into playthings and broke
them when tired; till the wrecks and
the hoard of your gifts grew immense,
hiding you, and the ceaseless expectation wore my heart out.

Take, oh take—has now become my
cry.

Shatter all from this beggar's bowl:
put out this lamp of the importunate
watcher: hold my hands, raise me from
the still-gathering heap of your gifts
into the bare infinity of your uncrowded
presence.

Rabindranath Tagore

THE WITNESS OF ISRAEL

MOSES AND THE BURNING BUSH

Moses was keeping the flock of Jethro his father-in-law, the priest of Midian; and he led the flock to the farthest end of the wilderness, and came to the mountain of God, unto Hereb.

And the angel of the Lord appeared unto him in a flame of fire out of the midst of a bush; and he looked, and, behold, the bush burned with fire, and the bush was not consumed.

And Moses said: "I will turn aside now, and see this great sight, why the bush is not burnt."

And when the Lord saw that he turned aside to see, God called unto him out of the midst of the bush, and said: "Moses, Moses." And he said: "Here am I."

And He said: "Draw not nigh hither; put off thy shoes from thy feet, for the place whereon thou standest is holy ground."

Moreover He said: "I am the God of thy father, the God of Abraham, the God of Isaac, and the God of Jacob." And Moses hid his face; for he was afraid to look upon God.

Exodus 3, 1–6

THE CLOUD ON THE MOUNTAIN

And the glory of the Lord abode upon Mount Sinai,

and the cloud covered it six days; and the seventh day He called unto Moses out of the midst of the cloud.

And the appearance of the glory of the Lord was like devouring fire on the top of the mount in the eyes of the children of Israel.

And Moses entered into the midst of the cloud, and went up into the mount; and Moses was in the mount forty days and forty nights.

Exodus 24, 16–18

THE FACE OF GOD

And it came to pass, when Moses entered into the Tent, the pillar of cloud descended, and stood at the door of the Tent; and (the Lord) spoke with Moses.

And when all the people saw the Pillar of cloud stand at the door of the Tent, all the people rose up and worshipped, every man at his tent door.

And the Lord spoke unto Moses face to face, as a man speaketh unto his friend . . .

And Moses said unto the Lord: . . . "Now therefore, I pray Thee, if I have found grace in Thy sight, show me now Thy ways, that I may know Thee, to the end that I may find grace in Thy sight; and consider that this nation is Thy people."

And He said: "My presence shall go with thee, and I will give thee rest." . . .

And he (Moses) said: "Show me, I pray Thee, Thy glory."

And He said: "I will make all My goodness pass before thee, and will proclaim the name of the Lord before thee; and I will be gracious to whom I will be gracious, and will show mercy on whom I will show mercy."

And He said: "Thou canst not see My face, for man shall not see Me and live."

And the Lord said: "Behold, there is a place by Me, and thou shalt stand upon the rock.

"And it shall come to pass, while My glory passeth by, that I will put thee in a cleft of the rock, and will cover thee with My hand until I have passed by.

"And I will take away My hand, and thou shalt see My back; but My face shall not be seen."

Exodus 33, 9–11; 13–14; 18–23

THE THRICE HOLY

In the year that king Uzziah died I saw the Lord sitting upon a throne high and lifted up, and His train filled the temple.

Above Him stood the seraphim; each one had six wings:
with twain he covered his face,
and with twain he covered his feet,
and with twain he did fly.
And one called unto another, and said:
Holy, holy, holy, is the Lord of hosts;
The whole earth is full of His glory.
And the posts of the door were moved at the voice of them that called, and the house was filled with smoke.
Then said I:
Woe is me! for I am undone;
Because I am a man of unclean lips,
And I dwell in the midst of a people of unclean lips;
For mine eyes have seen the King,
The Lord of hosts.
Then flew unto me one of the seraphim, with a glowing stone in his hand, which he had taken with the tongs from off the altar;
and he touched my mouth with it, and said:
Lo, this hath touched thy lips;
And thine iniquity is taken away,
And thy sin expiated.

Isaias 6, 1–7

THE SPIRIT ENTERED INTO ME

And I looked, and, behold, a stormy wind came out of the
    north,
a great cloud, with a fire flashing up, so that a brightness
was round about it; and out of the midst thereof as the
    colour
of electrum, out of the midst of the fire.
And out of the midst thereof came the likeness of
four living creatures. And this was their appearance:
they had the likeness of a man.
And every one had four faces, and every one of them had
    four wings.

And when they went, I heard the noise of their wings
like the noise of great waters,
like the voice of the Almighty,
a noise of tumult like the noise of a host;
when they stood, they let down their wings.
For, when there was a voice above the firmament that
    was over their heads,
as they stood, they let down their wings.
And above the firmament that was over their heads
was the likeness of a throne,
as the appearance of a sapphire stone;
and upon the likeness of the throne
was a likeness
as the appearance of a man upon it above.

As the appearance of the bow that is in the cloud in the
    day of rain,
so was the appearance of the brightness round about.
This was the appearance of the likeness
of the glory of the Lord.
And when I saw it, I fell upon my face,
and I heard a voice of one that spoke.

And He said unto me:
"Son of man, stand upon thy feet, and I will speak with
　　thee."
And the spirit entered into me
when He spoke unto me, and set me upon my feet;
and I heard Him that spoke unto me.

Ezechiel 1, 4–6; 24–26; 28; 2, 1–2

THE WORD OF THE ANCIENT OF DAYS

I beheld
　　　　Till thrones were placed,
　　　　And one that was ancient of days did sit:
　　　　His raiment was as white snow,
　　　　And the hair of his head like pure wool;
　　　　His throne was fiery flames,
　　　　And the wheels thereof burning fire.

　　　　A fiery stream issued
　　　　And came forth from before him;
　　　　Thousand thousands ministered unto him,
　　　　And ten thousand times ten thousand stood be-
　　　　　　fore him;
　　　　The judgment was set,
　　　　And the books were opened.

　　　　I saw in the night visions,
　　　　And, behold, there came with the clouds of heaven
　　　　One like unto a son of man,
　　　　And he came even to the Ancient of days,
　　　　And he was brought near before Him.

　　　　And there was given him dominion,
　　　　And glory, and a kingdom,
　　　　That all the peoples, nations, and languages
　　　　Should serve him;

His dominion is an everlasting dominion,
Which shall not pass away,
And his kingdom that which shall not be destroyed.

Daniel 7, 9–10; 13–14

THOU ART A HIDDEN GOD

And it came to pass, when Moses came down from Mount Sinai with the two tables of the testimony in Moses' hand, when he came down from the mount, that Moses knew not that the skin of his face sent forth beams while He talked with him.

And when Aaron and all the children of Israel saw Moses, behold, the skin of his face sent forth beams; and they were afraid to come nigh him.

And Moses called unto them; and Aaron and all the rulers of the congregation returned unto him; and Moses spoke to them.

And afterward all the children of Israel came nigh, and he gave them in commandment all that the Lord had spoken with him in Mount Sinai.

And when Moses had done speaking with them, he put a veil on his face.

Exodus 34, 29–33

Verily thou art a hidden God,
The God of Israel, the Saviour.

Isaias 45, 15

Clouds and darkness are round about him:
Justice and judgment are the establishment of his throne.
Psalm 96, 2

To us, then, God has made a revelation of it through his Spirit; there is no depth in God's nature so deep that the Spirit cannot find it out. Who else can know a man's thoughts, except the man's own spirit that is within him? So no one else can know God's thoughts, but the Spirit of God. And what we have received is no spirit of worldly wisdom; it is the Spirit that comes from God, to make us understand God's gifts to us; gifts which we make known, not in such words as human wisdom teaches, but in words taught us by the Spirit, matching what is spiritual with what is spiritual. Mere man with his natural gifts cannot take in the thoughts of God's Spirit; they seem mere folly to him, and he cannot grasp them, because they demand a scrutiny which is spiritual. Whereas the man who has spiritual gifts can scrutinise everything, without being subject, himself, to any other man's scrutiny.

I Corinthians 2, 10–15

Who shall see him and declare him? and
Who shall magnify him as he is from the beginning?

Ecclesiasticus 43, 35

He made darkness His secret place; His pavilion round
    about Him
Were dark waters and thick clouds of the skies.

Psalm 17, 12

When one speaks lovingly of God, all human words are like blinded lions seeking a spring in the desert.

Léon Bloy

And if anyone, when he has seen God, understands what he has seen, it is never God that he has seen, but some one of those things of His which exist and are known.

Dionysius the Areopagite

THE BLINDED SOUL

Still, Thou art hidden, O Lord, from my soul in Thy light and Thy blessedness; and therefore my soul still walks in darkness and wretchedness. For it looks, and does not see Thy beauty. It hearkens, and does not hear Thy harmony. It smells, and does not perceive Thy fragrance. It tastes, and does not recognise Thy sweetness. It touches, and does not feel Thy pleasantness. For Thou hast these attributes in Thyself, Lord God, after Thine ineffable manner, who hast given them to objects created by Thee, after their sensible manner; but the sinful senses of my soul have grown rigid and dull, and have been obstructed by their long listlessness.

Saint Anselm of Canterbury

GOD IS ALL

In my opinion that great man, Moses, learned in a vision that none of the objects which we perceive with our senses or understand with our mind truly exist in themselves, with exception of that supreme being which is the cause of all others, and on which they depend. Indeed in no other being is it possible to discover a nature so independent that it could exist without partaking in that one and only true being. It alone remains immutable through every change, whether it be for the better or for the worse, it never increases and never decreases, for it could never be evil, and therefore not become worse, nor could it become better. It alone stands in need of nothing, but all

things are in need of it. It alone all things require, in it
alone all things partake, but that of which they partake
is never diminished.

Saint Gregory of Nyssa

GOD IS WONDROUSLY ABOVE CHANGE

We may not think that God's rest affects Him one way,
and His work another, He is never affected, nor does His
nature admit anything that has not been ever in Him. That
which is affected suffers, and that which suffers is mutable.
For His leisure is not idle, slothful, nor sluggish, nor is
His work painful, busy or industrious. He can ever rest
working, and work resting. He can apply an eternal will
to a new work, and begins not to work now because He
repents that He wrought not before. But if He rested first
and wrought after (which I see not how man can conceive), this first and after were in things that first had no
being, and afterwards had. But there was neither precedence nor subsequence in Him to alter or abolish His will,
but all that ever He created was in His unchanged fixed
will eternally one and the same: first willing that they
should not be, and afterwards willing that they should
be, and so they were not, during His pleasure, and began
to be, at His pleasure. Wondrously showing to such as
can conceive it that He needed none of these creatures,
but created them of His pure goodness, having continued
no less blessed without them, from all unbegun eternity.

Saint Augustine

WHAT IS THE DIVINE DARKNESS?

Trinity, which exceedeth all Being, Deity, and Goodness! Thou that instructeth Christians in Thy heavenly
wisdom! Guide us to that topmost height of mystic love

which exceedeth light and more than exceedeth knowledge, where the simple, absolute, and unchangeable mysteries of heavenly Truth lie hidden in the dazzling obscurity of the secret Silence, outshining all brilliance with the intensity of their darkness, and surcharging our blinded intellects with the utter impalpable and invisible fairness of glories which exceed all beauty! Such is my prayer; and thee, dear Timothy, I counsel that in the earnest exercise of mystical contemplation thou leave the senses and the activities of the intellect and all things that the senses of the intellect can perceive, and all things in this world of nothingness, or in that world of being, and that, thine understanding being laid to rest, thou strain (so far as thou mayest) towards a union with Him whom neither being nor understanding can contain. For, by the unceasing and absolute renunciation of thyself and all things, thou shalt in pureness cast all things aside, and be released from all, and so shalt be led upwards to the Ray of that divine Darkness, which exceedeth all existence.

These things thou must not disclose to any of the uninitiated, by whom I mean those who cling to the objects of human thought, and imagine there is no superessential reality beyond, and fancy that they know by human understanding Him that has made Darkness His secret place. And if the Divine Initiation is beyond such men as these, what can be said of others yet more incapable thereof, who describe the Transcendent Cause of all things by qualities drawn from the lowest order of being, while they deny that it is in any way superior to the various ungodly delusions which they fondly invent in ignorance of this truth? That while It possesses all the positive attributes of the universe (being the Universal Cause), yet in a stricter sense It does not possess them, since It transcends them all, wherefore there is no contradiction between affirming and denying that It has them inasmuch as It precedes and surpasses all deprivation, being beyond all positive and negative distinction.

God, the Good cause, exceedeth all things in a super-essential manner, and is revealed in Its naked truth to those alone who pass right through the opposition of fair and foul, and pass beyond the topmost altitudes of the holy ascent and leave behind them all divine enlightenment and voices and heavenly utterances and plunge into the Darkness where truly dwells, as saith the Scripture, that One which is beyond all things. For not without reason is the blessed Moses bidden first to undergo purification himself and then to separate himself from those who have not undergone it; and after all purification he hears the many-voiced trumpets and sees many lights flash forth with pure and diverse-streaming rays, and then stands separate from the multitudes and with the chosen priests presses forward to the topmost pinnacle of the Divine Ascent. Nevertheless, he meets not with God Himself, yet he beholds—not Him indeed (for He is invisible)—but the place wherein He dwells. And this I take to signify that the divinest and the highest of the things perceived by the eye of the body or the mind are but the symbolic language of things subordinate to Him who Himself transcendeth them all. Through these things His incomprehensible presence is shown walking upon those heights of His holy places which are perceived by the mind; and then It breaks forth, even from the things that are beheld and from those that behold them, and plunges the true initiate into the Darkness of Unknowing wherein he renounces all the apprehensions of his understanding and is enwrapped in that which is wholly intangible and invisible, belonging wholly to Him that is beyond all things and to none else (whether himself or another), and being through the passive stillness of all his reasoning powers united by his highest faculty to Him that is wholly Unknowable, of whom thus by a rejection of all knowledge he possesses a knowledge that exceeds his understanding.

Dionysius the Areopagite

AT BEST, GOD IS SEEN ONLY IN SHADOWS

Not only do we see God at best only in shadows, but we cannot bring even those shadows together, for they flit to and fro, and are never present to us at once. We can indeed combine the various matters which we know of Him by an act of the intellect, and treat them theologically, but such theological combinations are no objects for the imagination to gaze upon. Our image of Him never is one, but broken into numberless partial aspects, independent each of each. As we cannot see the whole starry firmament at once, but have to turn ourselves from east to west, and then round to east again, sighting first one constellation and then another, and losing these in order to gain those, so it is, and much more, with such real apprehensions as we can secure of the Divine Nature. We know one truth about Him and another truth—but we cannot image both of them together; we cannot bring them before us by one act of the mind; we drop the one while we turn to take up the other. Both of them are fully dwelt on and enjoyed when they are viewed in combination . . . Break a ray of light into its constituent colours, each is beautiful, each may be enjoyed; attempt to unite them, and perhaps you produce only a dirty white. The pure and indivisible Light is seen only by the blessed inhabitants of heaven; here we have but such faint reflections of it as its diffraction supplies; but they are sufficient for faith and devotion. Attempt to combine them into one, and you gain nothing but a mystery, which you can describe as a notion, but cannot depict as an imagination . . . We must contemplate the God of our conscience as a Living Being, as one Object and Reality, under the aspect of this or that attribute. We must patiently rest in the thought of the Eternal, Omnipresent and All-knowing, rather than of Eternity, Omnipresence and Omniscience; and we must not hurry on and force a series of deductions, which, if they are to be realised, must distil like dew into our minds, and form themselves spontaneously there, by a calm contemplation and gradual understanding of their premises.

Cardinal Newman

DARKENED BY SIN AND DAZZLED BY THY LIGHT

Hast thou found what thou didst seek, my soul? Thou didst seek God. Thou hast found him to be a being which is the highest of all beings, a being than which nothing better can be conceived; that this being is life itself, light, wisdom, goodness, eternal blessedness and blessed eternity; and that it is everywhere and always.

For if thou hast not found thy God, how is he this being which thou hast found, and which thou hast conceived him to be, with so certain truth and so true certainty? But if thou hast found him, why is it that thou dost not feel thou hast found him? Why, O Lord, our God, does not my soul feel thee, if it hath found thee? Or, has it not found him whom it found to be light and truth? For how did it understand this, except by seeing light and truth? Or, could it understand anything at all of thee, except through thy light and thy truth?

Hence, if it has seen light and truth, it has seen thee; if it has not seen thee, it has not seen light and truth. Or, is what it has seen both light and truth, and still it has not yet seen thee, because it has seen thee only in part, but has not seen thee as thou art? Lord my God, my creator and renewer, speak to the desire of my soul, what thou art other than it hath seen, that it may clearly see what it desires. It strains to see thee more; and sees nothing beyond this which it hath seen, except darkness. Nay, it does not see darkness, of which there is none in thee; but it sees that it cannot see farther, because of its own darkness.

Why is this, Lord, why is this? Is the eye of the soul darkened by its infirmity, or dazzled by thy glory? Surely it is both darkened in itself and dazzled by thee. Doubtless it is both obscured by its own insignificance and over-whelmed by thy infinity. Truly, it is both contracted by its own narrowness and overcome by thy greatness.

For how great is that light from which shines every truth that gives light to the rational mind? How great is that truth in which is everything that is true, and outside which is only nothingness and the false? How boundless is the truth which sees at one glance whatsoever has been made and by whom, and through whom, and how it has been made from nothing? What purity, what certainty, what splendour where it is? Assuredly more than a creature can conceive.

Saint Anselm of Canterbury

THE UNSPEAKABLE MAJESTY OF GOD

Who but speaks of Him? Where, whether men read, or reason, or ask, or answer, or praise, or sing, or preach (after whatever fashion), nay, or even blaspheme, where is He not named? And while there is not but speaks of Him, who can receive Him so as He ought to be under-stood albeit He be never absent from the mouths and ears of men? Where is the man whose mental eye can reach Him? Where the man who would have known Him to be Trinity unless it had been His own will to be known as such? And who of mankind is now silent on that Trinity, and yet who of mankind can conceive of the Trinity as do the angels? The very things, then, that concern God's eternity, truth, holiness are evermore unreservedly and openly spoken, by some are understood aright, by others amiss: nay, by some are understood, by others not under-stood. For to understand amiss is not to understand. But even by them of whom they are understood aright, they are seen by some with less, by others with more of mental vividness, yet by none of mankind are they received as they are by the angels. Therefore, in the very mind, in the inner man, there is a sort of growth, not only to the passing from milk to meat but also to the taking of that meat more and more abundantly. A growth, however, not in dimensions of size but in luminous intelligence; because the meat itself is intellectual light. That you may grow, then, and the more you grow, may receive more and more, you must ask and hope not of the teacher who makes a sound in ears, who from without planteth and watereth, but of Him who giveth the increase.

Saint Augustine

KNOWING IN PART, DARKLY

LOOKING FROM AFAR

Looking from afar, behold I see the
power of God approaching and a mist
covering all the earth.
Go forth to meet him and say:
Tell us if thou art he who as king
shall rule the people Israel.
All children of earth and all sons of men,
rich men and poor,
Go into the highway to meet him and say:
Answer us, thou who art king of Israel,
thou who leadest Joseph like a sheep,
Tell us if thou art he.
Lift up your gates, ye princes,
and be ye lifted up, eternal gates,
and the king of glory shall enter.
Glory be to the Father and to the Son
and to the Holy Spirit.
Looking from afar, behold I see the
power of God approaching and a mist
covering all the earth.
Go forth to meet him and say:
Tell us if thou art he
Who as king shall rule the people Israel.

Roman Breviary

GOD BEYOND HIS CREATURES

See where you do not see, hear where no sound comes
    through,
Go where you cannot go, and God will speak to you.

SILENT PRAYER

We cannot speak of God, He is beyond compare,
And so we can adore Him best with silent prayer.

WHATEVER YOU WANT IS IN YOU

In you is hell's abyss, in you is heaven's grace,
What you elect and want you have in any place.

ALL WORKS ARE THE SAME

Do not select: at God's command the angels bring
A load of dung as lief as rest themselves and sing.

WORKING AND RESTING ARE BOTH GOD-LIKE

Would God not rather have us work than rest, you ask?
I say: like God one shall both rest and do one's task.

Angelus Silesius

WE HAVE NOT EYES KEEN ENOUGH

Religion has (as it were) its very life in what are para-
doxes and contradictions in the eye of reason. It is a seeming inconsistency how we can pray for Christ's coming,
yet wish time to "work out our salvation" and "make our
calling and election sure." It was a seeming contradic-

tion how good men were to desire His first coming, yet were unable to abide it; how the Apostles feared, yet rejoiced after His resurrection. And so it is a paradox how the Christian should in all things be sorrowful yet always rejoicing, and dying yet living, and having nothing yet possessing all things. Such seeming contradictions arise from the want of depth in our minds to master the whole truth. We have not eyes keen enough to follow out the lines of God's providence and will, which meet at length though at first sight they seem parallel.

Cardinal Newman

O DEPTH OF WISDOM . . .

As the soul cleansed and purified finds no place wherein to rest but God, this being its end by creation, so the soul in a state of sin finds no place for it but hell, this being its end by the appointment of God. No sooner, then, does the soul leave the body in mortal sin than it goes straight to hell as to its allotted place, with no other guide than the nature of sin; and should a soul not find itself thus prevented by the justice of God, but excluded altogether from His appointment, it would endure a still greater hell—for God's appointment partakes of His mercy, and is less severe than the sin deserves; as it is, the soul, finding no place suited to it, nor any lesser pain provided for it by God, casts itself into hell as into its proper place. Thus, with regard to purgatory, when the soul leaves the body, and finds itself out of that state of purity in which it was created, seeing the hindrance, and that it can only be removed by purgatory, without a moment's hesitation it plunges therein: and were there no such means provided to remove the impediment, it would forthwith beget within itself a hell worse than purgatory, because by reason of this impediment it would see itself unable to reach God, its last end: and this hindrance would be so full of pain, that, in comparison with it, purgatory, though, as I have said, it be like hell, would not be worth a thought, but be even as nothing.

Again I say that, on God's part, I see Paradise has no gate, but that whosoever will may enter therein; for God is all mercy, and stands with open arms to admit us to His glory. But still I see that the Being of God is so pure (far more than one can imagine), that should a soul see in itself even the least mote of imperfection, it would rather cast itself into a thousand hells than go with that spot into the presence of the Divine Majesty. Therefore, seeing purgatory ordained to take away such blemishes, it plunges therein, and deems it a great mercy that it can thus remove them. I see any soul with the least stain of imperfection accept it as a mercy, not thinking it of any moment when compared with being kept from its Love. It appears to me that the greatest pain the souls in purgatory endure proceeds from their being sensible of something in themselves displeasing to God, and that it has been done voluntarily against so much goodness; for, being in a state of grace, they know the truth, and how grievous is any obstacle which does not let them approach God.

Saint Catherine of Genoa

One day, the 6th December, 1273, as he was celebrating Mass in the chapel of St. Nicholas, a great change came over him. From that moment onward he ceased to write or to dictate . . . Reginald ventured to complain: "I can do no more," said his master. Reginald insisted: "Reginald, I can do no more; such things have been revealed to me that everything I have written seems to me rubbish. Now, after the end of my work, I must await the end of my life."

Saint Thomas Aquinas
as related by Jacques Maritain

After the death of the Doctor, Brother Reginald, having returned to Naples and resumed his lectures, exclaimed with many tears: "My brothers, while he was still in life, my Master forbade me to disclose the admirable things concerning him whereof I have been witness. One of these things was that he had acquired his science not by human industry but by the merit of prayer, for whenever he wished to study, discuss, read, write, or dictate, he first had recourse to prayer in private, and poured forth his soul with tears in order to discover the divine secrets, and by the merits of this prayer his doubts were removed and he issued therefrom fully instructed."

Saint Thomas Aquinas
as related by Peter Calo

A VISION

I saw what seemed to be a great iron-coloured mountain. On it sat someone in such a glory of light that his radiance dazzled me. On either side a wing both broad and long was spread like a gentle shadow.

Before him, at the foot of the mountain, stood a shape covered over and over with eye upon eye, so that this multitude of eyes prevented me from seeing anything that resembled a human form. In front of this shape there was another, that seemed a boy in a pale garment and shod with white. Upon its head he (who sat on the mountain) shed such a flood of splendour that I could not see its face. He who sat on the mountain also bred sparks of living light and cast them about both shapes in a lovely stream. In the mountain there were many windows that framed the heads of men, white and wan.

Then suddenly, he upon the mountain called in a loud and penetrating voice:

"O frail man! dust of the dust of the earth, ash of ashes, cry out and tell of the coming of pure salvation, so that those may be instructed who see into the very marrow of the Scriptures and still will not proclaim or preach them because their blood is tepid and they are dulled to the cause of God. Open to them the house of secrets, for they are hesitant and hide it in remote fields and garner no fruit. Grow into a fountain of plenty, flow out in mystical teachings so that those who would hold you in contempt because of the fall of Eve be shaken by the tide of your waters. For it is not from man that you have this insight and this depth. You receive it from above, from that sacred Judge on High, where the serene intercourse between shining shapes will beam in the clearest light. Arise then, and speak, and give tiding of what has been revealed to you with the supreme strength and help of God! For He who governs all His creatures in goodness and might, He pervades all who fear Him and serve Him in love and delight and humility with the clarity of heaven, and guides the patient pilgrim on the right path to the joyful beholding of eternity."

The great iron-coloured mountain symbolises the power and the constancy of God's eternal kingdom that cannot be destroyed by the impact of unsteadfast mutability. And he, who is seated on the mountain, and dazzles your sight with his glory, reflects him in the realm of the Blessed, who rules the circle of earth, lifted in the rays of changeless serenity and intangible to the mind of man. The long and broad wings, like shadows on either side, symbolise protection, tender and mild, that curbs with warning and also with chastisement. They are the adequate symbols of the ineffable nature of unerring justice that weighs all in her scales.

At the foot of the mountain stands the shape covered over and over with eye upon eye. In deep humility and oblivious of self, it recognises the kingdom of God and, sheltered in the fear of the Lord, toils among men eagerly and persistently, with the clear gaze of a good and just purpose. It has such hosts of eyes that you cannot see anything resembling a human form. Thanks to this sight that pierces through all things, it has so utterly overcome that forgetfulness of what is right and Godly that sweeps over men so often when they are overwhelmed by the tedium of living, that its wakefulness can no longer be clouded by weak and earthly questioning.

Beside this shape is another, that of a boy in a pale garment and shod with white. For those who fear God precede, and the poor in spirit follow. For who fears God with devotion is also informed with the bliss of the poor in spirit that does not ask for pride or a boastful heart, but loves simplicity and soberness. Inconspicuously clothed in devotion, as in a pale and insignificant garment, it ascribes its good works not to itself but to God, and joyfully follows in the candid footsteps of God's Son. He who is seated on the mountain sheds such splendour upon its head that you cannot see its face. For the serene visitation of Him who governs all creatures in a praiseworthy fashion pours forth strength and power in such abundance that a weak mortal cannot grasp such a lavishing of heavenly riches upon the poverty of man.

From him who is seated on the mountain fly many sparks of live fire that flit about the shapes in utter loveliness. This means: God Almighty exhales various and strong forces that shine in divine clearness and, as surrounding helpers and protectors, caress and anoint with fiery touch those who truly fear God and submit with faithful love to poorness of spirit.

In the mountain many windows can be seen that frame the heads of men, white or wan. This means: at such a lofty height, the striving and the doing of men cannot be kept secret or hidden from the incomparably deep and sharp recognition of God. Often through themselves they reveal a pale coolness or a warm glow of their being, now men whose heart and hand is weary and who sink into ignominious sleep, and now men who are wakeful and honourably vigilant. Thus says Solomon in witness of my words: "He becometh poor that dealeth with a slack hand; but the hand of the diligent maketh rich" (*Proverbs* 10,

4). This means: that man has made himself weak and poor who did not want to conquer his own sin, or to forgive the sins of others, who has never been filled with the miraculous works of beatitude. But he who has wrought at the great work of salvation, is a runner on the path of truth who reaches toward the fountain of glory that yields him the most precious treasures of heaven and earth. Whoever, then, has for his own the knowledge of the Holy Ghost and the plumed pinions of faith, let him not transgress my admonitions, but savour and absorb them in his soul.

Saint Hildegarde of Bingen

THE DESIRE OF SEEING GOD

Thus saith pain: "Woe to me that I have been created, woe, that I live! Who will help me? Who will free me? If God knew me I should not be in such great perils. What good is it to me that I trust in God? Even if I rejoice with Him, He does not take away from me evil . . . If He were my God, why did He hide from me all His grace? If He did me some good, I would know Him. But I know not even what I am myself. Hapless I was created and hapless I was born, and I live without consolation. Alas, what is life without joy? Why was I born, since nothing that is good is at hand?"

From the cloud Hildegarde heard a voice giving pain this answer: "O, blind and deaf art thou! Thou knowest not what thou sayest. God has created man light, but because of his disloyalty the serpent has led him into this sea of misery. Now, look at the sun, the moon, the stars, at all the green ornamentation of the earth and consider what prosperity God gives man with them, while man sins against God with much temerity . . . Who else but God has given thee these things which thou hast in this life as good things? While day hastens towards thee, thou callest it night. Salvation is nigh to thee and thou deemest it damnation. When things go well with thee in all manner, thou sayest, it is bad. How hellish thou art.

"But I have heaven, for all God's creation I see in the true way . . . The roses, the lilies, and all greenery, I gather them up to my bosom gently and I praise all God's works while thou pluckest from them pain on pain and art sad in all thy deeds. Thou art like hell's spirits who always deny God in all their deeds. Not I: I offer all my works to God, for there is a way of mourning that is rejoicing and there is a way of rejoicing in which the soul prospers; nor are they like night and day in their change. But as God constituted night and day thus also man's deeds are fashioned. For when greed has built her castle God tears it down quickly! When the flesh longs after dissipation God casts it down and scourges it! When lust in its hollow glory dares to soar to heaven God smites it and scatters it. And this is but just and right. Behold, how it is with birds and the evil worms of the earth, how they are useful or useless and how they devour one another. Thus it is with the happiness and the unhappiness of the world. One should not altogether throw them out, but the useful purge the useless, the useless cleanse the useful, as gold is purified in the furnace. Thou conformest to the useless part, not I. For I reckon on the useful and useless things as God constituted them. The soul is the witness of heaven, the body witness of the earth . . . Dost thou see how foolish and blind is what thou sayest?"

Saint Hildegarde of Bingen

REFLECTION ON A GREAT MYSTERY

As I knelt by the Crib of our Lord at Bethlehem I saw a most beautiful Maiden, covered with a white mantle and a robe of fine texture. The time of her delivery seemed to be at hand. A venerable old man accompanied her. An ox and an ass were with them. When they had come into the cave, and the old man had tethered the ox and the ass to the manger, he went out and returned with a lighted torch which he fastened to the wall, and then he went out again so as not to be present at the birth of the Child.

Then Our Lady laid aside her white mantle, took off her shoes from her feet and the veil from her head so that she was clad only in her light robe. Her beautiful golden hair hung down over her shoulders. Then she took out two linen cloths and two woollen ones, very clean and white, to wrap the Child in as soon as He was born, and two smaller pieces of linen to swathe His head. When all things were prepared Our Lady knelt down with her back against the Manger, her fact uplifted and turned eastward. Her hands were raised, her eyes fixed above, her whole being absorbed in ecstatic contemplation, bathed in heavenly rapture. And in a moment as she prayed she had brought forth her Son, from whom shone a light so great and so wonderful that the rays of the sun cannot be compared to it. The torch brought by St. Joseph seemed to be extinguished, so far did that Divine light outshine all light which is of earth. The infant was born so suddenly, so instantaneously, that I saw not how it happened. I only saw the Divine Child lying naked, white and shining on the ground. Then I heard the most wonderful singing of angels. When Our Lady, whose form was exceedingly delicate, slender, graceful, saw that her Child was born she bent her head, folded her hands, and adored the Infant with the deepest reverence and devotion. Then the Child began to weep and tremble with cold on the hard ground where He lay. He moved a little and stretched His tender limbs as though He desired the comfort of His Mother's caresses. The Mother took the Child in her arms, pressed Him to her heart and warmed Him against her face and bosom with great gladness and tender motherly pity. Then she sat down on the ground, laid the Child on her lap, and began to swathe Him very carefully. First she wrapt Him in linen and then in the woollen cloths, binding His tender body and little arms with the swaddling bands which were sewn to the four corners of the outer woollen cloth. Then she wrapt and bound His head in the two smaller linen cloths which she had laid beside her. When all this was done the venerable old man came in again, and falling on his knees adored the Child with tears of joy. Then the Virgin rose with the Infant in her arms, and she and St. Joseph together laid Him in the Manger and worshipped Him with great joy and gladness of heart.

Saint Brigid of Sweden

THE HEAVENS PROCLAIM THY GLORY

When I behold thy heavens, the work of thy fingers,
The moon and the stars, which thou hast established,
What is man, that thou shouldst be mindful of him,
Or the son of man, that thou shouldst regard him?

Yet hast thou made him but little lower than God,
Thou crownest him with glory and honour,
Thou settest him over the works of thy hands,
Thou hast put all things beneath his feet.

Psalm 8, 4–8

Thine are the heavens, and thine is the earth:
The world and the fulness thereof thou hast founded:
The north and the sea thou hast created.
Thabor and Hermon rejoice in thy name.

Psalm 88, 12–13

In the beginning, O Lord, thou foundedst the earth:
and the heavens are the works of thy hands.

They shall perish but thou remainest;
and all of them shall grow old like a garment:

and as a vesture thou shalt change them, and they shall be
changed.

But thou art always the selfsame, and thy years shall not
fail.

Psalm 101, 26–28

The Heavens proclaim the glory of God
And the firmament showeth his handiwork.

Psalm 18, 1

There are great and wonderful works:
a variety of beasts, and of all living things,
and the monstrous creatures of whales.

Ecclesiasticus 43, 27

From the foundations of the world men have caught
sight of his invisible nature, his eternal power and his
divineness, as they are known through his creatures.

Romans 1, 20

All things whatsoever observe a
mutual order; and this the form that maketh
the universe like unto God.

Herein the exalted creatures trace the impress of
the Eternal Worth, which is the goal whereto
was made the norm now spoken of.

In the order of which I speak all things incline,
by diverse lots, more near and less unto their
principle.

Dante

See now the height and breadth of the Eternal Worth,
since it hath made itself so many mirrors wherein it break-
eth, remaining in itself one as before.

Dante

Yea! Lord, whom I have not praised in the sun and moon and stars of light—Lord, whom I have forgotten in the spendthrift southern sun and the sun-like moon of Hindustan, and the myriad stars of mid-tropics—I undo and recall my past forgetfulness by praising thee now in the fire and hail, the snow and vapour, the stormy winds that fulfil thy word. Visit me and my aching limbs with any pain and I will seek to turn it into praise. Add new horrors to the gloom and loneliness of night by overshadowing my soul; and, with thy gracious help, I will sing to thee and to thy mercy songs in the night.

Sir Lawrence Shipley

A CANTICLE OF BROTHER SUN

Most high, omnipotent and gracious Lord,
Yours are the glory and honour, praises and all benediction,
Only to You, most High, do they belong,
And none is worthy that he mention You.
Be praised, my Lord, in what You have created,
Above all else in Brother, Messer Sun,
For he lights up the day
And he is beautiful and radiates splendour,
Of You, Most High, he gives signification.
Be praised, my Lord, in Sister Moon and the Stars.
You shaped them in the heavens: clear and beautiful and precious.
Be praised, my Lord, in Brother Wind,
And in the air and clouds and fair and other weathers,
Through which You give Your creatures sustenance.
Be praised, my Lord, in Sister Water,
Who is very useful and humble, precious and chaste.
Be praised, my Lord, in Brother Fire,
Through whom You light up the night,
And who is beautiful and strong, robust and jocund.

Be praised, my Lord, in our Sister Mother Earth,
Who governs and sustains us,
And brings forth varied fruits and gaudy flowers and
    grass.
Be praised, my Lord, in those who forgive for love of
    You,
And bear infirmity and tribulation,
Blessèd who bear them with a peaceful heart!
Because by You, Most High, they will be crowned.
Be praised, my Lord, in our Sister Bodily Death,
Whom no one living can escape.
Alas! for those who die in mortal sin!
Blessèd are they that find themselves in Your most holy
    will!
To them the second death shall bring no harm.
Praise and extol my Lord, and give Him thanks,
And serve Him in profound humility. Amen.

Saint Francis of Assisi

EPISODE OF THE FOUNTAIN

It happened on a certain day, between the Festival of
the Resurrection and the Ascension, that I went into the
court before Prime and seated myself near the fountain,
and I began to consider the beauty of the place, which
charmed me on account of the clear and flowing stream,
the verdure of the trees which surrounded it, and the
flight of the birds, and particularly of the doves—above all
the sweet calm—and considering within myself what would
make this place most useful to me, I thought that it would
be the friendship of a wise and intimate companion, who
would sweeten my solitude or render it more useful to
others, when Thou, my Lord and my God, who art a torrent of inestimable pleasure, after having inspired me with
the first impulse of this desire, Thou didst will to be also
the end of it, inspiring me with the thought that if, by

continual gratitude, I returned Thy graces to Thee, as a stream returns to its source; if increasing in the love of virtue, I put forth, like the trees, the flowers of good works; furthermore, if, despising the things of the earth, I fly upwards freely, like the birds, and thus free my senses from the distraction of exterior things, my soul would then be empty, and my heart would be an agreeable abode for Thee.

As I was occupied with the recollection of these things during the same day, having knelt after Vespers for my evening prayer before retiring to rest, this passage of the Gospel came suddenly to my mind: "If any man love Me, he will keep My Word, and My Father will love him, and We will come to him and will take up Our abode with him." At these words, my worthless heart perceived Thee, O my most sweet God and my delight, present therein . . . although my mind takes pleasure in wandering after and in distracting itself with perishable things, yet . . . when I return into my heart, I find Thee there; so that I cannot complain that Thou hast left me, even for a moment, from that time until this year, which is the ninth since I received this grace, except once when I perceived that Thou didst leave me for the space of eleven days . . . and it appeared to me that this happened on account of worldly conversation . . . Then Thy sweetest humanity and Thy stupendous charity moved Thee to seek me when I had reached such a pitch of madness that I thought no more of the greatness of the treasure I had lost, and for the loss of which I do not remember to have felt any grief at that time, nor even to have the desire of recovering it. I cannot now be sufficiently amazed at the mania which possessed my soul . . . Draw and unite me entirely to Thyself, that I may remain inseparably attached to Thee, even when I am obliged to attend to exterior duties for the good of my neighbour, and that afterwards I may return again to seek Thee within me when I have accomplished them for Thy glory in the most perfect manner possible, even as the winds, when agitated by a tempest, return again to their former calm when it has ceased; that Thou mayest find me as zealous in labouring for Thee as Thou hast been assiduous in helping me; and that by this means Thou mayest elevate me to the highest degree of perfection, to which Thy justice can permit Thy mercy to raise so carnal and rebellious a creature.

Saint Gertrude of Helfta

CHRISTIAN PLATONISM

For it is one thing to call and to maintain the creature in being from the innermost and highest point of causation, which He alone does who is God the Creator; but it is quite another thing to apply some form of operation from without on to the faculties and possibilities scattered abroad by Him that that which is created may experience a certain influence at this time or at that, or in this way or in that. For all these things from their origin and beginning have been created into a kind of texture of the elements. They come forth to operation whenever the opportunity is present. For as mothers are pregnant with young, so the world itself is pregnant with the causes of things that are born; which do not enter being except from the assent of that highest essence in which nothing either springs up or dies, either begins to be or ceases to exist. But the applying from without of adventitious causes which, although not natural, yet are to be applied according to nature in order that those things which are contained and hidden in the secret bosom of nature may break forth and be outwardly created in some way by the unfolding of the proper measures and numbers and weights which they have received in secret from Him "who has ordered all things in measure and number and weight" (*Wisdom* 11, 20): this is not only in the power of bad angels, but also of bad men. Only he is creator who shapes these seminal principles (as I have suggested in the story of Jacob).

Saint Augustine

GOD'S GRANDEUR

The world is charged with the grandeur of God.
It will flame out, like shining from shook foil;
   It gathers to a greatness, like the ooze of oil
Crushed. Why do men then now not reck his rod?
Generations have trod, have trod, have trod;
   And all is seared with trade; bleared, smeared with
      toil;
   And wears man's smudge and shares man's smell: the
      soil
Is bare now, nor can foot feel, being shod.

And for all this, nature is never spent;
   There lives the dearest freshness deep down things;
And though the last lights off the black West went
   Oh, morning, at the brown brink eastward, springs—
Because the Holy Ghost over the bent
   World broods with warm breast and with ah! bright
     wings.

Gerard Manley Hopkins

THE RESTLESS HEART

As the hart panteth after the water brooks,
So panteth my soul after Thee, O God.
My soul thirsteth for God, for the living God:
"When shall I come and appear before God?"
My tears have been my food day and night,
While they say unto me all the day: "Where is thy God?"
These things I remember, and pour out my soul within me,
How I passed on with the throng, and led them to the
    house of God,
With the voice of joy and praise, a multitude keeping
    holyday.

Why art thou cast down, O my soul?
And why moanest thou within me?
Hope thou in God; for I shall yet praise Him
For the salvation of His countenance.

O my God, my soul is cast down within me;
Therefore do I remember Thee from the land of Jordan,
And the Hermons, from the hill Mizar.

Deep calleth unto deep at the voice of Thy cataracts;
All Thy waves and Thy billows are gone over me.
By day the Lord will command His loving-kindness,
And in the night His song shall be with me,
Even a prayer unto the God of my life.

I will say unto God my Rock: "Why hast Thou forgotten
me?
Why go I mourning under the oppression of the enemy?"
As with a crushing in my bones, mine adversaries taunt
me;
While they say unto me all the day: "Where is thy God?"

Why art thou cast down, O my soul?
And why moanest thou within me?
Hope thou in God; for I shall yet praise Him,
The salvation of my countenance, and my God.

Psalm 41

For my days are vanished like smoke:
and my bones are grown dry like fuel for the fire.

I am smitten as grass, and my heart is withered;
because I forgot to eat my bread.

Through the voice of my groaning, my bone
hath cleaved to my flesh.

I am become like a pelican of the wilderness:
I am like an owl in the ruin.

I watch and am become as a sparrow,
all alone on the house-top.

Psalm 101, 4–8

The thirst, born with us and ne'er failing, for
the god-like realm bore us swift almost as
ye see the heaven.

Dante

THIRSTING HEART

*Great art Thou, O Lord, and greatly to be praised; great
is Thy power, and of Thy Wisdom there is no number.*

Yet man desires to praise Thee. He is but a tiny part of all that Thou hast created. He bears about him his mortality, the witness of his sinfulness, the witness that *Thou dost resist the proud:* yet this tiny part of all that Thou hast created desires to praise Thee.

Thou dost so excite him that to praise Thee is his joy. For Thou hast made us for Thyself and our hearts are restless till they rest in Thee. Grant me, O Lord, to know which is the soul's first movement toward Thee—to implore Thy aid or to utter its praise of Thee; and whether it must know Thee before it can implore. For it would seem clear that no one can call upon Thee without knowing Thee, for if he did he might invoke another than Thee, knowing no better. Yet may it be that a man must implore Thee before he can know Thee? But, *how shall they call on Him in Whom they have not believed? or how shall they believe without a preacher?* And *they shall praise the Lord that seek Him;* for those that seek shall find; and finding Him they will praise Him. I will seek Thee, Lord, by praying for Thy aid, and I will utter my prayer believing in Thee: for Thou hast been preached to us. My faith, Lord, cries to Thee, the faith that Thou hast given me, that Thou hast inbreathed in me through the humanity of Thy Son and by the ministry of Thy Preacher.

But how can I call unto my God, my God and Lord? For in calling unto Him, I am calling Him to me: and what room is there in me for my God, the God who made heaven and earth? Is there anything in me, O God, that can contain You? All heaven and earth cannot contain You for You made them, and me in them. Yet, since nothing that is could exist without You, You must in some way be in all that is: therefore also in me, since I am. And if You are already in me, since otherwise I should not be, why do I cry to You to enter into me? Even if I were in Hell You would be there *For if I go down into hell, Thou art there also.* Thus, O God, I should be nothing, utterly nothing, unless You were in me—or rather unless I were in You, *of Whom and by Whom and in Whom are all things.* So it is, Lord, and so I ask: Why do I call You to come to me, since I am in You? Or where else are You that You can come to me? Where shall I go, beyond the bounds of heaven and earth, that God may come to me, since He has said: *Heaven and earth do I fill.*

Who shall grant me to rest in Thee? By whose gift shalt Thou enter into my heart and fill it so compellingly that I shall turn no more to my sins but embrace Thee, my only good? What art Thou to me? Have mercy, that I may speak. What rather am I to Thee, that Thou shouldst demand my love and if I love Thee not be angry and threaten such great woes? Surely not to love Thee is already a great woe. For Thy mercies' sake, O Lord my God, tell me what Thou art to me. Say unto my soul, *I am Thy salvation.* So speak that I may hear, Lord, my heart is listening; open it that it may hear Thee say to my soul, *I am Thy salvation.* Hearing that word, let me come in haste to lay hold upon Thee. Hide not Thy face from me. Let me see Thy face even if I die, lest I die with longing to see it.

The house of my soul is too small to receive Thee: let it be enlarged by Thee. It is all in ruins: do Thou repair it. There are things in it that must offend Thy gaze, I confess and know. But who shall cleanse it? or to what other besides Thee shall I cry out: *From my secret sins cleanse me, O Lord, and from those of others spare Thy servant? I believe and therefore do I speak.* Lord, Thou knowest, *Have I not confessed against myself my transgressions against Thee, and Thou, my God, hast forgiven the iniquities of my heart? I contend not in judgment with Thee,* who art the truth; and I have no will to deceive myself, *lest my iniquity lie unto itself.* Therefore I contend not in judgment with Thee, for *if Thou, O Lord, wilt mark iniquities, Lord, who shall endure it?*

Saint Augustine

THRUSTING TOWARDS THE SUMMIT

Now do I see that never can our intellect be
sated, unless that Truth shine on it, beyond
which no truth hath range.

Therein it resteth as a wild beast in his den so
soon as it hath reached it; and reach it may;
else were all longing futile.

Wherefore there springeth, like a shoot,
questioning at the foot of truth; which is a thing
that thrusteth us towards the summit, on from
ridge to ridge.

Dante

THERE IS NONE GOOD BUT ONE

Thou hearest of good and dost pant for it: thou hearest
of good and sighest for it: and even whenever thou sin-
nest, it is perhaps because thou art mistaken in the eagerness of thy choice of good; and in this thou art liable to
condemnation, that thou hearest not the good counsel of
God, as to what ought to be spurned, and what to be
chosen; in that perhaps thou neglectest to learn, if thou
wast deceived in thy choice of good. Wherever thou sin-
nest, thou art as it were seeking for a good, longing for
refreshment. These objects of thy search are good; but
unto thee they will be evil, if He by whom they were
made good be forsaken. Seek thy own good, O soul. For
one thing is good to one creature, another to another, and
all creatures have a certain good of their own, to the completeness and perfection of their nature. There is a difference as to what is essential to each imperfect thing, in
order that it may be made perfect; seek for thy own good.
There is none good but One, that is, God. The highest

good is thy good. What then is wanting unto him to whom the highest good is good? For there are inferior goods, which are good to different creatures respectively. What, brethren, is good unto the cattle, save to fill the belly, prevent want, to sleep, to indulge themselves, to exist, to be in health, to propagate? This is good for them: and within certain bounds it hath an allotted measure of good, granted by God, the Creator of all things. Dost thou seek such a good as this? God giveth also this: but do not pursue it alone. Canst thou, a coheir of Christ, rejoice in fellowship with cattle? Raise thy hope to the good of all goods. He will be thy good, by whom thou in thy kind were made good. For God made all things very good. If therefore we say that That good, which is God, is very good, it hath already been said of the creation: God made everything very good. What therefore is that good whereof it is said, There is none good but One, that is, God? Do we say that it is very good? We call to mind that this is said of the whole creation, God made all things very good. What then are we to say? Our words are wanting, but not our feeling. Let us remember the Psalm lately treated of: we cannot express our feeling, let us shout for joy. God is good. What sort of good, who can say? Lo, we cannot say, and we are not allowed to be silent. If then we cannot say, and for our joy are not able to be silent, let us neither speak nor be silent. What then are we to do, neither speaking nor silent? Let us shout for joy. Jubilate unto the God of our salvation. Jubilate unto God, every land. What meaneth Jubilate? Utter the ineffable accents of your joy, and let your delight burst forth before Him. And what will this burst be after the full feast, if even now after slight refreshment the soul is so much affected? What will it be, when it shall be done after our redemption from all corruption, as is said in this Psalm, He shall satisfy thy longing with good things?

Saint Augustine

THE COLLAR

I struck the board, and cry'd, "No more,
    I will abroad."
What, shall I ever sigh and pine?
My lines and life are free; free as the road,
Loose as the wind, as large as store.
    Shall I be still in suit?
Have I no harvest but a thorn
To let me blood, and not restore
What I have lost with cordial fruit?
    Sure there was wine
Before my sighs did dry it; there was corn
Before my tears did drown it;
Is the year only lost to me?
Have I no bays to crown it?
No flowers, no garlands gay? all blasted,
    All wasted?
Not so, my heart; but there is fruit,
    And thou hast hands.
Recover all thy sigh-blown age
On double pleasures; leave thy cold dispute
Of what is fit and not; forsake thy cage,
    Thy rope of sands
Which petty thoughts have made: and made to thee
Good cable, to enforce and draw,
    And be thy law
While thou didst wink and wouldst not see.
    Away: take heed:
    I will abroad.
Call in thy death's-head there, tie up thy fears,
    He that forbears
To suit and serve his need
    Deserves his load.
But as I rav'd and grew more fierce and wild
    At every word,

Methought I heard one calling, "Child":
  And I replied, "My Lord."

George Herbert

FOR HIM OUR HEARTS SIGH

Arrest ye in your courses, oh, wild and foolish souls,
rein in your steps, retire within yourselves, and, rising to
the loftiest point of your intellect, you will touch Supreme
Unity by uniting all that is of you with It, and comprehend
somewhat of the Infinity comprehending you.

It is for Him that our hearts sigh by impulses prompt
and inexplicable, because, flashed up to infinity, the sensitive apex of the soul approaches this Indivisible through
a conception surpassing reason and a love outrunning the
questings of knowledge.

Yves of Paris

THE SOUL BEFORE GOD

Take me away, and in the lowest deep
  There let me be,
And there in hope the lone night-watches keep,
  Told out for me.
There, motionless and happy in my pain,
  Lone, not forlorn—
There will I sing my sad perpetual strain,
  Until the morn.
There will I sing, and soothe my stricken breast,
  Which ne'er can cease
To throb, and pine, and languish, till possest
  Of its Sole Peace.
There will I sing my absent Lord and Love:—
  Take me away,
That sooner I may rise, and go above,
And see Him in the truth of everlasting day.

Cardinal Newman

THOU HAST MADE US FOR THEE, O GOD

For thus saith the Lord to the house of Israel:
See ye me, and you shall live.

Amos 5, 4

My soul hath stuck close to thee:
thy right hand hath received me.

Psalm 62, 9

For God created man incorruptible,
and to the image of his own likeness he made him.

Wisdom 2, 23

He who secures his own life will lose it; it is the man
who loses his life for my sake that will secure it.

Matthew 10, 39

All those who from the first were known to him, he has
destined from the first to be moulded into the image of
his Son, who is thus to become the eldest-born among
many brethren.

Romans 8, 29

So Paul stood up in full view of the Areopagus, and said, Men of Athens, wherever I look I find you scrupulously religious. Why, in examining your monuments as I passed by them, I found among others an alter which bore the inscription, To the unknown God. And it is this unknown object of your devotion that I am revealing to you. The God who made the world and all that is in it, that God who is Lord of heaven and earth, does not dwell in temples that our hands have made; no human handicraft can do him service, as if he stood in need of anything, he, who gives to all of us life and breath and all we have. It is he who has made, of one single stock, all the nations that were to dwell over the whole face of the earth. And he has given to each the cycles it was to pass through and the fixed limits of its habitation, leaving them to search for God; would they somehow grope their way towards him? Would they find him? And yet, after all, he is not far from any one of us; it is in him that we live, and move, and have our being; thus some of your own poets have told us, For indeed, we are his children. Why then, if we are the children of God, we must not imagine that the divine nature can be represented in gold, or silver, or stone, carved by man's art and thought. God has shut his eyes to these passing follies of ours; now, he calls upon all men, everywhere, to repent, because he has fixed a day when he will pronounce just judgment on the whole world. And the man whom he has appointed for that end he has accredited to all of us, by raising him up from the dead.

When resurrection from the dead was mentioned, some mocked, while others said, We must hear more from thee about this. So Paul went away from among them.

Acts 17, 22–33

All forces have a meaning and a task. And this is to satisfy eternal truth.

Suso

When we feel within ourselves that we desire God, then God has touched the mainspring of power, and through this touch it swings beyond itself and towards God.

Theologia Germanica

Not all the time can the soul live in the thought of God's condescending friendship, for nature would run the risk of seeking itself through it. Nor can it constantly cling to the thought of the cross, for it would crush nature. But it could and should abide in God, in God alone! God above all graces, God above every cross!

Lucie Christine

LOVE IS THE NATURE OF THE SOUL

The fish will never drown within the tide,
Nor birds fall from the air on which they ride.
The flame will not corrode or blacken gold,
For fire burns it pure and clean,
Gives it a shining colour.
To all His creatures God has granted
To live according to their nature.
How then could I deny my breath and bone?
In all things I submit to God alone,
Who is my father by nature,
Who is my brother by His humanhood,
Who is my bridegroom by His love,
And from the outset I am all His own.

Mechtild of Magdeburg

OF THE TRUE GOD

One thing is certain: you can love only what is good. The earth is good with the height of its mountains, the depths of its valleys, and the level stretches of its fields. And a country estate is good in its charm and fruitfulness. And a well-proportioned house is good in its spacious brightness. And living creatures are good with their live bodies, and the gentle air is good, and well-tasting and wholesome food. And sturdy health is good, without pain and weariness, and the countenance of man is good, the well-shaped face with its vividness and its clear, fresh colours. And the heart of a friend is good with its sweet sympathy and its steadfast love. And a man of honesty and integrity is good, and riches are good, that let us live effortlessly. And the sky is good with its sun, and moon, and stars. And angels are good in their holy submission, and the word is good that tenderly teaches and fittingly admonishes the listener. And the song is good in the pleasing sound of its rhythms and the earnestness of its deep meaning. And how much, how much else! This is good and that is good. But put this and that aside and look, if you can, upon the true Good. For then you will see God who is good, not through another good, but who is the good of all good. Yes, of all the things I have enumerated and others we may see or think of, we could not choose between them and call one better than another if we were not permeated with the concept of the true Good, measured against which we now affirm a thing, and now place one thing above another. This is how we should love God: not as we love any good thing, as this or that, but as the true good in itself. For the soul has an urge to a good which is beyond its judgment, and can be embraced only by love, and what is this, if not God? Not the good soul, not the good angel, not the good heavens, but only the good of good.

Perhaps this will show more clearly what I want to say. If, for example, I hear someone say, "good soul," the fact that there are two words gives me a twofold impression: there is a soul and it is good. The soul has done nothing towards being a soul, and nothing existed that the soul could have wrought. But to be a "good soul" that, I believe, requires an act of the will. Not that whatever has made the soul a soul is not something good—for how else could it be called, and properly called, better than the body?—but the soul is called a "not yet good" soul because it has still to perform the act of the will through which it receives its higher value. If it is unable to perform this act of will it is justly regarded as guilty, and with good reason is called a soul that is "not good." For then it is far remote from the soul that performs this act of will, and is just as reprehensible as the other is praiseworthy. But the soul only arrives at the goal of being a "good" soul if it is full of zeal, and keeps itself free of everything that is alien to its being. To accomplish this, where shall we turn if not to the highest good toward which it reaches with its innermost urge and love? . . .

There is no life that does not spring from God. For God is the highest life and the source of all life. And no kind of life, in so far as it is life, is evil. It is evil only in so far as it clings to death. Worthlessness alone is the death of life, and takes its name from being worth nothing . . . That life, then, that voluntarily deserts Him who has made it, and Whose spirit was precious to it, that life that, contrary to the law of God, sought to find the highest preciousness in the world of carnal matters, above which God had placed it—that life clings to nothingness and is, therefore, worth nothing. . . .

Blessed is only he who has the highest good that can be grasped and held only in that truth which we call wisdom. Before we reach this life of bliss, the concept of blessedness is graven in our spirit and through it, we know and we say concerning ourselves, in perfect certainty that is beyond all doubt: we want to be blessed. Thus, before we are wise the concept of wisdom is graven in our spirit, and because of it everyone, in answer to the question whether he would be wise or no, will say beyond doubt and clearly: I would!

Saint Augustine

I would that I were home again
Where comforts of the world are vain.

I mean in heaven, that I might
Eternally have God in sight.

My soul, rejoice, my soul, prepare!
The angels all await you there.

You will go home the sooner when
You find how small's the world of men.

At home there is no death, but life,
And perfect bliss withouten strife.

Heinrich of Lauffenberg

NATURAL INCLINATION TO LOVE GOD ABOVE ALL THINGS

Although the state of human nature may not be now
endowed with its original health and rectitude . . . it is on
the contrary gravely depraved by sin, yet the sacred inclination to love God above all things has remained in us,
as well as the natural light by which we recognise that
His Sovereign Goodness is loving over all; it is impossible
that a man attentively thinking of God, nay, even only
casually talking of Him, should not feel a certain impulse
of love springing from the depths of his heart by the secret
trend of nature, by which, at the earliest awareness of
this First and Sovereign Object, the will is awakened and
prompted to delight itself in Him. With partridges, it often
occurs that some steal the eggs of others, in order to brood
. . . and it is a strange but nevertheless well-attested fact
that when the chick hatched and nourished under the
wing of the thievish partridge first hears the cry of the
true mother . . . it forthwith quits its thievish partridge,

and hurries to meet and follow its own parent, drawn by its correspondence with her, which had remained hidden and as though sleeping in the depths of its nature, until the encounter of each with each . . . Thus it is with our heart, for although hatched, nourished and brought up among things temporal, low and transitory, and, so to speak, under the wings of nature, yet at the first look it casts towards God, at the first consciousness inspired by Him, the natural inborn inclination to love Him, slumbering and imperceptible till now, awakes in an instant unawares, as a spark among ashes, and affecting the will, gives it an impulse of the supreme love due to the Sovereign and First Principle of all things.

Saint Francis de Sales

GOD INTIMATELY IN US

God exists in all things, not as a part of their essence or as one of their accidents, but He exists in them as an agent is present in that which it works upon. For an agent must be in immediate relation with that upon which it works, it must touch it by its efficacious power; from which Aristotle demonstrates in his *Physics* that the thing moved and the mover must exist at one and the same time. Now since God is existence itself by His own essence, it follows that created existence must be His proper effect, in the same way as to ignite is the proper effect of fire. This effect God produces in things not only when they are first given being, but as long as they conserve it; in the same way as light is produced by the sun as long as the earth remains illuminated. Thus, so long as a thing exists, so long is God present to its being. But the being of a thing is that which is most intimate to it, it is that which most deeply resides in it, since being is the form of all that which it encloses. Hence God is in all things, and is intimately in them.

Saint Thomas Aquinas

OUR SOUL LIKENED TO THE DIVINE PERSON

Grace renders the soul like to God. Thus when the soul has become similar to the Divine Person through grace, then, but only then, is the Divine Person sent to her. Since the Holy Ghost is love, the soul is assimilated to Him through charity: this supernatural virtue thus enters, intellectually, in the mission of the Holy Ghost. As for the Son, He is the Word, and the Word that breathes forth love. "By the Word," says Saint Augustine, in *On the Trinity*, 9, 10, "we mean knowledge joined with love." The Son is not sent to perfect understanding, but to give it the kind of perfection that gives birth to love. In *John* 6, 45, the Master says: "Every one that hath heard of the Father and hath learned cometh to Me"; and the Prophet, in *Psalm* 38, 4: "My heart grew hot within me: and in my meditation a fire shall flame out." We must understand these words of Saint Augustine: "The Son is sent in an invisible manner, whenever He is known and perceived." That last participle says more than the first: *perceiving* implies a certain experimental knowledge. In the same way, the word *wisdom* implies the idea of science and savour; and the Holy Spirit says in *Ecclesiasticus* 6, 23: "The wisdom of doctrine is according to her name."

Saint Thomas Aquinas

CARRION COMFORT

Not, I'll not, carrion comfort, Despair, not feast on thee;
Not untwist—slack they may be—these last strands of man
In me or, most weary, cry I can no more. I can;
Can something, hope, wish day come, not choose not to be.
But ah, but O thou terrible, why wouldst thou rude on me
Thy wring-world right foot rock? lay a lionlimb against
     me? scan
With darksome devouring eyes my bruisèd bones? and fan,

O in turns of tempest, me heaped there; me frantic to
    avoid thee and flee?
Why? That my chaff might fly; my grain lie, sheer and
    clear.
Nay in all that toil, that coil, since (seems) I kissed the
    rod,
Hand rather, my heart lo! lapped strength, stole joy, would
    laugh, cheer.
Cheer whom though? the hero whose heaven-handling
    flung me, foot trod
Me? or me that fought him? O which one? is it each one?
    That night, that year
Of now done darkness I wretch lay wrestling with (my
    God!) my God.

Gerard Manley Hopkins

SECOND PART

All things are but loss

DETACHMENT

Blessed are the poor in spirit;
the kingdom of heaven is theirs.

Matthew 5, 3

ALL WEAL IN ONE

In One is all my peace, in One my weal is done,
Though many things be lost to me, I run to One.

THE SPIRITUAL PEAK

I am a peak in God, and upward must I pace
Upon myself, that God may show His tender face.

LET THE SOMETHING FALL

Man, if you love some thing, you love no thing at all,
God is not this or that, so let the Something fall.

Angelus Silesius

ALONE WITH THE ALONE

Leave me alone, sheltered in my cell. Leave me with
God who alone is my benign. Go away, remove yourself

farther, leave me alone, let me die before God who created me. Nobody may knock at my door, nobody raise his voice. None of my acquaintances and friends may visit me, none shall draw away my mind from the contemplation of the good and beautiful Lord. Nobody hands me food, nobody brings me drink: I am satisfied to abide before the face of my God, my merciful God, my benign God, who came down on earth to call the sinners and to bring them within Him into heavenly life. I do not want to see any longer the light of this world nor the sun itself nor what inhabits the world. For I see my God, I see my King, I see the true Light and the Creator of all light. I see the source of all good. I see the maker and cause of all things. I behold the Beginning which has no beginning by whom all things were made, by whom all things live and are filled with good. If He wills, all ceases and withers away. How could I leave my cell for the things I have left? Leave me! I shall lament and deplore the nights and the days which I lost, when I gazed at this world, at the sun, at this light of the world of the senses, so dark: it does not enlighten the soul. In it live those who are slaves of their eyes and when, in death, they have passed away they will be like those who are now seeing. Once also I enjoyed myself in all fashions as a tramp. I believed there was no other light which might be the vital life, as we said, and altogether the cause of all essence that is and will be. I was like an "atheos," a man without God, when I did not know my God.

But now, after it pleased the unspeakable Mercy to let itself be seen by me and to reveal itself to me, the unworthy one, I see and truly know that He is the God of the universe, the God of all who are in the world. None of the children of man has seen Him face to face. For He is outside of the world, outside of light and darkness, outside of mind and intellect.

Thus I too have left the world of the senses, living in the gaze of Him.

Therefore you who are dominated by your senses, leave

me in peace. Let me lock my cell and sit therein. And if
I dig into the earth to hide myself within, and if I lead
my life there away from the world, and if I desire to die
for love of Him gazing at the eternal Creator and Lord—
leave me do it!

What good could the world offer me? What can they
now give me, those out in the world? Nothing indeed!
Naked they live in tombs, naked they will rise again and
all will be judged: for they have all left Christ, I say, the
true Life, the Light of the world. They all loved darkness,
and have chosen to walk in it—all those who have not received the light that shone in the world, the light which
the world cannot comprehend and cannot see.

Therefore leave me, leave me alone, I beg of you, that
I may weep and seek Him, until He is given me and I
may see Him in His fulness. Yea, He is not only seen or
contemplated: He communicates Himself, He makes His
abode and remains and is like a treasure hidden in the
bosom. He who bears Him has spiritual lust and He who
sees Him shouts in his heart and deems that He ought to
be visible to all even though He is hidden. But not all
see and touch Him. No thief nor robber can tear Him
away or abscond Him, even if one strangles him who carries Him . . . Nor does one see Him with eyes or seize
Him with hands. While He is totally attainable, He is yet
at the same time unattainable. Yea, hands* of the worthy
hold Him—flee ye unworthy!—and He lies in the hand as
a something—O miracle—and yet not as something, for He
is above all names. How incomprehensible . . .

Why do we let ourselves perturb, why do we permit
ourselves to be deceived, why do we thirst after light here,
light which serves our sensual nature, while we are endowed with a spiritual reason? Why do we return to the
perishable, withering things of this life, although we are
endowed with an immaterial, immortal soul? We are fools!
We live ourselves into these things with admiring eyes

* This statement refers to communion, which in this period
of church history was received in the hands of the faithful.

and we grope after iron instead of gold, after the sweets
of children instead of the precious pearl! We seek not the
little mustard seed which is greater and more precious
than all that eyes can see and all invisible things! Why
do we not compare and then give all for it? Why do we let
ourselves be deceived and why do we wish to remain in
life? Believe me: if it cost the death of death to purchase
this little seed, the price would not be too high.

Woe to them who do not carry this seed in their heart!
A great hunger will befall them. Woe to them who did
not see it sprout! They will stand there in their nakedness,
like trees which have lost their leaves . . . And I, too,
am among them, slothful, constant only in inconstancy.

But Thou, O undivided Triune, O universal One, O
Light, for whom there never was a name and never will
be one, O Being, who hast so many names after Thy
works, in which Thou workest everything, O sole Glory,
O Origin, Might and Kingdom, O Light, in whom all is
one, will, word and command and strength and virtue—
have mercy on me who am cast down.

Symeon the Younger

DETACHMENT

I have read many writings of heathen philosophers and
sages, of the old covenant and of the new, and have
sought earnestly and with all diligence which is the best
and highest virtue whereby a man may knit himself most
narrowly to God and wherein he is most like to his exemplar, as he was in God, wherein was no difference between
himself and God, ere God created creature. And having
approfounded all these scriptures to the best of my ability,
I find it is none other than absolute detachment from all
creatures.

Peradventure thou wilt say, What then is detachment
that it should be so noble in itself?—True detachment

means a mind as little moved by what befalls, by joy and
sorrow, honour and disgrace, as a broad mountain by a
gentle breeze. Such motionless detachment makes a man
superlatively Godlike. For that God is God is due to his
motionless detachment, and it is from his detachment that
he gets his purity and his simplicity and his immutability.
If then a man is going to be like God so far as any creature can resemble God, it will be by detachment. This
leads to purity and from purity to simplicity and from
simplicity to immovability; and it is these three which
constitute the likeness between man and God, which likeness is in grace, for it is grace which draws a man away
from mortal things and purges him from things corruptible.
I would have you know that to be empty of creatures is
to be full of God and to be full of creatures is to be empty
of God.

Now it must be remembered that in this immutable detachment God has stood for aye and does still stand.
Know also, that when God created the heavens and the
earth he might not have been making anything at all for
all that it affected his detachment. Nay, I say more:
prayers and good works wrought by a man in time affect
no more the divine detachment than if no prayers nor
virtuous works had come to pass in time; nor is God any
kindlier disposed towards that wight than if his prayers
and deeds had all been left undone. Further, I declare,
when the Son in his Godhead was pleased to be made man
and was and suffered martyrdom, God's motionless detachment was no more disturbed than if he had never
been made man.

Haply thou wilt say, I gather then that prayers and virtuous deeds are all in vain; God takes too little interest in
them to be affected by them. And yet they say God
likes to be entreated upon all occasions.

Now mark, and realise if possible, that in his first eternal
glance (if a first glance may be assumed) God saw all
things as they would happen and he saw in that same
glance both when and how he would make creatures. He

saw the humblest prayer that would be offered, the least good deed that anyone would do, and saw withal which prayers and which devotions he would hear. He saw that to-morrow thou shalt call upon him earnestly, urgently entreating him; and not for the first time to-morrow will God grant thy supplication and thy prayer: he has granted it already in his eternity ere ever thou becamest man. Suppose thy prayer is foolish or lacking earnestness, God will deny it thee not then, he has denied it thee already in his eternity. Thus God, who has seen everything in that first eternal glance, in no wise acts from any why at all, for everything is a foregone conclusion.

What then, I ask, is the object of absolute detachment? I answer, that the object of absolute detachment is neither this nor that. It is absolutely nothing, for it is the culminating point where God can do precisely as he will. God cannot have his way in every heart, for though God is almighty yet he cannot work except where he finds readiness or makes it. I add, or makes it, by reason of St. Paul, in whom he found no readiness, but whom he did make ready by infusion of his grace; wherefore I affirm, God works according to the aptitude he finds. He works differently in man and in a stone, and for this we have a natural analogy. If you heat a baker's oven and place in it the dough, some made of barley, some of oats and some of wheat and some of rye, then albeit in the oven the heat is all the same it does not tell alike on all the doughs, but one yields a fine bread, another one more coarse and a third coarser still. The heat is not to blame: it is the material which differs. Nor does God tell alike on every heart but according to the readiness and the capacity he finds. In any heart containing this or that there is something to hinder God's highest operation. For a heart to be perfectly ready it has to be perfectly empty, this being its condition of maximum capacity. To take another common illustration: suppose I want to write on a white tablet, then anything already written there, however excellent it be, will interfere and hinder me from writing; ere I can write I must erase completely whatever is already on the tablet, which is never better fitted for me to write upon than when there is nothing there at all. And so for God to write his very best within my heart everything dubbed this or that must be ousted from my heart, leaving it quite without attachment. God is free to work his sovereign will when the object of this solitary heart is neither this nor that.

Then again I ask, What is the prayer of the solitary heart? I answer, that detachment and emptiness cannot pray at all, for whoso prays desires of God something: something added to him or something taken from him. But the heart detached has no desire for anything nor has it anything to be delivered from. So it has no prayers at all; its only prayer consists in being uniform with God. In this sense we may take St. Dionysius' comment on the saying of St. Paul, "Many there be that run, but one receiveth the prize." All the powers of the soul competing for the crown which falls to the essence alone. According to Dionysius this running is none other than the flight from creature to union with uncreated nature. Attaining this the soul loses her name; God absorbs her in himself so that as self she comes to naught, just as the sunlight swallows up the dawn and naughts it. To this pass nothing brings the soul but absolute detachment. And here it is germane to quote St. Augustine's dictum: "The soul has a private door into divine nature at the point where for her things all come to naught." This door on earth is none other than absolute detachment. At the height of her detachment she is ignorant with knowing, loveless with loving, dark with enlightenment.

Here too we might cite a master's words, Blessed are the spiritual poor who have abandoned unto God all things as he possessed them when we existed not. This none can do but a heart wholly without attachment.

That God would sooner be in a solitary heart than any other, I argue in this fashion. Starting from thy question,

What does God seek in all things? I answer in his words out of the Book of Wisdom, "In all things I seek rest." Now there is nowhere perfect rest save in a heart detached. Ergo, God is happier there than in any other thing or virtue. Know that the more we are disposed to receive the inflowing God, the more happy we shall be: perfect receptivity gives perfect felicity. Now one makes oneself receptive to the influence of God only by dint of uniformity with God; as a man's uniformity with God, so is his sense of the inflow of God. Uniformity comes of subjection to God, and the more one is subject to creature the less one is uniform with God. But the heart which is quite detached and all devoid of creatures, being utterly subject to God and uniform with God in the highest measure, is wholly receptive of his divine inflow. Hence St. Paul's exhortation to "Put on Christ," *i.e.* uniformity with Christ. For know, when Christ was made man it was not a certain man that he assumed, he assumed human nature. Do thou go out of all things, then there remains alone what Christ put on and thou hast put on Christ.

Whoso has a mind to know the excellence and use of absolute detachment let him lay to heart Christ's words to his disciples touching his manhood: "It is good for you that I go away; if I go not away the comforter cannot come unto you"; as though to say, ye have too much love for my visible form for the perfect love of the Holy Ghost to be yours. Wherefore discard the form and unite with the formless essence, for God's ghostly comfort is intangible and is not offered save to those alone who despise all mortal consolations.

List ye, good people all: there is none happier than he who stands in uttermost detachment. No temporal, carnal pleasure but brings some ghostly mischief in its train, for the flesh lusts after things that run counter to the spirit and spirit lusts for things that are repugnant to the flesh. He who sows the tares of love in flesh reaps death, but he who sows good love-seed in the spirit reaps of the spirit eternal life. The more man flees from creatures the faster hastens to him their creator. Consider, all ye thoughtful souls! If even the love which it is given us to feel for the bodily form of Christ can keep us from receiving the Holy Ghost, then how much more must we be kept from getting God by inordinate love of creature comforts? Detachment is the best of all, for it cleanses the soul, clarifies the mind, kindles the heart and wakes the spirit; it quickens desire and enhances virtue giving intuition of God; it detaches creature and makes her one with God; for love disjoined from God is as water in the fire, but love in union is like the honeycomb in honey. Harkee, all rational souls! The swiftest steed to bear you to your goal is suffering; none shall ever taste eternal bliss but those who stand with Christ in depths of bitterness. Nothing is more gall-bitter than suffering, nothing so honey-sweet as to have suffered. The most sure foundation for this perfection is humility, for he whose nature here creeps in deepest depths shall soar in spirit to highest height of Deity; for joy brings sorrow and sorrow brings joy. Men's ways are manifold: one lives thus, another thus. He who would attain unto the highest life while here in time, let him take in a few words culled out of all the scriptures the summary philosophy which I will now set down.

Keep thyself detached from all mankind; keep thyself devoid of all incoming images; emancipate thyself from everything which entails addition, attachment or encumbrance, and address thy mind at all times to a saving contemplation wherein thou bearest God fixed within thy heart as the object from which its eyes do never waver; any other discipline, fasts, vigils, prayers, or whatever it may be, subordinate to this as to its end, using thereof no more than shall answer for this purpose, so shalt thou win the goal of all perfections.

Here someone may object, But who can persist in unwavering contemplation of the divine object? I answer, no one living here in time. This is told thee merely so that thou mayest know the highest, that whereon thy aspirations and desires should be set. But when this vision is withheld from thee, thou, being a good man, shalt think to have been robbed of thy eternal bliss and then do thou forthwith return into the same that it may come to thee again; and withal it does behove thee to keep strict watch upon thy thoughts at all times, there letting, as far as possible, their goal and refuge be. Lord God, glory be to thee eternally. Amen.

Meister Eckhart

DIVERSITIES BETWEEN NATURE AND GRACE

My son, mark diligently the stirrings of nature and grace; for in a very contrary yet subtle manner do they move, so that they can hardly be distinguished but by him that is spiritually and inwardly enlightened. All men indeed desire that which is good, and pretend some good in their words and deeds; and therefore under the show of good, many are deceived.

Nature is crafty, and seduceth many, ensnareth and deceiveth them, and always proposeth herself for her end and object. But grace walketh in simplicity, abstaineth from all show of evil, sheltereth not herself under deceits, doeth all things purely for God's sake, in whom also she finally resteth.

Nature is unwilling and loth to die, or to be kept down, or to be overcome, or to be in subjection, or readily to be subdued. But grace studieth self-mortification, resisteth sensuality, seeketh to be in subjection, is desirous to be kept under, and wisheth not to use her own liberty. She loveth to be kept under discipline, and desireth not to rule over any, but always to live and remain and be under God, and for God's sake is ready humbly to bow down unto all.

Nature striveth for her own advantage, and considereth what profit she may reap by another. Grace considereth not what is profitable and convenient unto herself, but rather what may be for the good of many. Nature willingly receiveth honour and reverence. Grace faithfully attributeth all honour and glory unto God. Nature feareth shame and contempt. Grace rejoiceth to suffer reproach for the Name of JESUS. Nature loveth leisure and bodily ease. Grace cannot be unemployed, but cheerfully embraceth labour.

Nature seeketh to have things that are curious and beautiful, and abhorreth those which are cheap and coarse. Grace delighteth in what is plain and humble, despiseth not rough things, and refuseth not to be clothed in that which is old and worn. Nature respecteth temporal things, rejoiceth at earthly gain, sorroweth for loss, is irritated by every little injurious word. Grace looketh to things eternal, cleaveth not to things temporal, is not disturbed at losses, nor soured with hard words; because she hath placed her treasure and joy in heaven, where nothing of it perisheth. Nature is covetous, doth more willingly receive than give, and loveth to have things private and her own. Grace is kind of heart, and ready to share with others, shunteth private interest, is content with a little, judgeth that it is more blessed to give than to receive.

Nature inclineth a man to the creature, to his own flesh, to vanities, and to wandering hither and thither. Grace draweth him unto God and to every virtue, renounceth the creature, hateth the desires of the flesh, restraineth wanderings abroad, blusheth to be seen in public. Nature is willing to have some outward solace, whereby she may receive delight of the senses. Grace seeketh consolation in God alone, and to have delight in the highest good above all visible things.

Nature turneth everything to her own gain and profit, she cannot bear to do anything without reward, but for every kindness she hopeth to obtain either what is equal, or what is better, or at least praise or favour; and is very earnest to have her works and gifts much valued. Grace seeketh no temporal things, nor desireth any other reward

save God alone, and asketh not more of temporal neces-
saries than what may serve her for the obtaining of things
eternal.

Nature rejoiceth to have many friends and kinsfolk, she
glorieth of noble place and noble birth, she smileth on the
powerful, fawneth upon the rich, applaudeth those who
are like herself. Grace loveth even her enemies, and is not
puffed up with multitude of friends; and thinketh not
greatly of high birth, unless it be joined with more exalted
virtue. Grace favoureth the poor rather than the rich,
sympathiseth more with the innocent than with the powerful, rejoiceth with the true man, not with the deceitful.
She is ever exhorting good men to strive for the best gifts;
and by all virtue to become like to the Son of God.

Nature quickly complaineth of want and of trouble.
Grace endureth need with firmness and constancy. Nature
referreth all things to herself, striveth and argueth for
herself. Grace bringeth back all to God, from whence
originally they proceed; she ascribeth no good to herself,
nor doth she arrogantly presume; she contendeth not,
nor preferreth her own opinion before others'; but in every
matter of sense and understanding she submitteth herself
unto the eternal wisdom and the divine judgment.

Nature is eager to know secrets, and to hear news; she
loveth to appear abroad and to make proof of many things
by her own senses; she desireth to be acknowledged, and
to do things for which she may be praised and admired.
Grace careth not to hear news, nor to understand curious
matters (because all this taketh its rise from the old corruption of man), seeing that upon earth there is nothing
new, nothing durable. Grace teacheth, therefore, to restrain the senses, to shun vain complacency and ostenta-
tion, humbly to hide those things that are worthy of admiration and praise, and from everything and in every
knowledge to seek profitable fruit, and the praise and
honour of God. She will not have herself nor that which
pertaineth to her publicly praised, but desireth that God

should be blessed in his gifts, because that of mere love he bestoweth all things.

This grace is a supernatural light, and a certain special gift of God, and the proper mark of the elect, and a pledge of everlasting salvation. It raiseth up a man from earthly things to love the things of heaven, and from being carnal maketh him a spiritual man. The more, therefore, nature is depressed and subdued, so much the more is grace infused, and every day by new visitations the inward man is created anew according to the image of God.

Imitatio Christi

SIMPLICITY

This exercise of the continual abandonment of oneself in the hands of God excellently comprehends within its perfect simplicity and purity all the perfection of other exercises; and while God leaves us the use of it, we must not change it. Spiritual lovers, the spouses of the Heavenly King, look at themselves from time to time, like doves that are near very pure waters, to see if they are ornamented so as to please their lover; and that is done by the examinations of conscience, in which they cleanse, purify, and adorn themselves as best they can, not to be perfect, not to satisfy themselves, not from the desire of advancing in virtue, but to obey their Spouse, from the reverence they bear Him, and from their extreme desire to please Him. But is it not a very pure and simple love, since they do not purify themselves in order to be pure, they do not adorn themselves in order to be beautiful, but only to please their Spouse, to whom if ugliness were equally agreeable, they would like it as well as beauty? And so these simple doves do not bestow very long nor very anxious pains on washing and adorning themselves; for the confidence their love gives them that they are greatly beloved, though unworthy (the confidence I say which their love gives them in the love and goodness of their lover), takes away all anxiety and mistrust lest they should not be beautiful enough; besides which, the desire of loving rather than of adorning themselves and preparing for love cuts short all careful solicitude, and makes them content themselves with a sweet and faithful preparation, made lovingly and with good will.

And to conclude this point, St. Francis, sending his children into the fields, on a journey, gave them instead of money, and for their whole provision, this advice: Cast your care on our Lord and He will feed you. I say the same to you, my very dear daughters, cast all your heart, your desires, your cares, and your affections on the paternal bosom of God, and He will lead you and carry you where His love wishes you to be.

Saint Francis de Sales

One day, before Matin, the sacristan saw him [Saint Thomas] raised nearly three feet above the ground and stood a long time gazing at him. Suddenly he heard a voice proceed from the image of the crucifix to which the Doctor was turned, praying in tears: "Thou hast written well of me, Thomas. What reward shall I give thee for thy work?"—"None but Thyself, O Lord!"

Saint Thomas Aquinas
as related by Jacques Maritain

BE THOU MY CHOOSER FOR ME

O my God, let me walk in the way of love which knoweth not how to seek self in anything whatsoever. Let this love wholly possess my soul and heart, which, I beseech Thee, may live and move only in, and out of, a pure and sincere love to Thee. Oh! that Thy pure love were so grounded and established in my heart that I might sigh and pant without ceasing after Thee, and be able in strength of this Thy love to live without all comfort and consolation, human or divine. O sight to be wished, desired, and longed for, because once to have seen Thee is to have learned all things! Nothing can bring us to this sight but love. But what love must it be? Not a sensible love only, a childish love, a love which seeketh itself more than the Beloved. No, it must be an ardent love, a pure love, a courageous love, a love of charity, a humble love, and a constant love, nor worn out with labours, nor daunted with any difficulties. O Lord, give this love into my soul, that I may never more live nor breathe but out of a most pure love of Thee, my All and only Good. Let me love Thee for Thyself, and nothing else but in and for Thee. Let me love nothing instead of Thee, for to give all for love is a most sweet bargain . . . Let Thy love work in me and by me, and let me love Thee as Thou wouldst be loved by me. I cannot tell how much love I would have of Thee, because I would love Thee beyond all that can be imagined or desired by me. Be Thou in this, as in all other things, my chooser for me, for Thou art my only choice, most dear to me. The more I shall love Thee, the more will my soul desire Thee, and desire to suffer for Thee.

Dame Gertrude More

STATE OF ABANDONMENT

"Offer a sacrifice of justice," says the Prophet, "and hope in the Lord." This means that the great and solid foundation of the spiritual life is to give oneself to God in order to be the subject of His good pleasure in everything internal and external, and afterwards to forget oneself so completely that one considers oneself as a thing sold and delivered to the purchaser to which one has no longer any right, in such a way that the good pleasure of God makes all our joy and His happiness, glory and being become our sole good.

This foundation being laid, the soul has nothing to do save to pass all her life in rejoicing that God is good, abandoning herself so completely to His good pleasure that she is equally content to do this or that, or the contrary, at the disposal of God, without reflecting on the use which His good pleasure makes of her.

To abandon oneself! This then is the great duty which remains to be fulfilled after we have acquitted ourselves faithfully of the duties of our state. The perfection with which this duty is accomplished will be the measure of our sanctity.

A holy soul is but a soul freely submitted to the Divine will with the help of grace. All that follows this simple acquiescence is the work of God and not of man. This soul should blindly resign herself in self-abandonment and universal indifference. This is the only disposition asked of her by God; the rest belongs to Him to choose and determine according to His designs, as an architect selects and marks the stones of the building he proposes to construct.

We should then love God and His order in everything, and we should love it as it presents itself, desiring nothing more. That these or those objects should be presented is no concern of the soul, but of God, and what He gives is best. The whole of spirituality can be expressed in abridged form in this maxim: we should abandon ourselves purely and entirely to the Order of God, and when we are in that Order we should with a complete self-forgetfulness be eternally busied with loving and obeying Him, without all these fears, reflections, returns on ourselves, and disquietudes which sometimes result from the care of our own salvation and perfection. Since God offers to manage our affairs for us, let us once and for all hand them over to His infinite wisdom, in order to occupy ourselves only with Himself and what belongs to Him.

Come, my soul, let us pass with head erect over all that

happens within us or outside us, remaining always content with God, content with what He does with us and with what He makes us do. Let us be very careful not to engage imprudently in that multitude of restless reflections which like so many paths leading nowhere present themselves to our mind to make it wander and stray endlessly to our sheer loss: let us pass this labyrinth of our own self-love by vaulting over it and not by following it out in all its interminable details.

Come, my soul, let us pass beyond our languors, our illnesses, our aridities, our inequalities of humour, our weaknesses of mind, the snares of the devil and of men with their suspicions, jealousies, sinister ideas and prejudices. Let us fly like the eagle above all these clouds, our gaze fixed on the sun and on its rays, which are our duties. We feel all these miseries, and it does not depend on us to be insensible to them, but let us remember that our life is not a life of feeling. Let us live in that higher region of the soul where the will of God produces His eternal operation, ever equal, ever uniform, ever immutable. In that spiritual home where the Uncreated, the Formless, the Ineffable, keeps the soul infinitely removed from all the specific detail of created shadows and atoms, we remain calm even when our senses are the prey of the tempest. We have become independent of the senses; their agitations and disquietudes, their comings and goings and the hundreds of metamorphoses they pass through do not trouble us any more than the clouds that darken the sky for a moment and disappear. We know that everything happens in the senses as in the air where all is without connection or order, in a state of perpetual change. God and His will is the eternal object which charms the heart in the state of faith, as in the state of glory He will be its true felicity; and the state of the heart in glory will have its effect on the whole of our material being, at present the prey of monsters, owls and weird beasts. Under these appearances, however terrible they may be, the Divine action will give to our being a heavenly power and make it as shining as the sun; for the faculties of the sensitive soul and of the body are prepared here below like gold, iron, fine linen and precious stones. Like the material substratum of these various things, they will only enjoy the splendour and purity of their form after much manipulation and when much has been destroyed and cut away. All that souls endure here below under the hand of God has no other purpose than to prepare them for this.

Father J. P. de Caussade

HOLY INDIFFERENCE

Nevertheless, I am continually with Thee;
Thou holdest my right hand.
Thou wilt guide me with Thy counsel,
And afterward receive me with glory.

Whom have I in heaven but Thee?
And beside Thee I desire none upon earth.
My flesh and my heart faileth;
But God is the rock of my heart and my portion for ever.

For, lo, they that go far from Thee shall perish;
Thou dost destroy all them that go astray from Thee.

But as for me, the nearness of God is my good;
I have made the Lord God my refuge,
That I may tell of all Thy works.

Psalm 72, 23–28

Only, brethren, I would say this; the time is drawing
to an end; nothing remains, but for those who have wives
to behave as though they had none; those who weep must
forget their tears, and those who rejoice their rejoicing,
and those who buy must renounce possession; and those
who take advantage of what the world offers must not
take full advantage of it; the fashion of this world is soon
to pass away. And I would have you free from concern.

I Corinthians 7, 29–32

I know what it is to be brought low, and what it is to have abundant means; I have been apprenticed to everything, having my fill and going hungry, living in plenty and living in want; nothing is beyond my powers, thanks to the strength God gives me.

Philippians 4, 12–13

That man is worse than luckless on the quay,
Who fished for truth and did not know the rules,
And comes home poorer than he went away.

Dante

Just as one who wheels a barrow does not employ it for his delight but only because it is useful, so the gifts of God should be nothing but useful to us, and we should take delight in God alone.

Blessed John Tauler

"Open thy mouth wide and I will fill it" (*Psalm* 80, 11). Desire is the mouth of the will. This mouth opens wide unless it be hindered or quenched with some morsel of joy. The instant desire seizes upon anything, it is narrowed. But except for God only, all serves to narrow.

Saint John of the Cross

Everyone remembers the story of St. Charles Borromaeus and his game of chess. While others talked about what they would do if they heard that they had to die within that very hour, the saint said he would continue his game of chess. For he had begun it only in honour of God, and he could wish for nothing better than to be called away in the midst of an action undertaken in the honour of God.

Frederick William Faber

PRAYER OF SIMPLICITY

My spirit in its extreme summit is in a very simple unity; it does not unite, for when it desires to make acts of union, which it too often wishes to do on certain occasions, it feels a strain, and perceives clearly that it cannot unite itself, but only remain united: the soul would not willingly stir thence. She neither thinks nor does anything, unless it be a certain deepening of her desire which goes on, as it were imperceptibly, that God should do with her and with all creatures, in all things, all that He wills. She would do this only for the morning exercise, for that of Holy Mass, for the preparation for Holy Communion, as a thanksgiving for all benefits; in fine, for all things, she would merely abide in this very simple unity of spirit with God, without extending her outlook elsewhere.

Saint Jane Frances de Chantal

REPOSE IN GOD

There are souls active, fertile, and abounding in considerations. There are souls who readily double and bend back upon themselves, who love to feel what they are doing, who wish to see and scrutinise what passes in them, turning their view ever on themselves to discover the progress they are making. And there are yet others who are not content to be content unless they feel, see, and relish their contentment; these are like to persons who being well protected against the cold would not believe it if they knew not how many garments they had on, or who, seeing their cabinets full of money, would not esteem themselves rich unless they knew the number of their coins.

Now all these spirits are ordinarily subject to be troubled in prayer, for if God deign award them the sacred repose of His presence, they voluntarily forsake it to note their own behaviour therein, and to examine whether they are really content, disquieting themselves to discern whether their tranquillity is really tranquil, and their quietude quiet: so that instead of sweetly occupying their will in tasting the sweets of the divine presence, they employ their understanding in reasoning upon the feelings they have; as a bride who should keep her attention on her wedding-ring without looking upon the bridegroom who gave it her. There is a great difference between being occupied with God, who gives us the contentment, and being busied with the contentment which God gives us.

The soul, then, to whom God gives holy, loving quiet in prayer, must abstain as far as she is able from looking upon herself or her repose, which to be preserved must not be curiously observed; for he who loves it too much loses it, and the right rule of loving it properly is not to love it too anxiously. And as a child who, to see where his feet are, has taken his head from his mother's breast, immediately returns to it because he dearly loves it; so if we perceive ourselves distracted, through a curiosity to know what we are doing in prayer, we must replace our hearts in the sweet and peaceable attention to God's presence from which we strayed. Yet we are not to apprehend any danger of losing this sacred repose by actions of body or mind which are not done from lightness or indiscretion. For, as the Blessed Mother St. Teresa says, it were a superstition to be so jealous of this repose as not to cough, spit or breathe for fear of losing it, since God who gives this peace does not withdraw it for such necessary movements, nor yet for those distractions and wanderings of the mind which are not voluntary: and the will having once tasted the divine presence does not cease to relish its sweetness, though the understanding or memory should make an escape and slip away after foreign and useless thoughts.

It is true the repose of the soul is not then so great as when the understanding and memory conspire with the will, yet it is a true spiritual tranquillity, since it continues to reign in the will, which is the mistress of all the other faculties. Indeed, we have seen a soul most strongly fixed and united to her God, who yet had her understanding and memory so free from all interior occupation that she understood very distinctly all that was said around her, and perfectly remembered it, though she could not answer, or loose herself from God, to whom she was fastened by the application of her will. And so attached, I tell you, that she could not be withdrawn from this sweet entertainment without experiencing a great grief, which provoked her to sighs: these indeed she gave in the very deepest of her consolation and quiet; as we see young children murmur and make little plaints when they have ardently desired milk, and begin to suck; or as Jacob did, who, in kissing the fair and chaste Rachel, lifting up his voice, wept, through the vehemence of the consolation and tenderness which he felt. This soul, then, of whom I speak, having only her will engaged, but her understanding, memory, hearing and imagination free, resembled, I think, the little child who, while sucking, might see and hear and even move his arms without leaving the dear breast.

However, the peace of the soul would be much greater and sweeter if there were no noise around her, nor occasion given of stirring herself either in body or mind, for she would greatly wish to be solely occupied in the sweetness of the divine presence; however, being sometimes unable to hinder distractions in her other faculties, she preserves peace in the will, at least. And note that then the will, being retained in quiet by the pleasure which it takes in the divine presence, does not move itself to bring back the other powers which are straying; because by undertaking this she would lose her repose, separating herself from her dearly beloved; and she would lose her labour if she ran hither and thither to catch these volatile powers, which also can never better be brought to their duty than by the perseverance of the will in holy quiet: for little by little all the faculties are attracted by the pleasure which the will receives, and of which she gives them a certain perception like perfumes which ex-

cite them to draw near her, to participate in the good
which she enjoys.

                                            Saint Francis de Sales

DO NOT ASK FOR OR SEEK THE FREE GIFTS OF GOD

Let us imagine we see two fountains with basins which
fill with water. I can find nothing more appropriate than
water by which to explain spiritual things, as I am very
ignorant and have poor wits to help me. Besides, I love
this element so much that I have studied it more attentively than other things. God, who is so great, so wise,
doubtless has, in all things He created, hidden secrets
which we should benefit greatly by knowing, as those say
who understand such matters. These two basins are filled
in different ways; the one with water from a distance,
flowing into it through many pipes and waterworks, while
the other basin is built near the source of the spring itself
and fills quite noiselessly. If the fountain is plentiful, like
the one we speak of, after the basin is full the water overflows in a great stream which flows continually. There is
no need here of any machinery, nor does the water run
through aqueducts.

. . . This is the difference between the two kinds of
prayer. The water running through the aqueducts seems
like sensible devotion, which is obtained through meditation. We gain it by our thoughts, by meditating on created
things, and by the labour of our minds; in short, it is the
result of our endeavours, and so makes the commotion
I spoke of, while bringing profit to the soul. The other
fountain is like divine consolations; it receives the water
from the source itself which signifies God; as usual, when
His Majesty wills to bestow on us any peace, calm, and
sweetness in the inmost depths of our being; I know
neither where nor how.

. . . This joy is not, like earthly happiness, at once felt
by the heart; gradually, after filling it to the brim, the

delight overflows throughout all the mansions and faculties, until at last it reaches the body. Therefore, I say it arises from God and ends in ourselves, for whoever experiences it will find that all the corporal part of our nature shares in this delight and sweetness. While writing this, I have been thinking that the verse "Thou hast dilated my heart" declares that the heart is dilated. This joy does not appear to me to originate in the heart, but in some more interior part of us and, as it were, in the depths of our being. I think this must be the centre of the soul, as I have since learnt and will explain later on. I discover secrets within us which often fill me with astonishment—how many more there must be unknown to me! O my Lord and my God! how stupendous is Thy grandeur! We are like so many foolish peasant lads: we think we know something of Thee; yet it must be as nothing, for there are mighty secrets even in ourselves of which we know naught. I say "as nothing" compared with all the secrets that lie hidden within Thee, yet how great are Thy mysteries we are acquainted with and can learn even by the study of Thy works!

Our Lord bestows a signal grace on the soul if it realises how great is this favour, and another great grace if it does not turn back on the right road. You are longing, my daughters, to enter into this state of prayer at once, and you are right, for, as I said, the soul cannot understand the value of the graces bestowed by God on it there, nor the love which draws Him ever closer to it: certainly we should desire to learn how to obtain this favour: I will tell you what I know about it, setting aside those cases in which God bestows these graces for no other reason than His own choice when we have no right to ask the why and wherefore.

Practise what I advised in the preceding mansions, then —humility, humility! for God lets Himself be vanquished by this and grants us all we ask. The first proof that you possess humility is that you neither think you now deserve these graces and consolations from God, nor that you ever will as long as you live. You ask me: "How shall we receive them, if we do not try to gain them?" I answer, that there is no surer way to obtain them than the one I have told you, therefore make no efforts to acquire them, for the following reasons. The first is, that the chief means of obtaining them is to love God without self-interest. The second, that it is a lack of humility to think that our wretched services can win so great a reward. The third, that the real preparation for them is to desire to suffer, and imitate our Lord, rather than to receive consolations after we have offended Him. The fourth reason is, that His Majesty has not promised to give us these favours in the same way as He has bound Himself to bestow eternal glory on us, if we keep His commandments. We can be saved without these special graces; He knows better than we do what is best for us and which of us love Him sincerely. I know for a certain truth, being acquainted with some who walk by the way of love (and therefore only seek to serve Christ crucified), that not only they neither ask for nor desire consolation, but they even beg Him not to give it them during this life: this is a fact. Fifth, we should but labour in vain; this water does not flow through aqueducts, like that of which we first spoke, and if the spring does not afford it, in vain shall we toil to obtain it. I mean, that, though we may meditate and try our hardest, and though we shed tears to gain it, we cannot make this water flow. God alone gives it to whom He chooses, and often when the soul is least thinking of it. We are His, my sisters, let Him do what He will with us, and lead us where He will. If we are really humble and annihilate ourselves, not only in our imagination (which often deceives us), but if we truly detach ourselves from all things, our Lord will not only grant us these favours but many others that we do not know even how to wish for.

Saint Teresa of Avila

THREE SPIRITUAL LAWS

It is well said that we must be always advancing, I answered; but we do not advance by the multitude of our pious exercises, as you think, but by the perfection with which we perform them, confiding more and more in our dear Spouse, and more and more distrusting ourselves. Last year you fasted three days in the week, and you took the discipline three times: if you were always to double your exercises, this year the whole week would be taken up, but next year what could you do? You would have to make nine days in the week, or else to fast twice a day. Great is the folly of those who amuse themselves with desiring to be martyred in the Indies, and do not apply themselves to what they have to do, according to their condition. But those also make a great mistake who want to eat more than they can digest. We have not enough spiritual heat to digest well all that we undertake for our perfection, and yet we will not give up our great anxiety and desire to do a great deal. To read many spiritual books, above all when they are new, to speak well about God, and all the most spiritual things, in order, we say, to excite ourselves to devotion, to hear many sermons, to hold conferences on all occasions, to communicate very often, to confess still oftener, to serve the sick, to speak well about all that passes in us, to show the desire we feel to become perfect, and as quickly as possible—are not these things very likely to perfect us, and to bring us to the end we are aiming at? Yes, provided that all is done as it has been commanded us, and always in dependence on the grace of God; that is to say, if we do not put our trust in all that, however good it may be, but in God, who alone can make us reap the fruit of all our exercises.

Saint Francis de Sales

FROM THE NEW SONG OF INNER FREEDOM

Unevenness no longer troubles me.
Wealth is the same to me as poverty.
Illusion I have cast away,
Without my self I long to stay.
Myself I leave,
Who lives beyond his thought, he shall not grieve.

You ask how from illusion I withdrew
When perfect union in myself I knew.
Only that union is not vain
That takes the sting from love and pain.
Myself I leave,
Who lives beyond his thought, he shall not grieve.

Since I was drowned in depths, nothing could force
My lips to speech, I lost my very tongue,
Thus God into Himself has taken me.
Myself I leave,
And in this darkness I no longer grieve.

Since now again my life is at its source,
I cannot age, I am for ever young,
The gifts of earth have all forsaken me,
Their powers leave,
Who lives beyond his thought, he shall not grieve.

Anonymous

HOW COULD HE GRIEVE WHO BEHOLDS GOD?

There was a sister whose name was Sister Else of
Neustadt. She had been in the convent for almost seventy
years. For some time before she died, she was confined
to her bed and became so lame that she could not walk
a step. And so she had to live in a separate cell and was

very lonely, since she had little conversation with people —only what was absolutely necessary. And that God is a friend of all those who dwell in misery, and of those who are cut off from bodily comfort He showed through this sister, as a sister who often went to her confirmed. This sister asked her whether she still thought of anything that was of this world. Then she answered: "I have forgotten all things, but I can think of God very well. All the world has forsaken me, and God alone has not forsaken me. He has always kept faith with me and dealt kindly with me. And especially since I have been so ill and weak, He has shown me special grace."

Then the sister asked her whether she grieved that her body was in a state of such pain and dependence, and that she was so utterly forsaken by people. She answered: "I feel as well as it is possible to feel on earth. God has made amends to me for my poor and wretched life, and will do so more and more. How could he grieve who beholds God? He makes the time pass quickly and pleasantly for me." Then the sister asked her whether she beheld our Lord with the outer or the inner eye. She answered: "I see Him in both ways, without and within." Then the sister asked her whether what she saw without was better than what she saw within, and what the inner vision was like. She answered: "What I see without is nothing compared to what I see within, for what I see within is a perfect and proud vision." And she continued: "It is a divine face of which no one can give tiding but he who has seen it, and even those who have seen it cannot describe it properly." And the sister asked her whether she could then think of anyone. She answered: "I cannot even think of myself. Where my senses and my heart go, save only to Him, I do not know. Then my soul rests in God, and knows all things in Him, and then I see the purity of my soul and that it is without stain." . . .

Then the sister asked what it was that she saw with her outer eye. She answered: "He appears as a beautiful and living youth, and my cell is filled with angels and saints. He is seated beside me and looks upon me in a very kindly way. But the angels stand around Him. He never comes alone, angels are always with Him. And He says to me: 'I shall come again and again, and I shall soon take you with Me and then I shall not part from you in all eternity.' And He clasps me in the clasp of His soul." Then the sister asked her what kind of garment He wore and mentioned several colours. But she could not compare the colour of the garment with any colour and said: "Everything that He wills appears upon Him." . . .

She had surrendered her will so completely to His will that she herself did not wish either to live or to die, but to be as He wished, and sometimes she said: "If it were pleasing to God and if it were His will, I should endure this pain even to the Day of Judgment." And when she was in a state of grace she was very merry and spoke of God in lovely words, and very often she repeated these words, in particular: "God is within me and I am within Him. He is mine and I am His. He is for me and I am for Him. My soul is beautiful and proud and confident, for God has lavished His mercy upon me and I am beloved by Him. This He has revealed to me in His glory." Then the sister asked her how He spoke when He talked to her. She answered: "His words are so full of love that no one can give any tiding of them. He can speak so that His words penetrate the soul and the depths of one's heart."

Often too she said: "God is in my heart and in my soul, and seldom goes from me. Only sometimes He escapes, and that is His right, and then my heart rushes after Him and I grow glad. And I say: 'My Love, my Heart's Delight!'" She spoke of God in many such words that were loving and serene. The sister also asked her how she knew that God was in her soul. She answered: "I know it through all the happiness and bliss that He brings with Him. He gladdens me and my heart grows wide, and He opens up my soul with the key of His divine mercy." Then the sister asked her how one might arrive at such intimacy with God. She answered: "It is possible if one loves Him in utter faithfulness and puts away all sin, and becomes nothing but the praise of God." . . .

When age and illness troubled her so much that she no longer wished to live, the sister said to her: "Alas! What is still alive in you?" She answered: "God lives within me and I in Him." And when she was about to die, the sister asked her how she felt. And she showed her as well as she could that she felt pain in her body, but that she rejoiced in her heart. The sister asked her whereat she rejoiced. She answered: "I rejoice because of God, because He is mine and I am His. He told me He would take me unto Himself and all the fear and terror that I had of death and pain have vanished from my heart." The sister also said to her: "How shall we, your special friends, conduct ourselves when you die?" She answered: "You shall laugh and be merry, for heaven is open to me." Then she closed her eyes and lay as if asleep. And the sister called to her and asked her whether she was asleep. She answered: "I am not asleep, I am resting in God." After this she began to feel very ill and approached death swiftly. Then the sister reminded her that she should not grieve at her pain and that God would soon put an end to it. Again she said that she would not grieve, no matter how long God might extend her pain, she would suffer it gladly. And so she died in holiness, and blissful in the faith that she would soon be with God.

Anna of Munzingen

LABOURING PILGRIMS

The life on earth does not yield the soul the essence of joy in God. And that is why even the greatest loveliness and delight that the soul enjoys is not God. God is beyond everything that can be grasped.

Saint John of the Cross

I also suffer now and then when, touched by the living light, I resound like the low tone of a trumpet.

Saint Hildegarde of Bingen

I see clearly that God reserved for Himself those who serve in secret. For He said to Elias: I love the unknown adorers in the world.

Pascal

If through our own spirit we recognise what is within ourselves, in that we receive the Spirit of God, we know what takes place in God, yet not everything, since we have not received Him in His entirety.

Saint Augustine

Why is it, Meister Eckhart asks, that people are so slow to look for God in earnest? His comment is: When one is looking for a thing and finds no trace of its existence one hunts half-heartedly and in distress. But lighting on some vestige of the quarry, the chase grows lively, blithe and keen. The man in quest of fire, cheered when he feels the heat, looks for its source with eagerness and pleasure. And so it is with those in quest of God: feeling none of the sweetness of God they grow listless, but sensing the sweetness of divinity they blithely pursue their search for God.

Meister Eckhart

SPIRITUAL LABOURS OF SPRING

Let every man now prepare for the approaching feast of the Holy Ghost, that he may receive Him with the best possible dispositions, keeping only God in view. Let each one search his whole way of life with all care, considering his interior soul, and whether anything dwells therein that is not God. This preparation will consist of four dispositions: detachment, self-renunciation, the interior spirit, and union with God.

A man should also be practised outwardly in natural virtues, and his lower spiritual powers in moral virtues. Then the Holy Ghost should be placed in possession of one's higher spiritual powers, to adorn them with the theological virtues. All this should be done with discretion and in right order in every respect. We should carefully examine if anything has found place in our life that is not entirely for God; and if so, then it should be at once condemned and reformed. We should imitate the farmer in the month of March; as the sun gains power he prunes his trees and he digs his ground and works his farm with great industry. So should we industriously dig up the ground of our soul and find out what is underneath the surface; we should prune the tree of our outward life of the senses, and we should clean out all weeds, as well as subject our lower powers to the higher ones. We must cut out the seven capital sins by the very roots. Pride should be exterminated inwardly and outwardly; and all avarice and hate and envy; all foul lust in body and soul, in heart and senses, in spirit and act must be totally expelled: no sloth of any kind must be allowed to lurk in the soul: all these evils must be cut away and totally rooted out. As yet the soul remains cold and hard, for although the sun grows warmer, it is yet far from summer's clear and genial light. But soon all is changed. The Divine sun begins to do its heavenly work in the well-prepared garden of the soul.

When, therefore, the genial sun of God's grace begins to shine brightly upon this well-cultivated garden, all the soul's inner and outer faculties being fully prepared, all its higher and lower tendencies directed towards Heaven, then indeed the sweet flowers of May begin to bloom, and all the welcome gifts of summertime. The eternal God causes the soul to blossom forth and to produce good fruit of virtue; and the joy in that soul no tongue can tell. For now the Holy Ghost is there, and His brightness shines directly upon the soul, yea, into its inmost depths. Well may He now be called the true Comforter, since His influence is so delicious. O how great a joy! O how rich a feast, the sweet odours of whose nourishing food excite the soul's deepest longing! These are granted in every plenty of enjoyment to the rightly prepared soul by the gentle Spirit of God. One drop of this Divine comfort is worth more than all the joys of created things put together; and it overpowers and quenches all longing for them whatsoever.

When a man feels this action of the Divine Comforter so wonderfully great and so unexpected, he would gladly sink down into its depths and rest and slumber in it for ever. He feels like St. Peter at the Lord's Transfiguration; it is good for him to be there, and he would set up three tabernacles of joy out of one drop of the happiness now granted him, and there dwell for ever. But such is not our Lord's will. When Peter said "It is good for us to be here," he was far from that degree in the spiritual life that his Lord would lead him to. So it is with souls in this stage: they think they have got all when they are in this brilliant sunshine of God's favour, and they would like to lie down and bask in it for ever. And all the souls who actually do so, remain stationary in their career. They amount to nothing unless they rise up and go forward.

To some of these it happens that they slip down into unlawful liberty. Their poor human nature turns inward and regards itself with self-complacency, a weakness toward which we are above all other things inclined. It is with them as with sick persons who trust too much to medicines. I have heard physicians say that men, finding relief in drugs, trust to them entirely and not at all to their natural forces, and that this breeds indolence. If a man is doubtful of all help from others, then he energetically sets to work to help himself. Remark, children, how this poisonous longing for ease and convenience penetrates everywhere in our natural life. And it is a thousand times worse in our spiritual life. When this very unusual joy is felt, the soul forthwith counts upon being sure to keep it. Earnest and faithful labour is now thought unnecessary; a soft lethargy possesses the spirit—no more activity of virtue, no more zealous toil, all is to be rest and peace. And this is Satan's chance. He comes to this soul, thus indolently reclining, and he insinuates into it a false sweetness, hoping to hold it fast in this wrong state of rest.

What shall we do, then? Shall we run away from this happiness? No, by no means. But, receiving it with much gratitude, we must humbly return it again into God's hands, praising Him in all sincerity, as we nevertheless protest ourselves to be wholly unworthy of such a favour. We should act like a young and robust traveller, but poor and hungry and thirsty as he starts on his journey. If he goes forward four miles and can only manage to get a meal to eat, he springs forward blithely and makes ten miles more. So let us do, when God feeds us with His sweet food of spiritual joy. Whatever good things such a man formerly did, he does more and better things now, loves

God more, praises and thanks Him more. He is more up-right, his heart is full of a more burning love, and thereby he becomes worthy of the gift of a yet deeper interior comfort. Just as we may fancy a man going to the Pope and giving him a florin, and receiving in return a hundred thousand, and getting the same exchange every time he gave a florin: so is the exchange between God and a rightly-guided soul. As often as he goes to God in all love and gratitude and humility, so often does God meet him on the instant with gifts and graces a thousandfold more precious than before. Thus it is that sweetness of devotion is made a help to us, and leads to greater good: we must use our spiritual gifts and not enjoy them. It is like riding in a waggon: we are there for the good of the journey and for the progress made, and not for the enjoyment of the waggon's soft seat. So let it be with God's gifts; draw the good out of them, leaving to God the joy. Hence St. Peter's warning to us to be sober and watchful; not to sink into the slumber of sensual pleasure, a state in which the soul is but half alive and is incapable of activity. The sober-minded man works right on courageously and intelligently: "Be sober and watch: because your adversary the devil, as a roaring lion, goeth about seeking whom he may devour; whom resist ye strong in faith" (*I Peter* 5, 8).

And again the Apostle bids us be "prudent and watch in prayers," that is, not to be so dull as to rest in anything that is not God; to keep the light of piety brightly burning; to keep a vigilant outlook over ourselves; always to long for God alone. It was on this account that our Saviour's disciples must give up the bodily presence of their Master, if they would receive the Holy Ghost. "If I go not," said He, "the Paraclete will not come to you" (*John* 16, 7). These loving disciples were so possessed of the visible presence of the Lord, that heart, soul, senses and faculties were entirely absorbed—inner and outer life all taken up. This condition must be changed, if they were to arrive at the true, spiritual, interior comfort of God—they must be cut off from the outward presence, no matter how bitter the stroke. Otherwise they should have remained in the lowest spiritual degree, that of the sensible life of religion. When they rose above the senses, it was to enter the religious life of the highest powers of the soul, in every way nobler and more delightful.

After that the soul enters further into its own deep interior, the very hidden shrine of God's presence within it. Divine sweetness is there and there only quite at home, there fully and essentially experienced. And there alone is the soul wide awake and watchful.

The Apostle bids us be sober, watchful and prayerful, for our "adversary the devil goeth about like a roaring lion." What prayer does he mean? That of the mouth? Reading the Psalms over and over? All that is truly prayer, but he means a yet higher prayer. It is the prayer our Lord meant when He said: "The true adorers shall adore the Father in spirit and in truth" (*John* 4, 23). Saints and divines teach us that prayer is the elevation of the soul to God. If thy prayer by word of mouth serves this purpose, well and good. But even so: if my clothing serves me, all the same it is not my own self. Thus does all prayer of the mouth serve true prayer; but in itself and taken alone it is not true prayer. For by true prayer the heart and soul of a man must go direct to God, and that is the essential thing. True prayer is this and nothing besides: a man's mind is totally subjected to God in loving desire and genuine humility.

Clergymen and members of orders are indeed especially bound at certain times to recite vocal prayers. But none of these prayers is so devout and lovely as the sacred prayer taught us by the supreme master of prayer Himself, namely the Pater Noster. That prayer approaches the nearest of all vocal prayer to the truest, the most essential. This prayer of spirit we lift up incessantly towards Heaven, and it lifts the soul with it straight up to God. And it is equally true to say that the soul penetrates into its own most sacred and interior depths, where alone it may form a union with God. Thus St. Augustine says:

"The soul has within itself a hidden abyss, and the things of time and of this world have no place therein, but only what is high above them and above all that concerns the body and its activities." In these heavenly abysses the soul finds all its sweetness, and there is the eternal abode of all Divine joys. In them the soul is still, fixed in God, cut off from creatures, and drawn into uncreated bliss. There is God Himself, acting, dwelling, ruling, granting the soul an incomparable Divine life. Into this life the soul melts away—into the infinite light and fire of love that God is by essence and by nature. Back and forth into this relation with God does such a man pass in prayer, as he pleads for every necessity of all Christendom, his holy petitions, his deep yearnings ever guided by God Himself. Thus does he pray for his friends on earth, even sinners, and for the souls in purgatory. The needs of every soul in holy Church are not beyond his help by counsel as well as by prayer. And yet such favoured spirits do not always pray exactly for this or that particular person or object. But with a certain kind of wide-sweeping universal and yet most simple prayer do they embrace all souls of men, just as I stand here and behold with one glance all of you sitting before me. They see all in the same Divine abyss, God's love, as in a Divine contemplation, and in the fire of Divine love—viewing thus as with one glance the necessities of all Christians. They may seem to themselves to be in and out of God in their soul's movements, and yet they are ever in Him, deep in the calm of fathomless love: therein is their life and being, therein all their life's activity. Nothing is to be discovered in them under any and all circumstances but a Divine existence; whether doing things or leaving them undone, everything tells of God. These are noble souls, necessary for holy Church, sanctifying and consoling all men, giving honour to God. Wherever they may be, God dwells in them and they in Him. May God help us to the methods and the devotion leading to such an end. Amen.

Blessed John Tauler

ON THE BENEFIT OF COMPOSURE PRACTISED WITHIN
AND WITHOUT

Mark well, that no man alive ever overcame himself so utterly that there was not something left to overcome. There are not many men who are well aware of this and who persevere. It is a fair give and take. For just as far as you go out of things with all that is yours, just as far does God enter into you with all that is His. So make a beginning and let it cost you all you can give. In this way you will find true peace and in no other.

People should not think so much about what they do, but rather should they think upon what they are. If only they themselves were good and their way of life, then their works would give forth a beautiful light. If yourself are just, then will your works be just. Do not think to found holiness upon doing; holiness must be founded upon being. Works do not make us holy. It is we who must make works holy. For no matter how holy works may be, they do not make us holy because we do them, but in so far as we within ourselves are as we should be, we make holy all that we do, whether it be eating, or sleeping, or waking, or what it may. Those whose nature is not great, no matter what they do, it will be as nothing.

Learn from this that one must make every endeavour to be good and that what one does is not so important, or what manner of works one performs, but what is the foundation of these works.

Meister Eckhart

ON REMOTENESS AND ON HAVING GOD

They asked me: there are some who withdraw rigorously from men and want to be alone, and regard this as the cause of their peace and that they are within the Church—is this the best way? I answered, no! And this is why:

He with whom all is well within himself, he will be well pleased in all places and with all kinds of people. But he with whom all is not well will not be well pleased in any place or with any person. He with whom all is well, he truly has God within himself. But whoever truly has God, has Him in all places, on the street and among people as well as in church, or in the wilderness, or in a cell. If he only has Him truly and has Him only—nothing can confuse such a man.

Why?

He has God only and thinks only of God, and all things are to him nothing but God. Such a man carries God into all of his works and into all places, and everything such a man does is nothing but God. For he who gives rise to works, such works are his more truly and more utterly than his who performs them. If then we think of God and of Him only, and think of Him truly, He gives rise to our works and nothing can hinder Him from doing those works —no place and no diversity. Thus, such a man cannot be confused. For he thinks of, and seeks, and is content with nothing but God who, through this thought, is united with such a man. And just as God cannot be distracted by diversity, so such a man can be neither distracted nor diverted, for he is one with the One, where all diversity is unity and university.

Man shall experience God in all things and shall accustom his heart to have God always present in his spirit, in his thought, and in his love. Have a care how you yearn to your God! As your heart is in church, and in your cell, so shall you keep it and carry it among people, and into an alien world and into unrest. And—as I have often said— when one speaks of remaining the same, that does not mean that all doing is the same, or all places, or all people. This would be very wrong. For it is better to pray than to spin, and the church is a worthier place than the street. But whatever you do, you yourself shall have the same heart and the same faithfulness, and the same earnestness towards your God. Verily, could you thus remain the same, then none could hinder you from having God present.

But whoever does not have God truly within himself, but is remote from God, so that he must always fetch Him from the outside, from here and there, and seeks Him in different ways, in a deed, or in a person, or in a place, he does not have God. And then it may easily come to pass that such a man finds obstacles, for he has not God within himself, and does not seek Him, and does not think of Him alone. And therefore, not only bad company is an obstacle to him but good company as well, and not only the street but also the church, and not only evil words and evil works but good words and good works as well. For the obstacle is within him, because for him not everything has become God. If everything were God to him, he would be pleased in all places and with all people. For God would be within him, and none could rob him of God, just as none could hinder him in his works.

What is this true having of God, this, that one really has Him?

This true having of God is a matter of the heart and of the intrinsic and conscious turning and striving to God, and certainly not of an even and constant thought of God. For to accomplish this would be impossible for the nature of man, and would be too difficult, and not even best. For man shall not merely think of God and let this suffice. When the thought vanishes, God vanishes also. But man shall be filled with the essence of God that is high above the thought of man, and above all things created. THAT God cannot vanish, unless man turn from Him voluntarily.

Whoever is thus filled with the essence of God grasps His Godhood, and God shines out to him in all things. For all things will seem to him related to God and God will appear to him in all things. God is awake within him at all times. He quietly turns from the outside world, and God who is present, God, the Beloved, invades him. Just as one who is burning with thirst, with a real thirst, may do other things than drink, and may even think of other things, but whatever he may do or with whomever he may be, with whatever wishes or thoughts, or whatever doing, he never fails to see the draught before him as long as he thirsts, and the greater his thirst, the greater and more intrinsic and intense and constant is his vision of the draught. And whoever loves something fervently and with all his strength, so that nothing but this delights him and touches his heart, so that he wants only this and nothing else, verily, wherever or with whomever he may be, or whatever he plans or does, he will never forget what he so loves, and in all things he will see the image of the One, and he will see it within him more clearly as his love grows deeper and deeper. Such a man does not seek rest, for he is not confused by any unrest.

Such a man is all the more the recipient of God's grace, in that to him all things are replete with God and more than just the things in themselves. But this, indeed, requires zeal and devotion and incessant care of our inner life, and a keen and clear and deep awareness that determines the response of the heart to men and to things. And man cannot learn this through flight, by fleeing from things and turning to solitude, away from all that is without, but he must acquire an inner solitude, no matter where or with whom he may be. He must learn to break through the shell of things and to grasp God therein, and to use all his power to shape God within himself to an image that does not fade.

Just like one who wants to learn to write! If he would master this skill he must practise much and often, no matter how difficult and tedious this may be or how impossible it may seem. If he only practises much and industriously he will learn and master this skill. First he must think of every letter separately and seize upon it firmly with his imagination. But when he has mastered the skill, he can give up imagining and thinking of the separate letters. He will write freely and easily, whether it be trivialities or bold thoughts that he would express by his skill. Now it is sufficient for him to know that he must use his skill, and

even though he does not think of it continually, indeed,
no matter what he may be thinking of, through his skill
he accomplishes his work.

Thus shall man also be pervaded with the presence of
God and shaped by the shape of his beloved God, and be
so fused with Him that God is present within him and
shines within him without any effort on his part, and that
he recognises the true nature of all things and remains
free from them. But to attain to this, he must first con-
centrate his thought and deliberately learn as a student
learns his skill.

Meister Eckhart

HOW MAN CAN DO HIS WORK MOST REASONABLY

The world is full of people, and if man but exerts his
will it is not difficult for him to reach a stage where the
things around him are no obstacles and do not leave a
lasting image within him. For when the heart is filled with
God, His creatures no longer have room in it. But we must
not be satisfied with this. In a higher sense, we should
make all things of use to us, no matter what they are or
where they are, whatever we see or hear, no matter how
different from us or how alien. Only then all will be well
with us and not before, and man shall never desist from
this task but grow in it incessantly and become richer with
true increase.

And in all his works and in all things, man should con-
sciously use his reason and always have a reasonable insight into himself, into his inner being, and grasp God
within all things in the highest possible sense. For man
shall be as the Lord said: You shall be as those who always wait and watch for their Lord. Verily, those who
wait are watchful and look about to see from where the
Lord, for whom they are waiting, is coming, and they
await Him in all that comes and, no matter how alien it
may be, they look for him to appear in it. So we, in all

things, should practise a constant expectation of our Lord. But for this zeal is necessary, and it demands all we can muster in thought and in strength. Thus it will be well with men and they will perceive God in all things alike, and find a portion of God in all things.

Often one work is not like the other. But he who performs his works with a like heart, verily, his works will all be alike. And he with whom all is well, if God is his very own, he will see the radiance of God in worldly things as purely as in the most divine. This does not mean that man should deliberately do something worldly or something wrong, for whatever reaches him from the world without, through his eyes or his ears, let him relate this to God. Whoever, then, sees God present in all and everything, and is in full possession of his reason and uses it, only he knows perfect peace and has found a true kingdom of heaven.

If all is to be well with man, then one of two things must befall: he must either learn to grasp God and merge Him in his work, or he must cease from doing any form of work. But since, in this life, man cannot exist without activity that is of many kinds and that is proper to man, man shall learn to possess God in all that comes to pass and not allow any work or any place to confuse him. And so when man sets out to work and to deal with people, he should first be gravely aware of God and hold Him fast in his heart and fuse Him with his every plan and thought, his will and strength, so that nothing else shall enter into him.

Meister Eckhart

WHAT MAN MUST DO WHEN GOD IS HIDDEN FROM HIM

You must know that a pure will cannot lose God. Sometimes, to be sure, the feeling heart believes He is not there and yields to the illusion that God has gone away. What must you do in such a case? Just what you would do if you were blessed with comfort. Learn to do the same when your suffering is greatest, and conduct yourself as you did when you were comforted. Some say: "We are of good will." But they are not following the will of God but their own will, and they wish to instruct our Lord that He must do thus and so. That is not good will.

In all things it is God's aim that we relinquish our will. When St. Paul held much converse with our Lord and our Lord with him, nothing availed until he relinquished his will and said: "What do you want me to do?" And then our Lord knew very well what He wanted him to do! And it was the same when the angel appeared to our Blessed Lady. All the words that she exchanged with him, and he with her, would not have made her the Mother of God. But as soon as she relinquished her will, then suddenly she became the true Mother of the everlasting Word, and conceived God, and God was her natural Son. And as far as we are concerned too, nothing in the world can make us into true men if we do not relinquish our own will. For, verily, unless we relinquish our own will in all things, we are not working together with God. Yes, I should even say that if we succeeded in relinquishing our entire will, and dared to give up all things within and without, we should then accomplish everything and not before.

One finds few such men. Whether they know it or not, most men would like to prosper so that they might enjoy great things, pleasure and possessions. But this is nothing but selfishness. You shall yield to God altogether and with all that you have, and you shall not ask what He does with that which is His own. It is true that thousands of men are dead and in heaven who have never completely given up their own will—only then can one have a true and perfect will if one goes over into the will of God and relinquishes one's own will completely—but the more nearly a man accomplishes this, the more deeply and truly is he fused with God. One Ave Maria recited in a spirit of abandoning oneself is of more avail than a thousand psalters

read without this spirit; yes, one step in this spirit were
better than a journey across the sea without it.

He, then, who has abandoned himself and all that is his,
will be truly and utterly fused with God. Wherever you
touched him you would come upon God, for he is wholly
in God, and God surrounds him as my cowl surrounds my
head, and whoever would touch me would first have to
touch my gown. And similarly, when I drink, the draught
must first pass over my tongue, for there the draught is
tasted. When the tongue is coated with bitterness, no matter how sweet the wine may be, it must grow bitter
through what it must pass to reach me. Verily, so he who
has completely abandoned his own self would be so completely surrounded with God that nothing created could
touch him without first touching upon God. And whatever was to reach him would have to pass God first, and
there it would get its savour and grow divine. No matter
how great a sorrow may be, if it comes by way of God,
God has already suffered it. Contempt becomes honour,
the bitter grows sweet, and deepest darkness turns to clearest light. Everything takes on the savour of God and becomes divine. For whatever befalls such a man is shaped
for him in God; he thinks nothing else and feels nothing
else, and thus he experiences God in all bitterness as well
as in supreme ecstasy.

It is when the light shines in darkness that we become
aware of it. Of what avail to man is the light of teaching
unless he make use of it? When they cower in darkness
and sorrow, then shall this light be revealed to them.

The more we would retain possession of ourselves, the
less we possess ourselves. He who has relinquished his self
will never lose God, and he will be aware of God in all
that he does. But if it came to pass that a man did something wrong or said something wrong or fell into some
other wrong-doing even though he set out upon his work
with God, then it is God's concern to take the wrong upon
Himself, and you must in no wise abandon your work.

Never in this life shall we be entirely safe from an evil

outcome of things. But because the rats have gotten into the wheat once is no reason to throw away the good wheat as well. Verily, if all is well with a man, and if he understands the ways of God, such interludes and such tribulation will grow into a blessing for him. Since for him who is righteous all things lead to righteousness, as St. Paul says, and also St. Augustine, yes, even sin.

Meister Eckhart

HOW ONE SHOULD IMITATE GOD AND OF THE RIGHT BEGINNING

He who would take upon himself a new life and work shall go to his God and ask of Him with great strength and devotion that He should dispose as He thinks best, and as it appears to Him most seemly and proper. But in doing this, he must not think of what he himself wishes, but only of God's will and nothing else. However God may dispose, let him accept it as coming from God and consider it best, and be wholly and ultimately content with it.

Even if it come to pass that later he may think some other way might have been better, let him remember: God has chosen this way for you and so it must be best. Let him have faith in God and see everything good in His chosen way, and accept all things, whatever they may be. For whatever good God has done and given in one way, one can find and receive on all good ways. In this one way, one can grasp all good ways and not only the special good of the one. For man can do only one thing, he cannot do all. It can only be one thing, but in the one all things should be comprised. For if someone wanted to do all, now this and now that, and leave his own way and take that of another because, suddenly, it pleased him better, that truly would lead to great fickleness. For sooner would that man be perfect who, leaving the world,

enters an order for the first time, than he who changes
from one order to another, no matter how holy he may
be. This comes of the change of way. Let a man take one
good way and remain in it and comprise in this all good
ways, and have faith that it comes from God, and do not
do one thing to-day and another to-morrow, and be without care that in going his way he neglect something else.
For if one is with God, one neglects nothing. Just as little
as God can neglect anything, just as little can he who is
with God neglect anything. And so, accept one thing from
God, and in it comprise all that is good.

But if this thing is incompatible and at strife with others,
this is a sure sign that it does not come from God. For one
good thing is never against another. As our Lord said:
"Every kingdom divided against itself is brought to desolation," and again: "He who is not with me is against me,
and he that gathereth not with me scattereth." And so
this may be a sure sign for you. If one good will not suffer
another good or perhaps a lesser good, or destroys it, then
it does not come from God. For good shall bring fruitfulness and not destruction.

To say it briefly and clearly so that there may be no
doubt: God in His faithfulness gives each man what is
best for him. And it is certainly true that He accepts none
that is fallen, if He might have had him upright. For God
in His Godhood sees each thing as it is at its best.

The question is asked: why does not God remove those
of whom He knows that they will fall from the grace of
baptism, so that they might die in their childhood and
before they are in full possession of their reason, since He
knows that they will fall and not rise again? For would
not this be best for them?

My answer is: God never destroys what is good, but
He fulfils. God never destroys nature but perfects it. Just
as grace does not destroy nature but perfects it. Now if
God destroyed nature in the beginning, He would do violence to it and wrong. And this He does not do. Man has
a free will with which he can choose good or evil. And

because God offers him death in ill-doing and life in righteousness, man is free and master of all his works, undestroyed and unvanquished.

And so there is nothing in God that destroys what has anything of its own, but He fulfils all things. And so we also must not destroy within ourselves a trifling and insignificant good for a greater, but we should bring the slight to its utmost perfection.

There was talk of a man who wanted to begin his life anew and I spoke in this way: man shall become a seeker of God in all things, and a finder of God at all times, and everywhere and among all people and in every way. And therein one can always and incessantly wax and grow and there shall be no end of waxing.

Meister Eckhart

ANSWER TO A TIMID WORKER

And then you say: "Yes, Lord, if only there were not one stumbling-stone, my weakness!"

If you have weaknesses, implore God often, if it would not be pleasing to Him and accrue to His honour, to take them from you, because you cannot do this yourself without Him. If He takes them from you, give Him thanks. And if He does not, you must suffer it, but no longer as sinful weakness, but as something you must practise greatly to overcome, whereby you may show your patience and win a reward. You shall be content, whether He gives you His gift or not.

He gives to each what is best and most seemly for him. If one wants to cut out a coat, one must cut it according to one's measure. For if it fits one it does not follow at all that it fits another. Each one must be measured, so that it may fit him. And so God gives each the very best according to His wisdom. Verily, who has faith in Him, he takes and has just as much from the smallest gift as from the greatest. If God wanted to give me what He gave St.

Paul, I should gladly take it if this were His will. But if He does not want to give me this—for it is His will that only a very few people experience this in their life-time—if, then, He does not give it to me, He will remain just as dear to me. I shall give Him just as great thanks and be just as content that He withholds it from me as if He gave it to me. For if I am as I should be in all other things, His withholding shall be just as sufficient and dear to me as His giving. Verily, the will of God shall suffice me in all things. Whatever He does or gives, His will shall be so precious to me and so dear to me, dearer than if He gave me a gift or wrought something within me.

And then you say: "I fear I am not zealous enough and not as careful as I wish to be."

This shall be a sorrow to you and you shall suffer it with patience and accept it as a spiritual exercise and be content. God is willing to suffer disgrace and all ills and to do without service and praise, if only those have peace who profess Him and who belong to Him. Why, then, should we not have peace, whatever He may give us or whatever we may have to do without? So it is written and so says our dearest Lord: "Blessed are they which are persecuted for righteousness' sake." Verily, if a thief who is to be hanged because he has well deserved this for his thefts, or if one who has done murder and, according to law, is to be stretched on the wheel, if these could realise within themselves: see, you must suffer this for the sake of righteousness that is justly meted out to you—at that moment they would be blessed! Verily, no matter how unrighteous we may be, if we accept from God whatever He may or may not do as just, and suffer for the sake of righteousness, then we are blessed. Therefore, lament no longer or, so I say to you, only lament that you still have too much. For he with whom all is as it should be will derive just as much from want as from possession.

And then you say: "God has wrought such great things in so many men, and they are garmented with God, and this means that God has wrought within them, and not they themselves."

Give thanks to God for their sake, and if He gives it to you also, accept it in the name of God. If He does not give it to you, you shall gladly suffer want of it, and profess only Him, untroubled as to whether your works are done by God or by yourself.

And do not trouble yourself what nature or what way God has given to some. If I were so good and so holy that I was raised among the saints, people would talk and ask whether what was within me was my own nature or the grace of God, and they would be confused thereat. But this would be wrong. Let God work within you and ascribe it to Him, and do not trouble yourself whether He works through His grace or through your nature, for both are His: nature and grace. What concern of yours is it, with what it pleases Him to work and what He works in you or in another? Let Him work however or wherever He pleases.

There was a man who wanted to provide water for his garden, and said: if I can only get water, it does not matter through what kind of pipe or gutter it runs, whether it be of iron, or wood, or stone, or otherwise if only I can get water. And so those do wrong who confuse their minds with the question as to how God works within them, through nature or through grace. Let Him do as He will, and be at peace!

For to the same extent that you are at peace, you are in God, and to the same extent that you are not at peace, you are remote from God. For if one is in God, one is at peace; and one is in God just as much as one is at peace. By this you shall always know to what extent you are in God, and if it is otherwise, whence comes your peace or your lack of peace. For if you cling to that which lacks peace, you must needs lack peace, for the lack of peace comes not from God, but from His creatures. Neither is there anything in God that need be feared. All that is in God is only to be loved. And so there is nothing in Him that need make us sad. Who knows only His will and His wish, he is at peace. And no one is at peace save he whose will is utterly one with God's will. May God grant us this union! Amen.

Meister Eckhart

OF SPIRITUAL ARIDITY VERSUS LUKEWARMNESS

But since aridities might frequently proceed, not from the night and purgation of the sensual desires, but from sins and imperfections, or from weakness and lukewarmness, or from some bad humour or indisposition of the body, I shall here set down certain signs by which it may be known if such aridity proceeds from the aforementioned purgation, or if it arises from any of the aforementioned sins. For the making of this distinction I find that there are three principal signs.

The first is whether, when a soul finds no pleasure or consolation in the things of God, it also fails to find it in anything created; for, as God sets the soul in the dark night to the end that He may quench and purge its sensual desire, He allows it not to find attraction or sweetness in anything whatsoever. Hence it may be laid down as very probable that aridity and insipidity proceed not from recently committed sins or imperfections. For, if this were so, the soul would feel in its nature some inclination or desire to taste other things than those of God; for, whenever the desire is allowed indulgence in any imperfection, it immediately feels inclined thereto, whether little or much, in proportion to the pleasure and the love that it had for it. Yet since this lack of enjoyment in things above or below might proceed from some indisposition or melancholy humour, which oftentimes makes it impossible for the soul to take pleasure in anything, it becomes necessary to apply the second sign and condition.

The second sign whereby a man may believe himself to be experiencing the said purgation is that ordinarily the memory is centred upon God with painful care and solicitude, thinking that it is not serving God but is backsliding, because it finds itself without sweetness in the things of God. And in such a case it is evident that this lack of sweetness and this aridity come not from weakness and lukewarmness; for it is the nature of lukewarmness not to care greatly or to have any inward solicitude for the things of God. There is thus a great difference between aridity and lukewarmness, for lukewarmness consists in great weakness and remissness in the will and in the spirit without solicitude as to serving God; whereas purgative aridity is ordinarily accompanied by solicitude with care and grief, as I say, because the soul is not serving God. And although this may sometimes be increased by melancholy or some other humour, it fails not for this reason to produce a purgative effect upon the desire, since the desire is deprived of all pleasure, and has its care centred upon God alone. For when mere humour is the cause, it spends itself in displeasure and ruin of the physical nature, and there are none of those desires to serve God which belong to purgative aridity. When the cause is aridity, it is true that the sensual part of the soul has fallen low, and is weak and feeble in its actions, by reason of the little pleasure which it finds in them; but the spirit, on the other hand, is ready and strong.

The third sign whereby this purgation of sense may be recognised is that the soul can no longer meditate or reflect in its sense of the imagination, as it was wont, however much it may of itself endeavour to do so. For God now begins to communicate Himself to it, no longer through sense, as He did aforetime, by means of reflections which joined and sundered its knowledge, but by pure spirit, into which consecutive reflections enter not; but He communicates Himself to it by an act of simple contemplation, to which neither the exterior nor the interior senses of the lower part of the soul can attain. From this time forward, therefore, imagination and fancy can find no support in any meditation, and can gain no foothold by means thereof.

Saint John of the Cross

TO BUY OUT TIME

How detached from everything that one feels or does must one be in order to walk by this path in which one lives on God only and one's present duty. We must cut off all more distant views, we must confine ourselves to the duty of the present moment without thinking of what preceded it or what will follow it.

I suppose, of course, that the law of God is secure, and also that the practice of self-abandonment has made your soul docile to Divine action. You will have a feeling that will cause you to say: I feel at present an affection for this person or book, I would like to give or receive this piece of advice, to make such or such a complaint, to open myself to this soul or receive confidences from her, to give or do this thing or the other. You should follow this movement by the impression of grace without supporting yourself an instant by your own reflections, reasonings or efforts. We must apply ourselves to things for the time that God wishes without mixing ourselves up in them personally. The will of God is applied to us in the state of which we are speaking; it should completely take the place of all our ordinary supports.

Each moment has its obligatory virtue to which the self-abandoned soul is faithful, yet she misses nothing of what she reads or hears; the most mortified novice does not fulfil her duties better; that is why these souls are now led to one book and now to another, or to make this or that remark on some trifling event. God gives them at one moment the desire to instruct themselves in what at another moment will support their virtue.

In all that they do, they feel only the attraction of the action without knowing why. All they can say reduces to this: I feel drawn to write, to read, to ask this question, to look at that object; I follow this *attrait,* and God who gives it me makes in my soul a reserve-fund of such things to be in the future the means of further *attraits* which enable me to make use of them in my own interest and that of others. This is what obliges such souls to be simple, gentle, supple and mobile, under the slightest, almost imperceptible impressions of the Divine breeze.

In the state of self-abandonment the one rule is the present moment. The soul is as light as a feather, as fluid as water, simple as a child, as easily moved as a ball, so as to receive and follow all the impressions of grace. Abandoned souls have no more hardness or consistency than melted metal. For just as metal takes all the shapes of the mould into which it is poured, these souls adapt and adjust themselves as easily to all the forms which God wishes to give them. In a word, their disposition resembles that of the air which is at the service of all who breathe it and of water which takes the form of every recipient.

They present themselves to God like a perfectly plain and simple canvas, without concerning themselves to know the subject which it may please God to paint in their souls, for they trust themselves to Him; they are abandoned and wholly occupied with their duty, think neither of themselves nor of what is necessary for them, nor of how they are to procure it.

The more, however, they apply themselves to their little job, so simple, so hidden, so contemptible as its outward appearances may be, the more God diversifies and beautifies it. On the background of simple love and obedience, His hands love to trace the most beautiful details, the most delicate and exquisite drawings, the most Divine figures . . . A canvas which is simply blindly abandoned to the painter's brush, merely receives each moment the impact of the brush. Similarly, if a stone could feel it would feel nothing but the cruel point of the tool destroying it, but in no case the figure of which it is tracing the lineaments.

Yes, dear souls, simple souls, leave to God what belongs to Him and remain loving and passive under His action. Hold for certain that what happens to you internally and externally is for the best. Leave God to act and abandon yourselves to Him. Let the point of the knife and the needle work. Let the brush of the Master cover you with a variety of colours which seem only to disfigure the canvas of your soul. Correspond with all these Divine operations by the uniform and simple disposition of a complete self-abandonment, self-forgetfulness and application to your duty. Keep to the line of your own advance and, without knowing the map of the country or the details, names and directions of the land you are passing through, walk blindly along that line and everything will be indicated to you if you remain passive. Seek only the Kingdom of God and His justice in love and obedience and all the rest will be given you.

One sees many souls who are disturbed and ask: Who will give us holiness, perfection, mortification, direction? Let them hunt up in books the precise terms and qualities of this wonderful business, its nature and its parts; as for you, remain in peace in the unity of God by your love and walk blindly in the clear straight path of your obligations. The angels are on your side in this night and their hands make a barrier around you. If God wishes more from you His inspiration will make you know it.

Father J. P. de Caussade

THE PRAYER OF ONE VERY ILL

Lord, the day is drawing to a close and, like all the other days, it leaves with me the impression of utter defeat. I have done nothing for You: neither have I said conscious prayers, nor performed works of charity, nor any work at all, work that is sacred for every Christian who understands its significance. I have not even been able to control that childish impatience and those foolish rancours that so often occupy the place that should be Yours in the "no man's land" of my emotions. It is in vain that I promise You to do better. I shall be no different to-morrow, nor on the day that follows.

When I retrace the course of my life, I am overwhelmed by the same impression of inadequacy. I have sought You in prayer and in the service of my neighbour, for we cannot separate You from our brothers any more than we can separate our body from our spirit. But in seeking You, do I not find myself? Do I not wish to satisfy myself? Those works that I secretly termed good and saintly dissolve in the light of approaching eternity, and I dare no longer lean on these supports that have lost their stability.

Even actual sufferings bring me no joy, because I bear them so badly. Perhaps we are all like this: incapable of discerning anything but our own wretchedness and our own despairing cowardice before the light of the Beyond that waxes on our horizon.

But it may be, O Lord, that this impression of privation is part of a divine plan. It may be that, in Your eyes, self-complacency is the most obnoxious of all fripperies, and that we must come before You naked so that You, You alone, may clothe us.

Marguerite Teilhard de Chardin

THE IMPORTANCE OF PATIENCE

When we enter on the path of virtue, we walk at first in darkness; but if we follow the leading of grace faithfully and perseveringly, we shall infallibly attain a great light both for our own guidance and for that of others.

We wish to become saints in a day; we have not patience to await the ordinary course of grace. This proceeds from our pride and cowardice. Let us only be faithful in co-operating with the graces which God offers us, and He will not fail to lead us to the fulfilment of His designs.

Father Louis Lallemant

AVERSIONS

When they say to me, "There is such a one whom we never see commit an imperfection," I ask directly, has she any office? If they answer me, "No," I do not make much account of her perfection; for there is a great difference between her virtue and that of another who is well tried, whether interiorly by temptations, or exteriorly by the contradictions she has to bear. For the virtue of strength and the strength of virtue are never acquired in time of peace, and while we are not tried by the contrary temptation. Those who are very gentle while they have not contradiction, and who have not acquired this virtue sword in hand, are indeed very exemplary, and very edifying; but if they are put to the proof, you will immediately see them disturbed, and they will show that their gentleness was not a strong and solid virtue, but imaginary rather than real. There is a great difference between the absence of a vice and the possession of the contrary virtue.

Saint Francis de Sales

A BROKEN HEART THOU WILT
NOT DESPISE

So it is, I tell you, in heaven; there will be more rejoicing over one sinner who repents, than over ninety-nine
souls that are justified, and have no need of repentance.

Luke 15, 7

The spirit you have now received is not, as of old, a
spirit of slavery, to govern you by fear; it is the spirit of
adoption, which makes us cry out, Abba, Father.

Romans 8, 15

And God, who can read our hearts, knows well what
the Spirit's intent is; for indeed it is according to the mind
of God that he makes intercession for the saints.

Meanwhile, we are well assured that everything helps
to secure the good of those who love God, those whom
he has called in fulfilment of his design. . . . He did not
even spare his own Son, but gave him up for us all; and
must not that gift be accompanied by the gift of all else?

Romans 8, 27–28; 32

The anguish of our Lord can only set you free
If first your heart becomes its own Gethsemane.

Angelus Silesius

He is not very annoyed to have fallen who remains prostrate in the mire.

Saint Bernard

FROM A LAST WILL

O my children, strive to possess this charity and judge not any man, even though ye should behold him commit a mortal sin. I do not say that sin should not be displeasing unto you and that ye should not hold it in the greatest horror, but I do say that ye should never judge sinners, and moreover I say that ye should never despise them, for ye know not the judgments of our Lord God; and many are there who do appear unto men to be condemned unto hell, but who are saved in the sight of God, and many who appear unto men to be saved are reprobate in the sight of God and condemned unto hell. I could tell you of some whom ye have despised, but of whom I have the sure hope that God will lead them back into His own Hand.

Blessed Angela of Foligno

WITHHOLD THY WRATH

Bedew us, heaven from above; ye clouds rain down the Just One.

Withhold Thy wrath from us, O Lord, and remember no more our evil-doing.

Lo, the city of the Holy One is made a desert, Sion a desert is become.

Jerusalem waste and desolate: the house of Thy hallowing presence, and of Thy glory, where of old our fathers sang Thy praises.

We all have sinned, and are become like unto one unclean.

We have fallen low, as a dying leaf falls earthward; and our iniquities, as a wind have swept us swiftly far.

Thou hast hidden Thy face from us, Thy people; Thou
   hast broken us by the weight of our own sinning.
Behold, O Lord, the affliction of Thy people. Send quickly
   Him who is to come. Send forth the Lamb who rules all
   earthly kingdoms, from Petra in the desert, to the Mount
   of the daughter of Sion; that He may take away the
   grievous yoke of our subjection.
Be ye comforted, be ye comforted, O ye My people: for
   most speedily comes salvation. Why are ye consumed
   with sorrowing, so that your grief has quite transformed
   you? I come to save, be no more fearful. For know ye
   not that I am your God and Master, Israel's Holy One,
   your sole Redeemer?

Advent Song

TRUE SORROW

Lord, my earthly nature is stood before my eyes
like a barren field
which hath few good plants grown in it.
Alas, sweetest Jesus and Christ,
now send me the sweet rain of thy manhood
and the hot sun of thy living Godhead
and the gentle dew of the holy Spirit
that I may wail and cry out the aches of my heart.

Mechtild of Magdeburg

ON THE DIGNITY OF TEMPORAL SUFFERING

The Servant: O Lord, it is so easy to talk, but the reality
is so difficult to endure, for it is so very painful.

Eternal Wisdom: If suffering gave no pain, it could not
be called suffering. There is nothing more painful than
suffering, and nothing more joyful than to have suffered.
Suffering is a short pain and a long joy. Suffering gives
to the sufferer pain here and joy hereafter. Suffering kills

suffering. Suffering is ordained that the sufferer may not suffer eternally. Hadst thou so much spiritual sweetness and divine consolation and heavenly delight as, at all times, to overflow with the divine dew, it would not be for thee so very meritorious of itself, since, for all this together, I should not have to thank thee so much as an affectionate suffering or patience in adversity, in which thou sufferest for My sake. Sooner will ten be perverted and ruined in the midst of a great delight and joyous sweetness than one in the midst of constant suffering and adversity. If thou hadst as much science as all the astronomers, if thou couldst discourse as ably of God as all the tongues of men and angels, and didst possess the treasures of knowledge of all the masters, not all this could avail to advance thee in a good life, so much as if thou didst give thyself up, and didst abandon thyself in all thy sufferings to God; for the former is common to the good and the bad, but the latter is proper to My elect alone. If anyone were able rightly to weigh time and eternity, he ought rather to desire to lie in a fiery furnace for a hundred years than to be deprived in eternity of the smallest reward for the smallest suffering; for this has an end, but the other is without end.

The Servant: Ah, sweet and dear Lord, how like a sweet harp are these words to a suffering mortal! Lord, Lord, wouldst Thou but cheer me thus and come to visit me in my sufferings, I should be glad to suffer; it would then be better for me to suffer than not to suffer.

Eternal Wisdom: Now, then, hearken to the sweet music of the distended strings of that Divine harp—a God-suffering man—how richly it sounds, how sweetly it vibrates. Before the world, suffering is a reproach, but before Me it is an infinite honour. Suffering is an extinguisher of My wrath, and an obtainer of My favour. Suffering makes a man in My sight worthy of love, for the sufferer is like Me. Suffering is a hidden treasure which no one can make good; and though a man might kneel before Me a hundred years to beg a friendly suffering, he nevertheless would not earn it. Suffering changes an earthly man into a heavenly man. Suffering brings with it the estrangement of the world, but confers, instead, My intimate familiarity. It lessens delight and increases grace. He to whom I am to show Myself a friend must be wholly disclaimed and abandoned by the world. Suffering is the surest way, the nearest way, and the shortest way. He who rightly knows how profitable suffering is, ought to receive it as a gift worthy of God.

Suso

ON EXCESS OF PENANCE

Some are beguiled with *overmuch abstinence from meat and drink and sleep.* That is a temptation of the devil, to make them fall in the midst of their work, so that they bring it not to an end as they should have done, if they had known reason and kept discretion. And so they lose their merit for their forwardness. This trap our enemy lays to take us with when we begin to hate wickedness and turn ourselves to God. Then many begin a thing that they may never bring to an end. Then they think they may do whatsoever their heart is set upon. But often they fall ere they reach half-way, and that thing which they thought was for them is hindering them. For we have a long way to heaven, and as many good deeds as we do, as many prayers as we make, and as many good thoughts as we think in truth and hope and charity, so many paces do we go heavenward. Then if we make ourselves so feeble that we may neither work nor pray as we should, nor think, are we not greatly to blame that fail when we have most need to be stalwart? And well I know that it is not God's will that we do so. For the prophet says: "Lord, I shall keep my strength to Thee." So that he might sustain God's service to his death-day, and not in a little and in a short time waste it and then lie wailing and groaning by the wall. And the peril is much more than men think. For St. Jerome says that he makes an offering of robbery who excessively torments his body with too little meat or sleep. And St. Bernard says: "Fasting and watching hinder not ghostly good, but help, if they be done *with discretion*—without that they are vices." Therefore it is not good to punish ourselves so much.

Richard Rolle

THE LUKEWARM PENITENTS

From the particular faults of good people, deliver us, O Lord! There are sacraments for sin, for lukewarmness there are none. Who does not know, that has ever ministered to souls, how even frequent communion hardens tepid hearts? Have you ever known ten persons plunged in lukewarmness who were cured? And what was it that cured nine out of the ten? The shame that followed falls into downright sin! Alas! this is a desperate game to play, to expect the prisons of hell to do the work of the medicines of heaven, and stake eternity on the experiment.

Frederick William Faber

GOD WRITES STRAIGHT ON CROOKED LINES

And therefore departure from God would be no vice unless in a nature whose property it was to abide with God. So that even the wicked will is a strong proof of the goodness of the nature. But God, as He is the Supremely good Creator of good natures, so is He of evil wills the most just Ruler; so that, while they make an ill use of good natures, He makes a good use even of evil wills. Accordingly, He caused the devil (good by God's creation, wicked by his own will) to be cast down from his high position, and to become the mockery of His angels—that is, He caused his temptations to benefit those whom he wishes to injure by them. And because God, when He created him, was certainly not ignorant of his future malignity, and foresaw the good which He Himself would bring out of his evil, therefore says the psalm "This dragon

whom Thou hast made to sport therein" (*Psalm* 103, 26),
that we may see that, even while God in His goodness
created him good, He yet had already foreseen and ar-
ranged how He would make use of him when he became
wicked.

Saint Augustine

THE GENTLE LORD

All that unites us to God, all that causes us to taste Him,
to delight in Him, to rejoice in His glory, and to love Him
so purely that we find our happiness in Him, and, not satisfied with reflections, with thoughts, with affections and
resolutions, leads us solidly to the practice of detachment
from self and from created things; all this is good, all this
is true prayer. We must take care not to torment our heads,
or over-excite our hearts; but to take whatever offers itself
to the soul's sight with humility and simplicity, without
those violent efforts which are rather imaginary than real
and well grounded; allowing ourselves to be drawn gently
to God, abandoning ourselves to the promptings of our
own spirit.

Bossuet

O FELIX CULPA!

It availed us nothing to be born
unless it had availed us to be redeemed.
O how admirable is thy goodness towards us!
O how inestimable is thy love!
Thou hast delivered up thy son
to redeem a slave.
O truly necessary sin of Adam,
which the death of Christ has blotted out!
O happy fault
that merited such and so great a redeemer!

Roman Missal

THE FLESH, ERROR AND SIN

And to the church's angel at Sardis write thus: A message to thee from him who bears the seven spirits of God, and the seven stars. I know of all thy doings, how thou dost pass for a living man, and all the while art a corpse. Rouse thyself, and rally whatever else still lives, but lives at the point of death. There are tasks my God expects of thee, and I find them unfulfilled. Remember how the gift, how the message came to thee; hold it fast, and repent. If thou failest in thy watch, I will come upon thee like a thief; thou shalt never know the hour of my coming to thee.

Apocalypse 3, 1–3

And indeed, for fear that these surpassing revelations should make me proud, I was given a sting to distress my outward nature, an angel of Satan sent to rebuff me. Three times it made me entreat the Lord to rid me of it; but he told me, My grace is enough for thee; my strength finds its full scope in thy weakness. More than ever, then, I delight to boast of the weaknesses that humiliate me, so that the strength of Christ may enshrine itself in me.

II Corinthians 12, 7–9

THE TWO SIDES OF RELIGION

Christianity, considered as a moral system, is made up of two elements, beauty and severity; whenever either is indulged to the loss and disparagement of the other, evil ensues. In heathen times, Greek and Barbarian in some sense divided these two between them; the latter were the slaves of dreary and cruel superstitions, and the former abandoned themselves to a joyous polytheism. And so, again, in these latter times, the two chief forms of heresy into which opposition to the primitive truth has developed were remarkable, at least in their origin three hundred years ago, and at times since, the one for an unrefined and self-indulgent religiousness, the other for a stern, dark, cruel spirit, very unamiable, yet still inspiring more respect than the other.

Religion has two sides, a severe side, and a beautiful; and we shall be sure to swerve from the narrow way which leads to life, if we indulge ourselves in what is beautiful while we put aside what is severe.

Cardinal Newman

THE HOSTILE BODY

I do not speak deliberately,
I speak since Love has bidden me.
When my life in God began,
When I turned from earth and man,
I looked upon my body
And saw it up in arms
Against my naked soul,
And full of power, rich in strength
And all the perfectness that Nature lends.
I saw it was my enemy,
And this I saw:
I must defeat myself to flee
Eternal death, and that would be
A battle unto victory.
I looked upon my soul and found it armed
With holy martyrdom of Jesus Christ, our Lord,
This was my sword.

I never lived at peace,
But feared unceasingly,
And all my youth struck mighty blows
Against the flesh.
What sighs and tears, confession, fasts, and vigils,
What scourging and what prayers constantly!

Mechtild of Magdeburg

ALL FLESH IS LIKE GRASS

It is always in season but now more than ever is it sea-
sonable to say: Vanity of vanities and all is vanity. . . .
Where is the gay torchlight now? Where are the clapping
hands and the dances and the assemblies and the festivals?
Where the green garlands and the curtains floating? Where
the cry of the town and the cheers of the hippodrome,
and the noisy flattering lungs of the spectators there? All
that is gone: a wind blew and on the sudden cast the
leaves and showed us the tree bare and all that was left
of it from the root upwards shaking—the gale that struck
it was so fearfully strong and threatened, indeed, to tear
it up root-whole, or shatter it this way and that, even to
the rending of the grain of the timber. Where now are the
friends, the make-believers, followers of the fashion?
Where are the suppers and feasts? Where the swarm of
hangers-on? The strong wine decanting all day long, the
cooks and the daintily dressed table, the attendants on
greatness and all the words and ways they have to please?
They were all night and dreaming: now it is day and they
are vanished. They were spring flowers, and, the spring
being over, they all are faded together. They were a
shadow, and it has travelled on beyond. They were smoke,
and it has gone out in the air. They were bubbles, and
are broken. They were cobwebs, and are swept away.
And so this spiritual refrain is left us to sing, coming in
again and again with: Vanity of vanities and all is vanity.

Oh this is the verse that should be written on walls, and in clothing and at markets and at home and by waysides and on doors and over entries and above all in the conscience of each, written wherever we look that we may read it whatever we do. While this swindle of the business of life and this wearing of masks and playing of characters is taken for truth by the many, this is the verse that every day, at dinner and supper and every meeting between men, I wish that each one of you could be bringing to his neighbour's ear and hearing from his neighbour's tongue: Vanity of vanities, all is vanity.

Saint John Chrysostom

THE WISDOM OF THIS WORLD IS NAUGHT

The reason for which it is necessary for the soul, in order to attain to Divine Union with God, to pass through this dark night of mortification of the desires and denial of pleasures in all things, is because all the affections which it has for creatures are pure darkness in the eyes of God, and, when the soul is clothed in these affections, it has no capacity for being enlightened and possessed by the pure and simple light of God, if it cast them not first from it; for light cannot agree with darkness; since, as St. John says: *Tenebrae eam non comprehenderunt.* That is: The darkness could not receive the light.

The reason is that contraries (even as philosophy teaches us) cannot co-exist in one person; and that darkness, which is affection for the creatures, and light, which is God, are contrary to each other, and have no likeness or accord between one another, even as St. Paul explained to the Corinthians, saying: *Quae conventio luci ad tenebras?* (II; 6, 14.) That is to say: What communion can there be between light and darkness? Hence it is that the light of Divine union cannot dwell in the soul if these affections first flee not away from it.

In order that we may the better prove what has been said, it must be known that the affection and attachment which the soul has for creatures renders the soul like to these creatures; and the greater is its affection, the closer is the quality and likeness between them; for love creates a likeness between that which loves and that which is loved. He that loves a creature becomes as low as is that creature, and, in some ways, lower; for love not only makes the lover equal to the object of his love, but even subjects him to it. Wherefore in the same way it comes to pass that the soul that loves anything else becomes incapable of pure union with God and transformation in Him. For the low estate of the creature is much less capable of union with the high estate of the Creator than is darkness with light. For all things of earth and heaven, compared with God, are nothing. The soul that is ravished by the graces and beauties of the creatures has only supreme misery and unattractiveness in the eyes of God; and thus it cannot be capable of the infinite grace and loveliness of God; for that which has no grace is far removed from that which is infinitely gracious; and all the goodness of the creatures of the world, in comparison with the infinite goodness of God, may be described as wickedness. For there is naught good, save only God. And therefore the soul that sets its heart upon the good things of the world is supremely evil in the eyes of God. And, even as wickedness comprehends not goodness, even so much a soul cannot be united with God, who is supreme goodness. All the wisdom of the world and human ability, compared with the infinite wisdom of God, are pure and supreme ignorance, even as St. Paul writes to the Corinthians, saying: *Sapientia hujus mundi stultitia est apud Deum.* The wisdom of this world is foolishness in the eyes of God.

Wherefore any soul that makes account of all its knowledge and ability in order to come to union with the wisdom of God is supremely ignorant in the eyes of God, and will remain far removed from that wisdom. For ignorance knows not what wisdom is, even as St. Paul says that this wisdom seems foolishness to God; since, in the eyes of God, those who consider themselves to be persons with a certain amount of knowledge are very ignorant, since the Apostle, writing to the Romans, says of them: Considering themselves to be wise they became foolish. And those alone gain the wisdom of God who are like ignorant children, and laying aside their knowledge, walk in His service with love. This manner of wisdom St. Paul taught likewise to the Corinthians: If any among you seemeth to be wise, let him become ignorant that he may be wise; for the wisdom of this world is foolishness with respect to God. So that in order to come to union with the wisdom of God, the soul has to proceed rather by unknowing than by knowing; and all the dominion and liberty of the world, compared with the liberty and dominion of the spirit of God, is the most abject slavery, affliction and captivity.

Wherefore the soul that is enamoured of prelacy, or of any such office, and longs for liberty of desire is considered and treated in the sight of God, not as a son, but as a base slave and captive, since it has not been willing to accept His holy doctrine, wherein He teaches us that he who would be greater must be less, and he who would be less must be greater. And therefore such a soul will be unable to attain to that true liberty of spirit which is encompassed in His Divine union. For slavery can have no part with liberty; and liberty cannot dwell in a heart that is subject to desires, for this is the heart of a slave; but it dwells in the free man, because he has the heart of a son. It is for this reason that Sarah bade her husband Abraham cast out the bondwoman and her son, saying that the son of the bondwoman should not be heir with the son of the free woman.

And all the delights and pleasures of the will in all the things of the world, in comparison with all those delights which are God, are supreme affliction, torment and bitterness. And thus he that sets his heart upon them is considered, in the sight of God, as worthy of supreme afflic-

tion, torment and bitterness; and thus he will be unable
to attain the delights of the embrace of union with God,
since he is worthy of affliction and bitterness. All the
wealth and glory of all the creatures in comparison with
the wealth which is God is supreme poverty and wretchedness. Thus the soul that loves and possesses creature
wealth is supremely poor and wretched in the sight of
God, and for this reason will be unable to attain to that
wealth and glory which is the state of transformation in
God; since that which is miserable and poor is supremely
far removed from that which is supremely rich and glorious.

Saint John of the Cross

VANITY

We call that glory vain which we assume to ourselves,
either for what is not in us, or for what is in us, and belongs to us, but deserves not that we should glory in it.
The nobility of our ancestors, the favour of great men,
and popular honour are things not in us, but either in our
progenitors or in the esteem of other men. Some become
proud and insolent, either by riding a good horse, wearing
a feather in their hat, or by being dressed in a fine suit
of clothes; but who does see the folly of this? for if there
be any glory in such things, the glory belongs to the horse,
the bird and the tailor; and what a meanness of heart
must it be to borrow esteem from a horse, from a feather,
or some ridiculous new fashion! Others value themselves
for a well-trimmed bearing, for curled locks, or soft hands;
or because they can dance, sing or play; but are not these
effeminate men who seek to raise their reputation by so
frivolous and foolish things? Others for a little learning
would be honoured and respected by the whole world, as
if everyone ought to become their pupil, and account them
his masters. These are called pedants. Others strut like
peacocks, contemplating their beauty and think themselves

admired by everyone. All this is extremely vain, foolish and impertinent; and the glory which is raised on so weak foundations is justly esteemed vain and frivolous.

Saint Francis de Sales

A SAINT'S HORROR OF SIN

If a man were to see the seriousness of a single sin, he would rather be in a fiery furnace, and remain there alive in body and soul, than endure it within him; and if the sea were a vast fire, he would rather cast himself into the midst thereof, right to the bottom, to flee from this sin, nor would he ever go out thence if he knew that on leaving he would have the sin within him.

Saint Catherine of Genoa

IT IS I WHO HEAL

"Be comforted. You would not seek me had you not found me.

"I thought of you in my agony. I shed so many drops of my blood for you.

"To think that you could perform this or that absent thing this is to tempt myself rather than to test you: I shall perform it within you when the time is come.

"Let yourself be guided by my rules. See how well I have guided the Virgin and the saints who have let me work in them.

"My Father loves all that I do.

"Do you always want me to shed the blood of my humanhood without shedding tears yourself?

"It is I who am responsible for your conversion. Have no fears and pray with confidence, as though it were for me.

"I am manifest to you through my word in the Gospels, through my spirit in the Church, through inspiration and my power in the priests, through my prayer in the Faithful.

"Physicians will not heal you, for in the end you will die. But it is I who heal and render the body immortal.

"Suffer chains and servitude of the body. For now I deliver you from spiritual servitude only.

"I am a better friend to you than this one or that one. For I have done more for you than they. They would not suffer for you as I have suffered for you and they would not die for your faithlessness and cruelty, as I have done and as I am ready to do, and as I do in the Elect and in the Holy Sacrament.

"If you knew your sins you would lose heart."

"I shall therefore lose it, Lord, for Your assurance convinces me of their heinousness."

"No, for I, through whom you have learned this, can heal you, and what I tell you is a sign that I want to heal you. You shall know your sins as you expiate them, and it shall be said to you: behold the sins that have been pardoned you. Do penance for your hidden sins, and for the concealed wickedness of those that you know."

"Lord, I give You all."

"I love you more ardently than you have loved your vices, *ut immundus pro luto.*

"Let the glory be mine and not yours, O worm and dust.

"Consult your advisor when the words I said lead you to evil, to vanity, or curiosity."

"I see the abyss of my pride, my curiosity, and my lust. I am in no harmony with God or with Jesus Christ the Just. But my sins have been visited upon Him and all our plagues have fallen upon Him. He is more abominable than I and, far from abhorring me, He regards it as an honour that I come to Him and assist Him. But He has healed Himself and He will heal me with all the more reason. My wounds must be added to His, and I must join myself with Him, and He will save me in saving Himself."

Pascal

GOD'S SCOURGE IN OUR SINS

Now you would fain say: the wicked are well off, they have it all their way, but not the good. Solomon saith: "The wicked man shall not say, what harm does it me that I do evil? It does not hurt me! Or who lets me feel it?" Whatever evil thou doest it is altogether thine own damage and enough woe will come to thee out of it. Be sure of that, by the truth eternal. In His wrath God could not afflict a sinner more by hellish pain than by letting it happen or occur that he sin without sending him suffering so hard that he forgets to sin. And if God gave him all the woes of the world to bear, it could not be a harsher scourge than being permitted to sin.

Meister Eckhart

ERROR DISGUISES ITSELF AS TRUTH

[For there *is* a certain show of beauty in sin.] Thus pride wears the mask of loftiness of spirit, although You alone, O God, are high over all. Ambition seeks only honour and glory, although You alone are to be honoured before all and glorious for ever. By cruelty the great seek to be feared, yet who is to be feared but God alone: from His power what can be wrested away, or when or where or how or by whom? The caresses by which the lustful seduce are a seeking for love: but nothing is more caressing than Your charity, nor is anything more healthfully loved than Your supremely lovely, supremely luminous Truth. Curiosity passes itself off as a desire for knowledge, whereas You supremely know all things. Ignorance and sheer stupidity hide under the names of simplicity and innocence: yet no being has simplicity like to Yours: and none is more innocent than You, for it is their own deeds that harm the wicked. Sloth pretends that it wants quietude: but what sure rest is there save the Lord? Luxuriousness would be called abundance and completeness; but You are the fulness and inexhaustible abundance of incorruptible delight. Wastefulness is a parody of generosity: but You are the infinitely generous giver of all good. Avarice wants to possess overmuch: but You possess all. Enviousness claims that it strives to excel: but what can excel before You? Anger clamours for just vengeance: but whose vengeance is so just as Yours? Fear is the recoil from a new and sudden threat to something one holds dear, and a cautious regard for one's own safety: but nothing new or sudden can happen to You, nothing can threaten Your hold upon things loved, and where is safety as secure as Yours? Grief pines at the loss of things in which desire delighted: for it wills to be like to You from whom nothing can be taken away.

Thus the soul is guilty of fornication when she turns from You and seeks from any other source what she will nowhere find pure and without taint unless she returns to You. Thus even those who go from You and stand up against You are still perversely imitating You. But by the mere fact of their imitation, they declare that You are the creator of all that is, and that there is nowhere for them to go where You are not.

So once again what did I love in that theft of mine? Of what excellence of my Lord was I making perverse and vicious imitation? Perhaps it was the thrill of acting against Your law—at least in appearance, since I had no power to do so in fact, the delight a prisoner might have in making some small gesture of liberty—getting a deceptive sense of omnipotence from doing something forbidden without immediate punishment. There was I a slave, fleeing from his Lord and pursuing his Lord's shadow. O rottenness, O monstrousness of life and abyss of death! Could you find pleasure only in what was forbidden, and only because it was forbidden?

Saint Augustine

ACEDIA, OR SPIRITUAL TEDIUM

Our sixth contending is with that which the Greeks call acedia, and which we may describe as tedium or perturbation of the heart. It is akin to dejection and especially felt by wandering monks and solitaries, a persistent and obnoxious enemy to such as dwell in the desert, disturbing the monk especially about midday, like a fever mounting at a regular time, and bringing its highest tide of inflammation at definite accustomed hours to the sick soul. And so some of the Fathers declare it to be the demon of noontide which is spoken of in the ninetieth Psalm.

When this besieges the unhappy mind, it begets aversion from the place, boredom with one's cell, and scorn and contempt for one's brethren, whether they be dwelling with one or some way off, as careless and unspiritually-minded persons. Also, towards any work that may be done within the enclosures of our own lair, we become listless and inert. It will not suffer us to stay in our cell, or to attend to our reading: we lament that in all this while, living in the same spot, we have made no progress, we sigh and complain that bereft of sympathetic fellowship we have no spiritual fruit; and bewail ourselves as empty of all spiritual profit, abiding vacant and useless in this place; and we that could guide others and be of value to multitudes have edified no man, enriched no man with our precept and example. We praise other and far distant monasteries, describing them as more helpful to one's progress, more congenial to one's soul's health. We paint the fellowship of the brethren there, its suavity, its richness in spiritual conversation, contrasting it with the harshness of all that is at hand where not only is there no edification to be had from any of the brethren who dwell here, but where one cannot even procure one's victuals without enormous toil. Finally we conclude that there is no health for us so long as we stay in this place, short of abandoning the cell wherein to tarry further will be only to perish with it, and betaking ourselves elsewhere as quickly as possible.

Towards eleven o'clock or midday it induces such lassitude of body and craving for food as one might feel after the exhaustion of a long journey and hard toil, or the postponing of a meal throughout a two or three days' fast. One gazes anxiously here and there, and sighs that no brother of any description is to be seen approaching: one is for ever in and out of one's cell, gazing at the sun as though it were tarrying to its setting; one's mind is in an irrational confusion, like the earth befogged in a mist, one is slothful and vacant in every spiritual activity, and no remedy, it seems, can be found for this state of siege than a visit from some brother, or the solace of sleep. Finally our malady suggests that in common courtesy one should salute the brethren and visit the sick, near or far. It dictates such offices of duty and piety as to seek out this relative or that, and make haste to visit him; or there is that religious or devout lady, destitute of any support from her family, whom it is a pious act to visit now and then and supply in holy wise with necessary comforts, neglected and despised as she is by her own relations: far better than to bestow one's pious labour upon those that sit without benefit or profit in one's cell . . .

The blessed Apostle, like a true physician of the spirit . . . busied himself to prevent the malady born of the spirit of acedia . . . "Study to be quiet . . . and to do your own business . . . and to work with your own hands, as is commended to you . . ."

And so the wise Fathers in Egypt would in no way suffer the monks, especially the younger, to be idle, measuring the state of their heart and their progress in patience and humility by their steadiness at work; and not only might they accept nothing from anyone towards their support, but out of their own toil they supplied such brethren as came by, or were from foreign parts, and did send huge stores of victuals and provisions throughout Libya, a barren and hungry land, and to those that pined in the squalor of the prisons in the towns . . . There was a saying approved by the ancient Fathers in Egypt: that a busy monk is besieged by a single devil; but an idle one destroyed by spirits innumerable.

So when the abbot Paul, revered among the Fathers, was living in that vast desert of Porphyrio, secure of his daily bread from the date palms and his small garden, and could have found no other way of keeping himself (for his dwelling in the desert was seven days' journey and more from any town or human habitation, so that more would be spent in conveying the merchandise than the work he had sweated on would fetch), nevertheless did he gather palm leaves, and every day exacted from himself just such a measure of work as though he lived by it. And when his cave would be filled with the work of a whole year, he would set fire to it, and burn each year the work so carefully wrought: and thereby he proved that without working with his hands a monk cannot endure to abide in his place, nor can he climb any nearer the summit of holiness: and though necessity of livelihood in no way demands it, let it be done for the sole purging of the heart, the steadying of thought, perseverance in the cell, and the conquest and final overthrow of acedia itself.

Cassian

THE RIGHT UNDERSTANDING OF EVIL

To You, then, evil utterly is not—and not only to You, but to Your whole creation likewise, evil is not: because there is nothing over and above Your creation that could break in or derange the order that You imposed upon it. But in certain of its parts there are some things which we call evil because they do not harmonise with other things; yet these same things do harmonise with still others and thus are good; and in themselves they are good. All these things which do not harmonise with one another, do suit well with that lower part of creation which we call the earth, which has its cloudy and windy sky in some way apt to it. God forbid that I should say: "I wish that these things were not"; because even if I saw only them, though I should want better things, yet even for them alone I should praise You: for that You are to be praised, things of earth show—*dragons, and all deeps, fire, hail, snow, ice, and stormy winds, which fulfil Thy word; mountains and all hills, fruitful trees and all cedars; beasts and all cattle, serpents and feathered fowl; kings of the earth and all people, princes and all judges of the earth; young men and maidens, old men and young, praise Thy name.* And since from the heavens, O our God, *all Thy angels praise Thee in the high places, and all Thy hosts, sun and moon, all the stars and lights, the heavens of heavens, and the waters that are above the heavens, praise Thy name*—I no longer desired better, because I had thought upon them all and with clearer judgment I realised that while certain higher things are better than lower things, yet all things together are better than the higher alone.

There is no sanity in those whom anything in creation displeases, any more than there was in me when I was displeased with many things that You had made. Because my soul did not dare to be displeased with my God, it would not allow that what displeased it was Yours. Thus it strayed off into the error of holding two substances, and it found no rest but talked wildly. Turning from that error it had made for itself a god occupying the infinite measures of all space, and had thought this god to be You, and had placed it in its heart, and thus had once again become the temple of its own idol, a temple abominable to You. But You caressed my head, though I knew it not, and closed my eyes that they should not see vanity; and I ceased from myself a little and found sleep from my madness. And from that sleep I awakened in You, and I saw You infinitely other; but that sight was not with the eyes of flesh.

And I looked upon other things, and I saw that they owed their being to You, and that all finite things are in You: but in a different manner, being in You not as in a place, but because You are and hold all things in the hand of Your truth, and all things are true inasmuch as they are: nor is falsehood anything, save that a thing is thought to be what it is not. And I observed that all things harmonised not only with their places but also with their times; and that You, who alone are eternal, did not begin to work after innumerable spaces of time had gone by: since all the spaces of time, spaces past, spaces to come, would neither go nor come if You did not operate and abide.

My own experience had shown me that there was nothing extraordinary in the same bread being loathsome to a sick palate and agreeable to a healthy, and in light being painful to sore eyes which is a joy to clear. Your justice displeases the wicked: but so do the viper and the smaller worms: yet these You have created good, and suited to the lower parts of Your creation—to which lower parts indeed the wicked themselves are well suited, insofar as they are unlike You, though they become suited to the higher parts as they grow more like You. So that when I now asked what is iniquity, I realised that it was not a substance but a swerving of the will which is turned towards lower things and away from You, O God, who are the supreme substance: so that it casts away what is most inward to it and swells greedily for outward things.

Saint Augustine

HELL'S TRUE MEANING

Saint Catherine of Genoa, in the course of one of her visions, argues with God about Hell; she is absolutely certain that the sinner will be better off if entrusted to *her* love. God gives her *carte blanche* and Catherine hastens to seize a thoroughly hardened sinner whom she pushes, and drives, and shoves, willy-nilly, into the very centre of Paradise, into the very heart of God, into the splendour of all light. Whereupon the soul thus commandeered into Paradise is violently angered, and protests: "Why, O God, didst thou deliver me over to this sentimental and foolish woman? What is my crime that now I must suffer a punishment which is spared even the Devil? No suffering in Hell could match the torture of being drowned in love when everything within me is hate, in purity when everything within me is corrupt." Catherine, undismayed, and thinking, no doubt, that with a little practice she will learn to handle souls, takes the sinner and places him outside of Paradise but also outside of Hell. A rending cry rises to God: "And now I am nowhere, now I am truly *lost*. I beg that I may be allowed to re-enter Hell where, through divine justice, I still form part of order. Thy justice, O God, which is a presence, lightens a little the terrible verdict of damnation; thine absence, thy punishment bring a little order into chaos—into negative and eternal absurdity."

Saint Catherine of Genoa
as related by Jean de Menasce

DIES IRAE

The day of wrath: on that dread day
The Cross her banners will display,
The world to ashes melt away.

How men will tremble then with fear
When they behold the Judge appear,
Who all their deeds will strictly hear.

The trumpet spreads the wondrous call,
On every tomb its echoes fall,
Before the throne it summons all.

Nature and Death will be appalled,
When all the dead, to life recalled,
Make answer, unto Judgment called.

The written book will then be brought,
Containing all that men have wrought,
From which their Judgment will be sought.

For when the Judge sits to arraign,
All hidden things will then be plain;
Nothing unpunished will remain.

Then, sinner, what will be my plea,
To whom appeal to succour me?
When barely safe the just may be?

King of most awful Majesty!
Who makes our salvation free,
Source of love! my Saviour be.

Remember, gracious Lord, I pray,
As Thou for me on earth didst stay,
Thou mayst not lose me on that day.

Me hast Thou sought thro' wearying strain,
Redeemed me by Thy Cross of pain—
Such suffering should not be in vain.

Righteous judgment of retribution,
Grant the gift of absolution,
Ere the day of execution.

I groan as tho' accused I stood,
My face suffused with guilty blood,
Spare Thy suppliant then, O God!

Thou who Mary has forgiven,
And the repentant robber shriven,
Some hope to me hast also given.

With feeble prayers to Thee I cry,
But on Thy goodness I rely,
Lest in eternal life I lie.

Among the sheep my place command,
Far from the goats I fain would stand,
Establish me at Thy right hand.

When the guilty are confounded,
And with cruel flames surrounded,
Let my call with saints be sounded.

Imploring, on my knees I bend,
My heart to ashes crushed—O lend
Thine aid and pity at my end.

When, on that dread day of weeping,
Man, arisen from death's sleeping,
Tried and judged, his doom is reaping,
Spare him, take him, in Thy keeping.

O Lord and Master, Jesus Blest,
Grant him then eternal rest.

Thomas a Celano

LITANIES

From needing danger, to bee good,
From owing thee yesterdaies teares to day,
From trusting so much to thy blood,
That in that hope, wee wound our soule away,

From bribing thee with Almes, to excuse
　　Some sinne more burdenous,
From light affecting, in religion, newes,
From thinking us all soule, neglecting thus
Our mutuall duties, Lord deliver us.

　From being anxious, or secure,
Dead clods of sadnesse, or light squibs of mirth,
　From thinking, that great courts immure
All, or no happinesse, or that this earth
　　Is only for our prison fram'd,
　　Or that thou art covetous
To them thou lovest, or that they are maim'd
From reaching this worlds sweet, who seek thee thus,
With all their might, Good Lord deliver us.

　That learning, thine Ambassador,
From thine allegeance wee never tempt,
　That beauty, paradises flower
For physicke made, from poyson be exempt,
　　That wit, borne apt high good to doe,
　　By dwelling lazily
On Natures nothing, be not nothing too,
That our affections kill us not, nor dye,
Heare us, weake ecchoes, O thou eare, and cry.

　Sonne of God heare us, and since thou
By taking our blood, owest it us againe,
　Gaine to thy self, or us allow;
And let not both us and thy selfe be slaine;
　　O Lambe of God, which took'st our sinne
　　Which could not stick to thee,
O let it not returne to us againe,
But Patient and Physition being free,
As sinne is nothing, let it no where be.

John Donne

THE DAY OF WRATH

Day of the king most righteous,
The day is nigh at hand,
The day of wrath and vengeance,
And darkness on the land.

Day of thick clouds and voices,
Of mighty thundering,
A day of narrow anguish
And bitter sorrowing.

The love of women's over,
And ended is desire,
Men's strike with men is quiet,
And the world lusts no more.

Saint Columba

LAW AND FREEDOM

And God spoke all these words, saying:

I am the Lord thy God, who brought thee out of the land of Egypt, out of the house of bondage.

Thou shalt have no other gods before me.

Thou shalt not make unto thee a graven image, nor any manner of likeness of any thing that is in heaven above, or that is in the earth beneath, or that is in the water under the earth;

Thou shalt not bow down unto them, nor serve them; for I the Lord thy God am a jealous God, visiting the iniquity of the fathers upon the children unto the third and fourth generation of them that hate me;

And showing mercy unto the thousandth generation of them that love me and keep my commandments.

Thou shalt not take the name of the Lord thy God in vain; for the Lord will not hold him guiltless that taketh his name in vain.

Remember the sabbath day, to keep it holy.

Six days shalt thou labour, and do all thy work;

But the seventh day is a sabbath unto the Lord thy God, in it thou shalt not do any manner of work, thou, nor thy son, nor thy daughter, nor thy man-servant, nor thy maid-servant, nor thy cattle, nor the stranger that is within thy gates.

For in six days the Lord made heaven and earth, the sea, and all that in them is, and rested on the seventh day; wherefore the Lord blessed the sabbath day, and hallowed it.

Honour thy father and thy mother, that thy days may be long upon the land which the Lord thy God giveth thee.

Thou shalt not murder.

Thou shalt not commit adultery.

Thou shalt not steal.

Thou shalt not bear false witness against thy neighbour.

Thou shalt not covet thy neighbour's house; thou shalt not covet thy neighbour's wife, nor his man-servant, nor his maid-servant, nor his ox, nor his ass, nor anything that is thy neighbour's.

And all the people perceived the thunderings, and the lightnings, and the voice of the horn, and the mountain smoking; and when the people saw it, they trembled, and stood afar off.

And they said unto Moses: Speak thou with us, and we will hear; but let not God speak with us, lest we die.

And Moses said unto the people: Fear not; for God is come to prove you, and that his fear may be before you, that ye sin not.

And the people stood afar off; but Moses drew near unto the thick darkness where God was.

Exodus 20, 1–18

Blessed is the man that feareth the Lord:
he shall delight exceedingly in his commandments.

Psalm 111, 1

To the righteous a light is risen up in darkness:
he is merciful, and compassionate and just.

Psalm 111, 4

Moses and Aaron among his priests:
And Samuel among them that call upon his name.
They called upon the Lord,
and he heard them.
He spoke to them in the pillar
of the cloud.
They kept his testimonies.
And the commandment which he gave them.

Psalm 98, 6–7

The Spirit himself thus assures our spirit, that we are children of God; and if we are his children, then we are his heirs too; heirs of God, sharing the inheritance of Christ; only we must share his sufferings if we are to share his glory. . . . When that is said, what follows? Who can be our adversary, if God is on our side? He did not even spare his own son, but gave him up for us all; and must not that gift be accompanied by the gift of all else? Who will come forward to accuse God's elect, when God acquits us? Who will pass sentence against us when Jesus Christ, who died, nay, has risen again, and sits at the right hand of God, is pleading for us? Who will separate us from the love of Christ? Will affliction, or distress, or persecution, or hunger, or nakedness, or peril, or the sword? For thy sake, says the scripture, we face death at every moment, reckoned no better than sheep marked down for slaughter. Yet in all this we are conquerors, through him who has granted us his love. Of this I am fully persuaded; neither death nor life, no angels or principalities or powers, neither what is present nor what is to come, no force whatever, neither the height above us nor the depth beneath us, nor any other created thing, will be able to separate us from the love of God, which comes to us in Christ Jesus our Lord.

Romans 8, 16–17; 31–39

OUR BLINDNESS TO FREEDOM

Some who are still steeped in the mire of an imperfect life go on, like frogs, sporting on green grass in the sunshine; that is to say, notwithstanding the impurity of their irreligion, and while they squat in the mud of their venial affections, they console themselves with the hope that God will be kind to them, a hope inspired rather by a gay optimism than by filial confidence. Now true servants of God regard all impure pleasures and creaturely quests as the depths of an ancient cistern defiled with slime, whence the pure water has long since flowed away.

Father Joseph Le Clerc du Tremblay
as quoted by Aldous Huxley in "Grey Eminence"

PRIDE AND FALSE FREEDOM

Now, after that a man hath walked in all the ways that lead him unto the truth, and exercised himself therein, not sparing his labour; now, as often and as long as he dreameth that his work is altogether finished, and he is by this time quite dead to the world, and come out from Self and giveth up to God alone, behold the devil cometh and soweth his seed in the man's heart. From this seed spring two fruits; the one is spiritual fulness or pride, the other is false, lawless freedom. These are two sisters who love to be together. Now, it beginneth in this wise; the Devil puffeth up the man till he thinketh himself to have climbed the topmost pinnacle, and to have come so near to heaven that he no longer needeth Scripture, nor teaching, nor this, nor that, but is altogether raised above any need.

Whereupon there ariseth a false peace and satisfaction with himself, and then it followeth that he saith and thinketh: "Yea, now I am above all other men, and know and understand more than anyone in the world; therefore it is certainly just and reasonable that I should be the lord and commander of all creatures, and that all creatures, and especially all men, should serve me and be subject unto me." And then he seeketh and desireth the same, and taketh it gladly from all creatures, especially men, and thinketh himself well worthy of all this, and that it is his due, and looketh on men as if they were beasts of the field, and thinketh himself worthy of all that ministereth to his body and life and nature, in profit, or joy, or pleasure, or even pastime and amusement, and he seeketh and taketh it wherever he findeth opportunity. And whatever is done or can be done for him seemeth to him all too little and too poor, for he thinketh himself worthy of still more and greater honour than can be rendered to him. And of all the men who serve him and are subject to him, even if they be downright thieves and murderers, he saith, nevertheless, that they are faithful, noble hearts, and have great love and faithfulness to the truth and to poor men. And such men are praised by him, and he seeketh them and followeth after them wherever they be. But he who doth not order himself according to the will of these high-minded men, nor is subject unto them, is not sought after by them, nay, more likely blamed and spoken ill of, even though he were as holy as St. Peter himself.

And seeing that this proud and puffed-up spirit think-eth that she needeth neither Scripture, nor instruction, nor anything of the kind, therefore she giveth no heed to the admonitions, order, laws and precepts of the holy Christian Church, nor to the Sacraments, but mocketh at them and at all men who walk according to these ordinances and hold them in reverence. Hereby we may plainly see that those two sisters dwell together.

Moreover, since this sheer pride thinketh to know and understand more than all men besides, therefore she chooseth to prate more than all other men, and would fain have her opinions and speeches to be alone regarded and listened to, and counteth all that others think and say to be wrong, and holdeth it in derision as a folly.

But it is quite otherwise where there is poorness of spirit

and true humility; and it is so because it is found and known of a truth that a man, of himself and his own power, is nothing, hath nothing, can do and is capable of nothing but only infirmity and evil. Hence followeth that the man findeth himself altogether unworthy of all that hath been or ever will be done for him by God or creatures, and that he is a debtor to God and also to all the creatures in God's stead, both to bear with, and to labour for, and to serve them. And therefore he doth not in any wise stand up for his own rights, but from the humility of his heart he saith, "It is just and reasonable that God and all creatures should be against me, and have a right over me, and to me, and that I should not be against anyone, nor have a right to anything." Hence it followeth that the man doth not and will not crave or beg for anything, either from God or creatures, beyond mere needful things, and for those only with shamefacedness, as a favour and not as a right. And he will not minister unto or gratify his body or any of his natural desires beyond what is needful, nor allow that any should help or serve him except in case of necessity, and then always in trembling; for he hath no right to anything and therefore he thinketh himself unworthy of anything.

So likewise all his own discourse, ways, words and works seem to this man a thing of naught and a folly. Therefore he speaketh little and doth not take upon himself to admonish or rebuke unless he be constrained thereto by love or faithfulness towards God, and even then he doth it in fear, and so little as may be.

Moreover, when a man hath this poor and humble spirit, he cometh to see and understand aright how that all men are bent upon themselves, and are inclined to evil and sin, and that on this account it is needful and profitable that there be order, custom, law and precepts, to the end that the blindness and foolishness of men may be corrected, and that vice and wickedness may be kept under, and constrained to seemliness. For without ordinances, men would be much more mischievous and ungovernable than dogs and cattle. And few have come to the knowledge of the truth but what have begun with holy practices and ordinances and exercised themselves therein so long as they knew nothing more nor better.

Therefore one who is poor in spirit and of a humble mind doth not despise or make light of law, order, precepts and holy customs, nor yet of those who observe and cleave wholly to them but with loving pity and gentle sorrow crieth: "Almighty Father, Thou Eternal Truth, I make my lament unto Thee, and it grieveth Thy Spirit too, that, through man's blindness, infirmity and sin, that is made needful and must be which indeed and in truth were neither needful nor right." (For those who are perfect are under no law. So order, laws, precepts and the like are merely an admonition to men who understand nothing better and know and perceive not wherefore all law and order is ordained.) And the perfect accept the law along with such ignorant men as understand and know nothing better, and practise it with them to the intent that they may be restrained thereby, and kept from evil ways, or, if it be possible, brought to something higher.

Theologia Germanica

SOME THINGS ARE FOR USE, OTHERS FOR ENJOYMENT

Some things, then, are to be enjoyed, others are to be used, still others enjoy and use. Those things which are objects of enjoyment make us happy. Those things which are objects of use assist and support us in our efforts after happiness so that we can attain the things that make us happy and rest in them. We ourselves again, who enjoy and use these things, being placed among both kinds of objects, if we set ourselves to enjoy those which we ought to use, are hindered in our course, and sometimes even led away from it; so that getting entangled in the love of lower gratifications we lag behind in, or even altogether turn back from, the pursuit of the real and proper objects of enjoyment.

DIFFERENCE BETWEEN USE AND ENJOYMENT

For to enjoy a thing is to rest with satisfaction in it for its own sake. To use, on the other hand, is to employ whatever means are at one's disposal to obtain what one desires if it is a proper object of desire; for an unlawful use ought rather to be called an abuse. Suppose we were wanderers in a strange country and could not live happily away from our fatherland, and that we felt wretched in our wandering, and wishing to put an end to our misery, determined to return home. We find that we must make use of some mode of conveyance, either by land or water, in order to reach that fatherland where our enjoyment is to commence. But the beauty of the country through which we pass and the very pleasure of the motion charm our hearts and, turning these things which we ought to use into objects of enjoyment, we become unwilling to hasten the end of our journey; and becoming engrossed in a fictitious delight, our thoughts are diverted from that home whose delights would make us truly happy. Such is a picture of our condition in this life of mortality. We have wandered far from God; and if we wish to return to our Father's home, this world must be used, not enjoyed, so that the invisible things of God may be clearly seen, being understood by the things that are made (*Romans* 1, 20)—that is, that by means of what is material and temporary we may lay hold upon that which is spiritual and eternal.

TRINITY TRUE OBJECT OF ENJOYMENT

The true objects of enjoyment, then, are the Father and the Son and the Holy Spirit, who are at the same time the Trinity, one Being, supreme above all, and common to all who enjoy Him, if He is an object and not rather the cause of all objects, or, indeed, even if He is the cause of all. For it is not easy to find a name that will suitably express so great excellence, unless it be better to speak in this way: the Trinity, one God, of whom are all things, through whom are all things, in whom are all things (*Romans* 11, 36): in the Father unity, in the Son equality, in the Holy Spirit the harmony of unity and equality; and these three attributes are all one because of the Father, all equal because of the Son, and all harmonious because of the Holy Spirit.

Saint Augustine

SPIRITUAL ADULTHOOD

Jesus be in your soul!

How long, daughter, do you suppose that you will be carried in the arms of others? I desire to see in you so great a detachment from creatures and an independence of them that hell itself would not suffice to trouble you. What are these uncalled-for tears that you are shedding nowadays? How much good time do you suppose you have wasted on these scruples? If you would communicate your trials to me, go to that spotless mirror of the Eternal Father, which is His Son, for in that mirror I behold your soul daily, and I doubt not but that you will come away from it comforted and will have no need to go begging at the doors of poor people.

Saint John of the Cross

ALL THINGS ARE BUT LOSS

And God did prove Abraham, and said unto him: "Abraham." And he said: "Here I am." And He said: "Take now thy son, thine only son, whom thou lovest, even Isaac, and get thee into the land of Moriah; and offer him there for a burnt offering upon one of the mountains which I will tell thee of." And Abraham rose early in the morning and saddled his ass, and took two young men with him and Isaac his son . . .

Genesis 22, 1–3

He is not worthy of me, that loves father or mother more; he is not worthy of me, that loves son or daughter more; he is not worthy of me, that does not take up his cross and follow me. He who secures his own life will lose it; it is the man who loses his life for my sake that will secure it.

Matthew 10, 37–39

And all this, which once stood to my credit, I now write down as loss, for the love of Christ. For that matter, there is nothing I do not write down as loss compared with the high privilege of knowing Christ Jesus, my Lord; for love of him I have lost everything, treat everything else as refuse, if I may have Christ to my credit. In him I would render my account, not claiming any justification that is my own work, given me by the law, but the justification

that comes from believing in Jesus Christ, God's gift on
condition of our faith.

Philippians 3, 7–9

THE CURING FEVER OF LOVE

As one that is possessed and burning with a fever loathes
and rejects the sweetest food or drink that you offer him
because he burns with the fever and is vehemently exercised by it, so those who burn with the heavenly, sacred,
solemn longing of the Spirit, and are smitten in soul with
love of the love of God, and are vehemently exercised by
the divine and heavenly fire which the Lord came to send
upon the earth, and desire that it should speedily be
kindled, and are aflame with the heavenly longing for
Christ, these, as we said before, consider all the glorious
and precious things of this age contemptible and hateful
by reason of the fire of the love of Christ, which holds
them fast and inflames them and burns them with a Godward disposition and with the heavenly good things of
love; from which nothing of all that are in heaven and
earth and under the earth shall be able to separate
them, as the apostle Paul testified, saying: Who shall separate us from the love of Christ? . . . .

But it is not possible that anyone should obtain the
possession of his own soul, and of the heavenly love of the
Spirit, unless he makes himself a stranger to all the things
of this age, and gives himself up to seeking the love of
Christ, and his mind stands clear of all material cares and
earthly distractions, in order that he may be wholly occupied with the one aim, directing these things by all the
commandments in order that his whole care and seeking,
and the engrossment and business of his soul, may be
about the search for the immaterial substance, how the
soul should be adorned with the commandments of the
virtues, and with the heavenly adornment of the Spirit,

and with the fellowship of the purity and sanctification of Christ—so that having renounced all and having cut himself free all round from the hindrances of earth and of material things, and set himself clear of fleshly love, whether it be the affection of parents or of kindred, the man may not permit his mind to be busied or distracted with any other thing, such as power, glory, honours, or fleshly friendships of the world, or any other earthly thoughts, but his mind may wholly and entirely take upon itself care and pains for the seeking of the immaterial substance of the soul, and may wholly and entirely endure in expectancy and waiting for the coming of the spirit; as the Lord says, "In your patience possess ye your souls," and again, "Seek the kingdom and all these things shall be added unto you."

Saint Macarius the Egyptian

A SOUL DRAWN TO GOD MASTERS THE BODY

All meditation in which the understanding works fatigues the body; other meditations there are, regulated and quiet, which are not trying to the understanding or wearisome to the interior spirit, and which are made without exterior or interior effort. These do not fatigue the body but rather give it rest, except in two cases: first, when it deprives you of the sustenance and recreation that must be given to the body. By loss of sustenance I mean when, through being absorbed in such meditations, one does not remember to give to the body its natural reflection, going beyond the appointed hours. By recreation I mean that we should at the proper times allow the intellect to dwell as it pleases on good and indifferent things, only avoiding always what is bad.

The second happens to many given to prayer and contemplation. It is that before they go to rest, through exces-

sive use of the understanding, they are afterwards unable
to sleep, their thoughts going continually back to the
things contemplated, or imagined. Hence the enemy endeavours to draw profit, making the body indisposed by
depriving it of sleep, a thing which must be altogether
avoided. With a healthy body you will be able to do
much, with a body unhealthy I do not know how much
may be possible. A sound state of body helps greatly to
do both much evil and much good; much evil in the case
of those whose will is depraved and whose habits are bad;
much good in those whose will is wholly applied to God
Our Lord and is confirmed in good habits. Consequently,
since I do not know what are your meditations or exercises, nor how long they last . . . I am not able to offer
any further suggestion more than what I have already
written. All that I confirm now more than ever; that is,
that you should bear in mind that your Lord loves you, a
truth of which I have no doubt, and that you should correspond with that same love, paying no attention whatsoever to bad, impure, or sensual thoughts, weaknesses or
even tepidity, so long as all these are contrary to your
will. Neither Saint Peter nor Saint Paul ever secured im-
munity from this trial; but though not all is gained, yet
much is gained by paying no attention to any part of it.
For just as my salvation will, please God, be secured by
the help of the good works of the good angels, so on the
same account I cannot be harmed by the evil thoughts
and weaknesses of which the bad angels, the world, and
the flesh are the cause. God Our Lord only wishes to see
my soul in conformity with His Divine Majesty; when the
soul is thus conformed, it makes the body act, whether it
will or no, in conformity with His divine will; and in this
consists both our greatest struggle and the pleasure of the
eternal and supreme goodness. Of whom we beg that
through His infinite pity and grace He may ever lead us
by the hand.

Saint Ignatius Loyola

HUNGER AND THIRST

The soul that really loves God and Christ, though it may do ten thousand righteousnesses, esteems itself as having wrought nothing, by reason of its insatiable aspiration after God. Though it should exhaust the body with fastings, with watchings, its attitude towards the virtues is as if it had not yet even begun to labour for them. Though divers gifts of the Spirit, or revelations and heavenly mysteries, should be vouchsafed to it, it feels in itself to have acquired nothing at all, by reason of its unlimited and insatiable love to the Lord. All day long, hungering and thirsting through faith and love, in persevering prayer, it continues to be insatiable for the mysteries of grace, and for the accomplishment of every virtue. It is smitten with passionate love of the heavenly Spirit. Continually stirring up within itself through grace an ardent aspiration for the heavenly Bridegroom, desiring to be perfectly admitted to the mystical, ineffable fellowship with Him in sanctification of the Spirit. The face of the soul is unveiled, and it gazes upon the heavenly Bridegroom face to face in a spiritual light that cannot be described, mingles with Him in all fulness of assurance, being conformed to His death, ever looking with great desire to die for Christ, and trusting with assurance to receive by the Spirit a perfect deliverance from sin and from the darkness of the passions; in order that having been cleansed by the Spirit, sanctified in soul and body, it may be permitted to become a clean vessel to receive the heavenly unction and to entertain the true King, even Christ; and then it is made meet for eternal life, being henceforward a clean dwelling-place of the Holy Ghost.

Saint Macarius the Egyptian

OUR ENTIRE BEING MUST BE FREED

Moses conquered by stretching out his arms, thus foreshadowing the mystery of the Cross by which we, the new Israel, also conquer, and when that is accomplished we shall at length attain to the vision of the supreme being. It is not only by a purity of body and soul brought about by certain ablutions that we are led to this vision, but also by the cleanness of our garments, so that not only what is hidden may be done becomingly and in accord with the dispositions of the soul, but also what is visible and manifest. True, a stain on a garment will not prevent us from ascending to God, but the pursuits which we have undertaken in this life are likened to a garment with which man is clothed. These pursuits, therefore, and this garb ought to be not soiled but clean. When this has been achieved employing all diligence and when cattle and brute beasts have been driven from the holy mountain, we may ascend it to behold the most exalted of all visions. This, in my opinion, shows that we ought all together to despise the knowledge acquired by our senses, namely the knowledge by which we contemplate things within the limits of our intelligence, because it is characteristic of the nature of the beast to be governed by sense-knowledge alone, without the use of intelligence. A beast is moved by desires originating in sight, or hearing or in one of the other senses, but not in will or intellect. Hence, all its motions and activities are of the senses. The vision, however, in which we contemplate God stands by itself and requires neither sight nor hearing. God is not perceived by the ordinary comprehension and process of knowledge, because "eye has not seen, nor ear heard," for He is not among the images that are wont to arise in the heart of man. Whoever, therefore, aspires to contemplation of God, let him cleanse his mind of every sensual and irrational emotion.

Saint Gregory of Nyssa

THE TRAP OF MEDIOCRITY

I know of no more common or easier mistake or one more difficult to remedy than that of setting a limit to love

and forming ideas that are totally inadequate for our service of God. It is a usual thing for people who have given
themselves to God, become monks or nuns, and wishing
to be saints, soon to circumscribe their ambitions, and instead of raising and extending the scope of their love, to
persuade themselves that it is not necessary to go to the
length of doing everything for God actually and in detail
as I have set forth. They even say that such an undertaking is illusory, and rarely set themselves to attempt it,
not reaching out towards perfection by recognising no
other motive than that of God Himself.

We may be assured that St. Ignatius Loyola and St.
Teresa avoided this temptation: the one saw the greater
glory of God as the end of all things, the other vowed
always to choose the more perfect way. Were I asked why,
seeing that so many people have undertaken the direct
service of God, there are so few saints, I would answer
that the chief reason is that they have given too big a
place in life to indifferent things. They do without thinking, naturally, and for their own satisfaction a thousand
little things, whatever little good there may be in them
being accepted without reference to God, and without any
effort to do all for Him or to stop short at what does not
conduce to His perfect service.

I will say frankly that among those I know serving God
some have a continual thirst for Him; they watch over the
purity of their motives and will not dwell for a moment
more than necessary on that which is solely human. But
I also know a large number who, in the midst of good
deeds, groan that they are against their own interest, who
are upset because they don't get in one place the appreci-
ation they receive in another, who are loud in praise of
their own mediocre attainments, who take comfort from
the thought that everybody cannot be perfect and that
God leaves us weak to keep us humble. This is true, but
there is a great difference between the weakness which
God leaves to the soul for our own good and the feebleness that is due to our own cowardice and irresolution.

These same people wilt under burden of their mortifications and exclaim: "I'm not one of these extraordinary souls. I haven't any mystical gifts. I don't fly so high. I stick to the well-beaten track of the common way," and persuade themselves that this is the spirit of their vocation. To them I say, "No, you haven't experienced these unions and heard these high calls of God, and perhaps this is why it is so difficult to calm you when you are put out by some little thing, as when you have been slighted. If you had a higher notion of perfection, if you looked always to God and found comfort only in Him, you might be admitted to these unions that make the heart so strong that nothing human can disturb it." It is not good to wish for visions, revelations, and such out-of-the-way things, but it is very good to have shown so great a liberality towards God as to deserve a similar return. If we choose poverty of spirit for His sake, our Lord gives us richness of spirit. This poverty consists in seeking self in nothing and in having a faith that enables us, at the word and example of Jesus and for His love, to throw aside the approval and comfort of men and all worldly advantages in order to accept the Cross and the duties of obedience.

Thereupon, without much reading and speculation and worrying of the head, the fountain of eternal life will flow for us; its Divine enlightening comes to the soul not in the form of logical conclusions, but like spurts of grace, rivers of peace, torrents of blessing, and the will feels its potent fires whose flames leap to the heavens.

Father J. J. Surin

ON SPIRITUAL POVERTY

The poor in spirit go out of themselves and all creatures: they are nothing, they have nothing, they do nothing, and these poor are not save that by grace they are God with God: which they are not aware of. St. Bernard says the

soul knows very well that her beloved cannot come to her
till everything is out of her. St. Augustine says, Well and
truly loves the man who loves where he well knows he is
not loved; that is the best of all loving. St. Paul, We know
right well that all things work together for good to them
that love God. And Christ said, Blessed are the poor in
spirit, God's kingdom is theirs.

They tell of various kinds of poverty of spirit. There
are four. What he refers to here is the first poverty of
spirit the soul knows when, illumined by the spirit of truth,
things that are not God weigh with her not a jot; as St.
Paul tells us, "All things are as dung to me." In this in-
digence she finds all creatures irksome.

In the second poverty she considers the merit of her
exemplar Christ and her own demerits and finds her own
works worthless, though they be the sum of men's achieve-
ments. Hence she laments her in the Book of Love, crying,
"The form of my beloved passed me by and I cannot follow him." To this passing she is self-condemned, following the spoor of her quarry, Christ. So sweet his scent, she
swoons away into forgetfulness of outward pain. As St.
Augustine says, The soul is where she loves rather than
where she is giving life, and St. Peter tells us that our
dwelling is in heaven.

The third poverty of spirit is that of the soul wherein
her own nature is slain; her own natural life is stone dead
and there is living in her nothing but the spirit of God. As
St. Paul declares, "I am dead, nevertheless I live; yet my
life Christ liveth in me." In this spiritual death she is grown
poor, for all she has to leave or give has been taken from
her; moreover, she is poor of her free will, for he is doing
with it what he will.

The fourth poverty is the incomprehensibility of God
in her mind, her inability to compass him whether with
knowledge or with works. But the deeper she gets the
more the incomprehensible splendour of the Deity is reflected in her poverty. For as far as with her inner man
she has gotten intuition of divinity so far as she follows

with her outer man the willing poverty of her pattern Jesus Christ; or in other words, the power of God having deprived her of all selfhood, she uses all creatures as she needs them, always without attachment, and if she has them not she can do as well without them and with the same detachment. She knows of nothing more that she can do but she rejoices in his incomprehensible truth and that created things are all as naught to him and that his love has taken to itself her naught which is cleaving to him like a tiny spark. It was this poverty St. Paul was in when he declared he "heard in God unspeakable things which it is not lawful for a man to utter." On that occasion he was knit to God so that neither life nor death could separate him from his love. Thus it befalls the soul perfectly lost in God—lost, not to creatures merely, but to herself as well, and aware of nothing but the pure, unclouded radiance of God's essence. Behold her lost in him, her heavenly joy, and all incapable of any real wrongdoing. The saints invariably say that nothing whatever can disturb the fixity they have in God. Real sin is any disobedience to the law of divine love, any departure from the life of Jesus Christ. He is the form and essence of all things. What, then, is real virtue? Anything wrought in the soul by divine love alone, for that effects naught but its like.

Such is the doctrine of spiritual poverty. Into this true poverty lead us, O superful goodness of God. Amen.

Meister Eckhart

PRAYER FOR THE TRUE THINGS

O God, who hast made ready for those that love Thee such good things as the eye has not seen; pour into our hearts such tender love for Thee, that loving Thee in all things and above all things, we may obtain Thy promises which surpass all desire.

Roman Missal

BUT ONE THING IS NEEDFUL

What is the nature of God's work? God's work is two-fold: that which remains within Him and that which flows out of Him. The work that remains within Him is God's being and nature, that which flows out of Him is His creation. And just as His creatures have flowed from God, in the same way they shall flow back into Him. And that is why God works in the soul, so that He may bring it back to the source from which it first flowed out, for all its own works are not enough to bring the soul back to its source. And, therefore, it is needful that man learns to receive the works of God so that these works may bring him to God again. That is why our Lord said: "But one thing is needful." And without this one thing no one can return to God.

As God comprises all things, so a man who is pure and poor comprises all virtue in a love that is simple and single, and in this love he performs all virtuous acts, and all the virtues are within him and exist side by side with poverty. For only he is poor in the right way to whom virtues have become as his own nature.

From the Book of the Poor in Spirit

A PRAYER

O everlasting Love, enflame my soul with the love of God, so that nothing save His embraces may set my heart on fire. O good Jesu, who shall make me to feel Thee here who mayest now be neither felt nor seen? Pour out of Thyself into the depths of my soul. Enter my heart and fill it with Thy sweetness. Refresh my mind with the strong wine of Thy love that, forgetting all evil and having only Thee, I may be glad and rejoice in Jesus my God. Leave me not, most sweet Lord, but stay with me for ever; for Thy presence is my only comfort and apart from Thee I am full of sorrow.

O Holy Ghost, that givest grace where Thou wilt, enter into my soul, and draw me to Thyself. Transform the nature which Thou hast given me by Thy grace, that my heart, filled with Thy joy, may despise the things of this world. May she receive spiritual gifts from Thee, the Giver, and entering by happiness into unspeakable light be all consumed by holy love. Burn up my inward parts and all my heart with the fire that burns for ever on Thine altar.

Come, I pray Thee, Thou sweet and true joy! Come, most sweet and most desired! Come, my Love who art my only comfort! Enter a soul that longs for Thee. Enflame with Thy divine fire all my heart; enlighten my inmost parts with Thy radiant light; feed me with Love.

Richard Rolle

THIRD PART

Apprehended by Jesus Christ

THE MYSTICAL BODY

He is the true likeness of the God we cannot see; his is that first birth which precedes every act of creation. Yes, in him all created things took their being, heavenly and earthly, visible and invisible; what are thrones and dominions, what are princedoms and powers? They were all created through him and in him; he takes precedence of all, and in him all subsist.

Colossians 1, 15–17

At the beginning of time the Word already was; and God had the Word abiding with him, and the Word was God. He abode, at the beginning of time, with God. It was through him that all things came into being, and without him came nothing that has come to be. In him there was life, and that life was the light of men. . . . There is one who enlightens every soul born into the world; he was the true Light. He, through whom the world was made, was in the world, and the world treated him as a stranger. He came to what was his own, and they who were his own gave him no welcome.

John 1, 1–4; 9–11

Use every kind of prayer and supplication; pray at all times in the spirit; keep awake to that end with all perseverance; offer your supplication for all the saints.

Ephesians 6, 18

And yet there are different kinds of gifts, though it is the same Spirit who gives them, just as there are different kinds of service, though it is the same Lord we serve, and different manifestations of power, though it is the same God who manifests his power everywhere in all of us. The revelation of the Spirit is imparted to each, to make the best advantage of it. One learns to speak with wisdom, by the power of the Spirit, another to speak with knowledge, with the same Spirit for his rule; one, through the same Spirit, is given faith; another, through the same Spirit, powers of healing; one can perform miracles, one can prophesy, another can test the spirit of the prophets; one can speak in different tongues, another can interpet the tongues; but all this is the work of one and the same Spirit, who distributes his gifts as he will to each severally.

A man's body is all one, though it has a number of different organs; and all this multitude of organs goes to make up one body; so it is with Christ.

I Corinthians 12, 4–12

And you are Christ's body, organs of it depending upon each other. God has given us different positions in the church; apostles first, then prophets, and thirdly teachers; then come miraculous powers, then gifts of healing, works of mercy, the management of affairs, speaking with different tongues, and interpreting prophecy. Are all of us apostles, all prophets, all teachers? Have all miraculous powers, or gifts of healing? Can all speak with tongues, can all interpret?

Prize the best gifts of heaven. Meanwhile, I can show you a way which is better than any other.

I may speak with every tongue that men and angels use; yet, if I lack charity, I am no better than echoing bronze, or the clash of cymbals. I may have powers of prophecy, no secret hidden from me, no knowledge too deep for me; I may have utter faith, so that I can move mountains; yet if I lack charity, I count for nothing. I may give away all that I have, to feed the poor; I may give myself up to be burnt at the stake; if I lack charity, it goes for nothing. Charity is patient, is kind; charity feels no envy; charity is never perverse or proud, never insolent; does not claim its rights, cannot be provoked, does not brood over an injury; takes no pleasure in wrongdoing, but rejoices at the victory of truth; sustains, believes, hopes, endures, to the last. The time will come when we shall outgrow prophecy, when speaking with tongues will come to an end, when knowledge will be swept away; we shall never have finished with charity. Our knowledge, our prophecy, are only glimpses of the truth; and these glimpses will be swept away when the time of fulfilment comes. (Just so, when I was a child, I talked like a child, I had the intelligence, the thoughts of a child; since I became a man, I have outgrown childish ways.) At present, we are looking at a confused reflection in a mirror; then, we shall see face to face; now, I have only glimpses of knowledge; then, I shall recognise God as he has recognised me. Meanwhile, faith, hope and charity persist, all three; but the greatest of them all is charity.

I Corinthians 12, 27–31; 13, 1–13

And moreover I tell you, that if two of you agree over any request that you make on earth, it will be granted them by my Father who is in heaven. Where two or three are gathered together in my name, I am there in the midst of them.

Matthew 18, 19–20

As in the body of man, the work of every member profits the entire body, so it is in the spiritual body, in the Church. And because all believers form One body, the good that is in each one is communicated to the others.

Saint Thomas Aquinas

When the members of Christ pray, they shall not separate from the head . . . God's Son alone shall plead for us, and plead within us, and be implored by us . . . He Himself is the Pleader in our midst.

Saint Augustine

Prayer is hindered by too little light and by too much. He who neither sees his sins nor confesses them is not illumined with light. But he for whom his sins loom so large that he despairs of forgiveness is drowned in light. Neither of these prays. What follows from this? The light must be gentle.

Saint Bernard

A LITANY

Heare us, O heare us Lord; to thee
A sinner is more musique, when he prayes,
    Than spheares, or Angels praises bee,
In Panegyrique Allelujaes;
    Heare us, for till thou heare us, Lord
    We know not what to say;
Thine eare to our sighes, teares, thoughts gives voice and
        word.
O Thou who Satan heard'st in Job's sicke day,
Heare thy self now, for thou in us dost pray.

John Donne

Verily, God has no need of His creatures, but everything created has need of Him.

Meister Eckhart

If, while the mouth prays, the heart is drawn to the prayer within, then do not resist but let your spirit glide into it silently. Even though the spoken prayer you had resolved to make is not completed, do not trouble yourself. For the devotions of the heart that you have made instead are much more pleasing to God, and more salutary for your soul.

Saint Francis de Sales

We are tempted to believe that we have ceased our prayers as soon as a certain joy we have felt in praying ceases. In order to recognise this error, we should reflect that the perfect prayer and the love of God are one and the same thing.

Fénelon

BLESSED CITY, JERUSALEM

Blessed city, Jerusalem,
Vision of peace,
Upbuilt in heaven
From living stones
And crowned by angels
As a bride and her train.

She comes, a new creation,
From heaven; a nuptial chamber
Waits, that, a bride,
She may wed Christ, the Lord.
Her walls, her courts
Are purest gold.

Pearls are the doors
To her sanctuary.
By dint of worth
Such may enter here
As have held fast
Christ's name in the world.

With beating, with pressure the polished stones
Are fitted in place
By the master's hand.
All things are set
In the holy house
To endure forever.

Christ is the stone set
For head of the corner,
He in the joined walls
Binds each to each.
Blessed Sion holds fast
Her faith in Him.

All God's elect
And holy city
Is filled with music
And joyous song,
Praising with fervour
One God in Three.

Monastic Breviary

Now I recognise what the Church is, and that she is infinitely higher than a mere assembly of people animated by the same feelings. Yes, she is the body of Jesus Christ, who, as her Head, is essentially united to her, and who has intimate relations with her, of which there is never any interruption. Now I recognise what an immense treasure of grace and good of all kinds the Church has received from God, which can only be communicated to me by her and through her.

Anna Katharina Emmerich

ANTIPHON FOR HOLY THURSDAY

Where charity and love are, there is God.
The love of Christ has gathered us together: Let us rejoice in Him and be glad.

Let us fear and love the living God, and let us love one another with a sincere heart.

Where charity and love are, there is God.

When, therefore, we are assembled in one, let us take heed, that we be not divided in mind. Let malignant quarrels and contentions cease, and let Christ our God dwell in the midst of us.

Where charity and love are, there is God.

Let us also with the blessed see Thy face in glory, O Christ our God, there to possess an immense and happy joy.

For infinite ages of ages. Amen.

Roman Missal

MEMBERSHIP IN GOD

Many may say: "My God": He belongs wholly to all, since He gave Himself to all for their delight. He gives Himself wholly in everything and to everyone. For those who say "My God" are not dividing Him among themselves. He is present everywhere. He fills everything. He is not more distinct close at hand, and less distinct at a distance, but He embraces everything, from one end of the earth to the other. He holds all in His strong clasp, He rules mildly—God belongs to all equally.

This light, my brothers, this palpable light, shines from the sky, dawns, circles, and sets, shifting from place to place, and yet the eyes of all creatures look to it and turn to it, and all possess it equally without dividing it up among themselves. No rich man can keep it within certain bounds, or take it from another, excluding or depriving the eyes of the poor. Thus everyone can say "My God." Has this one less? Has that one more? Perhaps of gold, but not of God!

Saint Augustine

THE PREFACE OF PENTECOST

It is truly right and fitting,
just and salutary,
that we thank Thee,
always and everywhere,
holy Lord, almighty Father, eternal God,
through Christ our Lord.
For He, ascending beyond all heavens
and sitting at Thy right hand,
has sent the Holy Spirit, as He had promised,
upon the children of His adoption.
Because of this the whole wide world exults,
profoundly glad.
The hosts of heaven even and the
angelic powers sing hymns
to Thy great glory, saying endlessly,
Holy, Holy, Holy the Lord God of Hosts!

Roman Missal

A VISION OF THE CHURCH

After that I saw as it were an image of a woman as
great as a great city. Her head wore a crown marvellously
worked; rays of glory, like sleeves, enveloped her arms
and cast radiance from heaven to earth. Her body was like
a net with a thousand meshes through which a multitude
might enter. She had neither legs nor feet, but remained
prostrate before the altar which is in the presence of God,
and she embraced it with extended hands. I was not able
to examine her clothing, for she was resplendent with
brightness and wholly surrounded by glory. On her breast
was seen a sparkling aurora of a brilliant red, and I heard
varied music singing in her honour the song of the shining
aurora.

And this image enfolded her splendour like a vesture

and said, "I must conceive and bring forth children." And immediately there ran, like lightning, a multitude of angels, preparing places within her for human beings whose coming was to be accomplished. Then I saw children, all black, moving on the ground and in the air as fish swimming in water, and entering into her womb through the meshes which were open for all who wished to enter. And she, trembling, drew them up and caused them to pass out through her mouth without suffering. And behold, in a serene light there appeared to me again the figure of a man, brilliant as a burning flame, like a vision that I had already had, who removed from each one of these children its black skin, which he threw far off out of the way; then she reclothed them with a white tunic, made their eyes glisten with a shining light, and said to each of them, "Cast away this old rag of sin and reclothe thyself with this new vesture of holiness, for the gates of thy inheritance are opened to thee. . . ."

Saint Hildegarde of Bingen

TE DEUM

We praise Thee, God,
We confess Thee, Lord.

The earth worships Thee,
Eternal Father.

All angels, all heavens,
All the powers of the universe:

Cherubim, seraphim
In endless song praise Thee:

Holy, holy, holy,
Lord God of Hosts.

Thy glory, Thy majesty
Fills earth and heaven.

The apostles together
In shining chorus,

The bands of prophets
Glorify Thee,

Armies elect
Of martyrs extol Thee.

To the ends of the earth
Holy Church confesses Thee,

The Father of infinite
Majesty,

Thy true, adorable
Only Son,

And the Holy Spirit,
The Comforter.

Thou, the Christ,
The king of glory,

Thou art the Father's
Eternal Son.

Thou didst not disdain
The womb of a virgin
To save men from sin.

Having conquered death's sting,
Thou hast opened a kingdom,
Thou hast opened heaven
To all who believe.

Thou dost sit at God's right
In Thy Father's glory.
From whence Thou wilt come,
We believe, as our judge.

Wherefore we pray thee,
Remember Thy servants,
Whom Thou hast redeemed
With Thy precious blood.

I have hoped in Thee, Lord;
I shall not be confounded
In eternity.

Roman Breviary

BLESSING DURING THE EUCHARIST

Let us pray, O God, who by Thy mighty power didst
make all things out of nothing; who having set in order
the beginnings of the universe and made man to God's
image, didst appoint woman to be his inseparable help-
meet, in such wise that the woman's body took its beginning from the flesh of man, thereby teaching that what
Thou hadst been pleased to institute from one principle
might never lawfully be put asunder. O God, who hast
hallowed wedlock by a mystery so excellent that in the
marriage-bond Thou didst foreshow the union of Christ
with the church. O God, by whom woman is joined to
man, and that fellowship which Thou didst ordain from
the beginning is endowed with a blessing which alone was
not taken away either by the punishment for the first sin
or by the sentence of the flood; look in Thy mercy upon
this Thy handmaid, who is to be joined in wedlock and
entreats protection and strength from Thee. Let the yoke
of love and of peace be upon her. True and chaste, let
her wed in Christ; and let her ever follow the pattern of
holy women: let her be dear to her husband like Rachel;

wise like Rebecca; long-lived and faithful like Sara. Let the father of sin work none of his evil deeds within her. Let her ever be knit to the faith and to the commandments. Let her be true to one wedlock and shun all sinful embraces. Let her fortify her weakness by strong discipline. Let her be grave in demeanour and honoured for her modesty. Let her be well taught in heavenly lore. Let her be fruitful in offspring. Let her life be good and sinless. May she win the rest of the blessed in the kingdom of heaven. May they both see their children's children unto the third and fourth generation, and may they reach the old age which they desire. Through the same Lord.

The Nuptial Mass, Roman Missal

LOVE YOUR NEIGHBOUR

Spread your charity over the whole world if you will love Christ, for the members of Christ are spread over the whole world.

If you love but a part you are separated; if you are separated you are not in the body; if you are not in the body you are not under the head.

What is the use of believing and blaspheming? You adore Him in the head, you blaspheme Him in the body. He loves His body. If you separate yourself of His body, the head does not for that matter separate itself from the body. In vain do you honour Me, the head cries to you from Heaven, in vain do you honour Me. It is as if somebody wanted to kiss your face while stepping on your feet. With his hobnailed boots he crushes your feet and tries to take hold of your head and kiss it; do you not interrupt his show of respect with the cry: "What are you doing, man? You are hurting me!"

Thus did Our Lord Jesus Christ, before ascending into Heaven, recommend to us His body through which He was to remain on earth. He could see that many would honour Him in His glory, but He could see that their honours would be of no use, for they would have contempt for His members on earth.

Saint Augustine

THE NEW CREATION:
OUR CONVERSATION
IS IN HEAVEN

Being what thou art, lukewarm, neither cold nor hot, thou wilt make me vomit thee out of my mouth. I am rich, thou sayest, I have come into my own; nothing, now, is wanting to me. And all the while, if thou didst but know it, it is thou who art wretched, thou who art to be pitied. Thou art a beggar, blind and naked; and my counsel to thee is, to come and buy from me what thou needest; gold, proved in the fire, to make thee rich, and white garments, to clothe thee, and cover up the nakedness which dishonours thee; rub salve, too, upon thy eyes, to restore them sight. It is those I love that I correct and chasten; kindle thy generosity, and repent. See where I stand at the door, knocking; if anyone listens to my voice and opens the door, I will come in to visit him, and take my supper with him, and he shall sup with me. Who wins the victory? I will let him share my throne with me; I too have won the victory, and now I sit sharing my Father's throne. Listen, you that have ears, to the message the Spirit has for the churches.

Apocalypse 3, 16–22

For me, life means Christ; death is a prize to be won. But what if living on in this mortal body is the only way to harvest what I have sown? Thus I cannot tell what to choose; I am hemmed in on both sides. I long to have done with it, and be with Christ, a better thing, much more than a better thing; and yet, for your sakes, that I should wait in the body is more urgent still.

Philippians 1, 21–24

And you must not fall in with the manners of this world; there must be an inward change, a remaking of your minds, so that you can satisfy yourselves what is God's will, the good thing, the desirable thing, the perfect thing.

Romans 12, 2

You must put aside, then, every trace of ill will and deceitfulness, your affectations, the grudges you bore, and all the slanderous talk; you are children new-born, and all your craving must be for the soul's pure milk, that will nurture you into salvation, once you have tasted, as you have surely tasted, the goodness of the Lord. Draw near to him; he is the living antitype of that stone which men rejected, which God has chosen and prized; you too must be built up on him, stones that live and breathe, into a spiritual fabric; you must be a holy priesthood, to offer up that spiritual sacrifice which God accepts through Jesus Christ. . . . You are a chosen race, a royal priesthood, a consecrated nation, a people God means to have for himself; it is yours to proclaim the exploits of the God who has called you out of darkness into his marvellous light.

I Peter 2, 1–5; 9

Since you have all been born anew with an immortal, imperishable birth, through the word of God who lives and abides for ever.

I Peter 1, 23

He too is that head whose body is the Church; it begins with him, since his was the first birth out of death; thus in every way the primacy was to become his. It was God's good pleasure to let all completeness dwell in him, and through him to win back all things, whether on earth or in heaven, into union with himself, making peace with them through his blood, shed on the cross.

Colossians 1, 18–20

GOD BE IN MY HEAD

God be in my head,
And in my understanding;
God be in mine eyes,
And in my looking;
God be in my mouth
And in my speaking;
God be in my heart,
And in my thinking;
God be at my end and at my departing.

Anonymous

Even if all teachers were dead and all books were burned, the holy life of Christ would still be teaching enough for us.

Blessed John Tauler

The composed "I" becomes an "I" according to Christ, of which Paul says in the Scriptures: I no longer live the life of the "I," Christ lives within me. And this I should call a greater "I."

Suso

Who desires to understand the words of Christ utterly and in all their beauty, he must endeavour to shape his life always and everywhere in accordance with that of Christ.

Imitatio Christi

"I shall place the candle in the holder, and a beam of knowledge will shine into all eyes that see it from afar."

Who shall be the holder and who the candle?

And the Lord said: "I am the light, and the holder is your heart."

Mechtild of Magdeburg

Do not show your inner reverence to the outside world save for a weighty reason. My secret belongs to me, said St. Bernard and St. Francis.

Saint Teresa of Avila

THE CROWN OF THE NEW CREATION

In this Shewing He brought our Blessed Lady to my understanding. I saw her ghostly, in bodily likeness: a simple maid and meek, young of age, and little waxen above a child, in the stature that she was when she conceived. Also God shewed in part the wisdom and the truth of her soul: wherein I understood the reverent beholding in which she beheld her God and Maker, marvelling with great reverence that He would be born of her that was a simple creature of His making. And this wisdom and truth —knowing the greatness of her Maker and the littleness of herself that was made—caused her to say full meekly to Gabriel: Lo me, God's handmaid! In this sight I understood truly that she is more than all that God made beneath her in worthiness and grace; for above her is nothing that is made but the blessed Manhood of Christ, as to my sight.

Juliana of Norwich

LETTER TO A NUN RECENTLY CLOTHED

"Regnum mundi et omnem ornatum saeculi contempsi propter amorem Domini mei Jesus Christi." The Kingdom

of this world and all secular array I have despised for the love of my master, Jesus Christ.

When I heard above me in the singing of this joyous stanza over the virginal exodus of a chosen bride of God from the false world into a heavenly life, I thought thus: It is joy to relinquish love if you choose yourself something more lovable. And this has happened to me to-day, forsooth! Therefore, false world, freely I bid thee farewell.

Behold all ye lovers of the play of the world! I possessed an hallucination. Where is now this image of hallucination, the promise of this dream? If I had held you, dame world, for a thousand years, what would it now be? Gone like the winking of an eye. Your nature's quality is to pass away. I thought I held thee in my arms: how thou didst vanish away! Him who will not leave thee, thou leavest; he who does not bid thee farewell, willingly, thou rewardest with an unpleasant parting. Woe, thou murderess! Therefore, farewell! May God be merciful on thee to-day and for evermore. Deceive whom thou wilt, thou canst no more deceive me.

"The kingdom of this world"—alas, my child in God Almighty, harken what I say to thee. Remember well: Thou hast given up all friends and honour and goods after long consideration and be firm in thy determination. Don't act like many a foolish maid who are like wild animals locked in a garden. The gates are shut, but they peek through the fences. Those who are half within and half without—woe! how they lose in their great work through small things. To serve God is for them like a prison, spiritual discipline is like a narrow stable. Because they cannot have the apple, they yearn after its odour. Instead of wreaths of roses they wear gay cloth, and as they cannot have red scarlet, they wrap themselves in white sackcloth. Not having the companionship of married life, they make themselves sorry with the destroyer of all spiritual life, wasting time and robbing their hearts with passing friendship. What they cannot have in deeds they enjoy in words, and what they cannot experience fills their minds. They pine away for longing and they coo with the images of their desires, as a thirsty pilgrim dreaming of cool water. And turning it hither and thither it vanishes and all that remains is an empty hand and a sad heart . . . Woe! God in Thy heavenly Kingdom, is this not a poor life, is it not the limbo near hell, not to be able to have the world and yet to be without God, to be dead to this world and yet to be lacking all spiritual consolation, to have lost on both sides, with God and with the world? How contemptibly they will face their fellows and the world at the end of times! How they will be eaten up by remorse because they have robbed themselves of such a great infinite good by such contemptible trifles! Alas, my child!

But to serve God freely and joyously with a pure heart, yea, what a delicious life it is! Ah, to embrace the delight and love of this supreme good with a full heart what a joy it is! You must know: even though there were no reward hereafter, it would be a reward in itself. Behold, they walk on earth and yet they dwell in heaven. Ah, purity, how beautiful thou art! To serve nobody, to love nobody but God, how free thou art! Ah, dear Lord, loving wisdom, to espouse Thee, to leave love for true love, how lovable it is!

Lord, they say, You give suffering. Yes, suffering, yea joyous suffering which makes me lovable to Thee, which makes me one with Thee. Lord, who lives in time without suffering? Truly, nobody on earth! It is true, my Lord, it hurts to tear oneself from things, in the beginning at least; but then it becomes a tolerable thing, and at good last it becomes delectable above all temporal enjoyments.

Suso

THE INVISIBLE KINGDOM

True Christians look just the same to the world as . . . the great mass of what are called respectable men . . .

who in their hearts are very different; they make no great show, they go on in the same quiet ordinary way as the others, but really they are training to be saints in Heaven. They do all they can to change themselves, to become like God, to obey God, to discipline themselves, to renounce the world; but they do it in secret, both because God tells them so to do and because they do not like it to be known. Moreover, there are a number of others between these two with more or less of worldliness and more or less of faith. Yet they all look about the same to common eyes, because true religion is a hidden life in the heart; and though it cannot exist without deeds, yet these are for the most part secret deeds, secret charities, secret prayers, secret self-denials, secret struggles, secret victories . . .

And yet, though we have no right to judge others, but must leave this to God, it is very certain that a really holy man, a true saint, though he looks like other men, still has a sort of secret power in him to attract others to him who are like-minded, and to influence all who have anything in them like him. And thus it often becomes a test, whether we are like-minded with the Saints of God, whether they have influence over us. And though we have seldom means of knowing at the time who are God's own saints, yet after all is over we have; and then on looking back at what is past, perhaps after they are dead and gone, if we knew them, we may ask ourselves what power they had over us, whether they attracted us, influenced us, humbled us, whether they made our hearts burn within us. Alas! too often we shall find that we were close to them for a long time, had means of knowing them and knew them not, and that is a heavy condemnation on us indeed . . . The holier a man is, the less he is understood by men of the world.

Cardinal Newman

THE SIMPLICITY OF THE RIGHTEOUS IS DERIDED

The simplicity of the righteous is made a subject of derision. The wisdom of this world hideth our true feelings by artifice, and useth language to conceal our thoughts; this is the wisdom which demonstrateth the truth of falsehood, and showeth the falsehood of the truth. This kind of shrewdness the young acquire by practice, and children pay for the learning of it. Those who are good at this look down upon their neighbours; those who are bad at it are humble and timid, and wonder at it in others; they regard this astuteness too, wrong though it be, with wistful admiration, under softened epithets. Unstraightforwardness is called good breeding. The principles of the world teach those who entertain them to try and rise to distinction, and when they have attained the bubble of glory which is so soon to pass away, to feel it sweet to have at their feet them on whom they may wreak rich revenge. These principles teach a man, as long as he is strong enough, to give way to nobody else, and, if he hath no chance by force, to try and attain his object by diplomacy.

The wisdom of the righteous is the contrary of all this. They seek to avoid deception, to give their thoughts a clear expression in their words, to love the truth because it is the truth, to avoid falsehood, and rather to suffer than to inflict evil. Such are they who seek not to avenge themselves for wrong, and deem it gain to be despised for the truth's sake. This their simplicity is made a subject of derision, for such as are wise in this world believe the purity of their virtue to be simple foolery. Whatsoever is done innocently, they consider without doubt stupid. Such works as the truth approveth are idiotic, when tried by carnal standards of wisdom. After all, what stupider thing is there in this world than to express our real thoughts in our words, to keep nothing quiet by skilful tact, to repay no injuries, to pray for them who curse us, to seek poverty, to give up property, to strive not with such as take from us, to turn the other cheek to the smiter?

Saint Gregory the Great

ALREADY WE SEE THROUGH THE MIST

The mind of the elect already bears down on all earthly desires beneath itself, already mounts above all the objects that it sees are of a nature to pass away, is already lifted up from the enjoyment of things external, and closely searches what are the invisible good things, and in doing the same is frequently carried away into the sweetness of heavenly contemplation; already it sees something of the inmost realities as it were through the mist, and with burning desire strives to be admitted to the spiritual ministries of the angels; it feeds on the taste of the unencompassed Light, and being carried beyond self, disdains to sink back again into self. But forasmuch as the corruptible body still weighs down the soul, it is not able to cleave for long to the Light which it sees in a momentary glimpse. For the mere infirmity of the flesh drags down the soul, as it mounts above itself, and brings it down sighing to think of low cares and wants.

Saint Gregory the Great

Eckhart said, There are people upon earth that bear our Lord in spirit as his mother did in flesh.

They asked him who these were? He answered, They being free from things do see in the mirror of truth whereto they are gotten all unknowing; on earth, their dwelling is in heaven and they are at peace: they go as little children.

Meister Eckhart

ALL IN GOD

The innocence of children is God's greatest glory. All one does during the day is agreeable to God—provided, of course, that it be done right. All is God's, all concerns God, all is done in the sight of God; the whole day is God's. All prayers are God's, all work is God's; all play is also God's—when it is time to play. I do not fear God, for He is our father. My father does not frighten me. Morning prayers and evening prayers, the morning Angelus and the evening Angelus, the day's three meals and four o'clock tea, appetite with meals, and grace before meals, work between meals, play when required and amusements when possible, prayers when getting up because the day is beginning, prayers when retiring because night is beginning, asking first, thanking after, always having a good disposition—it is for all these things taken together and for all these things taken one after the other that we have been put on earth, it is all these things together and all these things taken one after the other which make up the day of God.

Charles Péguy

THE BIRTH OF THE ETERNAL WORD IN THE SOUL

Now we will speak of the coming of our Lord Jesus Christ as he is born to-day at this holy season of the Virgin Mary his blessed mother and again as he is born of grace in the perfect soul, for that is the whole end of Christ's work on earth; and we shall ask questions from which any pious man may tell whether the eternal Word is born in him or no.

The first question is, how to prepare for the interior speaking of the eternal Word.—Several things are needed. First, purity of life and mind. Next, the peace and freedom of a still and silent heart which is speaking to no creature and is spoken to by none, whether of the senses or the spirit. And now for a hard saying which few will understand: while the soul is speaking her own word and her noble word, the Father cannot speak his Word in her; while the soul is begetting her own son, *i.e.* the noblest work of her own understanding, the Father is not able to beget his Son in her to her best advantage. Thirdly, the soul must forsake herself in order to conceive the eternal Word like St. Paul and Mary, God's mother, in whom the eternal Word was uttered perfectly. The mind must die to itself, disowning itself and becoming God's own. Fourthly, the mind must lift up its intellect and see, for seeing is the lustiest work and noblest of which the soul is capable. Mark how eagerly he comes; he says, "Behold I stand at the door and knock!" Fifthly, it behoves us greatly to desire this birth, for desire is the root of all virtue and goodness.

The second question is, what is God's birth in the soul? God's birth in the soul is nothing else than a special divine motion in a special heavenly mode whereby God wrests the spirit from the tumult of creaturely unrest into his motionless unity where God can communicate himself to the soul in his divinity. There man enjoys his Word in the Father in its first discriminate emanation and with the Father as essential Person and in the Holy Ghost as the limit set to their eternal bliss, and it is in the soul as the reflection of her intellectual prototype and in all creatures as the preserver of their being. For God speaks his Word in every creature, but no creature is aware of it save rational creatures only. The soul is reborn into God when she turns to God and pursues his eternal Word right into his paternal heart where God makes naked revelation of his birth to the soul. The soul falls upon this birth which is revealed to her, with love and knowledge. As the Father comes into the soul in his Word, so in the Word the soul is returned into the Father. That we may eternally play this game in God, God help us.

The third question is, can any man be so well prepared that God is obliged to speak his eternal Word in him? We know that God must fulfil two obligations. First, when God is pledged and bound to the soul by the bonds of mutual love. Then God never fails the soul provided she is ready; he is obliged of mutual necessity to give himself to her, as Christ said to Zaccheus, "This day I must abide with thee in thine house." There is another word that must be spoken. Every good thing communicates itself to whatever is able to receive it; it would therefore be contrary to God's goodness to withhold himself from us if we can take him in. And there is a third compulsory utterance, that of some cause or force which is inadmissible in God. Theologians tell us that works wrought by the soul with God and in his grace God rewards or not just as he chooses, for such works are creature and finite and befall in time. They are too insignificant and vile to deserve reward from God at all. But the work God does in us without our co-operation, where the soul's work fails and God's activity prevails, in that the soul is merely passive and God is the only one who works. Works wrought thus by God in the soul it is his bounden duty to requite with his own self, for these works are so divine, so eternal, so immense and so nearly touch God's honour, he has no guerdon for them but himself. These souls are the noblest product of this life, and it is of them St. John declares, "Blessed are the dead that die in the Lord." The outward world is dead to them as they are also to the world. Their outward man can no more clash with their inner man than the dead can with the living, and this is due to the gift of God and interior prayer and profound humility. Which God grant us.

The fourth question is, what particular place or power of the soul is the eternal Word born in? The philosophers and saints have many fine sayings about this. Some say, in the intellect, for that is most like God. Some say, in the will, for that is the free power of the soul. A third school teaches, in the soul-spark, because that is most nigh to God. A fourth, in the arcanum of the mind, for it is there that God is most at home. A fifth school says (and it is with this one that I hold) that it is born in the innermost being of the soul and all her powers are made aware of it in a divine savour, each power in its own mode, but intellect is the highest power of the soul and therewith the soul grasps the divine good. Free will is the power of relishing the divine good which intellect makes known to it. The spark of the soul is the light of God's reflection, which is always looking back to God. The arcanum of the mind is the sum-total, as it were, of all the divine good and divine gifts in the innermost essence of the soul, which is as a bottomless well of divine goodness. Which may God grant us.

The fifth question is, what part does the mind play in this birth? It enters a condition of complete passivity, leaving God to work his will in perfect liberty. Perhaps it may be asked, Is the mind aware that God is working in it? I answer: Virtue, all good works wrought by God in man, fervour and devotion, for example, a man will be aware of, for with works of this kind there is very often the evidence of the senses. But when the divine good overwhelms with its riches the appetitive faculty and the light of God raises the intellect to a higher power, coercing or carrying the mind into his divine countenance, then the mind pays no more attention to creatures: she is standing face to face with the highest truth. Which may God give us.

Meister Eckhart

TRUE KNOWLEDGE IS A PRINCIPLE OF LOVE

"Everyone who loves is born of God and knows God. He who does not love does not know God; for God is love." Thus writes St. John in his First Epistle (4, 7–8). As we meditate on this passage in the light of Johannine thought, the connection between the three themes, "Birth, knowledge, love," becomes clear. On the mystical plane they are equivalents. The knowledge of God comes through being His sons, born of Him by grace, and such sonship is through love. How would it be possible to know God without loving Him? There is no knowledge of good as such, as desirable and pursuable, without love. The deeper the knowledge, the stronger the love; the keener the love, the more intimate and close-cleaving the knowledge.

Those who make of knowledge a purely representational faculty, those who translate it into an existential judgment, without cleaving heat or without repulsion, abstract from reality, ignoring the finalistic character of knowledge, leaving out of count the movement of sympathy towards truth, of recoil from error as such, and the desire to seek that grain of truth that every error contains. Knowledge is a principle of love; the knowledge of the true good, insofar as it is real and full knowledge, is undoubtedly love. To know God is equivalent to establishing a relationship with Him, inasmuch as we recognise Him as our Creator, our first principle and our last end. Revelation presents Him to us as Father, Redeemer, Comforter, who makes us partakers of His divine life itself. Love is the same knowledge realised in the relationship of sons to their father.

Those philosophers who conceive of a strictly rational God as prime mover, as creator or rather as architect of the universe, reduce the relationship of man with God to a metaphysical dependency. This relationship is stripped of any cleaving will, of any sense of love; there is no communion in it. The God of whom we conceive is the God to whom the prophet Jeremias said: "But Thou, O Lord, art among us, and Thy name is called upon by us: Forsake us not" (14, 9); He is the same of whom St. Paul affirmed to the Athenians on the Areopagus: "For in Him we live and move and have our being, as indeed some of your own poets have said. For we are also His offspring" (Acts 17, 28). The presence, the participation of God, His being in the midst of us, His dwelling within us, are all approximate expressions of His intimacy with us, so that we may say that in Him is our life, our activity, our being.

Don Luigi Sturzo

THE FIRE OF DIVINE LOVE

I saw a very dazzling light that hovered over dense darkness. Within this light there was a tabernacle full of splendour, and above this tabernacle was our Saviour in His sacred human form, and His holy wounds streamed forth rays that garmented the saints with wonderful glory. A great number of saints surrounded Him. The Queen of Heaven was also there, and on her head she wore her three crowns from which beams of vivid light emanated. Then I saw other souls that were still one with their bodies. They entered this fire and left it again. Now this fire was the symbol of divine love. I was curious to know who these souls were that I beheld pass through the flame. I was told they belonged to living men who persevered in holy love, and that they came to renew holy love in this furnace. I was contemplating this beautiful spectacle with great joy, when Mary Magdalen, the fervent friend of Jesus, came accompanied by Saint Agnes to bid me draw closer to this beautiful fire, and had me climb to a high place from where I could see everything as well as I might wish. I saw a throng of Holy Virgins, all of whom wore upon their heads crowns of singular beauty. They took one another by the hand, and led by Magdalen, they entered the fire and went forth from it singing.

Saint Frances of Rome

HYMN TO CHRIST

King of saints, almighty Word,
Of the Father highest Lord;

Wisdom's head and chief;
Assuagement of all grief;
Lord of all time and space,
Jesus, Saviour of our race;
Shepherd, who dost us keep;
   Husbandman, who tillest,
Bit to restrain us, Rudder
   To guide us as Thou willest;
Of the all-holy flock celestial wing;
Fisher of men whom Thou to life dost bring
From evil sea of sin,
   And from the billowy strife,
Gathering pure fishes in,
   Caught with sweet bait of life:
Lead us, Shepherd of the sheep,
   Reason-gifted, holy One;
King of youths, whom Thou dost keep,
   So that they pollution shun:
Steps of Christ, celestial Way;
   Word eternal, Age unending;
Life that never can decay;
   Fount of mercy, virtue-sending;
Life august of those who raise,
Unto God their hymn of praise,
               Jesus Christ!

               Clement of Alexandria

THE TWO WAYS: MARTHA AND MARY

We belong to God, and a man must have knowledge of God if he is to listen to us; if he does not belong to God, he does not listen to us at all. That is the test by which we distinguish the true Spirit from the false spirit. . . . We have learned to recognise the love God has in our regard, to recognise it, and to make it our belief. God is love; he who dwells in love dwells in God, and God in him. . . . Love has no room for fear; and indeed, love drives out fear when it is perfect love, since fear only serves for correction. The man who is still afraid has not yet reached the full measure of love.

I John 4, 6; 16; 18

There was a man called Nicodemus, a Pharisee, and one of the rulers of the Jews, who came to see Jesus by night; Master, he said to him, we know that thou hast come from God to teach us; no one, unless God were with him, could do the miracles which thou doest. Jesus answered him, Believe me when I tell thee this; a man cannot see the kingdom of God without being born anew.

John 3, 1–3

ON THE TWO WAYS

The Church knoweth of two different lives which God hath revealed and blessed: one is the life of faith, the other the life of knowledge; one the life of this pilgrimage, the other the life of the eternal mansions; one the life of work, the other the life of rest; one the life of the journey, the other the life of home; one the life of action, the other the life of contemplation. The one escheweth evil and doeth good; the other hath no evil to eschew, and only an exceeding joy to enjoy. The one striveth with the enemy, the other hath no enemies, and reigneth.

The one succoureth the needy; the other is where there are no needy to succour. The one forgiveth them that trespass against it, that its own trespasses may be forgiven; the other neither hath trespasses to forgive nor to be forgiven. The one is chastened with evil, lest it be exalted above measure by good; the other enjoyeth such a fulness of grace that it feeleth no evil, and cleaveth so firmly unto the Highest Good that it hath no temptation to pride.

Wherefore the one is good, but still sorrowful; the other is better and perfectly blessed. And of these two lives there are types, of the one in the Apostle Peter, of the other in John. The one laboureth here even unto the end, and findeth its end hereafter; the other stretcheth out into the hereafter, and in eternity findeth no end. Therefore is it said unto the one, "Follow Me"; but to the other, "If I will that he tarry till I come, what is that to thee? Follow thou Me." What is the meaning of these words? who can know? who can understand? what is it? is it "Follow thou Me, imitating Me in the bearing of earthly sorrow; let him tarry till I come again, bringing the everlasting reward"?

Saint Augustine

MARTHA'S SERVICE

None is permitted to lead a life of pure contemplation in such a way that in his leisure he would not mind his neighbour's needs. On the other hand, no man should be busy in such a manner as to have no desire to contemplate God. His leisure should not be a rest without action, but either searching or finding of truth, and this in a way which would profit his neighbour through our own growth and personal stability.

There are two lives represented in Christ's body: one temporal, in which we labour; the other eternal, in which we contemplate God's delight. The first Christ represented to us in His passion, the other in His resurrection.

Two persons were in the house at Bethany, both blameless, both praiseworthy, two ways of life and with them the source of life: Martha, an image of the present life; and Mary, signifying the future life. Both were friends of the Lord, both lovable, both His disciples. What Martha did, we are. What Mary did, we are in hope of. Let us do one well, so that we obtain the fulness of the other.

Even the names of those women in the Old Testament, wives of Jacob, serve here as an illustration: Lea, the first wife of Jacob, is this: the labour of our mortal life, which we live in faith, performing many deeds in hardship, never really knowing how they will finally turn out to be of profit to those of whom we try to take good care . . . That is why it is also said of her that she had poor eyesight, "For the thoughts of mortal man are anguish and his foresight is uncertain" . . . But the hope of eternal vision which enjoys secure, joyful knowledge of the truth—that is Rachel, who is also called the beautiful, bright-eyed one. She is loved by all whose life is dedicated to holy wisdom. For her sake we are in the service of grace . . . Or who loves in his works of justice the labours of toil and suffering? Who would wish for such a life for its own sake? As little as Jacob loved Lea for her own sake, he should tolerate her according to God's will, since he cannot love her herself, in order to reach Rachel through her. And she was recommended to him also because she bore many children . . .

It is true that man, if it were at all possible, would attain to the delights of beautiful and perfect wisdom at once without first having to bear toils of work and suffering. But this cannot be in this land of mortal man . . . First in man's right education comes the right mind of toil in many labours, before the blissful happiness of knowing truth can enter . . . If you cannot love Lea for her own sake, you should love her for her children . . . Contemplative life strives to contemplate what is hidden to mortal flesh and desires to be free from all business, and therefore it is sterile.

If our Mary chose the best part which will not be taken from her, shall we then think that Martha's service was blamed, the service of a woman who tended with care as a host should and who received the Lord Himself as a guest? How could such a one merit rebuke who was moved by joy over her prominent guest? If that were true men might as well drop everything they are doing for the needy. They might choose the better part for themselves which will not be taken away from them. They might give all their time to God's word, sigh for the sweetness of His doctrine, be trained to the science of salvation! What do they care which stranger has come, who was without bread, who was without clothes, who needed a visit, whose chains needed to be loosened, who had no burial? Cease the works of mercy, only wisdom needs to be attended to! If this is the better part, why don't we all choose it?

No, it is not so! Listen to the Lord: "Thou carest for many things, one is necessary. Mary has chosen the better part. Thou, Martha, hast not chosen a bad part, even though she chose the better part." Let us dedicate ourselves to the manifold request: it is necessary service for beings who have to preserve their bodies. Holy leisure demands that we tend the truth, right toiling is demanded by love.

All honest work is good. The patriarchs tended their flocks, the Greek philosophers were often cobblers, Jesus' foster-father was a carpenter. It is true that work is nobler if not forced upon us by the inexorable needs of our body, but suffices also to the spirit striving after the high things.

Righteous, unselfish, peaceful and calm work in temporal things makes us worthy of eternal things. Only we should not let ourselves be held by it, we should not cleave and cling to it. Toil should not engulf us while it grows, should not ensnare us as it unravels itself. We should attain a certain freedom from perishable things and strive after the unchanging, eternal, certain values, superior to the merely earthly things. Our doing should be such as to attain a calm peacefulness instead of degenerating into a restless hurry. Mild and calm according to the image of Christ be the labour of the soul which desires rest to accomplish her task, not lazy, not careless, but as it is written: "In meekness perfect good works."

On to certain talents piety and a peaceful heart must be added. Without them no inner understanding of such sublime things is gained. A calm heart is needed, an humble and pious belief, a reverent dedication of the mind. And mark well: in this province the same rules as in bodily life do not prevail: sleep makes fit to work—it is all reversed: good work leads to rest that always wakes.

Saint Augustine

THE MORE PERFECT MUST BE HUMBLE

. . . And God forbid that I should in this work say anything that might be taken in condemnation of any of the servants of God in any degree, and in particular of His special saint. For one thinketh that she should be full well held excused of her complaint, taking regard to the time and the manner in which she said it. For of that she said her unknowing was the cause. And no wonder, though she knew not at that time how Mary was occupied; for I trow that before she had little heard of such perfection. And also, that she said was but courteously and in few words: and therefore she should always be held excused.

And so me thinketh that these worldly living men and

women of active life should also full well be held excused
of their complaining words touched before, although they
say rudely what they say; having regard to their ignorance. Right as Martha knew full little what Mary her
sister did when she complained of her to our Lord; right
so in the same manner these folk nowadays know full little,
or else naught, what these young disciples of God mean
when they set them from the business of this world, and
draw them to be God's special servants in holiness and
rightfulness of spirit. And if they knew, truly I daresay
that they would neither do nor say as they say. And therefore me thinketh that they should always be held excused:
because they know no better living than that they live in
themselves. And also when I think on mine innumerable
faults, the which I have made myself before this time in
words and deeds for default of knowing, me thinketh then,
if I would be held excused by God for mine ignorant faults,
that I should charitably and pitifully have other men's
ignorant words and deeds always excused. And surely else
do I not to others as I would they did to me.

The Cloud of Unknowing

THE TWO CALLINGS

Children, look at the human body, with all its different
members and senses, each part having its separate office.
Not any sense or member usurps the office of any other,
or acts otherwise than as God has ordained for it. So are
we all members of the same body, and of this body Christ
is the head. Now, the eye in the body of holy Church,
that is her teachers. It is an office that does not concern
you, for we ordinary Christians must note carefully what
our place is, the office to which our Lord has called us,
and in the performance of whose duties we are firmly
joined to the Head, our Lord, by means of His holy grace.
For no matter how insignificant the work may seem, if it

be that of a member of Christ's body, then it is done by the grace of the Holy Ghost to the profit of men's souls.

Well then, we live among the lowest members. One can spin, another can make shoes, some being skilful at one trade, others at another. And these are all graces that are made active by the operation of the Spirit of God. If I were not a priest, and were only a brother in a community, I should consider it a great thing to be able to make shoes, and I would be very glad to earn my bread by the labour of my hands. Children, the foot or hand should not wish to be the eye, but each should fulfil the office assigned by God; for however lowly that may seem, it could not be done by the other members. Thus our sisters do their part, as, for example, in piously chanting the psalms. St. Augustine says: "God is a most simple being; and yet He works in a most manifold way, being all things in each single thing, and one in all of them together." Every least little work of ours comes to us as a duty from God and each has its particular grace. Let us do it gladly for the sake of all our brethren, who cannot do it as appropriately as we. Thus do we all mutually exchange grace for grace. Believe me, the man who does not pray nor work for his neighbour's sake, shall have much to answer for before God when, as the Gospel tells us, it will be said to him: "Give an account of thy stewardship." And each of us is appointed as a steward to do a certain work for God, and to render account of the same.

How does it happen, then, that so many complain that their occupation in life hinders their serving God? God makes no limitations to His service, and how, then, does it happen that thy conscience is afflicted at having to do what He appoints for thee? Dear children, make up your minds that it is not your occupation, but your own ill-regulated way of performing it that disturbs your interior peace. Do thy duty rightly; have God alone in view; be disengaged from all self-conceit and self-love; look not to what is pleasant or unpleasant as thy end in doing or not doing; fear nothing and desire nothing but God; seek no profit, think of no joy in thy work; regard nothing except what is wholly for God's honour: act this way, and it is impossible that thou shouldst feel distress of conscience in thy usual occupations. It is a shame for any spiritual man to have it said of him that he is disorderly in doing his daily round of duty, for one soon perceives this defect —the work is not done in God, nor is it done to the benefit of his neighbour.

By this slovenly carelessness thou makest manifest that it is not for and in God thou art labouring; and herein is shown the cause of thy unrest of soul. Our Lord did not reprove Martha on account of her work, for that was holy; He chided her for her excessive solicitude. A man should practise approved spiritual exercises, attend to his bounden duty, and then cast all his care upon God, attending meanwhile to his obligations diligently and in all calmness of mind. And he should be careful to remain at home in his own spirit, looking often there in search of God, with inward intentness and very devoutly, meanwhile carefully attending to every call of duty in his external life. And besides, he should carefully watch for the inspiration of the Holy Ghost, whether to action or to suffering for God's sake. By this means he does or he leaves undone according to the guidance of the Holy Ghost, now resting quiet and again pushing onward: such is the way to fulfil thy part in life in all godliness and peace.

If there is any poor, old, feeble, helpless creature, do thou run quickly to his help. One should outdo the other in this work of charity, thus bearing one another's burdens. If thou failest in this, be sure that God will bestow the privilege on another with all the accompanying graces, leaving thee empty. Dost thou feel a special joy in any work? Be on thy guard carefully—do the work for God alone, be not carried away by thy feelings. Here then, children, is the way to acquire virtue, and a very necessary way if thou wouldst come to God. Do not dream that I am counselling quiet waiting for God, I mean sitting down idle till God shall come and infuse virtue into thy soul.

Put no trust in immature virtue, unearned virtue. If a man claims that the Father and the Son and the Holy Ghost have taken up their abode within him, there is nothing in what he says, unless he has attained to this state by devout exercises of religion, interior as well as exterior, the same that we have been considering. A farmer stands and threshes his grain with his flail uplifted, and suddenly falls into a trance; now the flail will fall on him and strike him, unless an angel from Heaven shall catch it. So with you. None like to thresh, all wish to be entranced—all the members of the body would be the eye, all for the contemplative and none for the active life. Now this is a sign of stupidity. I knew a man who was a very dear friend of God, and who was a ploughman all the days of his life—more than forty years, and indeed, he is the same yet. Well, he once asked our Lord whether or not he should give up his labour and spend his time in church. The Lord said to him: "No, thou shalt eat thy bread in the sweat of thy brow, and in that service thou shalt do honour to My precious blood." And yet everyone, each following his own pious method, should daily and nightly retire apart and sink down into the depths of his soul, choosing therefor a proper time and place. Those who are so far advanced as to go to God direct and without the images of the imagination should follow their method; others, in turn, are helped by a different one; for we cannot all be eyes in the Lord's body. Each one for himself must thus pray just as God ordains, and in deep love and quiet peace. Whosoever serves God as He wills, to him shall God respond according to that man's own will. But if one serves God according to his own will, him shall God treat, not as he would wish to be treated, but as God in His justice deems best.

Children, it is in this self-departure, this going forth from self-will, that the essential peace of the soul is born within us, which means the acquisition of well-seasoned virtue. Believe me, that essential peace never comes otherwise—it is false to assert such a thing. Outwardly practised and inwardly cherished virtue produces peace of soul; though it is to be said that the peace that arises from the more interior exercises of religion is a treasure of which no man can rob you. Men wise in their own conceit will bid you do this and do that to become perfect—and it is all a set of observances of their own contrivance.

Blessed John Tauler

THE GULF BETWEEN GOD AND US

By Thee we cross the gulf that lies between Thee and us. The Living God is life-giving. Thou art the Fount and Centre, as well as the Seat of all good . . . Remaining one and sole and infinitely removed from all things, still Thou art the fulness of all things, in Thee they consist, of Thee they partake, and into Thee, retaining their own individuality, they are absorbed. And thus, while we droop and decay in our own nature, we live by Thy breath; and Thy grace enables us to endure Thy presence.

Cardinal Newman

A MODERN MARY

We went for a walk, fourteen of us. I notice that to associate with many Marthas, men and women, does not affect me (from the point of view of union with God). One leaves them to talk, putting in a word here and there, but in reality one remains quite free to continue in prayer. But to be with one Martha only, what a terrible thing! Being only two, one is obliged to talk nearly all the time. Assuredly this does not hinder one from being united to God; but to speak of Him is not the same thing as to speak to Him, and dare one speak of Him as much, and in the manner one would like? For my part, I never dare tell anyone how much I love Him, fearing lest people may be too scandalised afterwards when they see all my imperfections. I find it a sort of martyrdom to remain thus shut up in myself, for it seems to me that were I to say what I think, I might contribute to make Him loved, and this would be my greatest happiness. Certainly God alone, or a soul enlightened and inflamed by His Spirit, would have the charity to understand how it is that I love Him so well and serve Him so badly. It is therefore a real solace to be able to write this or sometimes to exchange spiritual confidences.

May God deign to give me a little of the virtue of these holy Marthas I speak of! It is an excellent thing for me to be with them, for the sight of their capacity and activity, which I shall never possess, keeps me humble. Never, with all the good will in the world, shall I ever arrive at their degree of merit in the accomplishment of their active duties. For some days past I have felt a certain sadness at hearing those virtues, of which I feel myself so little capable, greatly eulogised, and I feared there might be some pride in this. I examined my conscience well, but could only find a regret at being able to do so little in that direction for my God, notwithstanding His graces and my continual efforts. Now this sadness has passed away. I am determined to do all I can to fulfil my daily duties well; I am content with my inferiority, and I think with love that, if my Jesus has chosen my soul to unite her intimately to Him, He has chosen me as being the smallest and the least gifted with those active talents which are so valuable in family life. I am therefore no longer tempted to discouragement. This is the sincere truth of my innermost soul known to God only.

I see also that, notwithstanding the great discretion of all those who surround me, they are very astonished to see that I always pray without a book. What can I do, O my God? I can do nothing, and no one in the world will ever be more astonished at it than I am . . .

I have made a long digression without having completed my account of yesterday's doings. I went to see that poor soul who had asked me to come and play a little to her on the piano. What a painful contrast between the gay task I had to perform and my sad feelings in that house where they seem to have lost the Faith. It was as if I had set myself to play to a corpse and I was praying for them the whole time. I had been obliged to go, for it would not have been advisable to let them think that piety is unamiable.

Lucie Christine

EUCHARISTIA

Come, let us sing praise to the Lord, let us shout with joy to God our Saviour! Let us come before Him with thanksgiving, and sing unto Him with psalms!

For the Lord is a great God, and a great king over all the gods: the Lord will not forsake His people. All the ends of the earth are in His hands and He looketh down on the highest mountains.

The sea is His, for He made it, and His hands formed the dry land. Come, let us adore and bow low before God, let us kneel before the Lord who made us; for He is the Lord, our God, and we His people and the sheep of His pasture.

Psalm 94, 1–7

He who eats my flesh, and drinks my blood, lives continually in me, and I in him.

John 6, 57

THE SLAIN LAMB

The deacon proclaims to the congregation:
Draw near with fear and partake in holiness.
The people come one by one and stand in front of the bema and the priest communicates them from the chalice in which is the sacred bread steeped in the wine and says each time:

The body and blood of our Lord and Saviour Jesus
Christ be to thee for salvation and for a guide to eternal
life.

The clerks sing:
Mother of faith,
thou shrine of holy spousals,
heavenly bridechamber

Home of thine immortal bridegroom
who hath adorned thee for ever

A marvellous second heaven art thou
FROM GLORY TO GLORY exalted

Which by the laver
Dost regenerate us children
Radiant like the light

Thou that dost distribute this spotless bread
and givest us to drink this pure blood

Who dost lift us up to an higher station
than the angels can attain unto.

Come then,
O children of the new Sion,
meet our Lord in Holiness.

O TASTE AND SEE
how GRACIOUS our Lord is
and mighty

The ancient tabernacle
was a type of you,
but ye are of higher pattern

It burst the adamantine gates:
ye raze the gates of hell
to their foundations

It parted Jordan:
ye cleave the sea
of universal sin

Its leader was Joshua the captain:
Thine is Jesus
the only son of the Father

THIS BREAD IS THE BODY OF CHRIST,
THIS CUP IS THE BLOOD OF THE NEW TESTAMENT

The greatest of mysteries
is revealed to us,
God Himself
is manifested to us herein

This is the same Christ
the divine Word
who sitteth at the right hand of the Father

And who
sacrificed here amongst us
TAKETH AWAY THE SIN OF THE WORLD

He is BLESSED FOR EVER
with the Father and the Spirit

Now and ever
for the time to come
and world without end.

The Armenian Liturgy

EUCHARISTIC PRAYER

When celebrating the eucharistic thanksgiving give ye
thanks thus. First, over the cup: We give Thee thanks, O

our Father, for the holy vine of Thy son David, which Thou madest known unto us through Thy Son Jesus; Thine is the glory for ever and ever. Then over the broken bread: We give Thee thanks, O our Father, for the life and knowledge which Thou didst make known unto us through Thy Son Jesus; Thine is the glory for ever and ever. As this broken bread was scattered upon the mountains and being gathered together become one, so may Thy Church be gathered together from the ends of the earth into Thy kingdom; for Thine is the glory and the power through Jesus Christ for ever and ever. But let no one eat or drink of this eucharistic thanksgiving, but they that have been baptised into the name of the Lord; for concerning this also the Lord hath said: Give not that which is holy to the dogs.

And after ye are filled thus give ye thanks: We give Thee thanks, Holy Father, for Thy holy name, which Thou hast made to dwell in our hearts, and for the knowledge and faith and immortality, which Thou hast made known unto us through Thy Son Jesus; thine is the glory for ever and ever. Thou, Almighty Master, didst create all things for Thy name's sake, and didst give food and drink unto men for enjoyment, that they might render thanks to Thee; and didst bestow upon us spiritual food and drink and eternal life through Thy Son. Before all things we give Thee thanks that Thou art powerful; Thine is the glory for ever and ever. Remember, Lord, Thy Church and deliver it from all evil and perfect it in Thy love; and gather it together from the four winds—the Church which has been sanctified—into Thy kingdom which Thou hast prepared for it; for Thine is the power and the glory for ever and ever. May grace come and may this world pass away. Hosanna to the God of David. If any man is holy, let him come; if any man is not, let him repent. Maran Atha, Amen.

But permit the prophets to offer thanksgiving as much as they desire . . .

Didache

PRAYER

O Sweet Lord Jesus Christ, pierce the marrow of my soul with the suave and beneficent blade of your love! Wound the entrails of my soul with your charity that is true and brotherly and apostolic, so that your divine love and my yearning for you will always and verily make my soul burn, and languish, and melt. How my soul sighs and swoons in the midst of your house! How it wants to melt and be with you! Let my soul always thirst for you alone, O bread of celestial life descended from heaven, bread of the angels, sustenance of saintly souls, our daily bread that is beyond mere substance and is possessed of all savour and sweetness, and inebriateness, and delight. You whom the angels long to behold shall be the perpetual food and drink of my heart. May your savour and your sweetness fill the entrails of my soul! May it always thirst for you, O fountain of life, O fountain of wisdom, O fountain of knowledge, O fountain of eternal light, O torrent of desire and fertility in the mansion of God! May my soul always rove around you, and seek you and find you! Let it turn to you and come to you! May you be the object of its thought and of its word. Let it sing your praise and the glory of your beloved name with humility and reserve, with love and delight, with ease and tenderness, with patience and peace, with success and perseverance unto the very end. You alone shall be all in all to me, you shall always be my hope, my confidence, my riches, my charm, my pleasure, my delight, my repose, my tranquillity, my peace, my suavity, my perfume, my sweetness, my refreshment, my nurture, my love, my thought, my support, my desire, my refuge, my succour, my patience, my treasure, my passion! My spirit and my heart shall always be fixed and locked and deeply rooted in you, and in you only! Amen.

Saint Bonaventure

TRANSFORMED INTO CHRIST'S BODY

So then, just as a cloud which is penetrated by the force and brightness of the sun's rays, filled and (if the word be allowable here) saturated with light, is itself like a sun, however it be looked at; just so, when Christ unites, not only His virtue and light, but His very Body and Spirit, with the faithful and just, and in some sort mingles His very Soul with their souls, and His Body with their bodies, in the way I have described, Christ looks out from their eyes, speaks with their tongues, works through their senses; their faces, their countenances, their movements are Christ, who thus occupies them wholly. So intimately does He take possession of them that, though His Nature in no way destroys or corrupts their own, there will be nothing seen in them at the Last Day, nor will any nature be found in them other than His Nature. There will be that one Nature in all; and both He and they will be one and the same in Himself.

Strong indeed . . . is that tie, and so fast a bond of union that in nothing which Nature has formed or art invented are the divers parts knit together with so fine and so invisible a bond as this. Indeed, it is like the union of matrimony, but so much the stronger and more excellent as the rite is the straighter and more pure. It is purer than betrothal or marriage after the flesh; and even so or more does it excel such marriage in the intimacy of its union . . . Here there is mutual affection between the wills of two persons; there all is one will and one desire. Here the body of the one is the master of the other; there, without destruction of her substance, Christ the Spouse transforms His Bride into His own Body, in the manner aforesaid. Here, men often stray; there, they walk ever securely. Here, we find continually anxiety and care, sworn foes of concord and union; there, that rest and security which helps and favours the state of those who atone. Here, the union of two is to bring into the world a third; there, one union leads to another, one embrace to another, and its fruits is oneness for evermore.

Here, happiness is but weak, delight of base alloy and brief duration; there, both are so great that they submerge alike body and soul—so noble, that they are glory—so pure, that sorrow neither precedes nor follows them, nor is joined nor mingled with them.

Luis de Leon

LONG HUNGER WASTED THE WORLD WANDERER

In the year of the Incarnation of our Lord 900 there appeared a marvellous sign in heaven. For the stars were seen to flow from the very height of heaven to the lowest horizon, wellnigh as though they crashed one upon the other. And upon this marvel followed woeful calamities, such as a most notable untowardness of the seasons and frequent tempests, rivers also overflowing their banks as in dread likeness of the Deluge and (what was yet more pestilent than these) ominous upheavals of men boasting themselves against God. In this same year, ere the intercalary days were ended, Fulk, the archbishop of Rheims, and the king Zvendibold were slain, and not many days before, I, Radbod the sinner, was judged worthy to be enrolled among the servants of the holy church of Utrecht: and O would that I be found worthy of that same company in the life eternal. This then shall be my epitaph:

"Hunger and thirst, O Christ, for sight of Thee,
Came between me and all the fears of earth.
Give Thou Thyself the Bread, Thyself the Wine,
Thou, sole provision for the unknown way.
Long hunger wasted the world wanderer,
With sight of Thee may he be satisfied."

Radbod

COME AND TASTE

There is this difference, dearly beloved brethren, between spiritual and earthly pleasures. So long as we do not yet enjoy them, earthly pleasures are greatly desired; but when they are partaken to the full our liking for them soon begins to pall. Spiritual joys, on the other hand, are a matter of indifference to us when we do not possess them, but once we begin to experience them, we are filled with desire; the more we enjoy them, the more we desire them. With pleasures of the body—it is desire that delights us, realisation which disappoints; with pleasures of the soul, desire is weak but spiritual experience is a source of the greatest joy . . . When our souls are full of spiritual joy we long for more, since by tasting it we learn to desire it more eagerly. We cannot love what we do not possess, because we do not know its savour. For who can love what he does not know? Therefore the Psalmist admonishes us, "Taste and see that the Lord is sweet." As if he were to say more explicitly, "You know not His sweetness if you have never tasted it; let then your heart but taste the Bread of Life, that coming to know its sweetness you may be able to love it." Man lost these delights when he sinned in Paradise; he went out from thence when he no longer opened his mouth to the heavenly food which filled him with spiritual joy. And so it comes to pass that we too, born into the miseries of this exile, find ourselves here below indifferent to our true good and not knowing what we should desire. This indifference is a malady which progresses as the soul withdraws itself from partaking of that heavenly food . . . As we do not wish to taste interiorly the spiritual sweetness which is offered to us, wretched as we are we love our own hunger.

Saint Gregory the Great

THE HOLY SIGN OF UNITY

Marvel and rejoice, we have become one with Christ!
He and we—that makes the perfect man.

Thus the Lord Jesus has given us a symbol of ourselves:
He wanted us to belong to Him. At His board He consecrated the holy symbol of peace and unity. In the communion of breaking bread and drinking wine, we behold
the communion of His body and His members: the Holy
Church in those who are predestined, called, sainted, and
glorified. Whoever receives the holy sign of unity and does
not keep within the bounds of peace, he has not received
a sign in favour of himself, but he receives testimony
against himself.

O secret of blessing, O sign of unity, O bond of love!

Saint Augustine

THE ALTAR IS CHRIST

This altar is composed of the very members of Christ,
and the Lord's body becomes an altar for thee. Venerate
it; for upon it, in the flesh, thou dost offer sacrifice to the
Lord. This altar is greater than the altar in this church,
and hence far greater than the altar of the Old Testament.

Do not protest! This stone altar is august because of
the Victim that rests upon it; but the altar of alms-giving
is more so because it is made of this very Victim. The
former is august because, though made of stone, it is sanctified by contact with the body of Christ; the latter, because it is the body of Christ. Therefore, my brother, it is
more venerable than the altar beside which thou art
standing.

What is Aaron when compared with this? What are
the crown, the bells, the Holy of holies? But why speak
of the altar of the Old Law when the altar of alms-giving
is so sublime in comparison with our own altar here? Thou

dost honour this altar because it receives the body of Christ. But the other, which is the body of Christ, you treat with ignominy and you look on indifferently while it perishes.

This altar you can see everywhere, in the streets and in the market place, and at any hour you may offer sacrifice thereon; for it too is a place of sacrifice. And, as the priest standing at the altar brings down the Spirit, so you too bring down the Spirit, like the oil which was poured out in abundance (upon the altar of the Old Law).

Saint John Chrysostom

THE BREAD OF MYSTERY

But why is this mystery accomplished with bread? Let us offer no reason of our own invention, but listen to the Apostle speak of this sacrament: "We many are one bread, one body" (*I Cor.* 10, 17). Understand this and rejoice. Unity, truth, piety, charity. "One bread." What is this one bread? It is one body formed of many. Remember that bread is not made of one grain, but of many. During the exorcisms you were ground like wheat; at baptism water was poured over you, as flour is mingled with water, and the Holy Spirit entered into you like the fire which bakes the bread. Be what you see, and receive what you are.

This is what the Apostle teaches concerning the bread. Though he does not say what we are to understand of the chalice, his meaning is easily seen. . . . Recall, my brothers, how wine is made. Many grapes hang from the vine, but the juice of all the grapes is fused into unity.

Thus did the Lord Christ manifest us in Himself. He willed that we should belong to Him, and He has consecrated on His altar the mystery of our peace and unity.

Saint Augustine

EASTER SUNDAY

Last night did Christ the Sun rise from the dark,
The mystic harvests of the fields of God,
And now the little wandering tribes of bees
Are brawling in the scarlet flowers abroad.
The winds are soft with birdsong; all night long
Darkling the nightingale her descant told,
And now inside church doors the happy folk
The Alleluia chant a hundredfold.
O father of Thy folk, be Thine by right
The Easter joy, the threshold of the light.

Sedulius Scottus

NOT HAVING OUR OWN
RIGHTEOUSNESS

I am the true vine, and it is my Father who tends it. The branch that yields no fruit in me, he cuts away; the branch that does yield fruit, he trims clean, so that it may yield more fruit. . . . The branch that does not live on in the vine can yield no fruit of itself; no more can you, if you do not live on in me. I am the vine, you are its branches; if a man lives on in me, and I in him, then he will yield abundant fruit; separated from me, you have no power to do anything. . . . I have bestowed my love upon you, just as my Father has bestowed his love upon me; live on, then, in my love.

John 15, 1–2; 4–5; 9

Love of our neighbour refrains from doing harm of any kind; that is why it fulfils all the demands of the law.

Romans 13, 10

If anybody claims to have superior knowledge, it means that he has not yet attained the knowledge which is true knowledge; it is only when a man loves God that God acknowledges him.

I Corinthians 8, 2–3

I have given way to vanity; it was you that drove me

to it; you ought to have given me credentials, instead of asking for them. No, I have done no less than the very greatest of the apostles, worthless as I am; I have earned the character of apostleship among you, by all the trials I have undergone, by signs and wonders and deeds of miracle.

II Corinthians 12, 11–12

IN GOD'S MIGHTY HAND

Certain souls, receiving no spiritual consolations, are humble, for they doubt whether it is not through their own fault, and are most anxious to improve. When they see anyone else weeping, unless they do the same, they think they must be much more backward than her in God's service, although perhaps they are more advanced, for tears, though a good sign, do not always indicate perfection. Humility, mortification, detachment, and other virtues are the safest: there is no cause for fear, nor need you doubt that you may become as perfect as the greatest contemplatives. St. Martha was holy, though we are never told she was a contemplative; would you not be content with resembling this blessed woman, who deserved to receive Christ our Lord so often into her home, where she feasted and served Him, and where He ate at her table, and even, perhaps, off her own plate? If she had always been enraptured, like the Magdalen, there would have been no one to offer food to this Divine Guest. Imagine, then, that this community is the house of St. Martha, where there must be different kinds of people. Let not the nun who is called to the active life murmur at others who are absorbed in contemplation, for she knows our Lord will defend them; as a rule, they themselves are silent, for the "better part" makes them oblivious of themselves and of all else. Remember that someone must cook the food, and think yourself favoured in being allowed to serve with Martha. Reflect that true humility consists in being willing and ready to do what our Lord asks of us: it always makes us consider ourselves unworthy to be reckoned among His servants.

If contemplation, mental and vocal prayer, nursing the sick, the work of the house, and the most menial labour, all serve this Guest who comes to eat and drink and converse with us, why should we choose to minister to Him in one way rather than in another? Not that I mean that we have any choice as to the labour we shall perform, but you should practise them all, for the decision does not rest with you but with our Lord. But if, after many years' trial, He makes it clear what place each is to fill, it would be a strange humility for you to choose for yourself. Leave that to the Master of the house: He is wise and powerful and knows what is best for you and for Himself.

You may be sure that if we do all we can and prepare ourselves for contemplation with all the perfection I have described, that if He does not grant it to us (though I believe, if our humility and detachment are sincere, He is sure to bestow this gift), He is keeping back these consolations in reserve only to give them to us all at once in Heaven. As I said elsewhere, He wishes to treat us as valiant women, giving us the cross His majesty ever bore Himself. What truer friendship can He show than to choose for us what He chose for Himself? Besides, perhaps we should not have gained so rich a reward by contemplation. His judgments are His own—we have no right to interfere with them. It is well the decision does not rest with us, for thinking it a more peaceful way, we should all immediately become contemplatives! What a gain is ours if, for fear of losing by it, we do not seek to gain by what we think is best; since God never permits the truly mortified soul to lose aught, save for its greater gain.

Saint Teresa of Avila

BE MORE TRUSTING IN GOD

May Jesus be in your grace. I give thanks to Him for giving me His grace, so that, as you say, I do not forget the poor, nor, as you say, do I live in ease, for it would cause me great pain to think that you believe what you say. That would be too bad at the end of so many marks of kindness, shown me when I least merited them. I have done anything but forget you; think, how could it be so with one who is in my soul as you are? While you are walking in this darkness and in these empty places of spiritual poverty, you think that everyone and everything is failing you; but that is not surprising, for at these times it seems to you that God too is failing you. But nothing is failing you, nor have you any need to consult me about anything, nor have you any reason to do so, nor do you know one, nor will you find one: this is merely suspicion without cause. He that seeks naught but God walks not in darkness, in whatever darkness and poverty he may find himself; and he that harbours no presumptuousness and desires not his own satisfaction, either as to God or as to the creatures, and works his own will in naughtsoever, has no need to stumble or to worry about anything. You are progressing well; remain in quietness and rejoice. Who are you to be anxious about yourself? A fine state you would get into if you did that!

Never have you been in a better state than now, for never have you been humbler or more submissive, nor have you ever counted yourself, and everything in the world, as of such little worth; nor have you ever known yourself to be so evil nor God to be so good, nor have you ever served God so purely and disinterestedly as now, nor do you any longer go, as perchance you were wont, after the imperfections of your will and your own interest. What do you desire? What kind of life do you imagine yourself as living in this world? How do you imagine yourself behaving? What do you think is meant by serving God, and abstaining from evil, keeping His commandments and walking in His ways as best we can? If this be done, what need is there of other apprehensions, or of any other illumination or sweetness whether from one source or from another? In these things as a rule the soul is never free from stumbling blocks and perils, and is deceived and fascinated by the objects of its understanding and desire and its very faculties cause it to stray. And thus God is granting the soul a great favour when He darkens the faculties and impoverishes the soul so that it may not be led astray by them; and how can it walk aright and not stray, save by following the straight road of the law of God and of the Church, and living only in true and dark faith and certain hope and perfect charity, and awaiting its blessings in the life to come, living here below as pilgrims, exiles and orphans, poor and desolate, with no road to follow and with naught beside, expecting to receive everything in Heaven?

Rejoice and put your trust in God, for He has given you signs that you can quite well do so, and indeed that you ought to do so; should you do otherwise, it will not be surprising if He is wroth at seeing you so foolish, when He is leading you by a road that is most meet for you and has set you in so sure a place. Desire no way of progress but this, and tranquillise your soul, for all is well with it, and communicate as is your wont. Confess when there is anything definite on your conscience; you have no need to talk of other things. When you have anything to say you will write about it to me, and write to me quickly, and more frequently, for you can do this through Dona Ana, when you cannot do it through the nuns.

Saint John of the Cross

MAKE YOURSELVES LITTLE

Do you desire to be great? Make yourselves little. There is a mysterious connection between real advancement and

self-abasement. If you minister to the humble and despised, if you feed the hungry, tend the sick, succour the
distressed; if you bear with the forward, submit to insult,
endure in gratitude, render good for evil, you are, as by
a divine charm, getting power over the world and rising
among the creatures. God has established this law. Thus
He does His wonderful works. His instruments are poor
and despised; the world hardly knows their names, or
not at all. They are busied about what the world thinks
to be petty actions, and no one minds them. They are ap-
parently set on no great works; nothing is seen to come
of what they do; they seem to fail. Nay, even as regards
religious objects which they themselves profess to desire,
there is no natural and visible connection between their
doings and sufferings and these desirable ends; but there
is an unseen connection in the kingdom of God. They rise
by falling. Plainly so, for no condescension can be so great
as that of our Lord Himself. Now the more they abase
themselves the more like they are to Him; and the more
like they are to Him, the greater must be their power
with Him . . . When a man discerns in himself most sin
and humbles himself most, when his comeliness seems to
him to vanish away and all his graces to wither, when
he feels disgust at himself, and revolts at the thought of
himself—seems to himself all dust and ashes, all foulness
and odiousness, then it is that he is really rising in the
kingdom of God.

Cardinal Newman

HUMILITY OF THE INTELLECT

All men naturally desire knowledge; but what availeth
knowledge without the fear of God? Surely, an humble
husbandman that serveth God is better than a proud philosopher who, neglecting himself, is occupied in studying
the course of the heavens? Whoso knoweth himself is
lowly in his own eyes, and delighteth not in the praises of

men. If I understood all things in the world, and had not charity, what would it avail me in the sight of God, who will judge me according to my deeds? Cease from an inordinate desire of knowledge, for therein is much distraction and deceit.

Learned men are anxious to seem learned to others, and to be called wise. There be many things to know which doth little or nothing profit the soul: and he is very unwise who minds other things more than those that tend to his salvation. Many words do not satisfy the soul; but a good life comforteth the mind, and a pure conscience giveth great confidence toward God. The more thou knowest, and the better thou understandest, the more strictly thou shalt be judged, unless thy life be also the more holy. Be therefore not elated in thine own mind because of any art or science, but rather let the knowledge given thee make thee afraid.

If thou thinkest that thou understandest and knowest much, yet know that there be many more things which thou knowest not, affect not to be overwise, but rather acknowledge thine own ignorance. Why wilt thou prefer thyself before others, seeing there be many more learned and more skilful in the Scripture than thou? If thou wilt know or learn anything profitably, desire to be unknown, and to be little esteemed.

The highest and most profitable lesson is the true knowledge and lowly esteem of ourselves. It is great wisdom and perfection to think nothing of ourselves, and to think always well and highly of others. If thou shouldest see another openly sin, or commit some heinous offence, yet oughtest thou not to think the better of thyself; for thou knowest not how long thou shalt be able to stand. We are all frail, but do thou esteem none more frail than thyself.

Imitatio Christi

ELEVATION IN HUMILITY

The Lord said to me: "Your whole life, your eating and drinking and sleeping, your whole bodily being, all this is pleasing unto me if you are in the state of love!" And again He spoke: "I shall do great things through you in the eyes of all peoples. Through you my name shall be known far and wide, and shall be glorified, praised, and exalted."

This and many other things of the same kind He said to me. But at His words, I thought of my sinning and my inadequacy and how little I deserved such proof of love. I began to cherish grave doubts of the truth of these words and my soul answered Him who had spoken to me: "If you were, indeed, the Holy Ghost, you would not say such things to me, for they are not so, and do not befit me. And I am, moreover, a frail mortal and might easily fall prey to vanity."

And He answered me: "Now think, and reflect whether it is really possible for you to have vain thoughts because of those words."

And I tried it in order to discover whether what had been spoken to me was the truth and whether he who spoke it was the Holy Ghost. And I gazed out upon the vineyards in order to free myself from the spell of the words. But wherever I gazed, I heard His voice: "Look and observe—all this I have created." And I felt unutterable ecstasy. But while I gazed I again became conscious of how much I had sinned in my life, and I saw within myself nothing but sin and inadequacy, and I was filled with humility as never before.

Blessed Angela of Foligno

CONFORMABLE UNTO HIS DEATH

Instead of making me a return of love, they detracted me: but I gave myself to prayer.

Psalm 108, 4

Your protest, your battle against sin, has not yet called for bloodshed; yet you have lost sight, already, of those words of comfort in which God addresses you as his sons; My son, do not undervalue the correction which the Lord sends thee, do not be unmanned when he reproves thy faults. It is where he loves that he bestows correction; there is no recognition for any child of his, without chastisement. Be patient, then, while correction lasts; God is treating you as his children. Was there ever a son whom his father did not correct?

Hebrews 12, 4–7

Then, like a good soldier of Christ Jesus, take thy share of hardship.

II Timothy 2, 3

To those who court their own ruin, the message of the cross is but folly; to us, who are on the way to salvation, it is the evidence of God's power. So we read in scripture, I will confound the wisdom of wise men, disappoint the calculations of the prudent. What has become of the wise men, the scribes, the philosophers of this age we live in?

Must we not say that God has turned our worldly wisdom to folly?

I Corinthians 1, 18–20

For ourselves, we are being hampered everywhere, yet still have room to breathe, are hard put to it, but never at a loss; persecution does not leave us unbefriended, nor crushing blow destroy us; we carry about continually in our bodies the dying state of Jesus, so that the living power of Jesus may be manifested in our bodies too.

II Corinthians 4, 8–10

No, we do not play the coward; though the outward part of our nature is being worn down, our inner life is refreshed from day to day. This light and momentary affliction brings with it a reward multiplied every way, loading us with everlasting glory; if only we will fix our eyes on what is unseen, not on what we can see. What we can see lasts but for a moment; what is unseen is eternal.

II Corinthians 4, 16–18

THE BELOVED AND THE LOVER

The Beloved clothed Himself in the garment of His Lover, that he might be His companion in glory for ever. So the Lover desired to wear crimson garments daily, that his dress might be like that of his Beloved.

The Lover wept and called upon his Beloved, until the Beloved came down from the heights of Heaven; and He came to earth to weep and suffer and die for the sake of love, and to teach men to know and love and praise His name.

As though mad went the Lover through a city, singing of his love; and they asked him if he had lost his senses. "My Beloved," he answered, "has taken my will, and I myself have yielded up to Him my understanding; so that there is left in me naught but memory, with which I remember my Beloved."

Ramon Lull

THE SYMBOLISM OF THE CRUCIFIXION

He had laid wood against wood, and hands against hands: His generously extended hands against those that reach out with greed; His nail-pierced hands against those that are fallen in discouragement; His hands that embrace the whole world against the hand that brought about Adam's banishment from Paradise.

Yesterday I hung on the Cross with Christ; to-day I am glorified with Him; yesterday I was dying with Him, to-day I am brought to life with Him; yesterday I was buried with Him, to-day I rise with Him.

Let us become like Christ, since Christ also became like us. Let us become gods for Him, since He became man for us.

Saint Gregory of Nyssa

LET ME BECOME THE WHEAT OF CHRIST

The farthest bounds of the universe shall profit me nothing, neither the kingdoms of this world. It is good for me to die for Jesus Christ rather than to reign over the farthest corners of the earth. Him I seek who died on our behalf; Him I desire who rose again (for our sake). The pangs of a new birth are upon me. Bear with me, brethren. Do not hinder me from living; do not desire my death. Bestow not on the world one who desireth to be God's, neither allure me with material things. Suffer me to receive the pure light. When I am come thither, then shall I be a man. Permit me to be an imitator of the passion of my God. If any man hath Him within himself, let him understand what I desire, and let him have fellow-feeling with me, for he knoweth the things which straiten me.

The prince of this world would fain tear me in pieces and corrupt my mind to Godward. Let not any of you, therefore, who are near abet him. Rather stand ye on my side, that is, on God's side. Speak not of Jesus Christ and withal desire the world. Let not envy have a home in you. Even though I myself when I am with you should beseech you, obey me not; but rather give credence to these things which I write to you. I write to you in the midst of life, yet lusting after death. My lust hath been crucified, and there is not fire of material longing in me, but only water living and speaking in me, saying within me, Come to the Father. I have no delight in the food of corruption or in the delights of this life. I desire the bread of God, which is the flesh of Christ, who was of the seed of David; and for a draught I desire His blood, which is love incorruptible.

I write to all the churches, and I bid all men know that of my own free will I die for God, unless you should hinder me. I exhort you, be ye not of an unseasonable kindness to me. Let me be given to the wild beasts, for through them I can attain unto God. I am God's wheat, and I am ground by the teeth of wild beasts that I may be found pure bread (of Christ). Rather entice the wild beasts, that they may become my sepulchre and may leave no part of my body behind, so that I may not, when I am fallen asleep, be burdensome to anyone. Then shall I be truly a disciple of Jesus Christ, when the world shall not so much as see my body. Supplicate the Lord for me, that through these instruments I may be found a sacrifice to God. I do not enjoin you as Peter and Paul did. They were Apostles, I am a convict; they were free, but I am a slave to this very hour. Yet if I shall suffer, then am I a freed-man of Jesus Christ, and I shall rise free in Him. Now I am learning in my bonds to put away every desire.

Saint Ignatius of Antioch

ST. FRANCIS OF ASSISI AND CHRIST

The day following, to wit, the day of the Most Holy Cross, St. Francis, on the morn before daybreak, knelt down betimes in prayer before the door of his cell; and turning his face eastwards, prayed in this wise, "O my Lord Jesus Christ, two graces do I pray Thee to grant unto me ere I die: the first, that while I live I may feel in my body and in my soul, so far as is possible, that sorrow, sweet Lord, that Thou didst suffer in the hour of Thy bitterest Passion; the second is, that I may feel in my heart, so far as may be possible, that exceeding love wherewith, O Son of God, Thou wast enkindled to endure willingly for us sinners agony so great." And remaining a long time thus praying, he knew that God would hear him; and that, so far as might be possible to a mere creature, thus far would it be vouchsafed to him to suffer the aforesaid things. St. Francis, having this promise, began to contemplate most devoutly the Passion of Christ and His infinite love; and the fervour of devotion waxed so within him that through love and through compassion he was wholly changed into Jesus. And being thus inflamed by this contemplation, he beheld, that same morning, a seraph with six resplendent and flaming wings come down from heaven; which seraph, with swift flight, drew nigh to St. Francis so that he could discern him, and he knew clearly that he had the form of a man crucified; and thus were his wings disposed: two wings were extended over his head; two were spread out in flight; and the other two covered the whole of the body. St. Francis, beholding this, was sore afraid, and yet was he filled with sweetness and sorrow mingled with wonder. Joy had he, exceeding great, at the gracious aspect of Christ that appeared to him thus familiarly and looked on him so graciously; but, on the other hand, seeing him nailed upon the cross, he suffered unspeakable grief and compassion. Thereafter, he marvelled greatly at so stupendous and unwonted a vision, well knowing that the infirmity of the Passion doth not accord with the immortality of the seraphic spirit. And being in this wonderment, it was revealed by the seraph who appeared to him, that that vision had been shown to him in such form, by divine providence, in order that he might understand he was to be changed into the express similitude of the crucified Christ in this wondrous vision, not by bodily martyrdom but by spiritual fire. Then the whole mount of La Verna seemed to flame forth with dazzling splendour, that shone and illumined all the mountains and the valleys round about, as it were the sun shining on the earth. Wherefore when the shepherds that were watching in that country saw the mountain aflame and so much brightness round about, they were sore afraid, according as they afterwards told the friars, and affirmed that that flame had endured over the mount of La Verna for the space of an hour or more. Likewise, certain muleteers that were going to Romagna, arose up at the brightness of this light which shone through the windows of the inns of that country, and thinking the sun had risen, saddled and loaded their beasts. And as they went their way, they saw the said light wane and the real sun rise. Now Christ appeared in that same seraphic vision, and revealed to St. Francis certain secret and high things that St. Francis would never, during his life, disclose to any man; but, after his death, he revealed them, according as is set forth hereafter. And the words were these, "Knowest thou," said Christ, "what I have done to thee? I have given thee the stigmas that are the marks of My Passion, in order that thou be My standard-bearer. And even as I, on the day of My death, descended into limbo and delivered all the souls I found there by virtue of these My stigmas, so do I grant to thee that every year, on the day of thy death, thou mayst go to purgatory and deliver all the souls thou shalt find there of thy three orders—Minors, Sisters, and Penitents—and others likewise that shall have had great devotion to thee, and thou shalt lead them up to the glory of paradise in order that thou be conformed to Me in thy death, even as thou art in thy life." This wondrous vision having vanished, after a great space, this secret converse left in the heart of St. Francis a burning flame of divine love, exceeding great, and in his flesh, a marvellous image and imprint of the Passion of Christ. For the marks of the nails began anon to be seen on the hands and on the feet of St. Francis, in the same manner as he had then seen them in the body of Jesus Christ crucified that had appeared to him in the form of a seraph: and thus his hands and feet seemed nailed through the middle with nails, the heads whereof were in the palms of his hands and in the soles of his feet, outside the flesh; and the points came out through the backs of the hands and the feet, so far, that they were bent back and clinched in such wise that one might easily have put a finger of the hand through the bent and clinched ends outside the flesh, even as through a ring: and the heads of the nails were round and black. In like fashion, the image of a lance-wound, unhealed, inflamed, and bleeding, was seen in his right side, whence thereafter blood came out many times from the holy breast of St. Francis and stained his tunic and his nether garments with blood. Wherefore his companions, before they learned these things from him, perceiving nevertheless that he never uncovered his hands or his feet, and that he could not put the soles of his feet to the ground, and finding thereafter that his tunic and nether garments were all bloody when they washed them, knew of a surety that he had the image and similitude of our Lord Jesus Christ crucified expressly imprinted on his hands and feet, and likewise on his side.

Fioretti

MORTIFICATION

The abbot Abraham . . . was silent for a long while, and then with a heavy sigh at last he spoke . . .

We could have built our cells in the valley of the Nile,

and had water at our door, nor been driven to bring it to our mouths from three miles off. . . . We are not ignorant that in our land there are fair and secret places, where there be fruit trees in plenty and the graciousness of gardens, and the richness of the land would give us our daily bread with very little bodily toil. . . . But we have despised all these and with them all the luxurious pleasure of the world: we have joy in this desolation and to all delight do we prefer the dread vastness of this solitude, nor do we weigh the riches of your glebe against these bitter sands. . . . It is a little thing that a monk should have made a single renunciation, that is, in the first days of his calling to have trampled on things present, unless he persist in renouncing them daily. Up to the very end of this life the word of the Prophet must be in our mouths: "And the day of man Thou knowest I have not desired." Whence the saying of the Lord in the Gospel, "If any man will come after Me, let him deny himself, and take up his cross daily, and follow Me."

Cassian

YOU FILL UP THE FULL MEASURE OF CHRIST'S PASSION

And so the passion of Christ is not in Christ alone; and yet the passion of Christ is in Christ alone. For if in Christ you consider both the Head and the body, then Christ's passion is in Christ alone; but if by Christ you mean only the Head, then Christ's passion is not in Christ alone. . . . Hence, if you are in the members of Christ, all you who hear me, and even you who hear me not (though you do hear me, if you are united with the members of Christ), whatever you suffer at the hands of those who are not among the members of Christ was lacking to the sufferings of Christ. It is added precisely because it was lacking. You fill up the measure, you do not cause it to overflow. You will suffer just so much as must be added of your

sufferings to the complete passion of Christ, who suffered
as our Head and who continues still to suffer in His members, that is, in us. Into this common treasury each pays
what he owes, and according to each one's ability we all
contribute our share of suffering. The full measure of the
Passion will not be attained until the end of the world.

Saint Augustine

THE EXTRAORDINARY ROAD

God leads His chosen children on extraordinary paths.
This is an extraordinary path,
A noble road
And a sacred way.
God Himself trod it:
That a person should suffer pain and
Yet be without guilt.
Free is the soul on this road
And without ache of heart,
For she willeth not otherwise than what her Lord
Who doth all things most well.

Mechtild of Magdeburg

CONFORMABLE UNTO HIS DEATH

The true Christian is ever dying while he lives; he is
on his bier, and the prayers for the sick are saying over
him. He has no work but that of making his peace with
God, and preparing for the judgment. He has no aim but
that of being found worthy to escape the things that shall
come to pass and to stand before the Son of man. And
therefore day by day he unlearns the love of this world,
and the desire of its praise; he can bear to belong to the
nameless family of God, and to seem to the world strange
in it and out of place, for so he is.

And when Christ comes at last, blessed indeed will be his lot. He has joined himself from the first to the conquering side; he has risked the present against the future, preferring the chance of eternity to the certainty of time; and then his reward will be but beginning, when that of the children of this world is come to an end.

Cardinal Newman

SOUL OF CHRIST, SANCTIFY ME!

Soul of Christ sanctify me
   through the riches of your inner life.
Body of Christ save me
   through the torment of your oblation.
Blood of Christ inebriate me
   through the warmth of the Heart from which you
   flowed.
Water from the side of Christ wash me
   through the impetus of your streaming.
Passion of Christ strengthen me
   through the might that endured you.
O good Jesus hear me
   because You are so unfathomably good.
In Your own wounds hide me
   because they are graven very deep.
Let me never be separated from You
   because it would be my eternal damnation.
From the evil enemy protect me
   because otherwise he will overwhelm me.
In the hour of death call me
   because my heart then will be filled with fear.
And suffer me then to come to You
   because You have loved me from the beginning.
That I may praise You with all Your Saints—
   You, my Lord and my God.

Anonymous

The cross meaneth that a truly independent man within and without at all times should stand in the surrender of self in all that God wills him to suffer.

Do not think that God will make thee just by a miracle. If He wished a beautiful rose to grow in the stark cold of winter He might do it well, but He doeth not such a thing, for He deemeth it His will that it be done in true order in May after the frost, by dew and many a rainfall ordained and framed to accomplish it.

Suso

Many souls cannot think of union but in terms of joy and consolation. They do not know the pure union of the will in suffering: that is why so few attain to lasting union.

Lucie Christine

I had the deep feeling—and I am deeply distressed not to be able to express it—that there is but one help. It is the absolute gift of oneself, such as Jesus practised it. One must allow oneself to be buffeted, spat upon, scourged, crucified . . . All else is vanity.

Léon Bloy

The Cloud of Unknowing

THE STILL SMALL VOICE

And Elias came thither unto a cave, and lodged there;
and, behold, the word of the Lord came to him,
and He said unto him:
"What dost thou here, Elias?"

And he said:
"I have been very jealous for the Lord, the God of hosts;
for the children of Israel have forsaken Thy covenant,
thrown down Thine altars,
and slain Thy prophets with the sword;
and I, even I only, am left;
and they seek my life, to take it away."

And He said:
"Go forth, and stand upon the mount before the Lord."
And, behold, the Lord passed by,
and a great and strong wind rent the mountains,
and broke in pieces the rocks before the Lord;
but the Lord was not in the wind;
and after the wind an earthquake;
but the Lord was not in the earthquake;
and after the earthquake a fire;
but the Lord was not in the fire;
and after the fire a still small voice.

III Kings 19, 9–12

The Word (Logos), the master and creator of all, is always born anew in the hearts of the saints.

From the Letter of Saint Hippolytus
of Rome to Diognetes

ETERNAL BIRTH

Does the soul bring forth the eternal Word in images or imageless? Remember this: When the soul resigns herself to God and is attuned with him and God undertakes her work, she is merely receptive and leaves God to act. Here the soul is pregnant without form or image, for anything conceived in form or image appertains to time and place and is akin to creatures; whence it follows that the more the work is of the soul, the less it is of God. The soul conceives more truly without images than in them, for this birth is more by way of Godhood than of selfhood. But we may still inquire in which image does the soul best succeed in giving birth to the eternal Word. There are three kinds of images. The first the soul takes in from without through the senses. The second the soul conjures up from within by thinking on the childhood of our Lord or on his martyrdom; but all images so obtained are called divine births in the soul. The third kind of images is given to the soul by God directly. It is in these last that the soul best conceives. According to another gloss, this happens when the mind engenders, feels and knows the eternal Word in its proper image as begotten by the Father in himself, supposing the soul able to attain thereto; or, the intellect failing her, when faring forth in faith and love, he reaches out to this same image: for in this final image the Eternal Word is born most perfectly of all.

Meister Eckhart

HOW THE WORD OF GOD SPEAKS UNTO THE HEART

This then, O God, was the Beginning in which You created Heaven and Earth: marvellously speaking and marvellously creating in Your Word, who is Your Son and Your Strength and Your Wisdom and Your Truth. Who shall understand this? Who shall relate it? What is that light which shines upon me but not continuously, and strikes upon my heart with no wounding? I draw back in terror: I am on fire with longing: terror in so far as I am different from it, longing in the degree of my likeness to it. It is Wisdom, Wisdom itself, which in those moments shines upon me, cleaving through my cloud. And the cloud returns to wrap me round once more as my strength is beaten down under its darkness and the weight of my sins: for *my strength is weakened through poverty,* so that I can no longer support my good, until Thou, Lord, who art merciful to my iniquities, shalt likewise heal my weakness: redeeming my life from corruption and crowning me with pity and compassion, and filling my desire with good things: *my youth shall be renewed like the eagle's. For we are saved by hope and we wait with patience for Thy promises.*

Let him who can hear Thy voice speaking within him; I, relying upon Thy inspired word, shall cry aloud: *How great are Thy words, O Lord! Thou hast made all things in wisdom.* Wisdom is "the Beginning": and it is in that Beginning that You made heaven and earth.

Saint Augustine

THE TOKEN OF TRUE CALLING

For from a young ghostly prentice in this work, the actual feeling thereof is oft-times for divers reasons. Sometime, so he shall not presume thereupon, and ween that it be in great part in his own power to have it when he liketh and as he liketh. And such a weening were pride. And evermore when the feeling of grace is withdrawn, pride is the cause, that is to say, not actual pride, but pride that should be, were it not that this feeling of grace were withdrawn. And thus ween oft-times some young fools that God is their enemy; when He is their full friend.

Sometimes it is withdrawn for their recklessness; and when it is thus, they feel soon afterwards a full bitter pain that biteth them full sore. Sometimes our Lord will delay it on purpose, because He will by such delaying make it grow and be more esteemed when it is new found and felt again that long had been lost. And this is one of the readiest and sovereignest tokens that a soul may have, in order to know whether he be called or not to work in this work; if he feel, after such a delaying and a long lacking of this work, that when it cometh suddenly as it doth—not purchased by any means—that he hath then a greater fervour of desire and a greater love-longing to work in this work than ever he had sorrow in the losing.

And if it be thus, surely it is a true token without error that he is called by God to work in this work, whatsoever that he be or hath been.

For not what thou art, nor what thou hast been, beholdeth God with His merciful eyes; but that thou wouldst be. And St. Gregory to witness that *all holy desires grow by delays, and if they wane by delays, then were they never holy desires.* For if a man feeleth ever less and less joy in new findings and sudden presentations of his old purposed desires, although they may be called natural desires of the good, nevertheless holy desires were they never. Of this holy desire speaketh Saint Austin and saith that *all the life of a good Christian is naught else but holy desire.*

The Cloud of Unknowing

SPIRITUAL FRAILTY

There are souls among those whom God leads by this way of simplicity, whom His divine goodness strips so extraordinarily of all satisfaction, desire and feeling that they had difficulty in enduring and in expressing themselves, because what passes in their interior life is so slight, so delicate and so imperceptible, being all at the extreme summit of the spirit, that they do not know how to speak of it. And these souls sometimes suffer greatly if their Superiors are not acquainted with their way, because, fearing to be useless and to be wasting time, they wish to achieve something, and rack their brains with reflections, so as to be able to observe what is going on within them; this is very prejudicial to them, and causes them to fall into great perplexities of mind which are difficult to unravel, unless they submit to discard these reflections entirely and to suffer with patience the pain that they feel—which pain is often due merely to their always wishing to be doing something, and not being content with what they have, and this disturbs their peace of mind and causes them to lose that very simple and very delicate interior occupation of their will.

Saint Jane Frances de Chantal

THE KIND HAND THAT SUSTAINS ALL THE WORLD

This sublime knowledge tends less to the satisfaction of curiosity than to the ruling of life . . . For when I am aware of a first principle, I adore a Goodness without bounds; and in humility of feeling hope all from this cause which has formed all out of nothing . . . When I contemplate a world that sprang from nothingness and which needs but an impulse to precipitate it into nothingness, I kiss the Hand which sustains it and gives it subsistence. All my love is His to whom belongeth all . . .

How sweet are the thoughts that transport my spirit
into that infinity which anticipated the world, accompanies it, and must succeed it!

Yves of Paris

HYMN TO THE PAEDAGOGUS

Teacher, to Thee a chaplet I present,
Woven of words culled from the spotless mead,
Where Thou dost feed Thy flocks; like to the bee,
That skilful worker, which from many a flower
Gathers its treasures, that she may convey
A luscious offering to the master's hand.
Though but the least, I am Thy servant still
(Seemly is praise to Thee for Thy behests).
O King, great Giver of good gifts to men,
Lord of the good, Father, of all the Maker,
Who heaven and heaven's adornment, by Thy word
Divine fitly disposed, alone didst make:
Who broughtest forth the sunshine and the day;
Who didst appoint their courses to the stars,
And how the earth and sea their place should keep;
And when the seasons, in their circling course,
Winter and summer, spring and autumn, each
Should come, according to well-ordered plan;
Out of a confused heap who didst create
This ordered sphere, and from the shapeless mass
Of matter didst the universe adorn—
Grant to me life, and be that life well spent,
Thy grace enjoying; let me act and speak
In all things as Thy Holy Scriptures teach;
Thee and Thy co-eternal Word, All-wise,
From Thee proceeding, ever may I praise;
Give me nor poverty nor wealth, but what is meet,
Father, in life, and then life's happy close.

Clement of Alexandria

PRAYER OF LOVE

Late have I loved Thee, O Beauty so ancient and so new; late have I loved Thee! For behold Thou wert within me, and I outside; and I sought Thee outside and in my unloveliness fell upon those lovely things that Thou hast made. Thou wert with me and I was not with Thee. I was kept from Thee by those things, yet had they not been in Thee, they would not have been at all. Thou didst call and cry to me and break open my deafness: and Thou didst send forth Thy beams and shine upon me and chase away my blindness: Thou didst breathe fragrance upon me, and I drew in my breath and do now pant for Thee: I tasted Thee, and now hunger and thirst for Thee: Thou didst touch me, and I have burned for Thy peace.

Saint Augustine

THE LOVING PURSUER

O Lord, thou hast searched me and thou hast known me:
Thou knowest my downsitting and my uprising.
Thou understandest my thought from afar off . . .
Thou hast hemmed me in behind and before,
And laid thy hand upon me . . .
Whither shall I go from thy spirit?
Or whither shall I flee from thy presence?
If I ascend up into heaven, thou art there:
If I make my bed in the netherworld, behold thou art
    there.
If I take the wings of the morning, and dwell in the
    uttermost part of the sea:
Even there would thy hand lead me and thy right hand
    would hold me.
And if I say, Surely the darkness will envelop me and the
    light about me shall be night.
Even the darkness is not too dark for thee, but the night
    shineth as the day;
The darkness is even as the light . . .
Search me, O God, and know my heart, try me and know
    my thoughts.
And see if there be any way in me that is grievous;
And lead me in the way everlasting.

Psalm 138

If any of you owns a hundred sheep, and has lost one
of them, does he not leave the other ninety-nine in the

wilderness, and go after the one which is lost until he finds
it? And when he does find it, he sets it on his shoulders,
rejoicing, and so goes home, and calls his friends and his
neighbours together; Rejoice with me, he says to them,
I have found my sheep that was lost. So it is, I tell you,
in heaven; there will be more rejoicing over one sinner
who repents, than over ninety-nine souls that are justified,
and have no need of repentance.

Luke 15, 4–7

When the fish is once caught on the hook, the fisher-
man has him, no matter how he may struggle and squirm.

Meister Eckhart

The Lord thy God is a consuming fire. In truth the fire
which is God consumes, to be sure, but it does not
destroy. It burns sweetly. It leaves one desolate unto bliss.

Saint Bernard

THE LOVE OF GOD

But what is it that I love when I love You? Not
the beauty of any bodily thing, nor the order of seasons,
not the brightness of light that rejoices the eye, nor the
sweet melodies of all songs, nor the sweet fragrance of
flowers and ointments and spices: not manna nor honey,
not the limbs that carnal love embraces. None of these
things do I love in loving my God. Yet in a sense I do love
light and melody and fragrance and food and embrace
when I love my God—the light and the voice and the
fragrance and the food and embrace in the soul, when that
shines upon my soul which no place can contain, that
voice sounds which no tongue can take from me, I breathe
that fragrance which no wind scatters, I eat the food
which is not lessened by eating, and I lie in the embrace

which satiety never comes to sunder. This it is that I love, when I love my God.

Saint Augustine

GOD'S LOVE SEEKS US OUT

If material things please you, then praise God for them, but turn back your love upon Him who made them: lest in the things that please you, you displease Him. If souls please you, then love them in God, because they are mutable in themselves but in Him firmly established: without Him they would pass and perish. Love them, I say, in Him, and draw as many souls with you to Him as you can, saying to them: "Him let us love: He made these things and is not far from them." For He did not simply make them and leave them: but as they are from Him so they are in Him. See where He is, wherever there is a savour of truth: He is in the most secret place of the heart, yet the heart has strayed from Him. O sinners, return to your own heart and abide in Him that made you. Stand with Him and you shall stand, rest in Him and you shall be at peace. Where are you going, to what bleak places? Where are you going? The good that you love is from Him: and insofar as it is likewise *for* Him it is good and lovely; but it will rightly be turned into bitterness if it is unrightly loved and He deserted by whom it is. What goal are you making for, wandering around and about by ways so hard and laborious? Rest is not where you seek it. Seek what you seek, but it is not where you seek it. You seek happiness of life in the land of death, and it is not there. For how shall there be happiness of life where there is no life?

But our Life came down to this our earth and took away our death, slew death with the abundance of His own life: and He thundered, calling to us to return to Him into that secret place from which He came forth to us—coming first into the Virgin's womb, where humanity was wedded to Him, our mortal flesh, though not ever to be mortal; and thence *like a bridegroom coming out of his bride chamber, rejoicing as a giant to run his course.* For He did not delay but rushed on, calling to us by what He said and what He did, calling to us by His death, life, descent, and ascension to return to Him. And He withdrew from our eyes, that we might return to our own heart and find Him. For He went away and behold He is still here. He would not be with us long, yet He did not leave us. He went back to that place which He had never left, for the world was made by Him. And He was in this world, and He came into this world to save sinners. Unto Him my soul confesses and He hears it, for it has sinned against Him. O ye sons of men, how long shall ye be so slow of heart? Even now when Life has come down to you, will you not ascend and live? But to what high place shall you climb, since you are in a high place and have *set your mouth against the heavens?* First descend that you may ascend, ascend to God. For in mounting up *against* God you fell. Tell the souls of men to weep in this valley of tears, and so bear them up with you to God, because it is by His Spirit that you are speaking this to them if in your speaking you are on fire with the fire of charity.

Saint Augustine

GOD'S LOVABLENESS

The Servant.—Lord, let me reflect on that Divine passage where Thou speakest of Thyself in the book of Wisdom: "Come over to Me, all ye that desire Me, and be filled with My fruits. I am the Mother of fair love: My spirit is sweet above honey and the honeycomb. Wine and music rejoice the heart, but the love of wisdom is above them both."

Ah, Lord! Thou canst show Thyself so lovely and so tender, that all hearts must needs languish for Thee and endure, for Thy sake, all the misery of tender desire; Thy words of love flow so sweetly out of Thy sweet mouth, and so powerfully affect many hearts in their days of youthful bloom, that perishable love is wholly extinguished in them. O my dear Lord, this it is for which my soul sighs, this it is which makes my spirit sad, this it is about which I would gladly hear Thee speak. Now, then, my only elected Comforter, speak one little word to my soul, to Thy poor handmaid; for lo! I am fallen softly asleep beneath Thy shadow, and my heart watcheth.

Eternal Wisdom.—Listen, then, My son, and see, incline to Me thy ears, enter wholly into thy interior, and forget thyself and all things. I am in Myself the incomprehensible good, which always was and always is, which never was and never will be uttered. I may indeed give Myself to men's hearts to be felt by them, but no tongue can truly express Me in words. And yet, when I, the Supernatural, immutable good, present Myself to every creature according to its capacity to be susceptible of Me, I bind the sun's splendour, as it were, in a cloth, and give thee spiritual perceptions of Me and of My sweet love in bodily words thus: I set Myself tenderly before the eyes of thy heart; now adorn and clothe thou Me in spiritual perceptions and represent Me as delicate and as comely as thy very heart could wish, and bestow on Me all those things that can move the heart to especial love and entire delight of soul. Lo! all and everything that thou and all men can possibly imagine of form, of elegance and grace is in Me far more ravishing than anyone can express, and in words like these do I choose to make Myself known. Now, listen further: I am of high birth, of noble race; I am the Eternal Word of the Fatherly Heart, in which, according to the love-abounding abyss of My natural Sonship in His sole paternity, I possess a gratefulness before His tender eyes in the sweet and bright-flaming love of the Holy Ghost. I am the throne of delight, I am the crown of salvation, My eyes are so clear, My mouth so tender, My cheeks so radiant and blooming, and all My figure so

fair and ravishing, yea, and so delicately formed, that if
a man were to lie in a glowing furnace till the day
of judgment, only to have one single glance at My beauty,
he would not deserve it. See, I am so deliciously adorned
in garments of light, I am so exquisitely set off with all
the blooming colours of living flowers, that all May-
blossoms, all the beautiful shrubs of all dewy fields, all
the tender buds of the sunny meads are but as rough
thistles compared to My adornment.

> In the Godhead I play the game of bliss,
> Such joy the angels find in this,
> That unto them a thousand years
> But as one little hour appears.

All the heavenly host follow Me entranced by new wonders, and behold Me; their eyes are fixed on Mine; their
hearts are inclined to Me, their minds bent on Me without intermission. Happy is he who, in joyous security, shall
take Me by My beautiful hand, and join in My sweet
diversions, and dance for ever the dance of joy amid the
ravishing delights of the kingdom of heaven! One little
word there spoken by My sweet mouth will far surpass the
singing of all angels, the music of all harps, the harmony
of all sweet strings. My faithfulness is so made to be loved,
so lovely am I to be embraced, and so tender for pure
languishing souls to kiss, that all hearts ought to break for
My possession. I am condescending and full of sympathy
and always present to the pure soul. I abide with her in
secret, at table, in bed, in the streets, in the fields. Turn
Myself whichever way I will, in Me there is nothing that
can displease, in Me is everything that can delight the
utmost wishes of thy heart and desires of the soul. Lo! I
am a good so pure that he who in his day only gets one
drop of Me regards all the pleasures and delights of this
world as nothing but bitterness; all its possessions and
honours as worthless, and only fit to be cast away; My
beloved ones are encompassed by My love, and are ab-

sorbed into the One Thing alone without imaged love and
without spoken words, and are taken and infused into that
good out of which they flowed. My love can also relieve
regenerate hearts from the heavy load of sin, and can give
a free, pure and gentle heart and create a clean conscience. Tell Me, what is there in all this world able to
outweigh this one thing? For he who gives his heart
wholly to Me lives joyfully, dies securely, and obtains
the kingdom of heaven here as well as hereafter.

Now, observe, I have assuredly given thee many words,
and yet My beauty has been as little touched by them as
the firmament by thy little finger, because no eye has ever
seen My beauty, nor ear heard it, neither has it ever entered any heart. Still let what I have said to thee be as a
device to show thee the difference between My sweet
love and false, perishable love.

The Servant.—Ah! Thou tender, delicious wild flower,
Thou delight of the heart in the embracing arms of the
pure loving soul, how familiar is all this to him who has
even once really felt Thee; but how strange is it to that
man who knows Thee not, whose heart and mind are still
of the body! O, Thou most heartfelt incomprehensible
good, this is a precious hour, this is a sweet moment, in
which I must open to Thee a secret wound which my
heart still bears from Thy sweet love. Lord, plurality in
love is like water in the fire. Lord, Thou knowest that
real fervent love cannot bear duality. Alas! Thou only
Lord of my heart and soul, my heart desires that Thou
shouldst have a particular love for me, and that I should
be particularly pleasing to Thy divine eyes. O Lord, Thou
hast so many hearts that ardently love Thee, and are of
much account with Thee. Alas! my sweet and tender
Lord, how stands it with me in this matter?

Eternal Wisdom.—My love is of that sort which is not
diminished in unity, nor confounded in multiplicity. I am
as entirely concerned and occupied with thee alone, with
the thought how I may at all times love thee alone, and

fulfil everything that appertains to thee, as though I were wholly disengaged from all other things.

The Servant.—O rare! O wonderful! whither am I borne, how am I gone astray! How is my soul utterly dissolved by the sweet friendly words of my beloved! . . . How very different is Thy love and the love of creatures! How false is everything that appears lovely in this world and gives itself out to be something, as soon as one really begins to know it! Lord, wherever I might cast my eyes I always found something to disgust me; for, if it was a fair image, it was void of grace; if it was fair and lovely, it had not the true way; or if it had indeed this, still, I always found something, either inwardly or outwardly, to which the entire inclination of my heart was secretly opposed. But Thou art beauty with infinite affability. Thou art grace in shape and form, the word with the way, nobility with virtue, riches with power, interior freedom and exterior brightness, and ONE thing Thou art which I have never found in time, namely, a power and faculty of perfectly satiating every wish and every ardent desire of a truly loving heart. The more one knows Thee, the more one loves Thee . . . Slay me, rather, in Thy love, O Lord, for from Thy feet I will never more be separated.

Eternal Wisdom.—I go forth to meet those who seek Me, and I receive with affectionate joy such as desire My love. All that thou canst ever experience of My sweet love in time is but as a little drop to the ocean of My love in eternity.

Suso

THE EMBRACE

The Soul.—What is that sweet thing that comes sometimes to touch me at the thought of God? It affects me with such vehemence and sweetness that I begin wholly to go out of myself and to be lifted up, whither I know not. Suddenly, I am renewed and changed; it is a state of inexpressible well-being. My consciousness rejoices. I lose the memory of my former trials, my soul rejoices, my mind becomes clearer, my heart is enflamed, my desires are satisfied. I feel myself transported into a new place, I know not where. I grasp something interiorly as if with the embraces of love. I do not know what it is, and yet I strive with all my strength to hold it and not to lose it. I struggle deliciously to prevent myself leaving this thing which I desire to embrace for ever, and I exult with ineffable intensity, as if I had at last found the goal of all my desires. I seek for nothing more. I wish for nothing more. All my aspiration is to continue at the point I have reached. Is it my Beloved? Tell me, I pray thee, if this be He, that when He return, I may conjure Him not to depart, and to establish in me His permanent dwelling-place.

The Man.—Yes, it is truly the Beloved who visits thee. But He comes invisible, hidden, incomprehensible. He comes to touch thee, not to be seen; to intimate His presence to thee, not to be understood; to make thee taste of Him, not to pour Himself out in His entirety; to draw thy affection, not to satisfy thy desire; to bestow the first-fruits of His love, not to communicate it in its fulness. Behold in this the most certain pledge of thy future marriage: that thou art destined to see Him and to possess Him eternally, because He already gives Himself to thee at times to taste; with what sweetness thou knowest. Therefore, in the times of His absence thou shalt console thyself; and during His visits thou shalt renew thy courage which is ever in need of heartening. We have spoken at great length, O my soul. I ask thee to think of none but Him, love none but Him, listen to none but Him, to take hold of none but Him, possess none but Him.

The Soul.—That indeed is what I desire, what I choose; that is what I long for from the depths of my heart.

Hugh of St. Victor

THE SOUL AND GOD

Your glory pours into my soul
Like sunlight against gold.
When may I rest within You, Lord?
My joys are manifold.
You garment Yourself in my soul,
And my soul is clothed in You;
That a parting must befall
Fills my heart with sorest rue.
If You loved me more I could
Surely go from here, and be
Where through all eternity
I might love You as I would.
I sang to You and still
It is not as I will.
But if You sang to me
Imperfectness would flee.

"When I glow
"When I glow
You must shine,
When I flow
You must be laved.
When you sigh
You draw my heart, God's heart, into yourself.
When you weep for me
I take you in my arms.
But when you love
We two shall be as one.
When we are one at last, then none
Can ever make us part again,
Unending, wishless rapture
Shall dwell between us twain."

Lord, thus I languish on,
In haste and in desire,
In hunger and in drouth,

Until that gracious hour
When from Your Godly mouth
Flows out the chosen word,
That none has ever heard,
Save for the soul that cast
The husk of earth at last,
And to Your mouth she lays her ear,
To her the finds of love grow clear.

Mechtild of Magdeburg

JESU, NOSTRA REDEMPTIO

Jesus, our redemption,
Our love, our longing,
God, Creator of all things
And man within time's limits:

What clemency moved Thee
To bear our guilt,
To bear bitter death,
To save us from death?

Hell's gates Thou hast entered,
Freeing Thy captive ones,
At the Father's right hand
Thou sittest victor triumphant.

Devotion impelled Thee
To conquer our evil,
To spare us, to choose us,
To show us Thy face.

Thou art our gladness,
Who wilt be our reward:
Be our glory in Thee
For all ages. Amen.

Monastic Breviary

THE CLEANSING

PURIFICATION

When with the help of God my self is purified,
To go to God I need not wander far and wide.

REVELATION

Ascend! If Christ shall fuse with you in sudden light
Then like His Three you must live up on Tabor's height.

HE TO WHOM ALL IS EQUAL BEHOLDS GOD

When all is nothingness to you, when you embrace
Nothing as all, you shall behold the Dearest Face.

Angelus Silesius

O GOD, BREAK THE TYRANNY OF CREATED THINGS!

O my God, whatever is nearer to me than Thou, things
of this earth, and things more naturally pleasing to me,
will be sure to interrupt the sight of Thee, unless Thy grace
interfere. Keep Thou my eyes, my ears, my heart, from
any such miserable tyranny. Break my bonds—raise my
heart. Keep my whole being fixed on Thee. Let me never

lose sight of Thee; and, while I gaze on Thee, let my love of Thee grow more and more every day.

Cardinal Newman

THE STRIPPING OF SELF

In order to arrive at having pleasure in everything,
Desire to have pleasure in nothing.

In order to arrive at possessing everything,
Desire to possess nothing.

In order to arrive at being everything,
Desire to be nothing.

In order to arrive at knowing everything,
Desire to know nothing.

In order to arrive at that wherein thou hast pleasure,
Thou must go by a way wherein thou hast no pleasure.

In order to arrive at that which thou knowest not,
Thou must go by a way that thou knowest not.

In order to arrive at that which thou possessest not,
Thou must go by a way that thou possessest not.

In order to arrive at that which thou art not,
Thou must go through that which thou art not.

When thou thinkest upon anything,
Thou ceasest to cast thyself upon the All.

For, in order to pass from all to the All,
Thou hast to deny thyself, wholly in all.

And, when thou comest to possess it wholly,
Thou must possess it without desiring anything.

For, if thou wilt have anything in all,
Thou hast not thy treasure purely in God.

In this detachment the spiritual soul finds its quiet and repose; for, since it covets nothing, nothing wearies it when it is lifted up, and nothing oppresses it when it is cast down, for it is in the centre of its humility; since, when it covets anything, at that very moment it becomes wearied.

Saint John of the Cross

EMPTY THY HEART OF CREATED THINGS

I never ask God to give himself to me: I beg of him to purify, to empty me. If I am empty, God of his very nature is obliged to give himself to me to fill me.

How to be pure? By steadfast longing for the one good, God to wit. How to acquire this longing? By self-denial and dislike of creatures; self-knowledge is the way, for creatures are all naught, they come to naught with lamentation and bitterness.

God being in himself pure good can nowhere dwell except in the pure soul: he overflows into her, whole he flows into her. What does emptiness mean? It means a turning from creatures: the heart uplifted to the perfect good so that creatures are no comfort, nor is there any want of them save inasmuch as the perfect good, God namely, is to be grasped therein. The clear eye tolerates the mote no more than does the pure soul aught that clouds, that comes between. Creatures as she enjoys them are all pure, for she enjoys creatures in God and God in creatures. She is so limpid she sees through herself; nor is God far to seek: she finds him in herself when in her natural purity she flows into the supernatural pure Godhead where she is in God and God in her and what she does she does in God and God does in her.

Meister Eckhart

HOW GOD OPERATES IN MAN

The first emotion that befalls a man by divine grace and draws the soul towards life, strikes the heart with the thought concerning the transitory character of this nature.

This thought is naturally connected with contempt of the world. And then begin all the beautiful emotions which educate unto life. That divine power which accompanies man makes as it were a foundation in him which desires to reveal life in him. As to this emotion which I mentioned, if a man does not extinguish it by clinging to the things of this world and to idle intercourse, and if he makes this emotion increase in his soul by perpetual concentration and by gazing at himself, he will bring himself near to that which no tongue is able to tell.

This thought is greatly hated by Satan and he strives with all his power to eradicate it from man. And if he were able to give him the kingdom of the whole earth in order to efface by thought of it from his mind this deliberation, he would not do otherwise. For Satan knows that if this recollection remains with him, his mind will no longer stay in this world of error, and his means will not reach man.

This sight is clad with fiery emotions, and he that has caught it will no longer contemplate the world nor remain with the body.

Verily, my beloved, if God should grant this veracious sight unto the children of man for a short time, the course of the world would stand still. It is a bond before which nature cannot stand upright. And he unto whom this intercourse with his soul is given—verily, it is a gift from God, stronger than all partial workings which in this middle state are presented unto those who with an upright heart desire repentance. It is especially given to him of whom God knows that he is worthy of the real transition from this world unto profitable life, because He finds good will in him. It will increase and remain with a man through his dwelling alone by himself. Let us ask this gift in prayer; and for the sake of this gift let us make long vigils. And as it is a gift without equal, let us keep watch with tears at the gate of our Lord, that He may give it to us. Further, we need not weary ourselves with the trouble of this world. This is the beginning of the impulse of life, which will fully bring about in a man the perfection of right-eousness.

On the second working upon man. When a man follows his discipline perfectly and when he has succeeded in rising above the degree of repentance, and when he is near to taste the contemplation of his service, when it is given him from above to taste the delight of spiritual knowledge, a second working, after the first, will take its origin here.

In the first place man is assured concerning God's care for him and illuminated concerning His love of the crea-tures—rational creatures—and His manifold care for the things which regard them. Then there arises in him that sweetness of God and the flame of His love which burns in the heart and kindles all the affections of body and soul. And this power he will perceive in all the species of the creation and all things which he meets. From time to time he will become drunk by it as by wine; his limbs will relax, his mind will stand still and his heart will follow God as a captive. And so he will be, as I have said, like a man drunk by wine. And according as his inner senses are strengthened, so this sight will be strengthened, and according as he is careful about discipline and watchful-ness and applies himself to recitation and prayer, so the power of sight will be founded and bound in him.

In truth, my brethren, he that reaches this from time to time will not remember that he is clad with a body, nor will he know that he is in the world. This is the be-ginning of spiritual sight in a man, and this is the prin-ciple of all intellectual revelations. By this the intellect will be educated unto hidden things and become ma-ture, and by this he will be gradually elevated unto other things which are higher than human nature. In short, by this will be conducted unto man all divine visions and spiritual revelations which the saints receive in this world. Thus nature can become acquainted with the gifts of revelation that happen in this life.

This is the root of our apperception in our Creator.

Blessed is he that has preserved this good seed when it fell in his soul, and has made it to increase without destroying it by idle things and by the distractions of that which is transitory.

Isaac of Nineveh

THE LOVE OF GOD IN PURGATORY

I see that God is in such perfect conformity with the soul that when He beholds it in the purity wherein it was created by His Divine Majesty, He imparts a certain attractive impulse of His burning love, enough to annihilate it, though it be immortal; and in this way so transforms the soul into Himself, its God, that it sees in itself nothing but God, who goes on thus attracting and inflaming it, until He has brought it to that state of existence whence it came forth—that is, the spotless purity wherein it was created. And when the soul, by interior illumination, perceives that God is drawing it with such loving ardour to Himself, straightway there springs up within it a corresponding fire of love for its most sweet Lord and God, which causes it wholly to melt away: it sees in the Divine light how considerately, and with what unfailing providence, God is ever leading it to its full perfection, and that He does it all through pure love; it finds itself stopped by sin, and unable to follow that heavenly attraction—I mean that look which God casts on it to bring it into union with Himself: and this sense of the grievousness of being kept from beholding the Divine light, coupled with that instinctive longing which would fain be without hindrance to follow the enticing look—these two things, I say, make up the pains of the souls in purgatory. Not that they think anything of their pains, however great they be; they think far more of the opposition they are making to the will of God, which they see clearly is burning intensely with pure love to them. God meanwhile goes on drawing the soul to Himself by His looks of love mightily, and, as it were, with undivided energy: this the soul knows well; and could it find another purgatory greater than this by which it could sooner remove so great an obstacle, it would immediately plunge therein, impelled by that conforming love which is between God and the soul.

Saint Catherine of Genoa

LIVING IN CHRIST

Man is the hand of God. Now let us mark: Where men are enlightened with the true light, they perceive that all which they might desire or choose is nothing to that which all creatures, as creatures, ever desired or chose or knew. Therefore they renounce all desire and choice, and commit and commend themselves and all things to the Eternal Goodness. Nevertheless, there remaineth in them a desire to go forward and get nearer to the Eternal Goodness; that is, to come to a clearer knowledge, and warmer love, and more comfortable assurance, and perfect obedience and subjection; so that every enlightened man could say: "I would fain be to the Eternal Goodness what His own hand is to a man." And he feareth always that he is not enough so, and longeth for the salvation of all men. And such men do not call this longing their own, nor take it unto themselves, for they know well that this desire is not of man but of the Eternal Goodness; for whatsoever is good shall no one take unto himself as his own, seeing that it belongeth to the Eternal Goodness only.

Moreover, these men are in a state of freedom, because they have lost the fear of pain or hell, and the hope of reward or heaven, but are living in pure submission to the Eternal Goodness, in the perfect freedom of fervent love. This mind was in Christ in perfection, and is also in His followers, in some more, and in some less. But it is a sorrow and shame to think that the Eternal Goodness is ever most graciously guiding and drawing us, and we will not yield to it. What is better and nobler than true poorness in spirit? Yet when that is held up before us, we will have none of it, but are always seeking ourselves, and our own things. We like to have our mouths always filled with good things that we may have in ourselves a lively taste of pleasure and sweetness. When this is so, we are well pleased, and think it standeth not amiss with us. (But we are yet a long way off from a perfect life. For when God will draw us up to something higher, that is, to an utter loss and forsaking of our own things, spiritual and natural, and withdraweth His comfort and sweetness from us, we faint and are troubled, and can in no wise bring our minds to it; and we forget God and neglect holy exercises, and fancy we are lost for ever.) This is a great error and a bad sign. For a true lover of God loveth Him or the Eternal Goodness alike, in having or in not having, in sweetness and bitterness; in good or evil report, and the like, for he seeketh alone the honour of God, and not his own, either in spiritual or natural things. And therefore he standeth alike unshaken in all things, at all seasons. (Hereby let every man prove himself how he standeth towards God, his Creator and Lord.)

Taken out of Hell and carried into Heaven. Christ's soul must needs descend into hell before it ascended into heaven. So must also the soul of man. But mark ye in what manner this cometh to pass. When a man truly perceiveth and considereth himself, who and what he is, and findeth himself utterly vile and wicked, and unworthy of all the comfort and kindness that he hath ever received from God, or from creatures, he falleth into such a deep abasement and despising of himself, that he thinketh himself unworthy that the earth should bear him, and it seemeth to him reasonable that all creatures in heaven and earth should rise up against him and avenge their Creator on him, and should punish and torment him; and that he were unworthy even of that. And it seemeth to him that he shall be eternally lost and damned, and a footstool to all the devils in hell, and that this is right and just (and all too little compared to his sins which he so often and in so many ways hath committed against God his Creator). And therefore also he will not and dare not desire any consolation or release, either from God or from any creature that is in heaven or on earth; but he is willing to be unconsoled and unreleased, and he doth not grieve over his condemnation and sufferings; for they are right and just, and not contrary to God, but according to the will of God. Therefore they are right in his eyes, and he hath nothing to say against them. Nothing grieveth him but his own guilt and wickedness; for that is not right and contrary to God, and for that cause he is grieved and troubled in spirit.

This is what is meant by true repentance for sin. And he who in this present time entereth into this hell, entereth afterward into the Kingdom of Heaven, and obtaineth a foretaste thereof which excelleth all the delight and joy which he ever hath had or could have in this present time from temporal things. But whilst a man is thus in hell, none may console him, neither God nor the creature, as it is written, "In hell there is no redemption." Of this state hath one said, "Let me perish, let me die! I live without hope; from within and from without I am condemned, let no one pray that I may be released."

Now God hath not forsaken a man in this hell, but He is laying His hand upon him, that the man may not desire nor regard anything but the Eternal Good only, and may come to know that that is so noble and surpassing a good that none can search out or express its bliss, consolation and joy, peace, rest and satisfaction. And then, when the man neither careth for, nor seeketh, nor desireth anything but the Eternal Good alone, and seeketh not himself, nor his own things, but the honour of God only, he is made a partaker of all manner of joy, bliss, peace, rest and consolation, and so the man is henceforth in the Kingdom of Heaven.

This hell and this heaven are two good, sage ways for a man in this present time, and happy is he who truly findeth them.

> For this hell shall pass away,
> But Heaven shall endure for aye.

Also let a man mark, when he is in this hell nothing may console him; and he cannot believe that he shall ever be released or comforted. But when he is in heaven, nothing can trouble him; he believeth also that none will ever be able to offend or trouble him, albeit it is indeed true, that after this hell he may be comforted and released, and after this heaven he may be troubled and left without consolation.

Again: this hell and this heaven come about a man in such sort that he knoweth not whence they come; and whether they come to him, or depart from him, he can of himself do nothing towards it. Of these things he can neither give nor take away from himself, bring them nor banish them, but as it is written, "the wind bloweth where it listeth, and thou hearest the sound thereof," that is to say, at this time present, "but thou knoweth not whence it cometh, nor whither it goeth." And when a man is in one of these two states, all is right with him, and he is as safe in hell as in heaven, and so long as a man is on earth, it is possible for him to pass oft-times from one into the other; nay even within the space of a day and night, and all without his own doing. But when a man is in neither of these two states, he holdeth converse with the creature, and wavereth hither and thither, and knoweth not what manner of man he is. Therefore he shall never forget either of them, but lay up the remembrance of them in his heart.

Touching true inward Peace. Many say they have no peace nor rest, but so many crosses and trials, afflictions and sorrows, that they know not how they shall ever get through them. Now he who in truth will perceive and take note perceiveth clearly that true peace and rest lie not in outward things; for if it were so, the Evil Spirit also would have peace when things go according to his will (which is nowise the case; for the prophet declareth, "There is no peace, saith my God, to the wicked"). And therefore we must consider and see what is that peace which Christ left to His disciples at the last, when He said: "My peace I leave with you, My peace I give unto you." We may perceive that in these words Christ did not mean a bodily and outward peace; for His beloved disciples, with all His friends and followers, have ever suffered from the beginning great affliction, persecution, nay, often martyrdom, as Christ Himself said: "In this world, ye shall have tribulation." But Christ meant that true, inward peace of the heart, which beginneth here, and endureth for ever hereafter. Therefore He said: "Not as the world giveth," for the world is false, and deceiveth in her gifts. (She promiseth much, and performeth little. Moreover there liveth no man on earth who may always have rest and peace without troubles and crosses, with whom things always go according to his will; there is always something to be suffered here, turn which way you will. And as soon as you are quit of one assault, perhaps two come in its place. Wherefore yield thyself willingly to them, and seek only that true peace of the heart, which none can take away from thee, that thou mayest overcome all assaults.)

Thus, then, Christ meant that inward peace which can break through all assaults and crosses of oppression, suffering, misery, humiliation and what more there may be of the like, so that a man may be joyful and patient therein, like the beloved disciples and followers of Christ. Now he who will in love give his whole diligence and might thereto will verily come to know that true and eternal peace which is God Himself, as far as it is possible to a creature; (insomuch that what was bitter to him before shall become sweet, and his heart shall remain un-

moved under all changes, at all times, and after this life
he shall attain unto everlasting peace).

Theologia Germanica

BORNE UP BY CHRIST

Let us therefore pray that we ourselves may be slain
through His power, and die to the world of the wickedness
of darkness, and that the spirit of sin may be destroyed
in us, and that we may put on and receive the soul of
the heavenly Spirit, and be translated from the wickedness
of darkness into the light of Christ, and may rest in life
through world after world. For as on the racecourse the
chariots run, and the one that gets the start on the other
is a clog, a check and a hindrance to the other, so that it
cannot make progress and get to victory first, so do the
thoughts of the soul and of sin run in man. If the thought
of sin happens to get the start, it clogs and hampers the
soul, so that it cannot get near to God and carry off the
victory from it. But where the Lord mounts and takes the
reins of the soul into His own hands, He always wins,
skilfully managing and guiding the chariot of the soul into
a heavenly and inspired mind for ever. He does not war
against wickedness; having always supreme power and
authority in Himself, He works the victory Himself. So
the Cherubim are driven, not where they are inclined of
themselves to go, but where the Rider or Charioteer di-
rects. Where He wills, they go, and He supports them.

Saint Macarius the Egyptian

THE DARK NIGHT

I sleep, but my heart waketh;
Hark! my beloved knocketh:
"Open to me, my sister, my love, my dove, my undefiled;
For my head is filled with dew,
My locks with the drops of the night."
I have put off my coat;
How shall I put it on?
I have washed my feet;
How shall I defile them?
My beloved put in his hands by the hole of the door,
And my heart was moved for him.
I rose up to open to my beloved;
And my hands dropped with myrrh,
And my fingers with flowing myrrh,
Upon the handles of the bar.
I opened to my beloved;
But my beloved had turned away, and was gone.
My soul failed me when he spoke.
I sought him, but I could not find him;
I called him, but he gave me no answer.
The Watchmen that go about the city found me,
They smote me, they wounded me;
The keepers of the walls took away my mantle from me.
"I adjure you, O daughters of Jerusalem,
If ye find my beloved,

What will ye tell him?
That I am love-sick."

Canticle of Canticles 5, 2–8

Save me, O God, for the waters are come in even unto
   the soul.
I am sunk in deep mire, where there is no standing;
I am come into deep waters and the flood overwhelmeth
   me.
I am weary with my crying, my throat is hoarse,
Mine eyes fail, while I wait for my God.

Psalm 68, 2–4

And now, in heaven, a great portent appeared; a
woman that wore the sun for her mantle, with the moon
under her feet, and a crown of twelve stars about her
head. She had a child in her womb, and was crying out
as she travailed, in great pain of her delivery. Then a second portent appeared in heaven; a great dragon was there,
fiery-red, with seven heads and ten horns, and on each
of the seven heads a royal diadem; his tail dragged down
a third part of the stars in heaven, and flung them to earth.
And he stood fronting the woman who was in childbirth,
ready to swallow up the child as soon as she bore it. She
bore a son, the son who is to herd the nations like sheep
with a crook of iron; and this child of hers was caught up
to God, right up to his throne, while the mother fled into
the wilderness, where God had prepared a place of refuge
for her, and there, for twelve hundred and sixty days,
she is to be kept safe.

Apocalypse 12, 1–6

When the spirit loses itself and is merged with Godhood pure and simple, then all its grandeur and perfection must not be interpreted as the transformation of its

earthly substance into Godhood, as if its very self were God . . . but it is due to the losing of itself to what it beholds . . . Then God has become all things to the spirit, and for the spirit; all things, as it were, have become God. For all things give reply to it in their capacity of being in God, and yet each thing remains what it is by nature.

Suso

We possess God, not in the sense that we become exactly as He, but in that we approach Him as closely as possible in a miraculous, spiritual manner, and that our innermost being is illumined and seized by His truth and His holiness.

Saint Augustine

The soul, in the preceding degrees, loves and is loved in return; she seeks and she is sought; she calls and is called. But in this, in an admirable and ineffable way, she lifts and is lifted up; she holds and is herself held; she clasps and she is closely embraced, and by the bond of love, she unites herself with God, with one, alone with Him.

Saint Thomas Aquinas

THE SONG OF THE SOUL

In darkness, on a night
Inflamed with love and sweet anxiety,
O daring! O delight!
I left—none noticed me—
My house was yielded to tranquillity.

In darkness, veiled from sight,
I took the secret stair unerringly,
O daring! O delight!
In dark and secrecy,
My house was yielded to tranquillity.

Upon that night of bliss,
When none beheld, I parted secretly,
Nor looked on that or this,
And nothing guided me
But light that brimmed my heart so ardently.

This was a surer guide
Than all the light of shining middle-day,
It took me to His side,
Who watched upon a way
On which I knew none else would ever stray.

O night that guided well!
O night of grace that day has never brought!
O night that in her spell
Beloved and Lover caught!
Into the Lover the beloved was wrought!

He lay upon the breast
I kept for Him immaculate and fair.
He closed His eyes in rest,
And I caressed Him there,
And fans of cedar branches moved the air.

And when the dawning flung
Her wind among His locks and spread them wide,
His gentle fingers clung
About my neck—O tide
Of ecstasy in which my senses died!

And then I bowed my head
On my Beloved, forgot my self, and all
Else ceased, my self I shed,
And shed was every pall:
Forgotten where the lilies hold in thrall.

Saint John of the Cross

THE DARK NIGHT OF THE SPIRIT AND OF THE SENSES

This night which, as we say, is contemplation, produces in spiritual persons two kinds of darkness or purgation, corresponding to the two parts of man's nature—namely, the sensual and spiritual. And thus the one night or purgation will be sensual, wherein the soul is purged according to sense, which is subdued to the spirit; and the other is a night or purgation which is spiritual; wherein the soul is purged and stripped according to the spirit, and subdued and made ready for the union of love with God. The night of sense is common and comes to many; these are the beginners; and of this night we shall first speak. The night of the spirit is the portion of very few, and these are they that are already practised and proficient, of whom we shall treat hereafter.

The first purgation or night is bitter and terrible to sense, as we shall now show. The second bears no comparison with it, for it is horrible and awful to the spirit, as we shall show presently. Since the night of the sense is first in order and comes first, we shall first of all say something about it briefly, since more is written of it, as of a thing that is more common; and we shall pass on to treat more fully of the spiritual night, since very little has been said of it, either in speech or in writing, and very little is known of it, even by experience.

The conduct of beginners upon the way of God is ignoble, and has much to do with their love of self and their own inclinations. God desires to lead them farther. He seeks to bring them out of that ignoble kind of love to a higher degree of love for Him, to free them from the ignoble exercises of sense and meditation (wherewith they go seeking God in so many ways that are unbefitting), and to lead them to a kind of spiritual exercise wherein they can commune with Him more abundantly and are freed more completely from imperfections. For they have now had practice for some time in the way of virtue and have persevered in meditation and prayer whereby, through the sweetness and pleasure that they found therein, they have lost their love of the things of the world and have gained some degree of spiritual strength in God; this has enabled them to some extent to refrain from creaturely desires, so that for God's sake they are now able to suffer a light burden and a little aridity without turning back to a time which they found more pleasant. When they are going about these spiritual exercises with the greatest delight and pleasure, and when they believe that the sun of Divine favour is shining most brightly upon them, God turns all this light of theirs into darkness, and shuts against them the door and the source of the sweet spiritual water which they were tasting in God whensoever and for as long as they desired. (For, as they were weak and tender, there was no door closed to them, as St. John says in the Apocalypse 3, 8.) And thus He leaves them so completely in the dark that they know not whither to go with their sensible imagination and meditation; for they cannot advance a step in meditation, as they were wont to do aforetime, their inward senses being submerged in this night, and left with such dryness that not only do they experience no pleasure and consolation in the spiritual things and good exercises wherein they were wont to find their delights and pleasures, but instead they find insipidity and bitterness in the said things. For, as I have said, God now sees that they have grown a little, and are becoming strong enough to lay aside their swaddling clothes and be taken from the gentle breast; so He sets them down from His arms and teaches them to walk on their own feet; which they feel to be very strange, for everything seems to be going wrong with them.

To recollected persons this commonly happens sooner after their beginnings than to others, inasmuch as they are freer from occasions of backsliding, and their desires turn more quickly from the things of the world, which is what is needful if they are to begin to enter this blessed night of the sense. Ordinarily, no great time passes after their beginnings before they begin to enter this night of the sense; and the great majority of them do in fact enter it, for they will generally be seen to fall into these aridities.

Saint John of the Cross

THE CLEANSING FIRE OF THE DARK NIGHT

For the greater clearness of what has been said, and of what has still to be said, it is well to observe at this point that this purgative and loving knowledge or Divine light whereof we here speak acts upon the soul which is purged and prepared for perfect union with it in the same way as fire acts upon a log of wood in order to transform it into itself; for material fire, acting upon wood, first of all begins to dry it, by driving out its moisture and causing it to shed the water which it contains within itself. Then it begins to make it black, dark and unsightly, and even to give forth a bad odour, and, as it dries it little by little, it brings out and drives away all the dark and unsightly accidents which are contrary to the nature of fire. And, finally, it begins to kindle it externally and give it heat, and at last transforms it into itself and makes it as beautiful as fire. In this respect, the wood has neither passivity nor activity of its own, save for its weight, which is greater, and its substance, which is denser, than that of fire, for it has in itself the properties and activities of fire. Thus it is dry and it dries; it is hot and heats; it is bright and gives brightness; and it is much less heavy than before. All these properties and effects are caused in it by the fire.

In this same way we have to philosophise with respect to this Divine fire of contemplative love, which, before it unites and transforms the soul in itself, first purges it of all its contrary accidents. It drives out its unsightliness, and makes it black and dark, so that it seems worse than before and more unsightly and abominable than it was wont to be. For this Divine purgation is removing all the evil and vicious humours which the soul has never perceived because they have been so deeply rooted and grounded in it; it has never realised, in fact, that it has had so much evil within itself. But now that they are to be driven forth and annihilated, these humours reveal themselves, and become visible to the soul because it is so brightly illumined by this dark light of Divine contemplation (although it is no worse than before, either in itself or in relation to God); and, as it sees in itself that which it saw not before, it is clear to it that it is not only unfit for God to see it, but that it deserves His abhorrence and that He does indeed abhor it. By this comparison we can now understand many things concerning what we are saying and purpose to say.

First, we can understand how the very light and the loving wisdom which are to be united with the soul and to transform it are the same that at the beginning purge and prepare it: even as the very fire which transforms the log of wood into itself, and makes it part of itself, is that which at the first was preparing it for that same purpose.

Secondly, we shall be able to see how these afflictions are not felt by the soul as coming from the said Wisdom, since, as the Wise Man says, all good things together come to the soul with her. They are felt as coming from the weakness and imperfection which belong to the soul; without such purgation, the soul cannot receive its Divine light, sweetness and delight, even as the log of wood, when the fire acts upon it, cannot immediately be transformed until it be made ready; wherefore the soul is greatly afflicted. This statement is fully supported by the Preacher, where he describes all that he suffered in order that he might attain to union with wisdom and to the fruition of it, saying thus: My soul hath wrestled with her and my bowels were moved in acquiring her; therefore it shall possess a good possession.

Thirdly, we can learn here incidentally in what manner

souls are afflicted in purgatory. For the fire would have no power over them, even though they came into contact with it, if they had no imperfections for which to suffer. These are the material upon which the fire of purgatory seizes; when that material is consumed there is naught else that can burn. So here, when the imperfections are consumed, the affliction of the soul ceases and its fruition remains.

The fourth thing that we shall learn here is the manner wherein the soul, as it becomes purged and purified by means of this fire of love, becomes ever more enkindled in love, just as the wood grows hotter in proportion as it becomes the better prepared by the fire. This enkindling of love, however, is not always felt by the soul, but only at times when contemplation assails it less vehemently, for then it has occasion to see, and ever to enjoy, the work which is being wrought in it, and which is then revealed to it. For it seems that the worker takes his hand from the work, and draws the iron out of the furnace, in order that something of the work which is being done may be seen; and then there is occasion for the soul to observe in itself the good which it saw not while the work was going on. In the same way, when the flame ceases to attack the wood, it is possible to see how much of it has been enkindled.

Fifthly, we shall also learn from this comparison what has been said above—namely, how true it is that after each of these periods of relief the soul suffers once again, more intensely and keenly than before. For after that revelation just referred to has been made, and after the more outward imperfections of the soul have been purified, the fire of love once again attacks that which is to be consumed and purified more inwardly. The suffering of the soul now becomes more intimate, subtle and spiritual, in proportion as it refines away the more intimate, subtle and spiritual imperfections, and those which are most deeply rooted in its inmost parts. And it is here just as with the wood, which, when the fire begins to penetrate it more deeply, acts with more force and vehemence in preparing its most inward part to possess it.

Sixthly, we shall likewise learn here the reason why it seems to the soul that all its good is over, and that it is full of evil, since naught comes to it at this time but bitterness; it is like the burning wood, which is touched by no air nor by aught else than by consuming fire. But when there occur other periods of relief like the first, the rejoicing of the soul will be more interior because the purification has been more interior also.

Seventhly, we shall learn that, although the soul has most ample joy at these periods (so much so that, as we said, it sometimes thinks that they can never return again, although it is certain that they will return quickly), it cannot fail to realise, if it is aware (and at times it is made aware) of a root of imperfection which remains, that its joy is incomplete, because a new assault seems to be threatening it; when this is so it happens quickly. Finally, that which still remains to be purged and enlightened most inwardly cannot well be concealed from the soul in view of its experience of its former purification; even as also in the wood it is the most inward part that remains longest unkindled, and the difference between it and that which has already been purged is clearly perceptible; and when this purification once more assails it most inwardly, it is no wonder if it seems to the soul once more that all its good is gone, and that it never expects it to return, since in its most inward sufferings all outward goodness is over for it.

Saint John of the Cross

GOD VEILS HIS MERCY

I knew nothing of myself. I only thought of Jesus and of my holy vows. The sisters did not understand me. I could not explain my state to them. I was too much within it. Had not God veiled many of the mercies He bestowed

on me, they would have begun to doubt me. In the midst
of all my pain and suffering I had such inner wealth as
never before. I felt more than blessed. I had a chair without a seat and a chair without a back in my cell, and yet
it was so well provided and splendid that I often seemed
to see all of heaven in it. At times, by night, in my cell,
I was elated by the mercy and love of the Lord and burst
into a flood of loving words, and spoke to Him as I had
done as a child, when people sometimes spied on me and
accused me of great impudence and audacity towards
God. And once, when I involuntarily replied that it
seemed greater audacity to receive the body of the Lord
without having spoken so intimately with Him, how
sternly was I reprimanded! And through all this I lived
at blessed peace with God and with all of His creatures.
When I was working in the garden, birds came to me and
perched on my head and shoulders, and together we sang
our praise of God. I always saw my guardian angel at
my side, and no matter how much the Evil One loosed
the powers of Hell against me, yes, even abused me with
tortures and blows, he could do me no real harm. I was
always forewarned and had help and protection. My
yearning for the Holy Sacrament was so irresistible that,
drawn toward it, I often left my cell by night, asleep, and
knelt or lay in the church, if it was open, or at the closed
church door or the church wall, even in severe winter
weather, rigid, with arms outstretched. And thus I was
found by the priest of the convent who came mercifully
earlier, to give me communion. But when he approached
and opened the church, I awoke and hastened to receive
communion and found my Lord and God. When I performed the duties of a sacristan, it seemed as though my
soul were suddenly snatched from me, and I climbed and
stood in high places in the church, on the window-sills,
projections and carvings that were impossible for a human being to reach by human powers alone. There I
cleaned and polished everything, and it always seemed
to me that good spirits were about me and sustained me

in those high places and helped me. I did not give it much thought, since I was accustomed to this from childhood on. I never felt alone for any length of time. We did everything together in such loving harmony. It was only among certain people that I felt lonely so that I wept like a child that wants to go home.

I saw very much that cannot be told. Who can tell with the tongue what he sees with more than his eyes? . . .

I do not see these things with my eyes, but it seems as though I saw them with my heart, in the very middle of my breast. And I break out in a sweat. But at the same moment I see all the persons and objects around me. But they do not know me, and neither do I know who and what they are. Even now that I speak, I have this inner sight . . . For several days I have been between this sight of the senses and beyond the senses. I must practise great restraint, for while I am speaking to others, I suddenly see quite different objects and images before me, and then I hear my own words as if they were those of another who speaks out of an empty barrel in a hollow and crude voice. It also seems to me as though I were inebriate and about to fall. My words to those with whom I am speaking flow on and are often more vivid than usual. But afterwards I do not know what I have said, although my speech was connected. It is difficult for me to maintain this double state. With my eyes I see what surrounds me, dimly, as one who is falling asleep and who sees the beginnings of a dream. But my inner eyes want to drag me away by force and what I see is clearer than with my natural sight, and it does not come through my eyes.

Anna Katharina Emmerich

PERSISTENT PRAYER

To persist in prayer without returns, this is not time lost, but a great gain. It is endeavour without thought of self and only for the glory of the Lord. Even though at first it seems that the effort is all in vain, it is not so, but it is as with children who work in their father's fields: they receive no daily wage, but when the year comes to an end, everything belongs to them . . .

He who sets out to pray must be as the husbandman. In the season of summer and fair weather he (as the ant) must not grow weary, so that he may be fed in the season of winter and stormy rains. He must have a full larder so that he may live and not (like the dumb beasts) die of hunger. For we must be prepared for the great storm of death and judgment.

In Albula I learned to know a certain saint who lived as it is fitting for a saint. After she had given away all for the sake of the Lord, she had left a cover to protect her from the cold, and this she gave also. Soon after this, God afflicted her with the greatest inner pain and a feeling of loneliness. Whereat she complained and said to Him: "Is this meet, dear Lord? You have taken all from me, and now You Yourself forsake me too!"

Here, then, God repaid the great services performed for Him, with sorrow. And there can, indeed, be no better payment, for the true meaning of it is that one is paid with the love of God.

Do not let your heart cling to inner solace. For that is in the manner of common soldiers: they demand their daily wage at once. Give your service as the noblest officers serve their king—for nothing!

Saint Teresa of Avila

THE TWOFOLD WAY

When the soul has naught to stay her, she is ready to pass into the image of God whereto none can attain be he not stripped of spiritual matter. Alas, how they obstruct this secret passage, those who so lightly stop in temporal things! Wherein I also acknowledge my wretchedness. In this sense St. Dionysius exhorted his disciples, saying, "And thou wouldst know the hidden mystery of God, transcend whatever hinder thy pure perception." When with her pure intellect now illumined with divine light, the naked soul sees God, then she knows herself. And when she sees how apt she is to him, how she is his and how they are both one, then, the burden of the body permitting, she remains thus always. This lofty intuition the soul has of the hidden mystery of God is that of which Job tells: "In the horror of a vision by night he cometh and whispereth into the ears of men." What does he mean by the horror? Solicitude for this perception of which we are speaking. The nocturnal vision is the revelation of the hidden truth. And the whispering is the flowing union wherein knower and known are one.

Meister Eckhart

THE WOUNDED HEART

Woe upon you, scribes and Pharisees, you hypocrites that build up the tombs of the prophets and engrave the monuments of the just; If we had lived in our fathers' times, you say, we would not have taken part in murdering the prophets. Why then, you bear witness of your own ancestry; it was your fathers who slaughtered the prophets; it is for you to complete your fathers' reckoning. Serpents that you are, brood of vipers, how should you escape from the award of hell? And now, behold, I am sending prophets and wise men and men of learning to preach to you; some of them you will put to death and crucify, some you will scourge in your synagogues, and persecute them from city to city; so that you will make yourselves answerable for all the blood of just men that is shed on the earth, from the blood of the just Abel to the blood of Zacharias the son of Barachias, whom you slew between the temple and the altar. Believe me, this generation shall be held answerable for all of it. Jerusalem, Jerusalem, still murdering the prophets, and stoning the messengers that are sent to thee, how often have I been ready to gather thy children together, as a hen gathers her chickens under her wings; and thou didst refuse it! Behold, your house is left to you, a house uninhabited. Believe me, you shall see nothing of me henceforward, until the time when you will be saying, Blessed is he that comes in the name of the Lord.

Matthew 23, 29–39

Hear, O ye heavens, and give ear, O earth, for the Lord hath spoken. I have brought up children and exalted them: but they have despised me. The ox knoweth his owner and the ass his master's crib: but Israel hath not known me and my people hath not understood.

Isaias 1, 2–3

How is the faithful city, that was full of judgment, become a harlot? Justice dwelt in it, but now murderers. Thy silver is turned into dross: thy wine is mingled with water. Thy princes are faithless, companions of thieves: they all love bribes, they run after rewards. They judge not for the fatherless: and the widow's cause cometh not in to them.

Isaias 1, 21–23

Many waters cannot quench charity, neither can the floods drown it: if a man should give all the substance of his house for love, he shall despise it as nothing.

Canticle of Canticles 8, 7

SONG OF LOVE

My song is a sighing, my life is spent in longing for the
   sight of my King, so fair in His brightness.
So fair in Thy beauty! Lead me to Thy light, and feed me
   on Thy love! Make me to grow swiftly in love and
   be Thou Thyself my prize.
When wilt Thou come, Jesus my joy, to save me from
   care and give Thyself to me, that I may see Thee
   evermore?
Could I but come to Thee, all my desires were fulfilled.
   I seek nothing but Thee alone, who art all my desire.

Jesus my Saviour! My comforter! Flower of all beauty!
My help and my succour! When may I see Thee in
Thy majesty?

When wilt Thou call me? I languish for Thy presence,
to see Thee above all things. Let not Thy love for
me fail! In my heart I see the canopy that shall cover
us both.

Now I grow pale and wan for love of my beloved Jesus
both God and man. Thy love did teach me when I
ran to Thee, wherefore now I know how to love Thee.

I sit and sing of the love-longing that is bred in my breast.
Jesus! Jesus! Jesus! Why am I not led to Thee?

Full well I know Thou seest my state. My thought is fixed
upon love. When I shall see Thee and dwell with
Thee, then shall I be filled and fed.

Jesus, Thy love is constant and Thou knowest best how
to love me. When shall my heart break forth to come
to Thee, my rest?

Jesus, Jesus, Jesus! I mourn for Thee! When may I turn
hence to Thee, my life and my living?

Jesus, my dear and my darling! My delight is to sing of
Thee. Jesus, my mirth and my melody! When wilt
Thou come, my King?

Jesus, my salvation and my sweetness, my hope and my
comfort! Jesus, I desire to die whenever it shall please
Thee. The longing that my Love has sent to me overwhelms me.

All woe is gone from me, since my breast has been inflamed with the love of Christ so sweet, whom I will
never leave, but do promise to love always.

For love can cure my evil and bring me to His bliss, and
give me Him for whom I sigh, Jesus, my love, my
sweeting.

A longing has come upon me that binds me day and night
until I shall see His face so fair and bright.

Jesus, my hope, my salvation, my only joy! Let not Thy
love cool, let me feel Thy love and dwell with Thee
in safety.

Jesus, with Thee alone I am great. I would rather die
    than possess all this world and have power over it.

When wilt Thou pity me, Jesus, that I may be with Thee,
    to love Thee and look upon Thee?

Do Thou ordain for me my settle and sit me thereon, for
    then we can never part.

And I shall sing of Thy love, in the light of the brightness
    of Heaven for ever and ever. Amen.

Richard Rolle

VISION OF AN ANGEL

Our Lord was pleased that I should have at times a
vision of this kind: I saw an angel close by me, on my left
side, in bodily form. This I am not accustomed to see, unless very rarely. Though I have visions of angels frequently, yet I see them only by an intellectual vision such
as I have spoken of before. It was our Lord's will that
in this vision I should see the angel in this wise. He was
not large, but small of stature and most beautiful—his face
burning as if he were one of the highest angels, who seem
to be all of fire: they must be those whom we call
cherubim. Their names they never tell me; but I see very
well that there is in heaven so great a difference between
one angel and another, and between those and the others,
that I cannot explain it.

I saw in his hand a long spear of gold, and at the iron's
point there seemed to be a little fire. He appeared to me
to be thrusting it time and again into my heart, and to
pierce my very entrails; when he drew it out, he seemed
to draw them out also, and to leave me all on fire with a
great love of God. The pain was so great that it made me
moan; and yet so surpassing was the sweetness of this
excessive pain that I could not wish to be rid of it. The
soul is satisfied now with nothing less than God. The pain
is not bodily but spiritual; though the body has its share

in it, even a large one. It is a caressing of love so sweet which now takes place between the soul and God, that I pray God of His goodness to make him experience it who may think that I am lying.

During the days that this lasted I went about as if beside myself. I wished to see and speak with no one, but only to cherish my pain, which was to me a greater bliss than all created things could give me.

Saint Teresa of Avila

THE KNOWLEDGE AND SAVOUR OF LOVE

To love and not to know
This is the wise soul's darkest woe.
To know and not to be aware
Is stifling hell in earthly air.
To savour without soaring free,
This is her utmost agony.

Mechtild of Magdeburg

AN ECSTATIC CONFESSION OF A SAINT FIGHTING FOR HER CHURCH

In the Name of Jesus Christ crucified and of Sweet Mary:

Dearest and sweetest father in Christ, sweet Jesus: I, Catherine, servant and slave of servants of Jesus Christ, write to you in His precious blood . . . wonderful mysteries has God wrought, from New Year's day till now; such that no tongue could suffice to tell them. But let us pass over all that time, and come to Sexagesima Sunday when occurred, as I am writing you briefly, those mysteries which you shall hear: never have I seemed to bear anything like them. For the pain in my heart was so great that the tunic which clothed me tore wherever I held it; and I circled around in the chapel like a person in spasms. He who had held me had surely taken away my life. Then, Monday coming, in the evening, I was constrained to write to Christ on earth* and to three cardinals. So I had myself helped, and went into the study. And when I had written to Christ on earth, I had no way of writing more, the pains had so greatly increased in my body. And, waiting a little, the terror of demons began, in such wise that they stunned me entirely; raging against me as if I, worm that I am, had been the means of taking from their hands what they had possessed a long time in Holy Church. So great was the terror, with the bodily pain, that I wanted to fly from the study and go to the chapel—as if the study had been the cause of my pains. So I rose up, and not being able to walk, I leaned on my spiritual son Barduccio. But suddenly I was thrown down; and lying there, it seemed to me as if my soul were parted from my body; not in such wise as when it really was parted, for then my soul tasted the good of the Immortals, receiving that Highest Good together with them; but this now seemed like a special case, for I did not seem to be in the body, but I saw my body as if it had been someone else. And my soul, seeing the grief of him who was with me, wished to know if I had any power over the body, to say to him: "Son, do not fear"; and I saw that I could not move the tongue or any member of it, any more than a body quite dead. Then I let the body stay just as it was; and the intellect was fixed on the abyss of the Trinity. Memory was full of recollection of the need of Holy Church and of all the Christian people; and I cried before His Face, and demanded divine help with assurance, offering to Him my desires, and constraining Him by the Blood of the Lamb and the pains that had been borne. And so eager was the demand that it seemed to me sure that He would not deny that petition. Then I asked for all you others, praying Him that He would fulfil in you

* *Pope Urban VI.*

His will and my desires. Then I asked that He would save me from eternal condemnation. And while I stayed thus for a very long time, so that the Family was mourning me as dead, at this point all the terror of the demons was gone away. The Presence of the Humble Lamb came before my soul, saying: "Fear not: for I will fulfil thy desires, and those of My other servants. I will that thou seest that I am a good master, who plays the potter, unmaking and remaking vessels as His pleasure is. These My vessels I know how to unmake and remake; and therefore I take the vessel of thy body, and remake it in the garden of Holy Church, in different wise than in past time." And as this Truth held me close, with ways and words most charming, which I pass over, the body began to breathe a little, and to show that the soul was returning to its vessel. Then I was full of wonder. And such pain remained in my heart that I have it there still. All pleasure and all refreshment and all food was then taken away from me. Being carried afterwards into a place above, the room appeared full of devils: they began to wage another battle, the most terrible that I ever had, trying to make me believe and see that I was not she who was in the body but an impure spirit. I, having invoked divine help with a sweet tenderness, refusing no labour, yet said: "God, listen for my help! Lord, haste Thee to help me! Thou hast permitted that I be alone in this battle, without the refreshment of the father of my soul, of whom I am deprived for my ingratitude."

Two nights and two days passed in these tempests. It is true that mind and desire received no break, but remained ever fixed on their object; but the body seemed almost to have failed. Afterwards on the Day of the Purification of Mary, I wished to hear Mass. Then all the mysteries were renewed; and God showed the great need that existed, as later appeared; for Rome has been on the point of revolution, backbiting disgracefully, and with much irreverence. Only that God has poured oil on their hearts, and I think the thing will have a good end. Then

God imposed this obedience on men, that during the whole
of this holy season of Lent, I should offer in sacrifice the
desires of all the Family, and have Mass celebrated before
Him with this one intention alone—that is, for Holy
Church—and that I should myself hear a Mass every morning at dawn—a thing which you know is impossible to me;
but in obedience to Him all things have been possible.
And this desire has become so much a part of my flesh,
that memory retains nothing else, intellect can see nothing
else, and will can desire nothing else. Not so much that
the soul turns aside from things here below for this reason
—but, conversing with the True Citizens, it neither can
nor will rejoice in their joy, but in their hunger, which
they still feel, and which they felt while pilgrims and way-
farers in this life.

In this way, and many others which I cannot tell, my
life is consumed and shed for this sweet Bride: I by this
road, and the glorious martyrs with blood. I pray the Divine Goodness soon to let me see the redemption of His
people. When it is the hour of terce, I rise from Mass,
and you would see a dead woman go to St. Peter's; and
I enter anew to labour in the ship of Holy Church. There
I stay thus till near the hour of vespers: and from this
place I would depart neither day nor night until I see this
people at least a little steadily established in peace with
their father. This body of mine remains without any food,
without even a drop of water: in such sweet physical tortures as I never at any time endured; insomuch that my
life hangs on a thread. Now I do not know what the Divine
Goodness will do with me: as far as my feelings go, I do
not say that I perceive His will in this matter; but as to
my physical sensations, it seems to me that this time I am
to confirm them with a new martyrdom, in the sweetness
of my soul—that is, for Holy Church; then, perhaps, He
will make me rise again with Him. He will put so an end
to my miseries and to my crucified desires, or He may
employ His usual ways to strengthen my body. I have
prayed and pray His mercy that His will be fulfilled in

me, and that He leave not you or the others orphans. But may He ever guide you in the way of the doctrine of Truth, with true and very perfect light. I am sure that He will do it . . .

Saint Catherine of Siena

MUTUALITY OF LOVE

I require that you should love Me with the same love with which I love you. This, indeed, you cannot do, because I loved you without being loved. All the love which you have for Me you owe to Me, so that it is not of grace that you love Me, but because you ought to do so. While I love you of grace, and not because I owe you My love. Therefore to Me, in person, you cannot repay the love which I require of you, and I have placed you in the midst of your fellows, that you may do to them that which you cannot do to Me, that is to say, that you may love your neighbour of free grace, without expecting any return from him, and what you do to him I count as done to Me . . .

Saint Catherine of Siena

CHRIST'S WOUNDS ARE ALL OPEN

. . . Name Jesus often, and invoke the aid of his passion, and implore him by his sufferings, and by his precious blood, and by his death on the cross. Fly into his wounds; creep into them with thy thought. They are all open. He loved us much who permitted such cavities to be made in him, that we might hide ourselves in them. And, with his precious blood, ensanguine thine heart. "Go into the rock," saith the prophet, "and hide thee in the pit which is dug in the earth"; that is, in the wounds of our Lord's flesh, which was as if dug into with the blunt nails, as he said long before in the Psalter, "They dug my feet and my hands." He did not say they "pierced" my feet and my hands, but "dug." For, according to this Latin, as our teachers say, the nails were so blunt that they digged his flesh, and broke the bones rather than pierced them, to torment him the sorer. He himself calleth thee toward those wounds. "My dove," saith our Lord, "come and hide thyself in the cavities of my limbs, and in the holes of my side."

The Nun's Rule

WOUNDED BY FLAMES IN GOD

The centre of the soul is God; and, when the soul has attained to Him according to the whole capacity of its being, and according to the force of its operation, it will have reached the last and the deepest centre of the soul, which will be when with all its powers it loves and understands and enjoys God; and so long as it attains not as far as this, although it be in God, who is its centre by grace and by His own communication, still, if it has the power of movement to go farther and strength to do more, and is not satisfied, then, although it is in the centre, it is not in the deepest centre, since it is capable of going still farther. Love unites the soul with God, and the more degrees of love the soul has, the more profoundly does it enter into God and the more is it centred in Him; and thus we can say that, as are the degrees of love of God, so are the centres, each one deeper than another, which the soul has in God; these are the many mansions which, He said, were in His Father's house. And thus the soul which has one degree of love is already in its centre in God, since one degree of love suffices for a soul to abide in Him through grace. If it have two degrees of love, it will have entered into another and a more interior centre with God; and, if it attain to three, it will have entered into the third. If it attain to the last degree, the love of God will succeed in wounding the soul even in its deepest centre—that is, in transforming and enlightening it as regards all the being and power and virtue of the soul, such as it is capable of receiving, until it be brought into such a state it appears to be God. In this state the soul is like the crystal that is clear and pure; the more degrees of light it receives the greater concentration of light there is in it, and this enlightenment continues to such a degree that at last it attains a point at which the light is centred in it with such abundance that it comes to appear to be wholly light, and cannot be distinguished from the light, for it is enlightened to the greatest possible extent and thus appears to be light itself.

And thus, when the soul says that the flame wounds it in its deepest centre, it means that it wounds it in the farthest point attained by its own substance and virtue and power. This it says to indicate the copiousness and abundance of its glory and delight, which is the greater and the more tender when the soul is the more fervently and substantially transformed and centred in God. This is something much greater than comes to pass in the ordinary union of love, because of the greater fervency of the fire, which here, as we say, gives forth living flame. For this soul, which is now in such sweetness and glory, and the soul that enjoys only the ordinary union of love, are in a certain way comparable respectively to the fire of God, which, says Isaias, is in Sion, and which signifies the Church Militant, and to the furnace of God, which was in Jerusalem and which signifies the vision of peace. For the soul in this state is like a furnace enkindled, the vision whereof is, as we say, the more peaceful and glorious and tender in proportion as the flame of this furnace is more vehemently enkindled than common fire. And thus, when the soul feels that this living flame is communicating all blessing to it after a living manner, because this Divine love brings everything with it, it says: "O living flame of love, that tenderly woundest." This is as though it were to say: O love enkindled, thou art tenderly glorifying me with thy loving movements in the greatest capacity and power of my soul, that is to say, art giving me Divine

intelligence according to the entire capacity of my understanding, and communicating love to me according to the
utmost power of my will, and delighting me in the substance of the soul with the affluence and copiousness of
the sweetness of Thy Divine contact and substantial union,
according to its utmost purity and the capacity of my
memory. This comes to pass in a greater degree than it is
possible for the soul to describe at the time when this flame
uprises in it.

Saint John of the Cross

THE BRIDE

By night on my bed I sought him
Whom my soul loveth;
I sought him, but I found him not.

I will rise now, and go about the city,
In the streets and in the broad ways,
I will seek him whom my soul loveth.
I sought him, but I found him not.

Canticle of Canticles 3, 1–2

Then I looked, and saw where the Lamb stood on mount
Sion, amidst a company of a hundred and forty-four thousand, with his name, and his Father's name, written on
their foreheads. And I heard a sound from heaven, louder
than water in full flood, or heavy thunder. This sound
which I heard seemed to come from harpers, playing on
their harps, as they sang a new song, there before the
throne, and the living figures, and the elders. It was a song
none else might learn to sing but the hundred and forty-
four thousand that came ransomed from the earth. These
have kept their virginity undefiled by the touch of woman;
these are the Lamb's attendants, wherever he goes; these
have been ransomed for God and the Lamb as the first-
fruits of mankind. Falsehood was not found on their lips;
they stand there untainted before the throne of God.

Apocalypse 14, 1–5

Then I saw a new heaven, and a new earth. The old heaven, the old earth had vanished, and there was no more sea. And I, John, saw in my vision that holy city which is the new Jerusalem, being sent down by God from heaven, all clothed in readiness, like a bride who has adorned herself to meet her husband. I heard, too, a voice which cried aloud from the throne, Here is God's tabernacle pitched among men; he will dwell with them, and they will be his own people, and he will be among them, their own God. He will wipe away every tear from their eyes, and there will be no more death, or mourning, or cries of distress, no more sorrow; those old things have passed away. And he who sat on the throne said, Behold, I make all things new. (These words I was bidden write down, words most sure and true.) And he said to me, It is over, I am Alpha, I am Omega, the beginning of all things and their end; those who are thirsty shall drink—it is my free gift—out of the spring whose water is life. Who wins the victory? He shall have his share in this; I will be his God, and he shall be my son. But not the cowards, not those who refuse belief, not those whose lives are abominable; not the murderers, the fornicators, the sorcerers, the idolaters, not those who are false in any of their dealings. Their lot awaits them in the lake that burns with fire and brimstone, and it is the second death.

And now an angel came and spoke to me, one of those seven who bear the seven cups charged with the seven last plagues. Come with me, he said, and I will show thee that bride, whose bridegroom is the Lamb. And he carried me off in a trance to a great mountain, high up, and there showed me the holy city Jerusalem, as it came down, sent by God, from heaven, clothed in God's glory. The light that shone over it was bright as any precious stone, as the jasper when it is most like crystal; and a great wall was raised high all round it, with twelve gates and twelve angels at the gates, and the names of the twelve tribes of Israel carved on the lintels; three gates on the east, three on the north, three on the south, three on the west. The city wall, too, had twelve foundation stones; and these, too, bore names, those of the Lamb's twelve apostles.

Apocalypse 21, 1–14

The Lover rose early and went to seek his Beloved. He found travellers on the road, and he asked if they had seen his Beloved. They answered him: "When did the eyes of thy mind lose sight of thy Beloved?" The Lover replied: "Since I first saw my Beloved in my thoughts, He has never been absent from the eyes of my body, for all things that I see picture to me my Beloved."

The bird sang in the garden of the Beloved. The Lover came and he said to the bird: "If we understand not one another's speech, we may make ourselves understood by love; for in thy song I see my Beloved before mine eyes."

Whether Lover and Beloved are near or far is all one; for their love mingles as water mingles with wine. They are linked as heat with light; they approach and are united as Essence and Being.

Ramon Lull

Love is chaste when we are devoted to God Himself, and have ceased to cherish those things He lets us taste through our senses. We follow Him, but not that we may have more loaves.

Fénelon

DESCRIPTION OF HIS OWN MYSTICAL EXPERIENCES

But bear now with my foolishness for a little. I wish to tell you, as I have promised, how such events have taken place in me. It is indeed a matter of no importance. But I put myself forward only that I may be of service to you, and if you derive any benefit, I am consoled for my egotism; if not, I shall have displayed my foolishness. I confess, then, though I say it in my foolishness, that the Word has visited me, and even very often. But although He has frequently entered into my soul, I have never at any time been sensible of the precise moment of His coming. I have felt that He was present; I remember that He has been with me; I have sometimes been able even to have a presentiment that He would come; but never to feel His coming or His departure. For whence He came to enter my soul, or whither He went on quitting it, by what means He has made entrance or departure, I confess that I know not even to this day . . . It is not by the eyes that He enters, for He is without colour; nor by the ears, for His coming is without sound; nor by the nostrils, for it is not with the air but with the mind that He is blended; nor again does He enter by the mouth, not being of a nature to be eaten or drunk; nor lastly is He capable of being traced by the touch, for He is intangible.

You will ask, then, how, since the ways of His access are thus incapable of being traced, I could know that He was present. But He is living and full of energy, and as soon as He has entered into me He has quickened my sleeping soul, has aroused and softened and goaded my heart, which was in a state of torpor and hard as stone. He has begun to pluck up and destroy, to plant and to build, to water the dry places, to illuminate the gloomy spots, to throw open those which were shut close, to inflame with warmth those which were cold, as also to straighten its crooked paths and make its rough places smooth, so that my soul might bless the Lord and all that is within me praise His Holy Name. Thus, then, the Bridegroom-Word, though He has several times entered into me, has never made His coming apparent to my sight, hearing, or touch. It was not by His motions that He was recognised by me, nor could I tell by any of my senses that He had penetrated to the depths of my being. It was, as I have already said, only by the movement of my heart that I was enabled to recognise His presence, and to know the might of His power by the sudden departure of vices and the strong restraint put upon all carnal affections. From the discovery and conviction of my secret faults I have had good reason to admire the depths of His wisdom; His goodness and kindness have become known in the amendment, whatever it may amount to, of my life; while in the renewal of the spirit of my mind, that is, of my inward man, I have perceived in some degree the loveliness of His beauty, and have been filled with amazement at the multitude of His greatness, as I meditated upon all these things.

But when the Word withdrew Himself, all these spiritual powers and faculties began to droop and languish, as if the fire had been withdrawn from a bubbling pot; and this is to me the sign of His departure. Then my soul is necessarily sad and depressed until He shall return and my heart grow warm within me, as it is wont, which indeed is the indication to me that He has come back again.

After having, then, such an experience of the Word, what wonder that I should adopt for my own the language of the Bride, who recalls Him when He has departed, since I am influenced by a desire, not indeed as powerful, but at least similar to hers. As long as I live that utterance shall be in my mind, and I will employ, for the recalling of the Word, that word of recall which I find here in the word "Return." And as often as He shall leave me, so often shall He be called back by my voice; nor will I cease to send my cries, as it were, after Him as He departs, expressing the ardent desire of my heart that He should return, that He should restore to me the joy of His salvation, restore to me Himself. I confess to you, my sons, that I take pleasure in nothing else in the meantime, until He is present who is alone pleasing to me.

Saint Bernard

A PERUVIAN SAINT'S EXPERIENCE

I was suspended in quiet contemplation, like a light uniting all things, when I saw a flash of wonderful splen-

dour. In the centre of the radiance was a rainbow of lucent
reflections and colours, and over it another of equal grandeur. Above the upper arch stood the Cross, touched with
purple and stained with blood, the nailholes visible. Within
the arches shone the human form of my Lord, Christ
ʹJesus, sending out rays of glory. He generously gave me
strength to look upon His beauty, for this time I saw Him
face to face! . . .

The arches were of fugitive colours, like none I see on
earth. And looking upon my Lord in their midst I felt
inexplicable flames of glory reach the depths of my soul,
so that I could almost think myself free of the prison
of this world.

Then, in the hands of the Lord, I saw a great scales,
with balances and squadrons of angels, illustrious with fes-
tive ornament, who bowed before the Divine Majesty.
They were joined by hosts of the souls of the blessed,
who made ceremonious reverence before the Saviour, and
then drew apart. The Angels, taking the balances, began
to load afflictions, laying some upon others as if they wished
to discover exactly the severity of each one, and when
they were perplexed by this, Christ intervened and took
upon Himself the office of arbiter. He made the scales
true, and from the piles upon the balances distributed
afflictions to the souls present there, setting aside for me
a heavy portion of adversity. Afterwards, placing new
weights upon the balances, blessings were heaped upon
blessings, and as the angels leaned to read the weight
Christ intervened again, His omnipotent arm alone being
equal to the task. He marked it exactly, and with great
attention divided among the souls as many blessings as He
had given them afflictions. To your handmaid He distributed inestimable riches. This done, the Saviour raised His
voice and said with majesty: "Know that the grace cor-
responds to tribulation. This is the one true Scales of Paradise." And when I heard Him speak I longed to rush out
into the plaza and tell all people the truth. My soul almost
left my body in its eager ardour, feeling that it could better

travel through every land on its mission alone. For no one
would cry out against his heavy cross if he knew the balances on which it has been weighed.

Saint Rose of Lima

SIX SONGS OF LOVE

THE TREASURE OF THE SOUL

Our Lord in the kingdom of heaven
Extols the soul that loves Him in the kingdom of earth,
And says: Behold! She who has wounded me
Is coming, she ascends!
She comes like a hunted stag
To the fount that is I.
She comes like an eagle soaring
From the depths to the height.
"Love quickens you and goads your wing,
My queen, what is it that you bring?"

> Lord, I bring you my treasure
> That is greater than mountains,
> That is wider than the world,
> Deeper than the sea,
> Higher than the clouds,
> Fairer than the sun,
> More manifold than the stars.
> It weighs heavier than all the earth.

"O image of my godhood,
  Honoured by my humanhood,
  Adorned with my holy spirit,
  What is the name of your treasure?"

> Lord, it is called my heart's delight,
> That I withheld from the world,

That I kept within myself
And denied to all creatures.
Now I can carry it no further.
Lord, where shall I lay it down?

"Nowhere shall you lay down your heart's delight
 But in my godly heart,
 And on my human breast.
 There shall my spirit kiss you,
 There only you shall rest."

GOD AND THE SOUL HOLD CONVERSE

O Emperor of all honours! O Crown of all princes!
O Wisdom of all masters! O Giver of all gifts!
O Deliverer from all bondage!

     "I come to my beloved
      As the dew to the flower."

What joyful vision! What lovely greeting!
What rapturous embrace!
Lord! your wonders have wounded me,
Your mercy has mowed me down.
O towering rock, so well and firmly wrought
That none may rest in you
Save dove and nightingale.

     "Welcome, sweet dove,
      You flew so high on earth
      That your wings are grown
      In the kingdom of heaven.
      Your savour is that of grapes,
      Your scent is that of balsam,
      Your radiance is like the sun,
      You are the waxing of my highest love."

O God who gushes His gifts!
O God who laves with his Love!

O God who sears with desire!
O God who melts in the fusion with His body!
O God who rests on my breast, I cannot breathe without
    you!

    "O beautiful rose among thorns!
      O bee that flew to the honey!
      O dove whose day is serene!
      O sun with beautiful sheen!
      O moon in the fulness of light!
      I cannot turn from you.
      You are my bed,
      My most secret rest,
      My want that grew and grew.
      My highest honour.
      You are the joy of my godhood,
      The solace of my humanhood,
      A river for my blaze."

You are my mountain of mirrors, the feast of my eyes,
The loss of myself, a tempest in my heart,
The fall and failing of my strength,
My greatest surety.

YEARNING FOR HOME

    Sick with love, with ailing heart,
    Pain, duress and bitter smart—
    Kept me all too long apart
    From my dearest Lord!
    How shall I do so long without you, Love?
    Ah! too far from you I grieve,
    Should you not receive
    My lament, O Lord, then I
    Must return to mourn and sigh,
    And wait and suffer, openly and veiled.
    For you, dear Lord, know very well
    How much with you I yearn to dwell.

LOVE'S LONGING

O could I die of love!
I would that this might be,
I saw the One I love,
With eyes that learned to see.
I saw within my soul
That He was waiting there,
A bride who welcomed her Beloved
Need never seek elsewhere.

THE POWER OF LONGING

Ah! Lord, if only once
It happened on a day
That to my heart's desire
I look on you, and lay
My arms around you lovingly,
The rapture of your holy love
Would flood my soul with ecstasy,
That men have known upon their earthly way!
And I would suffer after this
More than the tongues of men can ever say.
A thousand deaths would be too light,
I yearn for you so greatly, Lord!
And wait for you so faithfully.
If you will suffer me, O Lord,
I shall pursue and seek you long, in agony.
For well I know: You, Lord, must be
The first to feel a want of me.

THE PAIN OF LOVE

O noble eagle! O sweet lamb!
O blaze of fire, kindle me!
How long shall I be cold and stark?
One hour is too long for me.

One day is like a thousand years.
If you should be remote from me
No more than a week and a day,
In Hell I should prefer to stay,
Where I already am
When God is alien to the loving soul.
That is pain beyond death,
And pain beyond all pain.
Believe me! Must the nightingale
Not sing her song
When Nature tells her loving tale?
To bid her hush were death indeed.
Ah! mighty Lord, have pity on my need!

Mechtild of Magdeburg

THE KNIGHT AND HIS CELESTIAL LADY

O Holy Virgin,
Keep my heart as that of a child,
Pure, fresh, and wide and glad,
Transparent as a spring.
Give me a simple heart,
That does not savour sadness,
A heart that glories when it gives itself,
A heart aware of frailty
And open to compassion,
A faithful and a generous heart
That remembers every benefit
And does not cherish rancour for a hurt.
Grant me a tender, humble heart,
That loves and asks for no return,
Happy to efface itself in another heart,
In the presence of your divine Son,
A heart great and indomitable,
That no ingratitude can lock,
And no indifference render slack,

A heart tormented with the glory of Jesus Christ,
And wounded by His love,
A wound that only shall be healed in heaven.

Father Léonce de Grandmaison

LOVING MADNESS

She was filled with perpetual fervour. Her heart melted,
she thought incessantly of God, she spoke incessantly of
God, and she wrought for God incessantly. Often it
seemed as though she had lost her senses and were entirely within God. At times her inner fire was so great
that she could not contain it within her breast: it flamed
in her face and poured into her actions and words. She,
who as a result of penance performed, usually looked
weak and feeble, pale and emaciated, grew strong when
these flames of love overwhelmed her. Her face became
rounder and fervent, her eyes were like two shining stars,
and her gaze was serene and joyful like that of a blessed
angel. Then she was restless and could not be still. To
pour out this fervour that she could no longer contain, she
was forced to bestir herself and she was strangely impelled
to move about. And so, at such times, one saw her moving quickly from place to place. She ran through the convent as if crazed with love, and cried in a loud voice:
"Love, love, love!" And since she could not endure this
conflagration of love, she said: "O Lord! No more love,
no more love!" . . . And she said to the sisters that followed her: "You do not know, beloved sisters, that my
Jesus is nothing but love, yes, mad with love. You are
mad with love, my Jesus, as I have said and as I shall always say. You are very lovely and joyous, you refresh and
solace, you nourish and unite. You are both pain and slak-
ing, toil and rest, life and death in one. Is there anything
that is not within you! You are wise and wilful, lofty and
unmeasurable, miraculous and unutterable." At other times

she was consumed with desire that this loving God might be known and adored by men, and turning her face to heaven, she said: "O Love, O Love, give me so strong a voice, O Lord, that when I call you love, I may be heard from East to West, and in all parts of the world, and even down to Hell, so that you may be known and adored as the true Love. O Love, you suffuse and transfix, you rend and bind, you govern all things, you are heaven and earth, fire and air, blood and water. You are both God and man."

Once she stripped an image of Jesus of its adornments and said: "For me you shall be naked, O my Jesus, for I cannot endure your boundless virtues and perfections. I want your naked, naked humanhood."

Saint Maria Maddalena de' Pazzi

CONSECRATION OF VIRGINS

As martyrdom, so is virginity a state of perfection in the mystical Body of Christ, the Church. Women who elect to enter this state of spiritual wedlock to the divine spouse, representing the Church and all mankind, betrothed to the Bridegroom on the Feast of the Epiphany—Hodie Caelesti Sponso iuncta est Ecclesia—are consecrated by the high priest, the bishop. Their veils, their rings and their wreaths are blessed. The bishop chants a solemn hymn of consecration, a preface:

Lord, through the gift of Thy spirit let there be in these (Thy loved ones) prudent modesty, wise kindliness, grave gentleness, chaste freedom. May they glow with love and delight in nothing apart from Thee. May they live worthily, may they desire no praise. May they glorify Thee in their holiness of body and purity of soul. May they fear Thee with love, may they serve Thee with love. Be Thou their honour, Thou their joy, Thou their will, Thou their comfort in delay; Thou their counsel in doubt; Thou their help in injury, patience in tribulation, abundance in poverty, food in famine, medicine in sickness. May they have all in Thee whom they wish to love above all. Through Thee, may they guard what they profess. The searcher of hearts delights rather in beauty of soul than of body. May they join the number of the wise maidens that they may await their heavenly spouse, their lamps burning with virtue prepared with oil, not troubled by the unexpected coming of the King, but secure, with light, and joined to the band of elect virgins. May they run joyously to meet Him; may they not be excluded with the foolish, but may they enter freely the royal gates with the wise virgins, and in the perpetual company of the Lamb may they remain pleasing, abiding in chastity. What hundredfold fruits are worthy to adorn this gift of virginity which you have made?

Then the bishop, taking his mitre, intones the schola, completing this response:

> Come, my elect,
> And I will set my throne in thee.
> Because the King has desired thy presence.
>
> Listen, daughter, and see,
> And incline thy ear
> Because the King has desired thy presence.

The nun sings:

I am a handmaid of Christ, therefore I show myself obedient in spirit.

> I have despised the kingdom of the world,
> And all the ornaments of time
> For the love of our Lord Jesus Christ:
> Whom I have seen,
> Whom I have loved,
> In whom I have believed,

In whom I have delighted,
My heart has uttered a good word.
I speak of my works to the King,
Whom I have seen,
Whom I have loved,
In whom I have believed,
In whom I have delighted.

BLESSING OF VEILS

God, the head of all the faithful and
Saviour of the whole body, bless with
Thy right hand this covering of veils
which, for Thy love and that of Thy
Mother, the most blessed Virgin Mary,
Thy handmaids are about to place
upon their heads: and with Thy
protection may they preserve in
purity of mind and body that which
is here mystically symbolised; so that
when they, thus prepared, come to
the everlasting reward of the Saints
they may deserve to enter with the prudent
virgins and Thee their leader the everlasting nuptials
of the blessed. Who livest and reignest
God for ever and ever. Amen.

The bishop veils the young nun with these words:

Receive this blessed veil by which you will learn to despise
the world and to dedicate yourselves truly, humbly, with
all your hearts for ever as spouses of Jesus Christ who will
defend you from evil and lead you to eternal life. Amen.

The nun answers:

He has placed His seal upon me that I may prefer no love
to Him.

This being done, they are led back by their superior to their places and two others, following in order, are presented to the bishop. They genuflect, chant and receive the veils as the first. All having been so clothed, the bishop, likewise putting down his mitre and standing before them, says:

Lord, may Thy devoted care guard Thy family that the holy virginity which through Thy inspiration they have assumed they may by Thy protection preserve.

The bishop, taking his mitre, intones the antiphon which the schola continues:

> Be betrothed, beloved, come;
> The winter has passed;
> The turtle dove sings;
> The vineyards burst into blossom.

When this is begun the bishop, with his mitre, seats himself. At the conclusion those who have received the veil are presented in order to him by their superior.

BLESSING OF RINGS

> Creator and preserver of the human race,
> giver of spiritual gifts and dispenser
> of human welfare; Thou, Lord, bestow
> Thy blessing upon these rings, that
> those who wear them, fortified by
> heavenly virtues, may preserve their
> perfect faith and sincere fidelity
> so that, brides of Christ, they may
> guard the intention of virginity which
> they have in mind and persevere
> in perpetual chastity. Through Christ
> our Lord. Amen.

The bishop takes the ring in his right hand and the right hand of the novice in his left hand. Putting the ring on the ring finger of the novice's right hand, he weds her to Jesus Christ, saying to each in turn:

I betroth you to Jesus Christ, Son of the Most High Father, who will keep you unharmed. Therefore receive this ring in token, this mark of the Holy Spirit that you shall be called the bride of God and if you serve Him faithfully you shall be crowned for all eternity.

> I am betrothed to Him
> Whom angels serve,
> Whose beauty amazes
> Sun and moon.

This having been sung, they are led back by their superior to their places. They genuflect together and extend their right hands, singing this antiphon:

> With His own ring my Lord Jesus Christ
> Has wed me
> And crowned me
> With a crown as His bride.

Then the bishop, with mitre likewise and standing before them, says:

May the maker of heaven and earth bless you, God the Father Almighty who deigned to choose you for the companionship of the Blessed Mary Mother of our Lord Jesus Christ so that you may preserve inviolate and unstained the virginity which you have professed before God and His angels: that you may keep your troth, that you may preserve patience so that you may merit to receive the crown of virginity.

> Come bride of Christ
> Receive the crown

Which the Lord has prepared
In eternity for you.

*The bishop, with mitre, is seated during this antiphon.
Two brides are presented to him with bridesmaids. They
genuflect. He, taking a crown or wreath, places it upon
the head of each bride in turn, saying:*

Receive this crown of virginal excellence so that as you
are crowned by our hands on earth you may deserve to
be crowned by Christ in honour and glory in heaven.

They chant two by two:

The robe with which the Lord has clothed me
Is a robe of splendour with gold interwoven,
And the necklace with which He has adorned me
Is beyond all price.

*They genuflect together and extend their right hands, sing-
ing this antiphon.*

Roman Pontifical

SPIRITUAL WEDLOCK

I saw how Jesus united with His bride in closest embrace. He laid His head over the head of His bride, His
eyes upon her eyes, His mouth upon her mouth, His feet
upon her feet, all His members upon hers so that His bride
became one with Him and wanted all her Bridegroom
wanted, saw all that her Bridegroom saw, and savoured
all that her Bridegroom savoured. And God wants nothing but that the soul unite with Him in such wise, and
that He may be utterly united with her. And when the
soul leans her head against the head of Jesus, she has no
other desire save to unite with God, and to have God unite
with her. God sees Himself in Himself alone and draws

His power from Himself alone, and He sees Himself in all His creatures, even in those that have no sensation, and in them He feels Himself through the power with which He gives them their being, and causes them to be of use and to bear fruit. Thus, when the eyes of the soul are upon those of Jesus, she beholds herself in God and God in all things.

After holy communion, I reflected upon the great union of the soul with God through the sacrament, and for an instant I felt wholly united with God, changed into God, and beyond all bodily sensation, so that had I been cast into a fiery oven and burned, I should have felt nothing at all. I did not know whether I was dead or alive, whether I was in the flesh or in the spirit, whether I was upon earth or in heaven. I only saw the whole glory of God, God in Himself. I only saw Him love Himself with pure love, recognise Himself in His boundlessness, embrace all things created with pure and boundless love. I saw One in Three, an undivided Trinity, a God infinite in love, supreme in goodness, unfathomable and impenetrable. And I was with Him and knew nothing of myself. I only saw that I was in God, but I did not see myself—only God!

Saint Maria Maddalena de' Pazzi

MYSTICAL MARRIAGE

The return of the soul is its conversion, that is, its turning to the Word to be reformed by Him and to be rendered conformable to Him. In what respect? In charity. It is that conformity which makes, as it were, a marriage between the soul and the Word when, being already like unto Him by its nature, it endeavours to show itself like unto Him by its will, and loves Him as it is loved by Him. And if this love is perfected the soul is wedded to the Word. What can be more full of happiness and joy than this conformity? What more to be desired than this love, which makes thee, O soul, no longer content with human guidance, to draw near with confidence thyself to the Word, to attach thyself with constancy to Him, to address Him familiarly and consult Him upon all subjects, to become as receptive in thy intelligence as fearless in thy desires? This is the contract of a marriage truly spiritual and sacred. And to say this is to say little: it is more than a contract, it is embracement. Embracement, surely, in which perfect correspondence of wills makes of two one spirit. Nor is it to be feared that the inequality of the two who are parties to it should render imperfect or halting in any respect this concurrence of wills; for love knows not reverence. Love receives its name from loving, not from honouring. Let one who is struck with dread, with astonishment, with fear, with admiration rest satisfied with honouring; but all these feelings are absent in him who loves. Love is filled with itself, and where love has come it overcomes and transforms all other feelings. Wherefore the soul that loves, loves, and knows naught else. He who justly deserves to be honoured justly deserves to be admired and wondered at; yet He loves rather to be loved. They are Bridegroom and Bride. What other bond or constraining force do you seek for between spouses than to be loved and to love? . . . God says: If I be Father, where is My honour? He says that as a Father. But if He declares Himself to be a Bridegroom, where is My love? For He had previously said: If I be Lord, where is My fear? God, then, requires that He should be feared as Lord, honoured as Father, but as Bridegroom loved. Which of these three is highest and most to be preferred? Surely it is love. Without it fear is painful and honour without attraction. . . . Neither of these will He receive if it be not seasoned with the honey of love. Love is sufficient by itself, it pleases by itself, and for its own sake. It is itself a merit, and itself its own recompense. Love seeks neither cause nor fruit beyond itself. Its fruit is its use. I love be-

cause I love; I love that I may love. Love, then, is a great
reality. It is the only one of all the movements, feelings,
and affections of the soul in which the creature is able to
respond to its Creator, though not upon equal terms, and
to repay like with like. For example, if God is wroth with
me, may I be similarly wroth with Him? Certainly not,
but I shall fear and tremble and implore pardon . . . But
how different is it with love! For when God loves, He
desires naught else than to be loved, because He loves
us for no other purpose than that He may be loved, knowing that those who love Him become blessed by their
love itself . . . Love that is pure is not mercenary; it does
not draw strength from hope, nor is it weakened by dis-
trust. This is the love of the Bride, because all that she is
is only love. The very being of the Bride and her only
hope is love. In this the Bride abounds; with this the
Bridegroom is content. He seeks for nothing else; she has
nothing else. Thence it is that He is Bridegroom and she
is Bride. This belongs exclusively to a wedded pair, and
to it none other attains, not even a son. The Bridegroom's
love, or rather the Bridegroom who is Love, requires
only love in return and faithfulness. Let it then be permitted to the Bride beloved to love in return. How could
the Bride not love, she who is the Bride of Love? How
could Love not be loved?

Rightly, then, does she renounce all other affections
and devote her whole self to Him alone who is Love, because she can make a return to Him by a love which is
reciprocal. For even when she has poured her whole self
forth in love, what would that be in comparison to the
ever-flowing Flood of that Fountain? Not with equal fulness flows the stream of love from the soul and the Word,
the Bride, and the Bridegroom, the creature and the Creator. What then? Shall the desire of her who is espoused
perish and become of none effect, because she is unable
to contend with a Giant who runs His course, to dispute
the palm of sweetness with honey, of gentleness with the

lamb, of brilliance with the sun, of love with Him who is Love? No. For although, being a creature, she loves less, because she is less; nevertheless, if she loves with her whole self nothing is wanting where all is given. Wherefore, as I have said, to love thus is to be wedded; because it is not possible to love thus and yet not to be greatly loved, and in the consent of the two parties consists a full and perfect marriage. Can anyone doubt that the soul is first loved by the Word, and more dearly? Assuredly it is both anticipated in loving and surpassed. Happy the soul whose favoured lot it is to be presented with the benediction of a delight so great. Happy the soul to which is granted the experience, the embracement of such sweetness, which is naught else than a love holy and chaste; a love sweet and delightful; a love as serene as it is sincere; a love mutual, intimate, powerful, which not in one flesh, but in one spirit joins together two, and makes them no more two, but one, according to St. Paul: "He that is joined to God is one spirit."

Saint Bernard

ECSTASIS: WORDS NO MAN CAN UTTER

If we are to boast (although boasting is out of place), I will go on to the visions and revelations the Lord has granted me. There is a man I know who was carried out of himself in Christ, fourteen years since; was his spirit in his body? I cannot tell. Was it apart from his body? I cannot tell; God knows. This man, at least, was carried up into the third heaven. I can only tell you that this man, with his spirit in his body, or with his spirit apart from his body, God knows which, not I, was carried up into Paradise, and heard mysteries which man is not allowed to utter. That is the man about whom I will boast; I will not boast about myself, except to tell you of my humiliations.

II Corinthians 12, 1–5

With Christ I hang upon the cross, and yet I am alive; or rather, not I; it is Christ that lives in me. True, I am living, here and now, this mortal life; but my real life is the faith I have in the Son of God, who loved me, and gave himself for me.

Galatians 2, 19–20

Saul, with every breath he drew, still threatened the disciples of the Lord with massacre; and now he went to the high priest and asked him for letters of commendation to the synagogues at Damascus, so that he could arrest all those he found there, men and women, who belonged to the way, and bring them back to Jerusalem. Then, on his journey, when he was nearly at Damascus, a light from heaven shown suddenly about him. He fell to the ground, and heard a voice saying to him, Saul, Saul, why dost thou persecute me? Who art thou, Lord? he asked. And he said, I am Jesus, whom Saul persecutes. This is a thankless task of thine, kicking against the goad. And he, dazed and trembling, asked, Lord, what wilt thou have me do? Then the Lord said to him, Rise up, and go into the city, and there thou shalt be told what thy work is. His companions stood in bewilderment, hearing the voice speak, but not seeing anyone. When he rose from the ground he could see nothing, although his eyes were open, and they had to lead him by the hand, to take him into Damascus. Here for three days he remained without sight, and neither ate nor drank.

Acts 9, 1–9

And there, on the Lord's day, I fell into a trance, and heard behind me a voice, loud as the call of a trumpet, which said, Write down all thou seest in a book, and send it to the seven churches in Asia, to Ephesus, and Smyrna, and Pergamum, and Thyatira, and Sardis, and Philadelphia, and Laodicea. So I turned, to see what voice it was that was speaking to me. And as I turned, I saw seven golden candlesticks, and in the midst of these seven golden candlesticks one who seemed like a son of man, clothed in a long garment, with a golden girdle about his breast. The hair on his head was like wool snow-white, and his eyes like flaming fire, his feet like orichalc melted in the crucible, and his voice like the sound of water in deep flood. In his right hand were seven stars; from his mouth came a sword sharpened at both its edges; and his face was like the sun when it shines at its full strength. At the sight of him, I fell down at his feet like a dead man; and he, laying his right hand on me, spoke thus: Do not be afraid; I am before all, I am at the end of all, and I live.

I, who underwent death, am alive, as thou seest, to endless ages, and I hold the keys of death and hell.

Apocalypse 1, 10–18

Jesus is honey in the mouth, music in the ear, a shout
of gladness in the heart.

Saint Bernard

ECSTASY

I may, then, without any absurdity, call the ecstasy of
the Bride a death, but one which delivers her not from
life, but from the snares of life. For in this life we proceed in the midst of snares; which, however, are not
feared as often as the soul, by some holy and vehement
thought, is carried away out of itself, provided that it so
far departs in mind and flies away that it transcends its
usual way of thought. For how should impurity be feared
where there is non-consciousness of life? For when the soul
is transported, though not from life, yet from consciousness of life, the temptations of life cannot be felt. It is a
good death which does not take away life, but changes it
into something better by which the body does not fall, but
the soul is elevated.

This is a death which is the lot of men. But may my
soul die the death also, if I may so speak, of the angels;
that, departing from the memory of things present, it may
divest itself not only of the desires but of the images of
things below and corporeal, and may have pure commerce with those with whom is the image of purity. Such
transport alone, or in the highest degree, is named contemplation. For while alive not to be held by the desire
of things is the part of human virtue; but in the processes
of thought, not to be enveloped by the images of bodies
is the part of angelic purity. But both are by divine gift,
both are "to be transported," both are to transcend your-

self; but one a long way, the other not long. You have not yet gone a long way unless you are able by purity of mind to fly over the phantasmata of corporeal images that rush in from all sides. Unless you have attained to this, do not promise yourself rest. You are mistaken if you think that short of this you will find a place of quiet, secret solitude, serene light, a dwelling of peace. But show me him who has arrived thither, and I will straightway confess that he is enjoying rest. This place is truly in solitude, this dwelling is in the light. Suppose, therefore, that the Bride has withdrawn into this solitude, and there through the delightfulness of the place has sweetly gone to sleep in the embrace of the Bridegroom, that is to say, has been transported in spirit as in an ecstasy, . . . as often as the Bride is transported in contemplation, so often is she associated with the august company of the blessed spirits.

Saint Bernard

MEMORIAL

In the year of grace 1654
Monday, 23 November, the day of St. Clement,
Pope and Martyr, and others in the Roman Martyrology,
the eve of St. Chrysogonus, Martyr, and others, etc. . . .
From about half-past ten in the evening
Till about half an hour after midnight

FIRE

God of Abraham. God of Isaac. God of Jacob
not of the philosophers and the learned.
Certitude joy certitude emotion sight joy
GOD OF JESUS CHRIST
Deum meum et Deum vestrum.
Thy God shall be my God.
Forgetfulness of the world and of everything other than
    GOD

He can be found only in the ways taught
in the Gospel. *Greatness* of the human soul.
Good Father, the world has not known
Thee, but I have known Thee.
Joy Joy Joy and tears of joy
I have separated myself from Thee
Dereliquerunt me fontem
my God wilt Thou leave me
let me not be eternally separated from Thee
They have life eternal, they that know Thee
Sole true God and He Whom Thou hast sent
JESUS CHRIST
JESUS CHRIST
I have separated myself from Him I have fled renounced
crucified Him

Pascal

ECSTASY

Accidentally casting my bodily eye upon a crucifix, my soul was so suddenly and sharply touched that I could no longer even look upon it outwardly, but beheld it interiorly. I was amazed to see the Second Person of the Most Holy Trinity served in this wise for my sins and those of mankind. It would be quite impossible for me to describe what passed within, particularly the excellence and dignity of this Second Person. This realisation was so vivid and so clear that she could not comprehend how, having many other means to redeem the world, He had deigned to abase aught so worthy and precious; till it pleased the same Lord to comfort the anguish in which I fell (and I believe that, if it had lasted longer, I could not have borne it) by enlightening me so efficaciously and clearly that I could no longer doubt that it was He Himself who dawned through these shadows of death, teaching me as a good father would his child or a master his disciple.

What is inward experience cannot be spoken or expressed.
I remember well that my soul admired His Wisdom, His
goodness, and particularly the excess of His love towards
mankind.

Madame Acarie

JOINED TO GOD IN THE DIVINE LIGHT

It is a great thing, an exceeding great thing, in the time
of this exile to be joined to God in the divine light by a
mystical and denuded union. This takes place where a
pure, humble, and resigned soul, burning with ardent
love, is carried above itself by the grace of God, and
through the brilliancy of the divine light shining on the
mind it loses all consideration and distinction of things,
and lays aside all, even the most excellent images, and
liquefied by love, and, as it were, reduced to nothing, it
melts away into God. It is then united to God without
any medium and becomes one spirit with Him, and is
transformed and changed into Him, as iron placed in the
fire is changed into fire, without ceasing to be iron. It becomes one with God, yet not so as to be of the same substance and nature as God . . . In the faculty of intellect
it perceives the surpassing illumination of the Sun of Justice, and learns divine truth; and in the faculty of love it
feels a certain glow of quiet love, or contact of the Holy
Spirit, like a living fountain, flowing with streams of
eternal sweetness; and thus it is introduced into sublime
union with God. The soul, having entered the vast
solitude of the Godhead, happily loses itself; and enlightened by the brightness of most lucid darkness, becomes
through knowledge as if without knowledge, and dwells
in a sort of wise ignorance. And although it knows not
what God is, to whom it is united by pure charity, although it sees not God as He is in His glory, it yet learns
by experience that He infinitely transcends all sensible
things, and all that can be apprehended by the human

intellect concerning Him. It knows God by this intimate embrace and contact better than the eyes of the body know the visible sun. This soul well knows what true contemplation is.

. . . When through love the soul goes beyond all working of the intellect and all images in the mind, and is rapt above itself, utterly leaving itself, it flows into God: then is God its peace and fulness. It loses itself in the infinite solitude and darkness of the Godhead; but so to lose itself is rather to find itself. The soul is, as it were, all God-coloured, because its essence is bathed in the Essence of God.

Louis de Blois

AS WOOD IN A FIRE

And if in Words or by outward demonstrations the delight of the soul may be described, all these words that signify the greatest possible delight may be used, for all of them describe it. From the smallest beginning it increases, little by little, and as the breath of fruition ever gathers in strength, the soul, like a ship with sails full spread, sails upon a sea of sweetness, till at last it is consumed in flames of fire most wondrously sweet, through the operation of the hidden sparks which in the beginning it received within itself.

Luis de Leon

HE AND I ARE ONE

We are the members of Christ, and Christ is our member. And my hand, the hand of one who is poorest of the poor, is Christ, and my foot is Christ. And I, the poorest of the poor, am the hand of Christ and the foot of Christ. I move my hand, and Christ moves, who is my hand. For you must know that divinity is undivided. I move my foot and my foot shines as He shines. Do not say that this is blasphemy, but confirm this, and adore Christ who has made you in this way. For you also, if such is your desire, will become one of His members. And so all the members of each one of us will become the members of Christ, and Christ our member, and He will make all that is ugly and ill-shapen, beautiful and well-shapen, in that He adorns it with the splendour and majesty of His Godhood. And we shall all become gods and intimately united with God, and our bodies will seem to us immaculate, and since we have partaken of the semblance of the whole body of Christ, each one of us shall possess all of Christ. For the One who has become many remains the One undivided, but each part is all of Christ.

Although the many cannot grasp you, verily, in some way you become small within my hands, and you lean down to my lips giving forth light like a shining udder and a sweetness of what is secret. And now give yourself to me that I may allay my hunger with you, that I kiss and clasp your unutterable glory, the light of your countenance, that I be filled, and may communicate to all others, and, when I have departed this life, I may enter into you in glory. May I become light of your light, and stand beside you and be free from care and affliction; liberate me also from the fear that I may not return to you. Give me this also, Lord, grant me this also, since you have given me, who am unworthy, all else. For this is the most needful, and in this is all. For though I behold you now, though now you take pity upon me, though now you illumine me and give me mystic teachings, and watch over me and protect me with your mighty hand, and succour me and drive the demons into flight and destroy them, and make all subject to me and proffer me all and fill me with all that is good—O God, I shall have no gain from all of this if you do not permit me to cross the threshold of death unashamed; if the prince of darkness, approaching me, does not behold your glory shed around me and is annihilated, he, the dark one, consumed by your unconquerable light, and with him all the hostile powers behold the symbols in the seal and are driven to flight, but I, trusting in your mercy and unafraid, cross the threshold and approach you and fall on my knees before you. What fruit shall I have of what befalls me now? Verily, none, but it will fan the fire that is within me still more.

Again I saw Him in my house. Among all those everyday things He appeared unexpectedly and became unutterably united and merged with me, and leaped over to me without anything in between, as fire to iron, as the light to glass. And He made me like fire and like light. And I became that which I saw before and beheld from afar. I do not know how to relate this miracle to you. And I could not understand and even now I do not entirely understand how He entered into me and how He was united with me. But now that I am united with Him, how can I tell you who He is, who has united with me and with whom I, in turn, am united? I fear that if I related it to you, you would not believe it and, falling from ignorance into blasphemy, my brother, you might lose your soul. He, with whom I am united, and I have become one. But how shall I call myself who was united with Him? God, who is twofold in nature and one in essence, made me also twofold, and endowed me with a twofold name. This is the distinction: I am man by nature, and God by the grace of God.

Again the light shines upon me. Again it flings wide the heavens, again it drives away the night. Again it reveals all things. Again I behold it alone. Again it leads me away from all that is visible, from all that is accessible to the senses, and tears me away from them. And He, who is above heaven, whom none has ever beheld, He again enters my spirit without leaving the heavens, without dividing the night, without bruising the air, without shattering the roof of the house, without breaking through anything, and light pours into the middle of my heart, although it remains as it was, O holy secret, and the light lifts me above everything. And I, who was in the midst of

all things, am outside of them, and I do not even know
if I am outside of my body. And now, verily, I am in that
place where there is only light, and where the light is simple, and in beholding it, I emerge in simplicity and
innocence.

Symeon the Younger

LANGUAGE FAILS

I see without sight, I understand without intelligence,
I feel without feeling, I taste without taste; I know neither
shape nor dimension, yet without seeing, I see so divine
a preparation that all words concerning perfection, cleanness or purity which I uttered before now seem to me
to be naught but mockery and fable in comparison with
this truth and honesty. The sun which had appeared bright
to me before now seems dark. That which seemed sweet
now seems bitter, because all sweetness and beauty become spoilt and corrupt by contact with creatures. Afterwards, when the creature is purged, purified, and transformed in God, then is seen that which is pure and true;
and this vision which strictly speaking is not seen, can
neither be thought nor spoken of.

Saint Catherine of Genoa

PRAYING IN A TRANSPORT OF MIND

. . . But how and in what way those very convictions
are produced from the inmost recesses of the soul it is no
less difficult to trace out. For often through some inexpressible delight and keenness of spirit the fruit of a most
salutary conviction arises so that it actually breaks forth
into shouts owing to the greatness of its uncontrollable
joy; and the delight of the heart and greatness of exulta-
tion make themselves heard even in the cell of a neighbour. But sometimes the mind hides itself in complete

silence within the secrets of profound quiet, so that the amazement of a sudden illumination chokes all sounds of words and the overawed spirit either keeps all its feelings to itself or loses them and pours forth its desires to God with groanings that cannot be uttered. But sometimes it is filled with such overwhelming conviction and grief that it cannot express it except by floods of tears.

. . . And that you may see the character of true prayer I will give you not my own opinion but that of the blessed Anthony: whom we have known sometimes to have been so persistent in prayer that often as he was praying in a transport of mind, when the sunrise began to appear we have heard him in the fervour of his spirit, declaiming: Why do you hinder me, O sun, who art arising from this very purpose—to withdraw me from the brightness of this true light? And his also is this heavenly and more than human utterance on the end of prayer: That is not, said he, a perfect prayer wherein a monk understands himself and the words which he prays.

Cassian

ONE MUST HUNT DOWN ONE'S NATURE

God deigns to enter into us and grants us the favour of entering into Him by mutual immersion and reciprocal flowing together, which is expressed in Holy Scripture, when God bids us open our mouth and promises to fill it. This dilation means that the soul should enlarge the whole capacity of her free will, that is to say, should produce acts of the greatest and most whole-hearted love she can conceive. And it is not enough to open one's mouth in an ordinary way, as one does for eating, speaking and breathing; one must be like a man who, after having run long and violently after something he desperately longs to catch, stands breathless, opens his mouth and feels his heart beating, as though he were ready to die. Some open their will to God as if to eat, that is to say, as if they were to receive some inward sweetness; others as though to talk and make discourses to God; others again as if to breathe, in order to give refreshment to a spirit suffocated by this world's cares. To do this is not to love God perfectly. One must expel the life of self-will in every panting breath, one must hunt down one's nature in an implacable course towards perfection, to the end that one may exhale and infuse one's whole being, open mouthed, into the mouth of God . . . Thus the Scripture says, according to the Hebrew, that Moses died upon the mouth of God . . . O sacred resting place of happy lassitudes! O treasure of eternal repose of which our soul bears within it all the depths and breadths, since God opens Himself unto her to exactly the same extent as she is willing to open herself unto Him.

Father Joseph Le Clerc du Tremblay,
quoted by Aldous Huxley in "Grey Eminence"

SENTIMENTS OF LOVE

Our Lord told me that the voice of His love would resound in my ears like the voice of thunder. The following night, in fact, what I should describe as a storm of divine love, if this word did not signify something tumultuous, burst upon me. Its sudden impetuosity, the all-powerful way in which it took possession of my whole being, the infinitely strong and sweet embrace with which God united my soul to Him, cannot be compared with anything that takes place in the other, inferior states of union.

Inundated on all sides by the infinite Being of God, in which she feels herself plunged, the soul implores God to take pity on her weakness. As I offered this prayer, beseeching His Divine Majesty to deign to consider that there was no proportion between the vehemence of His love and the weakness of my poor heart, I felt within me a new invasion of this love; and out of the heart of these seas of celestial flame that inundated me on all sides, I heard the voice of this great God who, with the accents of an immense love, complained that men did not love Him sufficiently. I understood that it was, so to speak, a solace to His heart to discharge into my heart all this great love for mankind with which He is filled, and which our coldness condemns to do itself a perpetual violence. My God! how terrible will this love be on the Day of Judgment, when, breaking the bounds by which the divine mercy restrains it, it will fall upon those mortals who have despised it.

. . . Issuing forth from this crucible of the divine love wherein the whole being melts, so to speak, like wax in the fire, how great is the pain to the poor soul when it is forced to descend once more to the accustomed routine of this miserable life! How great the pain, especially, on seeing this divine and holy action succeeded by the warring action of the evil one! . . . Just as the soul has felt herself penetrated in all her being by the intimate operation of God, even so she sees herself exposed in her exterior being to the persecuting attack of her enemy the devil . . . When subjected to this action we no longer know where to retreat in order to evade his pursuit which seems momentarily to thrust the soul to the edge of the abyss.

Father Lyonnard

SHAPELESS BEAUTY

What I saw was without form or shape and nevertheless it was beautiful and pleasant to see. Without colour, it had the grace of all the colours. What I saw was not a Light like that of the sun or of the day, yet it shed a wonderful clarity, and from it proceeded all earthly and spiritual light. What I saw occupied no space, yet filled everything. It moved not, yet it animated and operated in all creation.

Marie Tessonier

SOBRIA EBRIETAS:
THE GREAT SILENCE

Joyful let us drink the sober drunkenness of the spirit.

Monastic Breviary

The Lord is in his holy temple: let all the earth keep silence before him.

Habacuc 2, 20

And they were all beside themselves with astonishment; Are they not all Galileans speaking? they asked. How is it that each of us hears them talking his own native tongue?

Acts 2, 7–8

So they were all beside themselves with perplexity, and asked one another, What can this mean? There were others who said, mockingly, They have had their fill of new wine.

But Peter, with the eleven apostles at his side, stood there and raised his voice to speak to them; Men of Judaea, he said, and all you who are dwelling in Jerusalem, I must tell you this; listen to what I have to say. These men are not drunk, as you suppose; it is only the third hour of the day. This is what was foretold by the prophet Joel: In the last times, God says, I will pour out my spirit upon all mankind, and your sons and daughters will be prophets. Your young men shall see visions, and your old men shall dream dreams; and I will pour out my spirit in those days upon my servants and handmaids, so that they will prophesy. I will show wonders in heaven above, and signs on the earth beneath, blood and fire and whirling smoke; the sun will be turned into darkness and the moon into blood, before the day of the Lord comes, great and glorious.

Acts 2, 12–20

The man who talks in a strange tongue is talking to God, not to men; nobody understands him, he is holding mysterious converse with his own spirit; whereas the prophet speaks to edify, to encourage, to comfort his fellow men.

I Corinthians 14, 2–3

. . . In the church, I would rather speak five words which my mind utters, for your instruction, than ten thousand in a strange tongue. Brethren, do not be content to think childish thoughts; keep the innocence of children, with the thoughts of grown men. We read in the law, I will speak to this people with an unknown tongue, with the lips of strangers, and even so they will not listen to me, says the Lord. Thus talking with a strange tongue is a sign given to unbelievers, not to the faithful; whereas prophecy is meant for the faithful, not for unbelievers. And now, what will happen if the uninstructed or the unbelievers come in when the whole church has met together, and find everyone speaking with strange tongues at once? Will they not say you are mad? Whereas, if some unbeliever or some uninstructed person comes in when all alike are prophesying, everyone will read his thoughts, everyone will scrutinise him, all that is kept hidden in his heart will be revealed; and so he will fall on his face and worship God, publicly confessing that God is indeed among you.

I Corinthians 14, 19–25

PRAISE OF GOD

O burning mountain, O chosen sun,
O perfect moon, O fathomless well,
O unattainable height, O clearness beyond measure,
O wisdom without end, O mercy without limit,
O strength beyond resistance, O crown of all majesty,
The humblest you created sings your praise.

Mechtild of Magdeburg

THE GOD OF DARKNESS

My soul was once lifted up, and I beheld God more clearly and more profoundly than ever before. And it was not love that I beheld; yes, I even lost the feeling of love and I became that which is not love.

And then I beheld Him in the midst of darkness. I say darkness because He is a treasure of such magnitude that neither reason nor thought can grasp Him, and nothing that belongs to the world of what can be thought and grasped reaches Him. Then the soul was filled with faith as firm as a rock, with nothing but strong, confident hope and nothing but steadfast certainty regarding God, so that all fear vanished. And I concentrated all my being on this treasure that is thus seen in darkness, and I was filled with the certainty of God that removes all doubt and for all time, all doubt that I truly possess God. And now my hope also is collected and strengthened in the treasure that works powerfully through darkness . . . When I behold Him, I possess all that I want to have and want to know, and I see an abundance of all riches. And it is impossible for me even to imagine that this treasure might be separated from the soul, or the soul from this treasure and all delight it accords. Rather does this treasure overwhelm the soul with unutterable ecstasy, so that it cannot express with its mouth or even grasp with the heart all it beholds.

It sees nothing and yet sees everything. And because this treasure is in darkness, we feel all the more that it is most certain and exceeding all else, and all the more so because we behold it as the most secret treasure of darkness.

And I beheld in this darkness that its treasure exceeds all other and indeed everything. Yes, everything else is darkness in its own way, and all that can be grasped with thought is less than this treasure. It is like this: when the soul beholds the power, and the wisdom, and the will of God, and all that I beheld in so unutterable and miraculous a fashion, all this is less than that most certain treasure. For this treasure that I behold is the whole, while everything else is only a part; and no matter how unutterable it may seem when we behold it, it yields bliss beyond measure, bliss that may even be of the body. But when God thus shows Himself as darkness, He works no smile upon the mouth, no glow or reverence in the heart, no leaping flame of love. The body does not tremble, it does not move or alter its condition as it is wont to do at such moments. And this is because the body does not see anything, only the soul beholds. The body rests and sleeps, and it is as if the tongue were cut off because it is incapable of uttering a single word.

Blessed Angela of Foligno

I SAW THE LORD FACE TO FACE

On the Second Sunday in Lent, as in the procession before Mass we were singing the response: Vidi Dominum facie ad faciem—I saw the Lord face to face—my soul found itself suddenly surrounded with a wondrous burst of light which was no other than that of Thy face which, according to the expression of St. Bernard, was not contained under any form, yet gave form to all else; which did not strike the eye of the body, but charmed that of the soul; which was lovable, not through the brightness of its colour, but through the gifts of its love. It is but Thou, my God, who canst know how not only my soul, but also all the powers of my heart found pleasure in this happy vision, in which the brightness of Thine eyes, like two suns, looked straight into my own . . .

When, then, as I have just said, Thou didst approach Thine adorable face, in which is found an abundant source of all joy, close to my own, so greatly unworthy to touch it, I perceived a gentle light proceeding from Thy divine eyes and passing through mine, spreading itself in every secret part of me, and seeming to fill all my members with a wonderful power and strength. At first it was as though it had dried up the marrow of my bones, and then, destroying the flesh and bones themselves, as if my whole substance were nothing else but this divine splendour which shone within it with greater allurement and beauty than is possible to tell, filling my soul with joy and incredible calmness.

Saint Gertrude of Helfta

WRESTLING WITH THE BLIND NAUGHT

And in the same manner, where another man would bid thee gather thy powers and thy wits wholly within thyself, and worship God there—although he saith full well and full truly: yea! and no man trulier if he be well conceived—yet for fear of deceit and bodily conceiving of his words, I care not bid thee do so. But thus will I bid thee. Look in nowise that thou be within thyself. And (to speak shortly) I will not that thou be without thyself, nor yet above, nor behind, nor on one side, nor on other.

"Where then," sayest thou, "shall I be? Nowhere, by thy tale!" Now truly thou sayest well; for there would I have thee. For why, nowhere bodily is everywhere ghostly. Look, then, busily that thy ghostly work be nowhere bodily; and then wheresoever that thing is on the which thou wilfully workest in thy mind in substance, surely there art thou in spirit, as verily as thy body is in that place that thou art bodily. And although thy bodily wits can find there nothing to feed them on, for they think it naught that thou dost, yea! do on then this naught, and do it for God's love. And let not therefore, but travail busily in that naught with a watchful desire to will to have God, whom no man may know. For I tell thee truly that I had rather be so nowhere bodily, wrestling with that blind naught, than to be so great a lord that I might when I would be everywhere bodily, merrily playing with all this aught as a lord with his own.

Let be this everywhere and this aught, in comparison of this nowhere and this naught. Reck thee never if thy wits cannot understand this naught; for surely I love it much the better. It is so worthy a thing in itself that they cannot understand it. This naught may better be felt than seen: for it is full blind and full dark to them that have but a little while looked thereupon. Nevertheless (if I shall trulier say), a soul is more blinded in feeling of it for abundance of ghostly light than for any darkness or wanting of bodily light. What is he that calleth it naught? Surely it is our outer man, and not our inner. Our inner man calleth it All; for by it he is well taught to understand all things bodily or ghostly, without any special beholding to any one thing by itself.

The Cloud of Unknowing

ALL IS MERGED

The faculties are there in an arrested condition, all fixed upon God, who draws them all equally to such contemplation. He it is who ravishes and absorbs them simply by the operation of His continual gaze—His gaze at the Soul and the Soul's gaze at Him. In this state there is neither creature nor created, neither knowledge nor ignorance, neither all nor nothing, neither limit nor name, nor kind, nor wonder, no difference between past, future, or even present, not even the eternal now. All is merged, confounded in that cloudy haze diffused by God, who thus has His pleasure in those souls within whom it pleases Him to work this noble operation.

Jean de Saint-Samson

GOD TOUCHES THE SOUL IMMEDIATELY

None but God alone can have access to the soul's essence. Creatures cannot have it, for they must stay outside among the soul's faculties, in which it beholds their image, and by means of which it gives them entrance. When the soul's faculties come into touch with creatures, these faculties form an image of them and present it to the soul, which in that way knows them. No deeper than this can creatures sink into the soul. Nor does the soul ever approach creatures except by willingly receiving an image of them, and by the presence of the same it is brought in contact with creatures. The soul forms the image from the thing itself by means of its own faculties; knowing, for example, and being joined to, a stone, a horse, or a man by the image thus made and perceived, the knowledge necessarily coming into the soul from outside through the senses. Hence it happens that nothing is so little known to the soul as its own real self. And hence a certain teacher says that the soul is unable to form or receive an image of its own self, for the reason that all images enter through the senses, and these cannot perceive the soul. It knows all other things, but itself it knows not. Of nothing is it so ignorant as of itself, and this is for lack of necessary intermediate image.

And be assured that when the soul is freed from all images and intermediaries, God can for that reason join it to Himself directly and without the interposition of anything whatsoever. Consider that whatever power thou dost claim for any human master, thou must own God to possess the same, and this beyond all measure. Now, the wider and mightier such a master is, the less does he need means and instruments to influence thee, and the simpler is his power. But man needs many means and instruments for his outer works, and between his planning and his performance there is much preparation. On the other hand, the moon and sun, in their masterful work of illuminating the world, need no longer than the twinkling of an eye to fill all the ends of the earth with light. And an angel needs even less means and uses fewer images; while the very highest seraph has but one single figure in which he knows and acts his part, though lesser spirits need a multiplicity of such aids. But God needs no aid of images or instruments at all, even of one. God acts upon the soul directly, without image or figure; yea, upon the soul's deepest depths, into which no image has ever penetrated, nor any being other than God's self. This no created thing can ever accomplish. God the Father thus begets His Son in the soul, and not as creatures act—by showing figure and likeness—but just as He begets Him in eternity.

And how is this Divine generation accomplished in the soul? Remember that God the Father has a knowledge of Himself which penetrates His being perfectly and without the interposition of any image; and it is thus that God the Father generates His Son in true unity of Divine nature. Now in no other manner does God the Father beget His Son in the essence and being of the soul, and in doing so unites Himself with the soul. But if in this Divine work there were any intermediary of figure or image, there could be no true and perfect union, and upon such a union depends all the soul's happiness.

But you may object that by nature the soul is ever full of images. I answer no; for if that were true the soul could never be happy, nor could God ever make a being capable of perfect bliss; nor would God be our greatest joy and last end—God, who is the beginning and the end of all. No creature can ever be the bliss of another creature, nor its perfection. The perfection of all virtue in this mortal life is followed by the perfection of immortal life hereafter, which consists in immediate union with God. If thou wouldst, therefore, enjoy here below a foretaste of thy future bliss, thou must needs retire inward and dwell in thy soul's depth and essence. There must it be that God will touch thee with His most simple being, without medium or similitude. No image is for its own sake, but only to show its original, coming from without by means of the senses acting on creatures; and as no creature can ever make us happy much less can any image of creatures.

And now let us consider our second question, namely: What shall one do to win and merit that this divine generation take place within his soul? Shall we co-operate by meditating on God, and this by means of similitudes? Or shall one rather rest in mental silence and wait for God in quiet of mind, leaving to Him alone all active working? And now let me repeat what I have said before: Such a matter as this concerns only perfect souls, who have already won to themselves, as it were essentially, all virtuous living, doing good without any effort—men who are living examples of the life and teaching of our Lord. Let such as these know that if they would be granted this divine life, their best and highest part is to be still and let God act and speak. When all the powers of a soul are withdrawn from all activity and all similitude of creatures, then in that soul shall the Divine Word be uttered (according to our text): "While all things were in quiet silence the Almighty Word leaped down from Heaven." Therefore, in proportion as thou dost earnestly gather inward all thy faculties in forgetfulness of all created things and of all their similitudes, being recollected in thyself in obliviousness of creatures, the nearer art thou to receive the generation of the Divine Word.

Blessed John Tauler

CHASTE RETIREMENT OF THE LOVING SOUL

Our Love demands one sole Infinite Object, into which it may withdraw and preserve our forces in their entirety.

Nevertheless, such acts of intellect and will dissipate these powers, and instead of bringing them into unity scatter them abroad. That is why the soul withdraws into herself, bidding reason hush, detaching herself from the elements infinite, immense, eternal, from all wisdom, might, goodness, and compassion; she, with pure and simple look, adores God.

She experiences a delicious sense of this Sovereign Goodness as though ravished by an All-Powerful transport above the world and nature; she beholds herself in the presence of an infinite and insupportable Radiance; as if exposed to an impetuous torrent of delights, as if over an abyss of favours of which she is at once in love and dread, for that she feels incapable of abandoning herself there without perishing. . . . But alas! this very dread separates her from that which she loves. This is why she speedily redoubles desire, losing and abandoning self, she resolves to cause nature to perish, by making fortunate shipwreck in the essence of life. At first the human heart, coming thus in contact with the Divine, suffers emotions like to those to be seen at the meeting of waters not yet mingling: then there is a calm, a mysterious silence, a tranquil tide of delight in which natural forces, as though absorbed in immensity, no longer retain their ordinary springs of action.

Memory finds itself deprived of all elements; judgment no longer hearkens to reason; the will alone is permitted to enter into those splendours ineffable, into those eternal pageants, there to become enriched with treasure inconceivable. At times she has share in a solemn festival, in holy tranquillity above the world's vicissitudes wherein the ordinary exercise of her forces is suspended, or again rapt in invisible fire enkindling her every enterprise. . . .

Yves of Paris

THE LOVING GAZE*

O SWEET AND DELECTABLE LIGHT

O sweet and delectable light, that is my infinite maker, enlighten the face and the vision of my inward eye with uncreated charity, and kindle my mind with Thy savour, that, thoroughly cleansed from uncleanness and made marvellous with Thy gifts, it may swiftly fly to the high mirth of love; that I may sit and rest in Thee, Jesus, rejoicing and going as it were, ravished with heavenly sweetness; and that, established in the beholding of heavenly things, I shall never be glad but in Divine things.

O Love everlasting, inflame my soul to love God, that nothing may burn in me but His embraces. O good Jesus, who shall grant me to feel Thee, who now neither may be felt nor seen? Shed Thyself into the entrails of my soul! Come into my heart and fill it with Thy most excellent sweetness. Inebriate my mind with the hot wine of Thy sweet love, that, forgetting all evils and all scornful visions and imaginations, and having Thee alone, I may be glad and rejoice in Jesus my God. Henceforward, sweetest Lord,

* This chapter is heavy with doctrine, but it is indispensable to any serious reader. While no attempt is made to give a full and systematic elaboration, nor to develop a private theory, outstanding examples have been included of the age of the Fathers, of Medieval spirituality, of the great Spanish age of classical mysticism, and of the devout mystics of France. Much of the remainder of the book should be read with this chapter as background.

The Editor

go not from me, but abide with me in Thy sweetness, for Thy presence alone is solace to me and Thine absence alone leaves me sad.

O holy Ghost, that givest grace where Thou wilt, come into me and ravish me to Thyself. The nature that Thou didst make, change with honeysweet gifts, that my soul, filled with Thy delightful joy, may despise and cast away all the things of this world, that it may receive ghostly gifts, given by Thee, and going with joyful songs into infinite light may be all melted in holy love. Burn with Thy fire my reins and my heart that on Thine altar shall burn for ever.

Come, I beseech Thee, O sweet and true Joy! Come, sweet and most desired! Come, my love, who art all my comfort! Come with mellifluous heat into a soul longing for Thee and yearning with sweetest ardour towards Thee. Kindle with Thy heat the whole of my heart, enlightening with Thy light my inmost parts; feed me with the honeysweet song of love, as much as the powers of my body and soul can endure.

Richard Rolle

FROM THE BEGINNING OF TIME

I thank You, O my light, eternal light, never failing light! You, the highest and most immutable good! I stand before You. I am Your poor and humble servant.

I thank You! Now I can see. I see the light that shines in the darkness.

And what do you see in this light?

I see how greatly You love me and that, if I remain in You, it is just as impossible that You should not love me at all times, and in all places, and in all ways, as that I should ever not love You.

And You give Yourself to me wholly, so that You are wholly and undividedly mine, as long as I am wholly and undividedly Yours. And if I am so wholly Yours, then this means that You have loved me from the beginning of time just as You have loved Yourself from the beginning of time. For this is nothing else than that You savour Yourself in me, and that through Your mercy I savour You in myself and myself in You.

And if I love myself in this wise, then I love none other than You, for You are in me and I in You like one whole and single thing that has sprung from union and cannot be divided in all eternity. And since everyone loves what is good and what is strong in the other, all this is nothing else than that You love Yourself.

But if I remain wholly and perfectly within You, I cannot perish, just as certainly as You are imperishable.

Gerlach Peters

HUMAN NATURE PURIFIED REFLECTS DIVINE NATURE

When we regard the embellishments detected in creatures, a certain notion is formed in our minds, not of the essence of the thing, but of the wisdom of Him who made all things wisely. The same is true if we consider the cause of our existence, because it was not by necessity that God was moved to create man, but by benevolent resolve. Again, in the same way we say that we see and contemplate God when we comprehend, not His nature, but His goodness. The same is true also of all other things that elevate the mind in order that it may consider what stands out by its excellence and is better and more exalted than all other things. All such we call the contemplation and knowledge of God, together with every sublime thought and consideration that brings God to our minds. Strength likewise and purity impress upon and form in our minds the vision and imagination that they belong to the same category, and that they are not mingled with the corresponding vices. The same is true of all such things in which certain divine and exalted concepts are detected. All that

I have just mentioned indicates how also our Lord told the truth when He promised that God would be seen by those who had a pure heart. Nor does St. Paul lie when he says in his Epistles that none has seen God, and that none is able to see Him. For He who is invisible by nature, while His existence is discovered through certain characteristics observed about Him, becomes visible by His causality and by His activity.

The idea of beatitude is not concerned exclusively with the fact that we are able to gather and affirm that an agent is such and such a being from his deeds and activities; after all, it is conceivable that the sages of this world may reach a grasp and understanding of divine wisdom and power by observing the organic harmony of the universe. But what is truly great in beatitude is to my mind something else, namely, the fact that it gives counsel and suggestions to those who are able to grasp and understand what is desired; furthermore, the consideration and intelligence that come to my mind through examples will also be explained by similitudes. Now, good bodily health is a boon in human life, but to possess it and not merely to know its nature is a blessing. If someone sings the praises of good health, but partakes of food that produces humours and illness, what then would be the use of the praises of good health while he is being consumed by ill health? Let us, therefore, interpret the sentence before us in the same way, because our Lord does not say that it is a blessing to know something about God, but to possess Him. Blessed are those who are endowed with a pure heart. To my mind it does not conflict with proposing to him whose mental vision has been clarified that he ought to contemplate God, which a word addressed to others expresses more clearly, namely where he says: The kingdom of God is within you, in order that we may become aware of the fact that he who has purged his heart of everything created and of every inordinate affection sees in his own beauty the image of divine nature. It seems to me that this word contains among the few things that it points out also a counsel something like this: O men, in whom there is some desire to contemplate the one true good, when you hear that divine majesty is raised and exalted above the heavens, that His glory is beyond explanation, that His beauty is unspeakable, and that His nature can neither be perceived nor comprehended, do not despair, because you are unable to see what you desire.

Saint Gregory of Nyssa

THE DEGREES OF PRAYER SEEN BY AN EARLY EASTERN SAINT

Sometimes from prayer a certain contemplation is born which makes prayer vanish from the lips. And he to whom this contemplation happens becomes as a corpse without soul, in ecstasy. This we call sight during prayer and not an image or form forged by phantasy . . . Also in this contemplation . . . there are degrees and differences in gifts. But till this point there is still prayer. For thought has not yet passed into the state where there is no prayer, but to a state superior to it. For the motions of the tongue and the heart during prayer are keys. What comes after them is the entering into the treasury. Here, then, all mouths and tongues are silent, and the heart, the treasurer of the thoughts, the mind, the governor of the senses, the daring spirit, that swift bird, and all their means and powers and the beseeching persuasions have to stand still there: for the master of the house has come.

For like as the whole force of the laws and commandments which God has laid down for mankind have their term in the purity of the heart, according to the words of the Fathers, so all kinds and habits of prayer with which mankind prays unto God have their term in pure prayer. Lamentations and self-humiliations and beseechings and inner supplications and sweet tears and all other habits which prayer possesses—as I have said—have their boundary, and the domain within which they are set into motion is pure prayer.

As soon as the spirit has crossed the boundary of pure prayer and proceeded onwards, there is neither prayer, nor emotions, nor tears, nor authority, nor freedom, nor beseechings, nor desire, nor longing after any of those things which are hoped for in this world or in the world to be.

Therefore there is no prayer beyond pure prayer, and all its emotions and habits by their authority with freedom conduct the spirit thus far and there is struggle in it; but beyond this limit it passes into ecstasy and is no longer prayer. From here onwards the spirit desists from prayer; there is sight, but the spirit does not pray.

Every kind of prayer which exists is set into motion by the impulses of the soul. But when the mind has entered the emotions of spirituality, then it can no longer pray.

Prayer is different from contemplation during prayer, though they are caused by each other. One is the seed; the other the load of the harvest borne by the hands, while the reaper is astonished by the indescribable sight of how from the mean and bare grains of seed glorious ears suddenly grow up before him. And during sight he remains without motion.

Every prayer is demand and request, or praise or thanksgiving. But judge whether there exists any of these modes, or demand of anything, when the mind has passed into this domain and has entered into this place.

I ask this of those who know the truth. It is not given to everyone to inquire into these distinctions, but only to those who have been personally witnesses and ministers of this matter or have been brought up in the presence of the spiritual authors of such experiences, and have received the truth from their mouth and have passed their days with such occupations, asking and answering concerning matters of truth. As among ten thousand men there is scarcely to be found a single one who has fulfilled the commandments and the laws to any extent and who has been deemed worthy of serenity of soul, so there is rarely to be found one among many who, on account of strenuous vigilance, has been deemed worthy of pure prayer, and who has made his way into this domain and been deemed worthy of this mystery. Not many are deemed worthy of pure prayer—only a few. But as to that mystery which lies beyond, there is scarcely to be found a single man in every generation who has drawn near to this knowledge of God's grace.

Prayer is a beseeching for, a caring for, a longing for something, either liberation from evil things here or in the world to come, or a desire for promised things, or a demand for something by which man wishes to be brought nearer unto God. In these emotions are included all habits of prayer. But its being pure or not depends upon the following circumstances: If, when the spirit is prepared to offer one of the emotions which I have enumerated, any foreign deliberation or distraction mingles itself with it, prayer is called non-pure, because it has brought upon the altar of the Lord an animal which it is not allowed to offer.

But when the spirit gives itself with longing to one of these emotions . . . at the time of the beseeching, and when on account of its alacrity the gaze of the emotion is directed by the eye of faith beyond the curtain of the heart, the entrances of the soul are closed thereby against the foreign deliberations which are called strangers whom the law does not allow to enter the tabernacle. This is called the accepted offering of the heart and pure prayer. Its boundaries are at this point. What lies beyond cannot be called prayer . . .

But sometimes they (the Holy Fathers) designate by spiritual prayer that which they sometimes call contemplation; and sometimes knowledge; and sometimes revelations of intelligible things. Dost thou see how the Fathers change their designations of spiritual things? This is because accurate designations can only be established concerning earthly things. The things of the world-to-be do not possess a true name but only cognition which is exalted above all names and signs and forms and colours and habits and composite denominations. When, therefore, the knowledge of the soul exalts itself above this circle of visible things, the Fathers use concerning this knowledge any designations they like, though no one does know the real names, in order that the psychic deliberations may be based on them. We use denominations and riddles, according to the word of the holy Dionysius, who says: We use signs and syllables, conventional names and words in behalf of the senses. But when by spiritual working our soul is moved unto divine things, then the senses and their workings are superfluous to us, as also the spiritual forces of the soul are superfluous as soon as our soul becomes the image of the Godhead through unification with the incomprehensible and radiant rays of the sublime—by those impulses which are not for the eyes . . .

As the saints in the world to come do not pray, there the mind being engulfed by the divine spirit, but they swell in ecstasy in that delightful glory, so the mind, when it has been made worthy of perceiving the future blessedness, will forget itself and all that is here, and it will not be moved any longer by the thought of anything . . .

All excellence whatever and all orders of prayer whatever, in body or in spirit, are in the realm of free will, as well as the mind that dominates the senses. But when the influence of the spirit reigns over the mind that regulates the senses and the deliberations, freedom is taken away from nature which no longer governs but is governed. And how could there be prayer at that time, when nature does not possess power over itself, but is conducted by an outward force without knowing whither? Nature, then, does not direct the emotions of the spirit according to its will, but captivity reigns over nature in that hour and conducts it there where sensual apperception ceases; because nature even has no will at that time, even to this extent that it does not know whether it is in or without the body, as Scripture testifies. Has, therefore, such a one prayer who is a captive to this degree and who even does not know himself? . . .

When there is no prayer, can then this unspeakable gift be designated by the name of prayer? The cause, as we say, is therein, that at the time of prayer this gift is granted unto those who are worthy. And in prayer it has its starting-point, because this glorious gift cannot be granted except at this time, according to the testimony of the Fathers . . .

If anyone asks: How is it that at this time only these great and unspeakable gifts are granted? we answer: Because at this time, more than in any other hour, man is concentrated and prepared to look unto God and to desire and to expect compassion from Him. In short, it is the time that the demand of him who is at the gate of the king and asks desiringly and beseechingly is likely to be heard. And what time is there when man is so cautious and fit and prepared as the time when he prays? Or should it be becoming that he should be deemed worthy of this at the time when he sleeps or settles any affair or is distracted of mind? However, the saints do not even know a time of idleness, because at all times they are occupied by spiritual things, for when they are not standing in preparation for prayer, they often meditate upon some stories of the scriptures, or their mind meditates in contemplation of the created things, or with other things meditation of which is profitable.

At the time of prayer the gaze of the spirit is exclusively fixed on God, and the tendency of its emotion is wholly directed towards Him, and it offers to Him the beseechings of the heart with the necessary zeal, with fervour and ardour. Therefore it is becoming that at this time, when a single thought dominates the soul, divine mercy should well forth from Him. For we see also that when we offer the visible sacrifice, while everyone is standing in prayer, supplicating and beseeching, the mind being concentrated upon God, the gift of the spirit descends upon the bread and wine which we lay on the altar . . .

What time is so holy and fit for sanctification and the receiving of gifts as the time of prayer, in which man speaks with God? At this time man utters his desires unto God, beseeching Him and speaking with Him, and his whole emotion and thought are concentrated from all sides upon Him with compulsion: of God alone he thinks, and Him alone he supplicates; his whole thought is absorbed in discourse with Him and his heart is full of Him. It is in this state, therefore, that the Holy Ghost joins with the things for which man prays some unattainable insights, which it stirs in him in accordance with his aptitude of being moved so that by these insights the emotion of prayer ceases, the mind is absorbed in ecstasy and the desired object of prayer is forgotten. The impulses are drowned in a heavy drunkenness and man is no longer in this world. Then there is no longer distinction of body or of soul, nor recollection of anything . . .

Prayer namely is steadfastness of mind which is terminated only by the light of the Holy Trinity through ecstasy. Thou seest how prayer is terminated when those insights which are born in the spirit from prayer pass into ecstasy, as I have said in the beginning of this treatise and in several places further on. . . .

Steadfastness of mind is highness of intelligible apperceptions which resembles the colour of the sky over which rises, at the time of prayer, the light of the Holy Trinity. When is a man deemed worthy of the whole of this grace such that during prayer he is exalted unto this height? Euagrius says: When the mind puts off the old man and puts on the new one by grace, then it also sees its steadfastness at the time of prayer, resembling sapphire or the colour of heaven, as the place of God was called by the elders of Israel, to whom it appeared on the mountain (cf. *Exodus* 24, 9–11).

So, as I have said, this gift is not to be called spiritual prayer, but what then? The fruit of pure prayer, which is engulfed in the spirit. The mind has ascended here above

prayer. And having found what is more excellent, it desists from prayer. And further there is no longer prayer,
but the gaze in ecstasy at the unattainable things which
do not belong to the world of mortals, and peace without
knowledge of any earthly thing. This is the well-known
ignorance concerning which Euagrius says: Blessed is he
who has reached, during prayer, unconsciousness which is
not to be surpassed.

Isaac of Nineveh

ADORNMENT OF SPIRITUAL MARRIAGE

The inward lover of God, who possesses God in fruitive
love, and himself in adhering and active love, and his
whole life in virtues according to righteousness; through
these three things, and by the mysterious revelation of
God, such an inward man enters into the God-seeing life.
Yea, the lover who is inward and righteous, him will it
please God in His freedom to choose and to lift up into a
superessential contemplation, in the Divine Light and according to the Divine Way. This contemplation sets us in
purity and clearness above all our understanding, for it is
a singular adornment and a heavenly crown, and besides
the eternal reward of all virtues and of our whole life.
And to it none can attain through knowledge and sub-
tlety, neither through any exercise whatsoever. Only he
with whom it pleases God to be united in His Spirit, and
whom it pleases Him to enlighten by Himself, can see
God, and no one else. The mysterious Divine Nature is
eternally and actively beholding and loving according to
the Persons, and has everlasting fruition in a mutual embrace of the Persons in the unity of the Essence. In this
embrace, in the essential Unity of God, all inward spirits
are one with God in the immersion of love; and are that
same one which the Essence is in Itself, according to the
mode of Eternal Bliss. And in this most high unity of the
Divine Nature, the heavenly Father is origin and begin-

ing of every work which is worked in heaven and on earth. And He says in the deep-sunken hiddenness of the spirit: BEHOLD, THE BRIDEGROOM COMETH; GO YE OUT TO MEET HIM.

These words we will now explain and set forth in their relation to that superessential contemplation which is the source of all holiness, and of all perfection of life to which one may attain. Few men can attain to this Divine seeing, because of their own incapacity and the mysteriousness of the light in which one sees. And therefore no one will thoroughly understand the meaning of it by any learning or subtle consideration of his own; for all words, and all that may be learnt and understood in a creaturely way, are foreign to, and far below, the truth which I mean. But he who is united with God, and is enlightened in this truth, he is able to understand the truth by itself. For to comprehend and to understand God above all similitudes, such as He is in Himself, is to be God with God, without intermediary, and without any otherness that can become a hindrance or an intermediary. And therefore I beg everyone who cannot understand this, or feel it in the fruitive unity of his spirit, that he be not offended at it, and leave it for that which it is: for that which I am going to say is true, and Christ, the Eternal Truth, has said it Himself in His teaching in many places, if we could but show and explain it rightly. And, therefore, whosoever wishes to understand this must have died to himself, and must live in God, and must turn his gaze to the eternal light in the ground of his spirit, where the Hidden Truth reveals Itself without means. For our Heavenly Father wills that we should see; for He is the Father of Light, and this is why He utters eternally, without intermediary and without interruption, in the hiddenness of our spirit, one unique and abysmal word, and no other. And in this word He utters Himself and all things. And this word is none other than: BEHOLD. And this is the coming forth and the birth of the Son of Eternal Light, in whom all blessedness is known and seen.

Now if the spirit would see God with God in this Divine light without means, there needs must be on the part of man three things.

The first is that he must be perfectly ordered from without in all the virtues, and within must be unencumbered, and as empty of every outward work as if he did not work at all: for if his emptiness is troubled within by some work of virtue, he has an image; and as long as this endures within him, he cannot contemplate.

Secondly, he must inwardly cleave to God, with adhering intention and love, even as a burning and glowing fire which can never more be quenched. As long as he feels himself to be in this state, he is able to contemplate.

Thirdly, he must have lost himself in a Waylessness and in a Darkness, in which all contemplative men wander in fruition and wherein they never again can find themselves in a creaturely way. In the abyss of this darkness, in which the loving spirit has died to itself, there begin the manifestation of God and eternal life. For in this darkness there shines and is born an incomprehensible Light, which is the Son of God, in whom we behold eternal life. And in this Light one becomes seeing; and this Divine Light is given to the simple sight of the spirit, where the spirit receives the brightness which is God Himself, above all gifts and every creaturely activity, in the idle emptiness in which the spirit has lost itself through fruitive love, and where it receives without means the brightness of God, and is changed without interruption into that brightness which it receives. Behold, this mysterious brightness, in which one sees everything that one can desire according to the emptiness of the spirit: this brightness is so great that the loving contemplative, in his ground wherein he rests, sees and feels nothing but an incomprehensible Light; and through that Simple Nudity which enfolds all things, he finds himself, and feels himself, to be that same Light by which he sees, and nothing else. And this is the first condition by which one becomes seeing in the Divine

Light. Blessed are the eyes which are thus seeing, for they possess eternal life.

Now the Spirit of God says in the secret outpouring of our spirit: Go YE OUT, in an eternal contemplation and fruition, according to the way of God. All the riches which are in God by nature we possess by way of love in God, and God in us, through the unmeasured love which is the Holy Ghost; for in this love one tastes of all that one can desire. And therefore through this love we are dead to ourselves, and have gone forth in loving immersion into Waylessness and Darkness. There the spirit is embraced by the Holy Trinity, and dwells for ever within the super-essential Unity, in rest and fruition. And in that same Unity, according to Its fruitfulness, the Father dwells in the Son, and the Son in the Father, and all creatures dwell in Both. And this is above the distinction of the Persons; for here by means of the reason we understand Father-hood and Sonhood as the lifegiving fruitfulness of the Divine Nature.

Here there arise and begin an eternal going out and an eternal work which is without beginning; for here there is a beginning with beginning. For, after the Almighty Father had perfectly comprehended Himself in the ground of His fruitfulness, so the Son, the Eternal Word of the Father, came forth as the second Person in the Godhead. And, through the Eternal Birth, all creatures have come forth in eternity, before they were created in time. So God has seen and known them in Himself, according to distinction, in living ideas, and in an otherness from Himself; but not as something other in all ways, for all that is in God is God. This eternal going out and this eternal life, which we have and are in God eternally, without ourselves, is the cause of our created being in time. And our created being abides in the Eternal Essence, and is one with it in its essential existence. And this eternal life and being, which we have and are in the eternal Wisdom of God, is like unto God. For it has an eternal immanence in the Divine Essence, without distinction; and through the birth of the Son it has an eternal outflowing in a distinction and otherness, according to the Eternal Idea. And through these two points it is so like unto God that He knows and reflects Himself in this likeness without cessation, according to the Essence and according to the Persons. For, though even here there are distinction and otherness according to intellectual perception, yet this likeness is one with that same Image of the Holy Trinity, which is the wisdom of God and in which God beholds Himself and all things in an eternal Now, without before and after. In a single seeing He beholds Himself and all things. And this is the Image and the Likeness of God, and our Image and our Likeness; for in it God reflects Himself and all things. In this Divine Image all creatures have an eternal life, outside themselves, as in their eternal Archetype; and after this eternal Image, and in this Likeness, we have been made by the Holy Trinity. And therefore God wills that we shall go forth from ourselves in this Divine Light, and shall reunite ourselves in a supernatural way with this Image, which is our proper life, and shall possess it with Him, in action and in fruition, in eternal bliss.

For we know well that the bosom of the Father is our ground and origin, in which we begin our being and our life. And from our proper ground, that is from the Father and from all that lives in Him, there shines forth an eternal brightness, which is the birth of the Son. And in this brightness, that is, in the Son, the Father knows Himself and all that lives in Him; for all that He has, and all that He is, He gives to the Son, save only the property of Fatherhood, which abides in Himself. And this is why all that lives in the Father, unmanifested in the Unity, is also in the Son actively poured forth into manifestation: and the simple ground of our Eternal Image ever remains in darkness and in waylessness, but the brightness without limit which streams forth from it, this reveals and brings forth within the Conditioned the hiddenness of God. And all those men who are raised up above their created being into a God-seeing life are one with this Divine brightness. And they are that brightness itself, and they see, feel, and find, even by means of this Divine Light, that, as regards their uncreated essence, they are that same onefold ground from which the brightness without limit shines forth in the Divine way, and which, according to the simplicity of the Essence, abides eternally onefold and wayless within. And this is why inward and God-seeing men will go out in the way of contemplation, above reason and above distinction and above their created being, through an eternal intuitive gazing. By means of this inborn light they are transfigured, and made one with that same light through which they see and which they see. And thus the God-seeing men follow after their Eternal Image, after which they have been made; and they behold God and all things, without distinction, in a simple seeing, in the Divine brightness. And this is the most noble and the most profitable contemplation to which one can attain in this life; for in this contemplation, a man best remains master of himself and free. And at each loving introversion he may grow in nobility of life beyond anything that we are able to understand; for he remains free and master of himself in inwardness and virtue. And this gazing at the Divine Light holds him up above all inwardness and all virtue and all merit, for it is the crown and the reward after which we strive, and which we have and possess now in this wise; for a God-seeing life is a heavenly life. But were we set free from this misery and this exile, so we should have, as regards our created being, a greater capacity to receive this brightness; and so the glory of God would shine through us in every way better and more nobly. This is the way above all ways, in which one goes out through Divine contemplation and an eternal intuitive gazing, and in which one is transfigured and transmuted in the Divine brightness. This going out of the God-seeing man is also in love; for through the fruition of love he rises above his created being, and finds and tastes the riches and the delights which are God Himself, and which

He causes to pour forth without interruption in the
hiddenness of the spirit, where the spirit is like unto the
nobility of God.

When the inward and God-seeing man has thus attained to his Eternal Image, and in this clearness, through
the Son, has entered into the bosom of the Father: then
he is enlightened by Divine truth, and he receives anew,
every moment, the Eternal Birth, and he goes forth according to the way of the light, in a Divine contemplation.

You should know that the heavenly Father, as a living
ground, with all that lives in Him, is actively turned towards His Son, as to His own Eternal Wisdom. And that
same Wisdom, with all that lives in It, is actively turned
back toward the Father, that is, towards that very ground
from which It comes forth. And in this meeting, there
comes forth the third Person, between the Father and the
Son; that is the Holy Ghost, Their mutual Love, who is
one with them Both in the same nature. And He enfolds
and drenches through both in action and fruition the
Father and the Son, and all that lives in Both, with such
great riches and such joy that as to this all creatures must
eternally be silent; for the incomprehensible wonder of
this love eternally transcends the understanding of all
creatures. But where this wonder is understood and tasted
without amazement, there the spirit dwells above itself,
and is one with the Spirit of God; and tastes and sees without measure, even as God, the riches which are the spirit
itself in the unity of the living ground, where it possesses
itself according to the way of its uncreated essence.

Now this rapturous meeting is incessantly and actively
renewed in us, according to the way of God; for the
Father gives Himself in the Son, and the Son gives Himself in the Father, in an eternal content and a loving embrace; and this renews itself every moment within the
bonds of love. For like as the Father incessantly beholds
all things in the birth of His Son, so all things are loved
anew by the Father and the Son in the outpouring of the

Holy Ghost. And this is the active meeting of the Father and of the Son, in which we are lovingly embraced by the Holy Ghost in eternal love.

Now this active meeting and this loving embrace are in their ground fruitive and wayless; for the abysmal Waylessness of God is so dark and so unconditioned that it swallows up in itself every divine way and activity, and all the attributes of the Persons, within the rich compass of the essential Unity; and it brings about a Divine fruition in the abyss of the Ineffable. And here there is a death in fruition, and a melting and dying into the Essential Nudity, where all the Divine names, and all conditions, and all the living images which are reflected in the mirror of Divine Truth, lapse in the Onefold and Ineffable, in waylessness and without reason. For in this unfathomable abyss of the Simplicity, all things are wrapped in fruitive bliss; and the abyss itself may not be comprehended, unless by the Essential Unity. To this the Persons, and all that lives in God, must give place; for here there is nought else but an eternal rest in the fruitive embrace of an outpouring Love. And this is that wayless being which all interior spirits have chosen above all other things. This is the dark silence in which all lovers lose themselves. But if we would prepare ourselves for it by means of the virtues, we should strip ourselves of all but our very bodies, and should flee forth into the wild Sea, whence no created thing can draw us back again.

May we possess in fruition the essential Unity, and clearly behold unity in the Trinity; this may Divine Love, which turns no beggar away, bestow upon us. Amen.

Blessed John Ruysbroeck

DEGREES OF PRAYER

A beginner must look upon himself as making a garden wherein our Lord may take His delight, but in a soil unfruitful and abounding in weeds. His Majesty roots up the weeds, and has to plant good herbs. Let us, then, take for granted that this is already done when a soul is determined to give itself to prayer and has begun the practice of it. We have, then, as good gardeners, by the help of God, to see that the plants grow, to water them carefully, that they may not die, but produce blossoms, which shall send forth much fragrance, refreshing to our Lord, so that He may come often for His pleasure into this garden and delight Himself in the midst of these virtues.

Let us now see how this garden is to be watered, that we may understand what we have to do: how much trouble it will cost us, whether the gain be greater than the trouble, or how long a time it will take us. It seems to me that the garden may be watered in four ways: by water taken out of a well, which is very laborious; or with water raised by means of an engine and buckets, drawn by a windlass—I have drawn it this way sometimes—it is a less troublesome way than the first, and gives more water; or by a stream or brook, whereby the garden is watered in a much better way—for the soil is more thoroughly saturated, and there is no necessity to water it so often, and the labour of the gardener is much less; or by showers of rain, when our Lord Himself waters it, without labour on our part—and this way is incomparably better than all the others of which I have spoken.

Of those who are beginners in prayer, we may say that they are those who draw the water up out of the well—a process which, as I have said, is very laborious; for they must be wearied in keeping the senses recollected, and this is a great labour, because the senses have been hitherto accustomed to distractions. It is necessary for beginners to accustom themselves to disregard what they hear or see, and to put it away from them during the time of prayer; they must be alone, and in retirement think over their past life. Though all must do this many times, beginners as well as those more advanced; all, however, must not do so equally, as I shall show hereafter.

Beginners at first suffer much because they are not convinced that they are penitent for their sins; and yet they are, because they are so sincerely resolved on serving God. They must strive to meditate on the life of Christ, and the understanding is wearied thereby. Thus far we can advance of ourselves—that is, by the grace of God—for without that, as everyone knows, we never can have one good thought.

What, then, will he do here who sees that, for many days, he is conscious only of aridity, disgust, dislike, and so great an unwillingness to go to the well for water that he would give it up altogether, if he did not remember that he has to please and serve the Lord of the garden; if he did not trust that his service was not in vain, and did not hope for some gain by a labour so great as that of lowering the bucket into the well so often, and drawing it up without water in it? It will happen that he is often unable to move his arms for that purpose or to have one good thought. Working with the understanding is drawing water out of the well.

What, then, once more, will the gardener do now? He must rejoice and take comfort, and consider it as the greatest favour to labour in the garden of so great an Emperor; and as he knows that he is pleasing Him in the matter—and his purpose must not be to please himself, but Him—let him praise Him greatly for the trust He has in him—for He sees that, without any recompense, he is taking so much care of that which has been confided to him; let him help Him to carry the Cross, and let him think how He carried it all His life long; let him not seek his kingdom here, not ever intermit his prayer; and so let him resolve, if this aridity should last even his whole life long, never to let Christ fall down beneath the Cross.

The time will come when he shall be paid once for all. Let him have no fear that his labour is in vain: he serves a good Master . . . These labours have their reward, I know it; for I am one who underwent them for many years. When I drew but one drop of water out of this blessed well, I considered it was a mercy of God . . .

It is certain that the love of God does not consist in tears, nor in this sweetness and tenderness which we for the most part desire, and with which we console ourselves; but rather in serving Him in Justice, fortitude, and humility. That seems to me to be a receiving rather than a giving of anything on our part . . . Some are distressed, thinking they are doing nothing; the understanding ceases from its acts, and they cannot bear it. Yet, perhaps, at that very time, the will is feeding and gathering strength, and they know it not . . .

His Majesty knoweth our misery and natural vileness better than we do ourselves. He knoweth that these souls long to be always thinking of Him and loving Him. It is this resolution that He seeks in us; the other anxieties which we inflict upon ourselves serve to no other end but to disquiet the soul . . . This poor prisoner of a soul shares in the misery of the body. The changes of the seasons, and the alterations of humours, very often compel it, without fault of its own, not to do what it would, but rather to suffer in every way. Meanwhile, the more we force the soul on these occasions, the greater the mischief, and the longer it lasts. Some discretion must be used, in order to ascertain whether ill-health be the occasion or not. The poor soul must not be stifled. Let those who thus suffer understand that they are ill; a change should be made in the hour of prayer, and oftentimes that change should be continued for some days . . .

His Majesty seeks and loves courageous souls; but they must be humble in their ways, and have no confidence in themselves. I never saw one of those lag behind on the road; and never a cowardly soul, though aided by humility, make that progress in many years which the former makes in a few. I am astonished at the great things done on this road by encouraging oneself to undertake great things, though we may not have the strength for them at once; the soul takes a flight upwards and ascends high, though, like a little bird whose wings are weak, it grows weary and rests . . .

It is of great consequence that the director should be prudent—I mean, of sound understanding—and a man of experience. If, in addition to this, he is a learned man, it is a very great matter. But if these three qualities cannot be had together, the first two are the most important, because learned men may be found with whom we can communicate when it is necessary. I mean, that for beginners learned men are of little use if they are not men of prayer. I do not say that they are to have nothing to do with learned men, because a spirituality the foundations of which do not rest on the truth I would rather were not accompanied by prayer. Learning is a great thing, for it teaches us who know so little, and enlightens us; so when we have come to the knowledge of the truths contained in the holy writings, we do what we ought to do. From silly devotions, God deliver us! . . .

A nun begins to practise prayer; if her director be silly, and if he should take it into his head, he will make her feel that it is better for her to obey him than her own superior. He will do all this without any evil purpose, thinking that he is doing right. For if he be not a religious himself, he will think this right enough. If his penitent be a married woman, he will tell her that it is better for her to give herself unto prayer when she ought to attend to her house, although she may thereby displease her husband. And so it is, he knows not how to make arrangements for time and business, so that everything may be done as it ought to be done; he has no light himself, and can therefore give none to others, however much he may wish to do so.

Though learning does not seem necessary for discretion, my opinion has always been, and will be, that every Christian soul should continue to be guided by a learned director if he can, and the more learned the better. They who walk in the way of prayer have the greater need of learning; and the more spiritual they are, the greater is that need. Let them not say that learned men not given to prayer are not fit counsellors for those who pray: that is a delusion. I have conversed with many; and now for some years I have sought them the more because of my greater need of them. I have always been fond of them; for though some of them have no experience, they do not dislike spirituality, neither are they ignorant of what it is, because in the sacred writings with which they are familiar they always find the truth about spirituality. I am certain myself that a person given to prayer who treats of these matters with learned men, unless he be deceived with his own consent, will never be carried away by any illusions of the devil. I believe that the evil spirits are exceedingly afraid of learned men who are humble and virtuous, knowing that they will be found out and defeated by them.

I have said this because there are opinions held to the effect that learned men, if they are not spiritual, are not suited for persons given to prayer. I have just said that a spiritual director is necessary; but if he be not a learned man, he is a great hindrance. It will help us much if we consult those who are learned, provided they be virtuous; even if they be not spiritual, they will be of service to me, and God will enable them to understand what they should teach; He will even make them spiritual in order that they may help us on. I do not say this without having had experience of it; and I have met with more than two.

Having spoken of the toilsome efforts and of the strength required for watering the garden when we have to draw the water out of the well, let us now speak of the second manner of drawing the water which the Lord of the vineyard has ordained; of the machine of wheel and buckets whereby the gardener may draw more water with less labour, and is able to take some rest without being continually at work. This, then, is what I am now going to describe; and I apply it to the prayer called the prayer of quiet.

Herein the soul begins to be recollected; it is now touching on the supernatural—for it never could by any efforts of its own attain to this . . . The water is nearer to it, for grace reveals itself more distinctly to the soul.

This is a gathering together of the faculties of the soul within itself in order that it may have the fruition of that contentment in greater sweetness; but the faculties are not lost, neither are they asleep; the will alone is occupied in such a way that, without knowing how it has become a captive, it gives a simple consent to become the prisoner of God; for it knows well what it is to be the captive of Him it loves . . .

As soon as the soul has arrived thus far, it begins to lose the desire of earthly things, and no wonder; for it sees clearly that even for a moment this joy is not to be had on earth; that there are no riches, no dominion, no honours, no delights that can for one instant, even for the twinkling of an eye, minister such a joy; for it is a true satisfaction, and the soul sees that it really does satisfy. Now, we who are on earth, as it seems to me, scarcely ever understand wherein our satisfaction lies, for it is always liable to disappointment; but in this, at that time, there is none; the disappointment cometh afterwards, when the soul sees that all is over, and that it has no power to recover it, neither does it know how; for if it cuts itself in pieces by penance and prayer, and every other kind of austerities, all would be of little use, if our Lord did not grant it. God, in His great mercy, will have the soul comprehend that His Majesty is so near to it that it need not send messengers to Him, but may speak to Him itself, and not with a loud crying, because so near is He already that He understands even the movements of its lips . . .

There are times in which the soul has no recollection of this garden; everything seems parched and there is no water to be had for preserving it—and in which it seems as if the soul had never possessed any virtue at all. This is the season of heavy trials; for our Lord will have the poor gardener suppose all the trouble he took in maintaining and watering the garden to have been taken to no purpose. Then is the time really for weeding and rooting out every plant, however small it may be, that is worthless, in the knowledge that no efforts of ours are sufficient if God withholds from us the waters of His grace; and in despising ourselves as being nothing, and even less than nothing. In this way we gain great humility—the flowers grow afresh.

This quiet and recollection of the soul makes itself in great measure felt in the satisfaction and peace attended with very great joy and repose of the faculties and most sweet delight, wherein the soul is established. It thinks, because it has not gone beyond it, that there is nothing further to wish for but that its abode might be there, and it would willingly say so with St. Peter. It dares not move nor stir, because it thinks that this blessing it has received must then escape out of its hands; now and then, it could wish it did not even breathe. The poor little soul is not aware that, as of itself it could do nothing to draw down this blessing on itself, it is still less able to retain it a moment longer than our Lord wills it should remain.

I have already said that, in the prior recollection and quiet, there is no failure of the powers of the soul; but the soul is so satisfied in God that, although two of its powers be distracted, yet, while the recollection lasts, as the will abides in union with God, so its peace and quiet are not disturbed; on the contrary, the will by degrees brings the understanding and the memory back again; for though the will is not yet altogether absorbed, it continues still occupied without knowing how, so that notwithstanding all the efforts of the memory and the understanding, they cannot rob it of its delight and joy— yea, rather it helps without any labour at all to keep this little spark of the love of God from being quenched.

The prayer of quiet, then, is a little spark of the true

love of Himself, which our Lord begins to enkindle in the soul; and His will is that the soul should understand what this love is by the joy it brings. This quiet and recollection and little spark, if it is the work of the Spirit of God, and not a sweetness supplied by Satan, or brought about by ourselves, produces great results. A person of experience, however, cannot possibly fail to understand at once that it is not a thing that can be acquired, were it not that our nature is so greedy of sweetness that it seeks for it in every way. But it becomes cold very soon; for, however much we try to make the fire burn, in order to obtain this sweetness, it does not appear that we do anything else but throw water on it, to put it out. This spark, then, given of God, however slight it may be, causes a great crackling; and if men do not quench it by their faults, it is the beginning of the great fire which sends forth—I shall speak of it in the proper place—the flames of that most vehement love of God which His Majesty will have perfect souls to possess.

This little spark is a sign or pledge which God gives to a soul, in token of His having chosen it for great things, if it will prepare to receive them. It is a great gift, much too great for me to be able to speak of it. It is a great sorrow to me; because, as I said before, I know that many souls come thus far, and that those who go farther, as they ought to go, are so few, that I am ashamed to say it. I do not mean that they are absolutely few; there must be many, because God is patient with us, for some reasons; I speak of what I have seen.

I should like much to recommend these souls to take care that they do not hide their talent; for it may be that God has chosen them to be the edification of many others, especially in these days, when the friends of God should be strong, in order that they may support the weak. Those who discern in themselves this grace must look upon themselves as such friends if they would fulfil the law which even the honourable friendship of the world respects; if not, as I have said just now, let them fear and

tremble, lest they should be doing mischief to themselves
—and God grant it should be to themselves only!

What the soul has to do at those seasons wherein it is
raised to the prayer of quiet is nothing more than to be
gentle and without noise. By noise, I mean going about
with the understanding in search of words and reflections
whereby to give God thanks for this grace, and heaping
up its sins and imperfections together to show that it
does not deserve it . . .

Let us now speak of the third water wherewith this
garden is watered—water running from a river or from a
brook—whereby the garden is watered with much less
trouble, although there is some in directing the water. In
this state our Lord will help the gardener, and in such a
way as to be, as it were, the Gardener Himself doing all
the work. It is a sleep of the powers of the soul, which are
not wholly lost, nor yet understanding how they are at
work. The pleasure, sweetness and delight are incomparably greater than in the former state of prayer; and the
reason is that the waters of grace have risen up to the
neck of the soul, so that it can neither advance nor retreat
—nor does it know how to do either; it seeks only the
fruition of exceeding bliss. It is like a dying man with the
candle in his hand, on the point of dying the death desired. It is rejoicing in this agony with the unutterable
joy; to me it seems to be nothing else but a death, as it
were, to all the things of this world, and a fruition of God.
I know of no other words whereby to describe it or to explain it; neither does the soul then know what to do—
for it knows not whether to speak or be silent, whether it
should laugh or weep. It is a glorious folly, a heavenly
madness, wherein true wisdom is acquired; and to the
soul a kind of fruition most full of delight.

It is now some five or six years, I believe, since our Lord
raised me to this state of prayer, in its fulness and that
more than once—and I never understood it and never
could explain it; and so I was resolved, when I should

come thus far in my story, to say very little or nothing at all. I knew well enough that it was not altogether the union of all the faculties, and yet most certainly it was higher than the previous state of prayer; but I confess that I could not determine and understand the difference . . .

The faculties are almost all completely in union, yet not so absorbed that they do not act. I have been singularly delighted in that I have been able to comprehend the matter at last. Blessed be our Lord who has thus consoled me!

The faculties of the soul now retain only the power of occupying themselves wholly with God; not one of them ventures to stir, neither can we move one of them without making great efforts to distract ourselves—and, indeed, I do not think we can do it at all at this time. Many words are then uttered in praise of God—but disorderly, unless it be that our Lord orders them Himself. At least, the understanding is utterly powerless here; the soul longs to send forth words of praise, but it has no control over itself—it is in a state of sweet restlessness. The flowers are already opening; they are beginning to send forth their fragrance.

The soul in this state would have all men behold it, and know of its bliss, to the praise of God, and help it to praise Him. It would have them to be partakers of its joy; for its joy is greater than it can bear. It seems to me that it is like the woman in the Gospel who would, or used to, call in her neighbours . . .

Finally, the virtues are now stronger than they were during the preceding prayer of quiet; for the soul sees itself to be other than it was, and it knows how it is beginning to do great things in the odour which the flowers send forth; it being our Lord's will that the flowers should open in order that the soul may believe itself to be in possession of virtue; though it sees most clearly that it cannot, and never could, acquire them in many years, and that the heavenly Gardener has given them to it in that instant . . .

This state of prayer seems to me to be a most distinct union of the whole soul with God, but for this, that His Majesty appears to give the faculties leave to be intent upon, and have the fruition of, the great work He is doing then. It happens at times, and indeed very often, that the will being in union, the soul should be aware of it, and see that the will is a captive and in joy, that the will alone is abiding in great peace—while, on the other hand, the understanding and the memory are so free that they can be employed in affairs and be occupied in the works of charity . . .

The soul, which would willingly neither stir nor move, is delighting in the holy repose of Mary; but in this prayer it can be like Martha also. Accordingly, the soul is, as it were, living the active and contemplative life at once, and is able to apply itself to works of charity and the affairs of its state, and to spiritual reading. Still, those who arrive at this state are not wholly masters of themselves, and are well aware that the better part of the soul is elsewhere. It is as if we were speaking to one person, and another speaking to us at the same time, while we ourselves are not perfectly attentive either to the one or the other.

May our Lord teach me the words whereby I may in some measure describe the fourth water. I have great need of His help—even more than I had while speaking of the last; for in that the soul still feels that it is not dead altogether. We may thus speak, seeing that to the world it is really dead. But, as I have said, it retains the sense to see that it is in the world, and to feel its own loneliness; and it makes use of that which is outward for the purpose of manifesting its feelings, at least by signs. In the whole of the prayer already spoken of, and in all the states of it, the gardener undergoes some labour: though in the later states the labour is attended with so much bliss and comfort of the soul that the soul would never willingly pass out of it—and thus the labour is not felt as labour, but as bliss.

In this the fourth state there is no sense of anything, only fruition, without understanding what that is the fruition of which is granted. It is understood that the fruition is of a certain good containing in itself all good together at once; but this good is not comprehended. The senses are all occupied in this fruition in such a way that not one of them is at liberty, so as to be able to attend to anything else, whether outward or inward.

The senses were permitted before, as I have said, to give some signs of the great joy they feel; but now, in this state, the joy of the soul is incomparably greater, and the power of showing it is still less; for there is no power in the body and the soul has none whereby this fruition can be made known. Everything of that kind would be a great hindrance, a torment and a disturbance of its rest. And I say, if it really be a union of all the faculties, that the soul, even if it wished—I mean, when it is in union—cannot make it known; and if it can, then it is not union at all.

How this, which we call union, is effected, and what it is, I cannot tell. Mystical theology explains it, and I do not know the terms of that science; nor can I understand what the mind is, nor how it differs from the soul or spirit either; all three seem to me but one; though I do know that the soul sometimes leaps forth out of itself, like a fire that is burning and is become a flame; and occasionally this fire increases violently—the flame ascends high above the fire; but it is not therefore a different thing: it is still the same flame of the same fire . . .

It is plain what union is—two distinct things becoming one. O my Lord, how good Thou art! Blessed be Thou for ever, O my God! Let all creatures love Thee who hast so loved us that we can truly speak of this communication which Thou hast with souls in this our exile! . . .

The soul, while thus seeking after God, is conscious with a joy excessive and sweet that it is, as it were, utterly fainting away in a kind of trance: breathing and all the bodily strength fail it, so that it cannot even move the hands without great pain; the eyes close involuntarily, and if they are open they are as if they saw nothing; nor is reading possible—the very letters seem strange, and cannot be distinguished—the letters, indeed, are visible, but, as the understanding furnishes no help, all reading is impracticable, though seriously attempted. The ear hears; but what is heard is not comprehended. The senses are of no use whatever except to hinder the soul's fruition, and so they rather hurt it. It is useless to try to speak, because it is not possible to conceive a word; nor, if it were conceived, is there strength sufficient to utter it; for all bodily strength vanishes, and that of the soul increases, to enable it the better to have the fruition of its joy. Great and most perceptible, also, is the outward joy now felt.

This prayer, however long it may last, does no harm— at least it has never done any to me; nor do I remember, however ill I might have been when our Lord had mercy upon me in this way, that I ever felt the worse for it—on the contrary, I was always better afterwards . . .

The truth is, it passes away so quickly in the beginning —at least, so it was with me—that neither by the outward signs nor by the failure of the senses, can it be perceived when it passes so quickly away. But it is plain, from the overflowing abundance of grace, that the brightness of the sun which had shone there must have been great, seeing that it has thus made the soul to melt away. And this is to be considered; for, as it seems to me, the period of time, however long it may have been, during which the faculties of the soul were entranced, is very short; if half an hour, that would be a long time . . .

Saint Teresa of Avila

ON THE PRAYER OF RECOLLECTION

In my opinion when God calls the soul into this state, as I said, it is best for it to endeavour, without force or disturbance, to keep free from wandering thoughts. No effort, however, should be made entirely to suspend the intellect and imagination from acting; it is well to remember God's presence and to consider who He is. If transported out of itself by what it feels, well and good, but let it not try to understand what is passing within it, for this favour is bestowed on the will, which should be left to enjoy it in peace, only occasionally making loving aspirations. Although, in this kind of prayer, the soul makes no effort to do so, yet often, for a very short time, the mind ceases to think at all. I explained elsewhere why this occurs during this spiritual state. On first speaking of the fourth mansions, I told you I had mentioned divine consolations before the prayer of recollection. The latter should have come first, as it is far inferior to consolations, of which it is the commencement. Recollection does not require us to give up meditation, nor to cease using our intellect. In the prayer of quiet, when the water flows from the spring itself and not through conduits, the mind ceases to act; it is forced to do so, although it does not understand what is happening, and so wanders hither and thither in bewilderment, finding no place for rest. The will, meanwhile, entirely united to God, is much disturbed by the tumult of the thoughts: no notice, however, should be taken of them, or they would cause the loss of a great part of the favour the soul is enjoying. Let the spirit ignore these distractions and abandon itself into the arms of divine love: His Majesty will teach it how best to act. His principal desire is that it should recognise its unworthiness of so great a good and should occupy itself in thanking Him for it.

In treating of the prayer of recollection, I have passed over in silence the effects and symptoms to be found in the souls thus favoured by God. Divine consolations evidently cause a dilation or enlargement of the soul. This may be compared to water flowing from a spring into a basin which has no outlet, but is constructed so as to increase in size in proportion to the quantity poured into it. God seems to work the same effect by this prayer, besides giving many other marvellous graces, so preparing and disposing the soul to contain all He intends giving it. After interior sweetness and dilation the soul is no longer as restrained as before in God's service, but possesses much more liberty of spirit. It is less distressed by the fear of hell, for though more anxious than ever not to offend God, it has lost servile fear and feels sure that one day it will possess its Lord. It no longer dreads the loss of health by austerities, and thinks there is nothing it could not do by His grace, being more desirous than before of doing penance. Greater indifference is felt for sufferings, because, faith being stronger, it trusts that if borne for God He will give the grace to endure them patiently. Indeed, such a one even longs for trials at times, having a most ardent desire to do something for His sake. As the soul better understands the divine Majesty, it realises more vividly its own baseness. Divine consolations show it how vile are earthly pleasures; gradually withdrawing itself from them, it gains more mastery over self. In short, the virtues are increased and it will not cease to advance in perfection, unless it turns from the right road and offends God. Should it act thus, it would lose everything, however high a state it may have reached.

It is not to be supposed that all these effects are produced merely by God having shown these favours once or twice. They must be received continually, for it is on their frequent reception that the whole welfare of the soul depends. I strongly urge those who have reached this state to avoid most carefully all occasions of offending God. The soul is not yet fully established in virtue, but is like a new-born babe, first feeding at its mother's breast: if it leaves her, what can it do but die? I greatly fear that when a soul to whom God has granted this favour discontinues prayer, except under urgent necessity, it will, unless it returns to the practice at once, go from bad to worse.

I realise what danger there is in such a case, and have had the grief of witnessing the fall of persons I knew, because they withdrew from Him who sought, with so much love, to make Himself their friend, as He proved by His treatment of them. I warn such persons not to run the risk of sinning; the devil would rather gain one of these souls than a large number to whom our Lord does not show such favours, for the former may cause him severe loss by leading others to follow their example, and may even render great service to the Church of God. If there were no other reason except that he saw the special love His Majesty bore these people, it would be enough to make him try to destroy God's work in them, so that they might be lost eternally. Therefore they suffer grievous temptations, and if they fall their fall is lower than others'.

. . . When the mind is not recollected nor even thinking of God, His Majesty arouses it suddenly, as if by a swiftly flashing comet, or by a clap of thunder, although no sound is heard. Yet the soul which God thus calls hears Him well enough—so well, indeed, that sometimes, especially at first, it trembles and even cries out, although it feels no pain. It is conscious of having received a wound of love, but cannot discover how nor who gave it, but recognises it as a most precious grace, and hopes the hurt will never heal.

The soul makes amorous complaints to its Bridegroom, even uttering them aloud; nor can it help itself, for it knows that, though He is present, He will not manifest Himself so that it may enjoy Him. This causes a pain, keen though sweet and delicious, from which the soul could not escape even if it wished; however, it never desires to do so. This favour is more delightful than the pleasing suspension of the faculties in the prayer of quiet, which is unaccompanied by pain.

I am much embarrassed, my sisters, as to how to make you understand this operation of love; I know not how to do so. It seems contradictory to say that the Beloved clearly shows He dwells in the soul and calls it with so unmistakable a sign, and a summons so penetrating, that the spirit cannot choose but hear it, while yet it appears that He resides in the seventh mansion. He speaks in this manner, which is not a set form of speech, and the inhabitants of the other mansions dare not stir, either with the senses or the imagination and the faculties.

O God Almighty! how great are Thy secrets, and how different are spiritual matters from anything that can be seen or heard in this world! I can find nothing to liken to these graces, though they are very insignificant compared with many others Thou dost bestow on souls. This favour has such a strong effect upon the spirit that it is consumed by desires, yet knows not what to ask, for it realises clearly that God is with it. You may inquire, if it realises this so clearly, what more does it desire, and why is it pained? What greater good can it seek? I cannot tell: I know this suffering seems to pierce the very heart, and when He who wounded it draws out the dart, He seems to draw the heart out too, so deep is the love it feels.

I have been thinking that God might be likened to a fire of burning coals, from which a little spark flies into the soul, which feels the heat, although there is not enough to consume it. The sensation is so delightful, that the spirit lingers in the pain produced by contact with the spark. This seems to me the best comparison I could find, for the pain is delicious and is not really pain at all, nor does it always continue in the same degree; sometimes it lasts for a long time, and on other occasions passes away at once. This is as our Lord chooses, for it cannot be obtained by any human means, and though it is felt for a long while, yet it comes and goes.

In short, it is never permanent and therefore does not wholly inflame the soul, except at times, when, as the soul is ready to take fire, the little spark suddenly dies out, leaving the heart longing to suffer anew the loving pangs it gave. There are no grounds for thinking this comes from any natural cause, nor that it proceeds from melancholy, or is a deceit of the devil, or perhaps a fancy. It is impossible not to see that this movement of the heart comes from God, who is unchangeable; besides, its effects do not resemble those of other devotions, in which the strong transport of joy may make us doubtful about the reality.

There is no suspension here, either of the senses or the other faculties: they wonder at what is happening, but cannot impede it. I do not think this delightful pain can either be increased or got rid of at will. Whoever has received this favour from our Lord will understand my meaning when she reads this; let her thank Him fervently: there is no need to fear any deception, but far more danger of not being sufficiently grateful for such a signal grace. Let her endeavour to serve Him and to amend her life in every respect, and she will see what will happen, and will obtain still higher gifts.

A person on whom this grace was bestowed passed several years without receiving any other favour and yet was perfectly satisfied, for even though she may have served God for very many years in the midst of severe trials, yet she was abundantly repaid in this way. May He be for ever blessed, Amen! You may wonder why we may feel more secure against deception concerning this favour than in other cases. I think it is . . . because the devil cannot give a delicious pain like this: he may cause a pleasure or delight which appears spiritual, but it is not in his power to add suffering to it, especially suffering of so keen a sort, united to peace and joy of soul. His power is limited to what is external; when he causes pain it is never accompanied with peace, but with anxieties and struggles.

Saint Teresa of Avila

THE BEGINNING OF CONTEMPLATION

When after a long cultivation of purity of heart, God would enter into a soul and manifest Himself to it openly by the gift of His Holy presence, which is the first in order of His supernatural gifts, the soul finds itself so delighted with this new state that it feels as if it had never known or loved God before. It is astounded at the blindness and stupidity of men; it condemns the indolence and languor in which we generally pass our lives; it deplores the losses it believes itself to have incurred by its slothfulness; it accounts the life it has hitherto led as not deserving the name of life, and that it is only just beginning to live.

In vain do we labour to have this sense of the presence of God unless He Himself bestows it upon us. It is a pure gift of His mercy. But when we have received it, by that presence and in that presence we see God and will of God in our actions, as we behold at one and the same time the light and the body which it enables us to see. This grace is the fruit of great purity of heart, and leads the soul to close union with God. He bestows it upon us when, on our part, we do what we can and ought to do.

Were we fully possessed with God, we should be able to practise incessant prayer. It occasionally happens that some passion, or resentment, or vexation of mind so possesses us that we are altogether engrossed by it for two or three days together, and think of scarcely anything else. Not an hour in the day passes without our experiencing this ill-feeling; and though we fancy we resist it, yet if God were to show us the real disposition of our heart, we should see that we had no desire to be free from it, and yielded it some sort of secret consent.

In like manner, if we had a tender devotion to our Lord, in the Holy Sacrament of the altar, we should think of Him a thousand times a day. If our heart were wholly occupied with God, we should cherish an unceasing remembrance of Him, and should experience no difficulty in realising His presence. Everything would serve to raise us to Him, and the least occasions would excite our fervour.

. . . We see in the First Epistle of St. Paul to the Corinthians that the most marvellous gifts of God were commonly granted to the first Christians—the gift of tongues, of healing the sick, of working miracles, of prophecy, and of discernment of spirits; and the holy Apostle exhorts the faithful to desire these spiritual gifts, and particularly that of prophecy, which consists not only in predicting things to come, but also in understanding the Scriptures, in expounding them, and instructing the people.

Nowadays, if anyone aspires after some gift of prayer a little above the common order, he is plainly told that such things are extraordinary gifts which God gives only when He will and to whom He will, and that we must not desire them nor ask for them: thus the door of these gifts is for ever shut against him. This is a great abuse. True it is that we must not ourselves intrude into these kinds of prayer; but at the same time we ought not to refuse them when God offers them, nor actually do anything which may have the effect of preventing His admitting us to them when He pleases.

Meditation wearies and fatigues the mind, and its acts are of short duration; but those of contemplation, even such as is of a common order, last whole hours without labour and without weariness; and in the purest souls contemplation may easily continue several days together in the very midst of the world and the engagements of business. In the state of glory the first act made by a holy soul on beholding the beatific vision will last to all eternity without satiety or fatigue, ever the same and ever new. Now contemplation is a participation in the state of glory. It resembles it in its facility and duration. It injures neither health nor strength.

Contemplation opens a new world to the soul, with the beauty of which it is enraptured. St. Teresa, when passing out of prayer, used to say that she came from a world incomparably more vast and beautiful than a thousand worlds such as this.

St. Bernard, returning from converse with God, went back with regret to the society of men, and dreaded attachment to creatures as hell itself. That holy priest, John of Avila, on leaving the altar, could scarcely endure intercourse with the world.

In contemplation a pure soul discovers without labour, or any exertion of its powers, truths which throw it into ecstasy, and which, withdrawing it from all the operations of the senses, cause it to experience within itself a foretaste of paradise.

Contemplation leads souls to heroic acts of charity, zeal, penance, and other virtues as, for example, martyrdom. The saints who had received this gift from God desired their sufferings to be increased tenfold; and to form these desires, they had not to undergo those struggles and repugnances which we commonly experience in our good resolutions. They found therein nothing but consolation.

Contemplation is a perception of God or of Divine things, simple, free, penetrating, and certain, proceeding from love, and tending to love.

This perception is simple. In contemplation we do not exercise reason as in meditation.

It is free: because to produce it the soul must be liberated from the least sins, irregular affections, eagerness, and unprofitable and disquieting cares. Without this, the understanding is like a bird, tied by the feet, which cannot fly unless it be set at liberty.

It is clear and penetrating, not as in the state of glory, but as compared with the knowledge we have by faith, which is always obscure. In meditation we see things only confusedly, as it were from afar off, and in a drier manner. Contemplation enables us to see them more distinctly, and as it were close at hand. It enables us to touch them, feel them, taste them, and have an inward experience of them. To meditate on hell, for instance, is to see a painted lion; to contemplate hell is to see a living lion.

It is certain: because its objects are the supernatural truths which the Divine light discloses to it; and when this disclosure is made immediately to the understanding, it is not liable to error. When it is made either through the senses or through the imagination, some illusion may at times mix with it.

It proceeds from love and tends to love. It is the employment of the purest and most perfect charity. Love is its principle, its exercise, and its term.

The gifts of the Holy Spirit which serve to contemplation are particularly those of understanding, wisdom, and knowledge in regard to the intellect; and those of piety and fear in regard to the will.

By the gift of knowledge, we know creatures, and despise them, beholding their frailty, their fleetingness, their nothingness. By the gift of wisdom we know the greatness of God and of heavenly things; and hence we are led to detach ourselves from all affection to creatures in order to unite ourselves solely to God. The effect is pretty much as when one has just been seeing the Louvre or some extraordinary picture. The mind, filled with these beautiful objects, deigns not so much as to cast a look at some peasant's hut or some schoolboy's daub. Thus a soul to which God manifests Himself in prayer ceases to find anything great on earth. St. Anthony possessed so rare a gift of contemplation that he passed whole nights in this holy exercise without perceiving that he spent a moment in it; and on receiving letters from the Emperor Constantine, did not deign even to send him one word in reply.

Father Louis Lallemant

CONCLUSION

Into Paradise

THE EXCELLENCE OF THE
KNOWLEDGE OF OUR LORD

For wisdom, which is the worker of all things, taught me . . .

For she is a vapour of the power of God, and a certain pure emanation of the glory of almighty God; and therefore no defiled thing cometh into her.

For she is the brightness of eternal light, and the unspotted mirror of God's majesty, and the image of his goodness.

And being but one, she can do all things: and remaining in herself the same, she reneweth all things, and through nations conveyeth herself into holy souls. She maketh the friends of God and prophets.

For God loveth none but him that dwelleth with wisdom.

Wisdom 7, 21; 25–28

And they to whom she shall show herself love her by the sight and the knowledge of her great works.

The fear of the Lord is the beginning of wisdom, and was created with the faithful in the womb. It walketh with chosen women, and is known with the just and faithful.

The fear of the Lord is the religiousness of knowledge.

Ecclesiasticus 1, 15–17

To disown the Son is to have no claim to the Father; it is by acknowledging the Son that we lay claim to the Father too. Enough for you, that the message which was first brought you should dwell in you. If that first message dwells in you, you too will dwell in the Son, and in the Father.

I John 2, 23–25

On me, least as I am of all the saints, he has bestowed this privilege, of making known to the Gentiles the unfathomable riches of Christ, of publishing to the world the plan of this mystery, kept hidden from the beginning of time in the all-creating mind of God.

Ephesians 3, 8–9

Whoever does not believe, will not experience, and who does not experience, will not know. For just as experiencing a thing far exceeds the mere hearing of it, so the knowledge of him who experiences is beyond the knowledge of him who hears.

Saint Anselm of Canterbury

All mystic charisms are worthless compared to the love of God. They are as a string of pearls adorning a hungry infant who does not heed the pearls but only wants his mother's breast.

Saint Macarius the Egyptian

The highest good can only be beheld by those who are very pure in spirit, and can only be tasted when the passions are as they should be. This is why St. Augustine prays: O Lord, let me taste in my will what I know in my mind, and feel through love what I grasp through awareness.

Saint Bonaventure

The Lord gives His blessing where He finds the vessels empty.

Imitatio Christi

OF THE DOCTRINE OF TRUTH

Happy is he whom truth by itself doth teach, not by figures and words that pass away, but as it is in itself. Our own opinion and our own sense do often deceive us, and they discern but little. What availeth it to cavil and dispute much about dark and hidden things, for ignorance of which we shall not be reproved at the day of judgment?

It is a great folly to neglect the things that are profitable and necessary, and to choose to dwell upon that which is curious and hurtful. We have eyes and see not. And what have we to do with *genera* and *species*? He to whom the Eternal Word speaketh is delivered from many an opinion. From one Word are all things, and all things utter one Word; and this is the *Beginning*, which also speaketh unto us. No man without that Word understandeth or judgeth rightly. He to whom all things are one, he who reduceth all things to one, and seeth all things in one may enjoy a quiet mind and remain at peace in God.

O God, who art the truth, make me one with Thee in everlasting love. It wearieth me often to read and hear many things: in Thee is all that I would have and can desire. Let all doctors hold their peace; let all creatures be silent in Thy sight; speak Thou alone unto me. The more a man is at one within himself, and becometh of single heart, so much the more and higher things doth he understand without labour; for that he receiveth the light of wisdom from above.

A pure, single, and stable spirit is not distracted, though it be employed in many works; for that it doth all to the honour of God, and being at rest within, seeketh not itself in anything it doth. Who hinder and trouble thee more than the unmortified affections of thine own heart? A good

and devout man arrangeth within himself beforehand
those things which he ought to do. Neither do they draw
him to the desires of an inordinate inclination, but he or-
dereth them according to the direction of right reason.
Who hath a greater combat than he that laboureth to
overcome himself? This ought to be our endeavour, to
conquer ourselves, and daily to wax stronger, and to grow
in holiness.

All perfection in this life hath some imperfection mixed
with it; and no knowledge of ours is without some darkness. A humble knowledge of thyself is a surer way to
God than a deep search after learning.

Yet learning is not to be blamed, nor the mere knowledge of anything whatsoever, for that is good in itself,
and ordained by God; but a good conscience and a virtuous life are always to be preferred before it. But because many endeavour rather to get knowledge than to
live well, therefore they are often deceived, and reap
either none or but little fruit. O, if man bestowed as much
labour in the rooting out of vices, and the planting of virtues, as they do in the moving of questions, neither would
so many evils be done, nor so great scandal be given in
the world. Truly, at the day of judgment we shall not be
examined as to what we have read, but as to what we
have done; not as to how well we have spoken, but as to
how religiously we have lived.

Tell me, where are all those Doctors and Masters with
whom thou wast well acquainted whilst they lived and
flourished in learning? Others occupy their places and
perhaps do scarce ever think of those who went before
them. In their lifetime they seemed something, but now
they are not spoken of.

O, how quickly doth the glory of the world pass away!
Would that their life had been answerable to their learning! Then had their study and reading been to good purpose. How many perish by reason of vain learning of this
world, who take little care of the serving of God? And

because they rather choose to be great than humble, therefore they become vain in their imaginations.

He is truly great that is little in himself, and that maketh no account of any height of honour. He is truly wise that accounteth all earthly things as dung, that he may win Christ. And he is truly learned that doth the will of God, and forsaketh his own will.

Imitatio Christi

CAN THE SOUL FORETASTE ETERNAL BLESSEDNESS?

It hath been asked whether it be possible for the soul, while it is yet in the body, to reach so high as to cast a glance into eternity, and receive a foretaste of eternal life and eternal blessedness. This is commonly denied; and truly so in a sense. For it indeed cannot be so long as the soul is taking heed to the body, and the things which minister and appertain thereto, and to time and the creature, and is disturbed and troubled and distracted thereby. For if the soul shall rise to such a state, she must be quite pure, wholly stripped and bare of all images, and be entirely separate from all creatures, and above all from herself. Now many think this is not to be done and is impossible in this present time. But St. Dionysius maintains that it is possible, as we find from his words in his Epistle to Timothy, in which he saith, "For the beholding of the hidden things of God, shalt thou forsake sense and the things of the flesh, and all that the senses can apprehend, and that reason of her own powers can bring forth, and all things created and uncreated that reason is able to comprehend and know, and shall take thy stand upon an utter abandonment of thyself, and as knowing none of the aforesaid things, and enter into union with Him who is, and who is above all existence and all knowledge." Now if he did not hold this to be possible in this present time, why should he teach it and enjoin it on us in this present time?

But it behoveth you to know that a master hath said on this passage of St. Dionysius, that it is possible, and may happen to a man often, till he become so accustomed to it as to be able to look into eternity whenever he will. (For when a thing is at first hard to a man and strange, and seemingly quite impossible, if he put all his strength and energy into it, and persevere therein, that will afterwards grow quite light and easy which he at first thought quite out of reach, seeing that it is of no use to begin any work unless it be brought to a good end.)

And a single one of these excellent glances is better, worthier, higher, and more pleasing to God than all that the creature can perform as a creature. (And as soon as a man turneth himself in spirit, and with his whole heart and mind entereth into the mind of God which is above time, all that he hath lost is restored in a moment. And if a man were to do thus a thousand times a day, each time a fresh and real union would take place; and in this sweet and divine work standeth the truest and fullest union that may be in this present time. For he who hath attained thereto asketh nothing further, for he hath found the Kingdom of Heaven and Eternal Life on earth.)

Theologia Germanica

EXPERIENCE AT MANRESA

One day, as St. Ignatius Loyola knelt on the steps of the monastery reciting the Hours of the Blessed Virgin, the eyes of his mind were opened, and he saw the Most Blessed Trinity as it were under the likeness of a triple plectrum, or of three spinet-keys.

At another time, the manner of God's creating the world was most clearly presented to his thought. He seemed to see something white, and rays proceeded from it, and out of it God shed forth light. He could not find words to explain it fully, nor remember the images whereby God imprinted it on his soul.

He saw it once at Jerusalem, and again when walking near Padua, after the same fashion, without distinction of members, he saw the Blessed Virgin Mary. He was no little comforted by these visions and often thought that even if Scripture had not taught those mysteries of faith, he would have been resolved to die for them after what he himself had seen.

There also (at Manresa) it was that when he was at Mass in the monastery, and when the Body of the Lord was lifted up, he saw with his mind's eye an appearance as of white rays descending from on high. And, not withstanding that after so long a time he could not call to mind and explain how he saw it, yet this time he saw clearly, namely, in what manner Jesus Christ our Lord is present in the Most Holy Sacrament.

He went to pray in a church a little more than a mile distant from Manresa, dedicated, I think, to St. Paul. The road led thither along a river bank. And on his way, being intent on prayer, he sat down, facing the stream which was running deep. While he was sitting there the eyes of his mind were opened, not so as to see any kind of vision, but so as to understand and comprehend spiritual things such as those pertaining to the mysteries of the Faith . . . and this with such clearness that for him all these things were made new. Neither could he give a plain account of each of them separately which, though they were many, he had yet comprehended, for a brightness so clear and penetrating illumined the darkness of his mind that if all the enlightenment and help he had received from God in the whole course of his life down to this sixty-second year, and over, and everything he had learnt were gathered into one heap, these all would appear less than he had been given at this one time.

Saint Ignatius Loyola

INTO PARADISE

GOD'S PRESENCE IN THE SOUL

Even though I was aware that I had a soul, I neither appreciated its worth nor remembered the One who lived in it, because I had allowed my eyes to be blinded by the vain things of this life. Truly it is wonderful that He, who by His vastness could fill a thousand and more worlds, should constrict Himself within a space so narrow [as a human soul]. He is Master, and thus is free to act; loving us as no one does, He fits us to His measure. In the beginning, for fear the soul should be dismayed to see that a thing so worthless as itself can contain the Infinite One, He does not manifest Himself; then, by degrees, He dilates it, as far as is necessary for it to contain all He intends to infuse into it.

Saint Teresa of Avila

THE JOY-GIVING PERFECTION OF GOD

Thou, Eternal Trinity, art my creator, and I am the work of Thy hands, and I know through the new creation which Thou hast given me in the blood of Thy Son that Thou art enamoured of the beauty of Thy workmanship. Oh, Abyss! Oh, Eternal Godhead! Oh, Sea Profound! What more couldst Thou give me than Thyself? Thou art the fire which ever burns, without being consumed; Thou consumest in Thy heat all the soul's self-love; Thou art the fire which takes away all cold; with Thy light Thou dost illuminate me so that I may know all Thy truth; Thou art that light above all light which illuminates supernaturally the eye of my intellect, clarifying the light of faith so abundantly and so perfectly that I may see that my soul is alive, and in this light receive Thee—the true light.

Saint Catherine of Siena

THE CHANGING OF OUR VILE BODY

If what we preach about Christ, then, is that he rose from the dead, how is it that some of you say the dead do not rise again? If the dead do not rise, then Christ has not risen either; and if Christ has not risen, then our preaching is groundless, and your faith, too, is groundless. Worse still, we are convicted of giving false testimony about God; we bore God witness that he had raised Christ up from the dead, and he has not raised him up, if it is true that the dead do not rise again. If the dead, I say, do not rise, then Christ has not risen either; and if Christ has not risen, all your faith is a delusion; you are back in your sins. It follows, too, that those who have gone to their rest in Christ have been lost. If the hope we have learned to repose in Christ belongs to this world only, then we are unhappy beyond all other men. But no, Christ has risen from the dead, the firstfruits of all those who have fallen asleep.

I Corinthians 15, 12–20

The sun has its own beauty, the moon has hers, the stars have theirs, one star even differs from another in its beauty. So it is with the resurrection of the dead. What is sown corruptible, rises incorruptible; what is sown unhonoured, rises in glory; what is sown in weakness, is raised in power; what is sown a natural body, rises a spiritual body.

I Corinthians 15, 41–44

Here is a secret I will make known to you; we shall all rise again, but not all of us will undergo the change I speak of. It will happen in a moment, in the twinkling of an eye, when the last trumpet sounds; the trumpet will sound, and the dead will rise again, free from corruption, and we shall find ourselves changed; this corruptible nature of ours must be clothed with incorruptible life, this mortal nature with immortality. Then, when this corruptible nature wears its incorruptible garment, this mortal nature its immortality, the saying of Scripture will come true, Death is swallowed up in victory. Where then, death, is thy victory; where, death, is thy sting? It is sin that gives death its sting, just as it is the law that gives sin its power; thanks be to God, then, who gives us victory through our Lord Jesus Christ.

I Corinthians 15, 51–57

Do not be surprised at that; the time is coming, when all those who are in their graves will hear his voice and will come out of them; those whose actions have been good, rising to new life.

John 5, 28–29

The bread which comes down from heaven is such that he who eats of it never dies. I myself am the living bread that has come down from heaven. If anyone eats of this bread, he shall live for ever. And now, what is this bread which I am to give? It is my flesh, given for the life of the world.

John 6, 50–52

Thy brother, Jesus said to her, will rise again. Martha said to him, I know well enough that he will rise again at the resurrection, when the last day comes. Jesus said to her, I am the resurrection and life; he who believes in me, though he is dead, will live on, and whoever has life, and has faith in me, to all eternity cannot die. Dost thou believe this? Yes, Lord, she told him, I have learned to believe that thou art the Christ; thou art the Son of the living God; it is for thy coming the world has waited.

John 11, 23–27

I never think upon eternity without receiving great comfort. For I say to myself: how could my soul grasp the idea of everlastingness, if the two were not related in some way? But as soon as I feel how close the yearning of my heart follows upon the thought of eternity, my happiness becomes incomparably greater. For I am certain that, according to his nature, man can yearn only for that which can be attained. And so my yearning makes me certain that I shall reach eternity.

Saint Francis de Sales

O age! Blessed time of life, I salute you even now! Men are afraid of you, but they should love you as the most happy time of life because you are its end. I shall love you as the dawning of the eternal day. I can already see my temples growing white under the touch of your harbingers, and a smile rises to my lips.

Lucie Christine

Now behold round about you a countless throng that drink from the living forth-gushing fountain of the heavens as much as their hearts desire. See how they gaze at the pure and limpid mirror of sheer Godhood in which all things become manifest and are revealed to them.

Suso

If centres of gravity increase their power of attracting bodies when the bodies draw near to one another, we must believe that Divine Compassion puts forth greater strength in the last moments of our life, drawing us to

Him, as to our centre, although we have oft flown off at
tangents from the circumference.

Yves of Paris

Have pity upon every man, Lord, in that hour when
he has finished his task and stands before Thee like a
child whose hands are being examined.

Paul Claudel

LOSING OURSELVES IN GOD

Since, however, Scripture says God hath made all
things for Himself, it will certainly come to pass that the
creature will at one time or other conform itself to its Author and be of one mind with Him. We ought therefore
to be transformed into this same disposition of soul, so
that as God has willed that everything should be for Himself, so we too may deliberately desire neither ourselves
nor any other thing to have been in the past, or to be in
the future, unless it be equally for His sake, to wit, for His
sole will, not for our own pleasure. A need satisfied
(calmed by satisfaction), or good fortune received will
not delight us so much as that His will is seen perfectly
fulfilled in us and by us; which, too, is what we daily ask
in prayer when we say: Thy will be done on earth as it
is in heaven. O love, holy and chaste! O sweet and pleasing affection! O pure and undefiled intention of the will!
The more surely undefiled and purer, as there is mixed
with it now nothing of its own; so much the sweeter and
more pleasing, as its every feeling is wholly divine. To be
thus affected is to become one with God. Just as a little
drop of water mixed with a lot of wine seems entirely to
lose its own identity, while it takes on the taste of wine
and its colour; just as iron, heated and glowing, looks very
much like fire, having divested itself of its original and
characteristic appearance; and just as air flooded with
the light of the sun is transformed into the same splendour

of light so that it appears not so much lighted up as to be light itself; so it will inevitably happen that in saints every human affection will then, in some ineffable manner, melt away from self and be entirely transfused into the will of God. Otherwise how will God . . . be all in all, if in man there is left anything at all of man himself. The substance, indeed, will remain, but in another form, another glory, and another power (i.e. a man's human nature and individual identity will remain, transfigured). When will this be? Who will see this? Who will possess it? When shall I come and appear before the face of God? O Lord, my God, my heart hath said to Thee: My face hath sought Thee. Thy face, O Lord, will I still seek. Will I, do you think, see Thy holy temple?

Saint Bernard

THE END OF THE GAME

O God, how soon we shall be in eternity! There we shall know how little it has to do with all the affairs of this world, and how little it matters whether we succeeded in them or not. And yet now we trouble ourselves about them as though they were, heaven knows, how important! When we were little children, how busily we fetched pieces of brick and wood and clay to build a little house or a hut. And if someone had broken it up, how we should have wept! But now we know very well that all this trumpery was of small account. The same will come to pass in heaven when we know that all the troubles of this world were only childish matters. And yet I would not set aside all care for these fripperies, for God has assigned them to us so that we may practise our soul; but I should like to remove from this care all passion and violence. Let us be childish, since we are children! But let us not catch cold in so being, and if someone comes and breaks up our little house and crosses our plans, let us not be too grieved thereat. But when the evening comes that brings us rest, when death approaches, then the little house does not matter at all. For then we must enter the house of our Father. So attend faithfully to your affairs, but be assured that there is no affair as important as that of your salvation and that nothing is so necessary for your salvation as that you keep your soul on the path that leads to true blessedness in God.

Saint Francis de Sales

YOU SHALL BE UNAFRAID IN THE FACE OF DEATH

One of the dearest of the servant Suso's spiritual children lay dying. And when he heard that she would surely die and that she was afraid of death, he wrote her this letter to comfort her:

My child, would God that I, your faithful father, could die for you, my dear and good child. Though I do not die in the body, my heart is dying for the child I love in my heart. It is true that I am not with you in the body, but my heart is at your deathbed and weeps bitterly and makes constant lament. Give me your feeble hand. And, if God bids you, die gladly and be firm in the Christian faith. Rejoice that your beautiful soul, which is a pure and reasonable spirit shaped to the pattern of God, is to be released from its narrow and wretched prison, and will then joyfully savour its blessedness without any hindrance, for God Himself says: "There shall no man see me and live."

There is one thing that makes many an inexperienced person fear death, and makes death bitter, and that is if he reviews the years of his life and all his wasted days, and he feels he is greatly in debt to God so that he is at a loss as to what he shall do on the Day of Judgment. But from the Scriptures and from truth, I will show you a sure way to avoid this and to feel secure.

If you have ever sinned, and few people are without

sin, you shall not fear too much because of this at the hour of your death. If it has been possible for you to receive extreme unction, as is right and fitting, then do one thing: take the crucifix and gaze upon it and clasp it to your heart, and bend into the bleeding wounds of His unfathomable mercy, and implore Him to wash away all your misdeeds with the blood of His wounds in His divine strength, according to His glory and your needs, and then believe my words: according to the Christian faith that cannot deceive, you may be certain that you will be purified of all dross, and die serenely.

There is one more thing you must think of at that hour so that you may scorn death the more. For know, there is a country where, when a man is born, all his friends are wont to come together and weep and cry out and conduct themselves without restraint. But when he dies, they laugh and rejoice, and what they mean by this is that nobody knows the great misfortunes that are destined to some, and that is why they weep at birth. But when death puts an end to life they rejoice.

If one considers it rightly, one may call man's birth into this miserable world death, because of the toil and suffering that await him. Thus the death of the body may be called a new birth, because the heavy body sinks away, and there is nothing that blocks the path to eternal bliss. He whose eyes have been opened to see this truth, for him death will be easier. But he who cannot see this, his lament will be great and the death he knows nothing of will be the bitterer. Behold what unhappiness there is in this world, and what sorrow, and fear, and suffering wherever one turns! And if there were nothing but the timid body and the timid soul, and the inconstancy of this changing world, one would desire to leave it. A man will meet ten sorrows before he encounter one joy. Many a man, if he were asked, would say: I never had even one good day on earth. The world is full of snares, and deceit, and faithlessness. None can trust another, for every man seeks only his profit. Whoever desires to live long in order to increase his fortune, he cannot be certain whether it is his fortune that will increase or his debts that are already great. He has an abundance of fortune who is permitted to gaze upon the lovely and tender face of his beautiful Lord for ever and ever, and O delight! to live among the cherished denizens of heaven! Though the hour of death be sore and bitter, everyone must face it when his time is come. No man has ever evaded the hour of death. He who is not prepared to-day will be even less prepared to-morrow: the older the worse! One finds many more who become worse than such as become better. Though the presence of death be bitter, it does, indeed, put an end to all bitterness.

Therefore, my child, turn your heart, and hands, and eyes toward your heavenly home and greet it with an avid heart, and commend your will to the will of God. Let not your soul be troubled. Whatever He may have in store for you, be it life or death, accept it as what is best, since it comes from God. For, although you may not know it at the moment, it is best. Do not be afraid: the holy angels are around you and with you. God, who is gentle and compassionate, will help you out of your anguish as a father, if you only trust in His goodness.

Suso

SAINT FRANCIS' DEATH

Then, as the hour of his departure was fast approaching, he made all the Brethren that were in the place be called unto him and, consoling them for his death with words of comfort, exhorted them with fatherly tenderness unto the love of God. He spake long of observing patience, and poverty, and fidelity unto the Holy Roman Church, placing the Holy Gospel before all other ordinances. Then as all the Brethren sat around him, he stretched his hands over them, crossing his arms in the likeness of the Cross, for that he did ever love that sign, and he blessed all the Brethren present and absent alike, in the might and in the Name of the Crucified. He added, moreover, "Be strong, all ye my sons, in the fear of the Lord, and abide therein for ever. And since temptations will come and trials draw nigh, blessed are they who shall continue in the work that they have begun. I for my part make haste to go unto God, unto whose grace I commend you all." When he had made an end of gentle exhortations after this wise, this man most beloved of God asked them to bring him the book of the Gospels, and to read unto him from the Gospel according unto John, beginning at that place, "Before the feast of the Passover." Then he himself, as best he could, brake forth into the words of that Psalm, "I cried unto the Lord with my voice, with my voice unto the Lord did I make supplications," and went through even unto the end, saying, "The righteous shall compass me about, for Thou shalt deal bountifully with me."

At length, when all the mysteries had been fulfilled in him, and his most holy spirit was freed from the flesh, and absorbed into the boundless depths of the divine glory, the blessed man fell to sleep in the Lord. One of his Brethren and disciples saw that blessed soul, under the likeness of a star exceeding bright, borne on a dazzling cloudlet over many waters, mounting in a straight course unto heaven, as though it were radiant with the dazzling whiteness of his exalted sanctity, and filled with the riches of divine wisdom and grace alike, by the which the holy man was found worthy to enter the abode of light and peace, where with Christ he resteth for evermore. Moreover, a Brother named Augustine, who was then minister of the Brethren in Terra di Lavoro, a holy and upright man, having come unto his last hour, and some time previously having lost the power of speech, in the hearing of them that stood by did on a sudden cry out and say, "Tarry with me, Father, tarry for me; lo, even now I am coming with thee!" When the Brethren asked and marvelled much unto whom he thus boldly spake, he made answer, "Did you not see our Father, Francis, who goeth unto heaven?" And forthwith his holy soul, departing from the body, followed the most holy Father.

The Bishop of Assisi at that time had gone on pilgrimage unto the Oratory of St. Michael on Monte Gargano, and unto him the Blessed Francis, appearing on the night of his departure, said, "Behold, I leave the world and go unto heaven." The Bishop, then, rising at dawn, related unto his companions that which he had seen, and returned unto Assisi; there, when he had made diligent enquiry, he learnt of a certainty that in that hour whereof the vision notified him, the Blessed Father had departed from this world.

At the hour of the passing of the holy man, the larks—birds that love the light, and dread the shades of twilight—flocked in great numbers unto the roof of the house, albeit the shades of night were then falling, and wheeling round it for a long while with songs even gladder than their wont, offered their witness, alike gracious and manifest, unto the glory of the Saint, who had been wont to call them unto the divine praises.

Saint Bonaventure

THE DEATH OF BLESSED ANGELA OF FOLIGNO

About the Feast of the Nativity of our Lord Jesus Christ (at which time she passed away unto Christ), as she lay very sick, she said, "The Word is made Flesh," and after a long silence, as though she were returning from some other place, she said, "Oh, every creature faileth, and the whole of the angelic understanding sufficeth not to comprehend this." Then she added, "My soul is washed and cleansed in the blood of Jesus Christ, the which was as fresh and warm as though it had but this moment issued from the body of the Crucified."

After this she said: "Christ Jesus, the Son of God, hath

now presented me unto the Father, and these words have been spoken unto me—

"'Oh bride and fair one, oh thou who art beloved of Me with perfect love, of a truth I would not that thou shouldst come unto Me with these exceeding great sufferings, but I would thou shouldst come with the utmost rejoicing and with joy unspeakable, even as it is seemly that the King should lead home the bride, whom He hath loved so long, and clothed with the royal robe.'

"And he showed me the robe, even as the bridegroom showeth it unto the bride whom he hath loved a long time. It was neither of purple nor of scarlet, nor of sendal, nor of samite, but it was a certain marvellous light which clothed the soul. And then He showed unto me the Bridegroom, the Eternal Word, so that now I do understand what thing the Word is and what it doth mean—that is to say, this Word which for my sake was made Flesh. And the Word entered into me and touched me throughout and embraced me, saying, 'Come, My love, My bride, beloved of Me with true delight—come, for all the saints do await thee with exceeding great joy.' And He said again unto me, 'I will not commit thee in charge unto the blessed angels or other saints that they should lead thee unto Me, but I will come personally and fetch thee and will raise thee unto Myself, for thou hast made thyself meet for Me and pleasing unto My Majesty.'"

Now when she was nigh unto the time of her passing away (being the day before it), she did often repeat, "Father, into Thy Hands I do commend my soul and my spirit." Once, after repeating these words, she said unto us who were present:

"Now hath an answer unto those words been given unto me, and it is this: 'It is impossible that in death thou shouldst lose that which hath been impressed upon thine heart in life.'" Then did we say unto her, "Wilt thou, then, depart and leave us?" And she made answer: "A long time have I hidden it from you, but now will I con-

ceal it no longer. I say unto you that I must needs depart."

And upon that same day ceased all those sufferings with
which for many days previously she had been grievously
tormented in all her limbs, both within and without, and
afflicted in many ways. And she did then lie in such
repose of the body and cheerfulness of spirit that she appeared as though she already tasted somewhat of the joy
which had been promised unto her.

Then did we ask of her whether that aforesaid joy had
yet been granted unto her, and she replied that the
above-mentioned joy had commenced.

Anonymous

LETTER ON HIS FATHER'S DEATH

Let us regard death in the light of what the Holy Spirit
has taught us. We have the priceless advantage of knowing that truly and effectively death is a penalty of sin,
imposed upon man to expiate his crime, and needful to
man to purge him of his sin. For only death can free the
soul of the lust of the body without which even the saints
did not come into this world. We know that life, and the
life of Christians, is a continual sacrifice that ends only
with death. We know that when Jesus Christ came to
earth He considered Himself and offered Himself to God
as a holocaust and a true victim; that His birth, His life,
His death, His resurrection, His ascension and His
presence in the Eucharist, and His everlasting sitting at
the right side, are nothing but a sole and unique sacrifice.
We know that what happened in Jesus Christ must happen in all His members.

Let us, then, say that life is a sacrifice, and that the in-
cidents of life impress the Christian spirit only in so far as
they interrupt or accomplish this sacrifice. Let us call
evil only that which makes the victim of God a victim of

the devil, but let us call good that which makes the victim
of the devil in Adam the victim of God. And by this
standard let us examine the nature of death.

For this examination we must have recourse to the person of Jesus Christ, for everything that is in men is
abominable. Just as God regards men only through the
mediator, Jesus Christ, men also shall not regard others
or themselves save mediately through Jesus Christ. For
if we do not pass through this medium, we shall discover
in ourselves nothing but real calamities or abominable
pleasure. But if we consider all things in Jesus Christ, we
shall find every consolation, every satisfaction, every
edification.

Let us consider death in Jesus Christ and not without
Jesus Christ. Without Jesus Christ, death is horrible, it is
hateful, it is the horror of nature. In Jesus Christ it is quite
otherwise: it is something to be loved, it is holy, it is the
joy of the faithful. Everything is sweet in Jesus Christ,
even death, and this is why He suffered and died—to
sanctify suffering and death, and that, as God and as man
He was all great and all humble—to sanctify in Himself
all things excepting sin, and to be a pattern for all the conditions of life . . .

From the very moment we enter the Church, which is
the world of the faithful and particularly of the elect, the
world which Jesus Christ entered from the very moment
of His incarnation, by a special privilege of the only Son
of God, we are offered up and sanctified. This sacrifice
continues through life and ends with death, in which the
soul, leaving behind it all vices and love of earth, with
which it is ever contaminated during this life, puts an end
to its immolation and is received in the bosom of God.

Let us not grieve like the pagans who have no hope.
We did not lose our father at the moment of his death: we
lost him, as it were, when he entered the Church through
baptism. From that time on he belonged to God. His life
was vowed to God. His actions were concerned with this

earth only for the sake of God. In his death he detached himself wholly from his sins, and it is now that he is received by God, and that his sacrifice is accomplished and crowned.

Thus he performed what he vowed. He has finished the work that God assigned to him. He has accomplished the only thing for which he was created. The will of God is accomplished in him, and his will is absorbed in God.

Pascal

CONVERSATION WITH MONICA ON THE KINGDOM OF HEAVEN

When the day was approaching on which she was to depart this life—a day that You knew though we did not— it came about, as I believe by Your secret arrangement, that she and I stood alone leaning in a window, which looked inwards to the garden within the house where we were staying, at Ostia on the Tiber; for there we were away from everybody, resting for the sea-voyage from the weariness of our long journey by land. There we walked together, she and I alone, in deep joy; and *forgetting the things that were behind and looking forward to those that were before,* we were discussing in the presence of Truth, which You are, what the eternal life of the saints could be like, *which eye has not seen nor ear heard, nor has it entered into the heart of man.* But with the mouth of our heart we panted for the high waters of Your fountain, the fountain of the life which is with You: that being sprinkled from that fountain according to our capacity, we might in some sense meditate upon so great a matter.

And our conversation had brought us to this point, that any pleasure whatsoever of the bodily senses, in any brightness whatsoever of corporeal light, seemed to us not worthy of comparison with the pleasure of that eternal

Light, not worthy even of mention. Rising as our love flamed upward towards that Selfsame, we passed in review the various levels of bodily things, up to the heavens themselves, whence sun and moon and stars shine upon this earth. And higher still we soared, thinking in our minds and speaking and marvelling at Your works: and so we came to our own souls, and went beyond them to come at last to that region of richness unending, from which you feed Israel for ever with the food of truth: and there life is that Wisdom by which all things are made, both the things that have been and the things that are yet to be. But this Wisdom itself is not made: it is as it has ever been, and so it shall be for ever: indeed, "has ever been" and "shall be for ever" have no place in it, but it simply is, for it is eternal: whereas "to have been" and "to be going to be" are not eternal. And while we were thus talking of His Wisdom and panting for it, with all the effort of our heart we did for one instant attain to touch it; then sighing, and leaving the first-fruits of our spirit bound to it, we returned to the sound of our own tongue, in which a word has both beginning and ending. For what is like to Your Word, Our Lord, who abides in Himself for ever, yet grows not old and makes all things new?

So we said: If to any man the tumult of the flesh grew silent, silent the images of earth and sea and air: and if the heavens grew silent, and the very soul grew silent to herself and by not thinking of self mounted beyond self: if all dreams and imagined visions grew silent, and every tongue and every sign and whatsoever is transient—for, indeed, if any man could hear them, he should hear them saying with one voice: We did not make ourselves, but He made us who abides for ever: but if, having uttered this and so set us to listening to Him who made them, they all grew silent, and in their silence He alone spoke to us, not by them but by Himself: so that we should hear His word, not by any tongue of flesh nor the voice of an angel nor the sound of thunder nor in the darkness of a parable, but that we should hear Himself whom in all these things we love, should hear Himself and not them: just as we two had but now reached forth and in a flash of the mind attained to touch the eternal Wisdom which abides over all: and if this could continue, and all other visions so different be quite taken away, and this one should so ravish and absorb and wrap the beholder in inward joys that his life should eternally be such as that one moment of understanding for which we had been sighing—would not this be: *Enter Thou into the joy of Thy Lord?* But when shall it be? Shall it be when *we shall all rise again* and *shall not all be changed?*

Such thoughts I uttered, though not in that order or in those actual words; but You know, O Lord, that on that day when we talked of these things the world with all its delights seemed cheap to us in comparison with what we talked of. And my mother said: "Son, for my own part I no longer find joy in anything in this world. What I am still doing here and why I am here I know not, now that I no longer hope for anything from this world. One thing there was, for which I desired to remain still a little longer in this life, that I should see you a Catholic before I died. This God has granted me in superabundance, in that I now see you His servant to the contempt of all worldly happiness. What, then, am I doing here?"

Saint Augustine

A CHRISTIAN IS ONE OF THE EVERLASTING COMPANY

See what a noble principle faith is. Faith alone lengthens a man's existence, and makes him, in his own feelings, live in the future and in the past. Men of this world are full of plans of the day. Even in religion they are ever coveting immediate results, and will do nothing at all unless they can do everything—can have their own way, choose their methods, and see the end. But the Christian throws himself fearlessly upon the future, because he believes in Him which is, and which was, and which is to come. He can endure to be one of an everlasting company while in this world, as well as in the next. He is content to begin and break off; to do his part and no more; to set about what others must accomplish; to sow where others must reap. None has finished his work, and cut it short in righteousness, but He who is One. We, His members, who have but a portion of His fulness, execute but a part of His purpose. One lays the foundation, and another builds thereupon; one levels the mountain, and another "brings forth the headstone with shoutings . . ."

Does it not seem a very strange thing that we should be fed, and lodged, and clothed in spiritual things by persons we never saw or heard of, and who never saw us, or could think of us, hundreds of years ago? Does it not seem strange that men should be able, not merely by acting on others, not by a continued influence carried on through many minds in a long succession, but by one simple and direct act, to come into contact with us and, as if with their own hand, to benefit us, who live centuries later? . . .

Little by little the work of grace went forward; and they could afford to take time about it, and be at pains to do it best, who had a promise that the gates of hell should not prevail against it.

Cardinal Newman

THE LAST CLEANSING

The souls in purgatory, as far as I can understand the matter, cannot but choose to be there; and this by God's ordinance, who has justly decreed it so. They cannot reflect within themselves and say, "I have done such and such sins, for which I deserve to be here"; nor can they say, "Would that I had not done them, that now I might go to Paradise"; nor yet say, "That soul is going out be-

fore me"; nor, "I shall go out before him." They can remember nothing of themselves or others, whether good
or evil, which might increase the pain they ordinarily endure; they are so completely satisfied with what God has
ordained for them, that He should be doing all that
pleases Him, and in the way it pleases Him, that they
are incapable of thinking of themselves even in the midst
of their greatest sufferings. They behold only the goodness
of God, whose mercy is so great in bringing men to Himself, that they cannot see anything that may affect them,
whether good or bad; if they could, they would not be in
pure charity. They do not know that their sufferings are
for the sake of their sins, nor can they keep in view the
sins themselves; for in doing so there would be an act of
imperfection, which could have no place where there
can be no longer any possibility of actually sinning.

Once, in passing out of this life, they perceive why they
have their purgatory; but never afterwards, otherwise self
would come in. Abiding, then, in charity, and not being
able to deviate therefrom by any real defect, they have
no will, no desire, nothing but the will of pure love; they
are in that fire of purgatory by the appointment of God,
which is all one with pure love; and they cannot in anything turn aside from it, because as they can no more
merit, so they can no more sin.

I do not believe it would be possible to find any joy
comparable to that of a soul in purgatory, except the joy
of the blessed in Paradise—a joy which goes on increasing
day by day, as God more and more flows in upon the soul,
which He does abundantly in proportion as every hindrance to His entrance is consumed away. The hindrance
is the rust of sin; the fire consumes the rust, and thus the
soul goes on laying itself open to the Divine inflowing.

It is as with a covered object. The object cannot respond to the rays of the sun, not because the sun ceases
to shine—for it shines without intermission—but because
the covering intervenes. Let the covering be destroyed,
again the object will be exposed to the sun, and will an-

swer to the rays which beat against it in proportion as the work of destruction advances. Thus the souls are covered by a rust—that is, sin—which is gradually consumed away by the fire of purgatory; the more it is consumed, the more they respond to God, their true Sun; their happiness increases as the rust falls off, and lays them open to the Divine ray; and so their happiness grows greater as the impediment grows less, till the time is accomplished. The pain, however, does not diminish, but only the time of remaining in that pain. As far as their will is concerned, these souls cannot acknowledge the pain as such, so completely are they satisfied with the ordinance of God, so entirely is their will one with it in pure charity. On the other hand, they suffer a torment so extreme that no tongue could describe it, no intellect could form the least idea of it, if God had not made it known by special grace; which idea, however, God's grace has shown my soul; but I cannot find words to express it with my tongue, yet the sight of it has never left my mind. I will describe it as I can: they will understand it whose intellect the Lord shall vouchsafe to open.

Saint Catherine of Genoa

EPITAPH

Here halt, I pray you, make a little stay,
O wayfarer, to read what I have writ,
And know by my fate what thy fate shall be.
What thou art now, wayfarer, world-renowned,
I was: what I am now, so shalt thou be.
The world's delight I followed with a heart
Unsatisfied: ashes am I, and dust.

Wherefore bethink thee rather of thy soul
Than of thy flesh:—this dieth, that abides.
Dost thou make wide thy fields? in this small house
Peace holds me now: no greater house for thee.

Wouldst have thy body clothed in royal red?
The worm is hungry for that body's meat.
Even as the flowers die in a cruel wind,
Even so, O flesh, shall perish all thy pride.

Now in thy turn, wayfarer, for this song
That I have made for thee, I pray you, say:
"Lord Christ, have mercy on Thy servant here,"
And may no hand disturb this sepulchre,
Until the trumpet rings from heaven's height,
"O thou that liest in the dust, arise,
The Judge of the unnumbered hosts is here!"

Alcuin was my name: learning I loved.
O thou that readest this, pray for my soul.

*Here lieth the Lord Abbot Alcuin of blessed memory,
who died in peace on the nineteenth of May, 804. And
when ye have read this, do ye all pray for him and say
"May the Lord give him eternal rest." Amen.*

Alcuin

HOLY, STRONG, IMMORTAL ONE

The heaven which so many lights made beautiful
from the deep mind which rolleth it,
taketh the image and thereof maketh the seal.

And as the soul within your dust, through
members differing and conformed to divers
powers, doth diffuse itself,

so doth the Intelligence deploy its goodness,
multiplied through the stars, revolving still
on its own unity.

Dante

GOD IS A LIVING GOD

God possesses life in the most perfect degree. A being
lives insofar as it acts of itself, without receiving movement from another cause; and the more it eminently possesses this spontaneity of action, the more is perfect life in
it. With regard to movement three things succeed each
other in action: first, the end moves the agent; then the
agent operates through its form and communicates its
efficaciousness to the instrument; then, at last, the instrument, which acts not through its form but through another
power, accomplishes the action. This being established,
let us say that certain beings do not move themselves in
respect to any form or end, but only to the execution of

the movement: such are plants, which move themselves, according to their inherent nature, only in the execution of the movements of growth and decay.

Other beings possess self-movement, not only regarding the execution of the movement, but also regarding the form which in them is the principle of action, and which they acquire by their own efforts: such are animals, with whom movement has its principle in the form given to them, not by nature, but by the senses. Thus, the more the nervous system is developed in animals, the more their movement is perfect. Those which have nothing but the sense of touch are limited to movements of expansion and contraction, such as the oyster, which is hardly above plants; those animals which, endowed with all the senses, are able to know far away objects as well as those they touch, possess local movement.

But if these animals receive through the senses the form which in them is the principle of movement, they nevertheless cannot propose to themselves the end of their action: nature imperiously marks out for them the goal they must attain, and instinct moves them to act according to the impressions they receive from the outside. We thus must place above these animals those that move themselves with regard to the end they propose themselves. This deliberate movement implies the existence of reason, for reason alone can know the relation between cause and effect; she alone can proportion means to an end. It thus appears that the most developed life is that where intelligence is found. Why? because in that case the power of self-movement is most perfect. Take man: in him the mind moves the sensitive faculties, and the sensitive faculties move the organs that execute movement: in the same way art rules the form of the palace, for instance, and the architect commands the working-men who execute its construction.

Yet if our intellect most often finds in itself the principle of its actions, it sometimes suffers impulses from nature: thus first principles bring about the assent of the intellect, and our last end has need of its will: the intellect moves itself with respect to some things, but it is moved by another power with respect to others. Thus if there existed a being whose being would be its knowledge, and which had of itself all that it has essentially, this being would possess life in the highest degree. Such a being is God; thus God has life in a supereminent manner. The Philosopher, therefore, after having shown that God is intelligent, concludes that He has perfect and eternal life, because His intelligence is always in act, and contains all perfections.

Saint Thomas Aquinas

GOD'S BIRTH IN US

I have been asked what God is doing in heaven. I answer He has been giving His Son birth eternally, is giving birth now and will go on giving birth for ever, the Father being in childbed in every virtuous soul. Blessed, thrice blessed is the man within whose soul the heavenly Father is thus brought to bed. All she surrenders to Him here she shall enjoy from Him in life eternal. God made the soul on purpose for her to bear His one-begotten Son. His ghostly birth in Mary was to God better pleasing than His nativity of her in flesh. When this birth happens nowadays in the good loving soul it gives God greater pleasure than His creation of the heavens and earth.

Meister Eckhart

THE SON IS BORN IN US

To-day the church celebrates three births, each of which is such a source of joy and delight that we should break forth into jubilation, love and thanksgiving, and whoever does not feel such sentiments should mistrust himself. The first birth and the most sublime is that whereby the

Heavenly Father begets His only Son in the Divine essence, and in the distinction of the Divine persons. The second birth is that which made Mary a mother in virginity most pure and inviolate. The third is that by which every day and every hour God is truly and spiritually begotten in our souls by grace and love. These three births are shown forth by the three masses of Christmas Day. The first is sung at midnight, commencing with the words: "Thou art My Son; this day have I begotten Thee" (*Psalm* 2, 7), that is to say in eternity.

This brings home to us the hidden birth accomplished in the darksome mystery of the inaccessible Divinity. The second mass begins with these words: "To-day light has shined upon us" (*Isaias* 9, 2). It figures the glory of human nature Divinely influenced by its union with the Word. That mass is celebrated partly in the night and partly in the day, because the birth it represents is partly known to us and partly unknown. The third mass is sung in the daytime, and begins with the words: "A Child is born to us, and a Son is given to us." It figures that mysterious birth which should happen, and does happen, every day and every instant in holy souls, when they dispose themselves for it by deep attention and sincere love; for one can never experience that birth except by the recollection of all one's powers. In that nativity God belongs to us and gives Himself to us so completely that nothing whatever is more our own than He is. And that is what those words say to us: "A Child is born to us, and a Son is given to us." He is, therefore, our own; He is ours totally and everywhere, for He is always being begotten within us.

Let us speak first of the ineffable birth represented by the third mass of Christmas, and let us explain how it may be brought about in us in a manner the most perfect and efficacious. To that end let us consider the qualities of that first generation, by which the Father begets the Son in eternity. The ineffable riches of the Divine good are so overflowing that God cannot contain Himself, and by His very nature He is forced to expend and communicate Himself. "It is God's nature to expend Himself," says St. Augustine. The Father has thus poured Himself out into the other two Divine persons; after that He communicated Himself to creatures. The same saint says further: "It is because God is good that we are good, and all the good that the creature has is good with the essential goodness of God." What, then, is the peculiar character of the Divine generation? The Father, inasmuch as He is Father, turns inward to Himself and His Divine intelligence; He sees Himself and penetrates Himself with a gaze which wholly embraces His Divine essence, and then, just as He sees and knows Himself, so does He utter Himself completely; and the act whereby He knows Himself and the Word whereby He utters Himself is also the act whereby He begets His Son in eternity.

Thus the Father Himself remains within Himself in the unity of His essence, and goes out of Himself in the distinction of persons. Again He returns into Himself, and therein He rests in unspeakable self-delight, and that self-delight goes forth and overflows in ineffable love, which is the Holy Spirit. Thus does God dwell within Himself and go forth out of Himself to return again into Himself. Therefore is all outgoing for the sake of ingoing again. And hence in the material universe is the movement of the heavenly spheres most noble and most perfect, because it unceasingly returns again to the origin and beginning from which it first set forth. And so also is the course of man ever noblest and most perfect when it returns again upon its source and origin.

The quality which the Heavenly Father has in this His incoming and outgoing, the same should every man have who will become the spiritual mother in this divine bringing forth. He must enter wholly into himself, and again go out of himself; as the soul has three noble powers, wherein it is the true image of the blessed Trinity—memory, understanding, and free will. Through these powers is the soul capable of receiving and clinging to God, and all that God is, has, and can bestow, and in this way it can

gaze upon Him in eternity. For the soul is created between
time and eternity; with its superior part it belongs to
eternity, and with the inferior—the sensitive, animal powers
—it belongs to time.

But both the higher and lower powers of the soul wander away into time and into the fleeting things of time,
and this is because of the kinship between its higher and
lower powers. Very easy is it in this straying thus to go
astray from eternity. If we would be born again with the
Divine birth, then we need to start back again, earnestly
struggle inward and there gather up all our powers, lower
and higher, if we would restore all dissipation of mind to
unity, since united forces are ever the strongest, and they
become united when drawn back from multiplicity. When
a hunter would hit the mark he shuts one eye in order
that with the other he may look straighter; when one
would think deeply about anything, he closes all his senses
and unites all his powers in his inmost soul, out of which,
as branches from a tree, all the senses go forth into activity. When all our powers of sense and motion are thus
by an inward movement assembled together in the highest
power, which is the force and foundation of them all, then
happens an outward, yea, an overflowing movement, beyond and above self, by which we renounce all ownership
of will, of appetite, and of activity. There remains for thee,
then, only a pure and clear intention to be of God and of
God's purposes, to be nothing whatever of self, or ever
to become anything of self, to be for Him alone, to give
room to Him alone, whether in things high or low, so that
He may work His will in thee and bring about His birth in
thee, and therein remain unhindered by thee to the end.

If two are to be made one, then must one stand passive
and the other active. If my eye is to receive an image,
it must be free from all other images; for if it already has
so much as one, it cannot see another, nor can the ear
hear a sound if it be occupied with one already. Any
power of receiving must first be empty before it can receive anything. Hence St. Augustine says: "Empty thyself

if thou wouldst be filled. Go forth, if thou wouldst enter in." And elsewhere he says: "O noble soul, O noble creature of God, wherefore goest thou outside thyself in search of Him who is always and most certainly within thee, and through whom thou art made a partaker of the divine nature? What hast thou to do or why dost thou concern thyself with creatures?"

When a man thus clears the ground and makes his soul ready, without doubt God must fill up the void. The very heavens would fall down to fill up empty space, and much rather will God not allow thee to remain empty, for that would be against His nature, His attributes; yea, and against His justice. If, therefore, thou wilt be silent, the Word of this Divine birth shall speak in thee and shall be heard; but, if thou speakest, be sure He will be silent. Thou canst not serve the Word better than by being silent and by listening. If thou goest out of self, He without doubt goeth in, and so it will be much or little of His entering in, according to much or little of thy going out.

An illustration of this going out of self is given in the book of Moses, how God made Abraham go forth from his country and his kinsfolk, so that He might show him all good things. The Divine birth in the soul of man—that means certainly all good things, and that alone is its meaning. The country or region out of which the soul must go—that means the body, with its lusts and concupiscences of whatever kind. The friends he must have—these are his inclinations and the sensitive or sensible powers with their images, which draw him on and fasten him down. These set love and pain in motion, joy and sorrow, longing and dread, care and frivolity. These friends are very near akin to us; against them we must be strictly on our guard if we would wholly elude them, and if we would have born in us the all-good that this Divine birth really is for us. A proverb says: A boy kept too much at home behaves like a calf when away from home, which means that men who have not gone beyond their natural life, nor raised themselves above what the senses furnish to be seen, heard, tasted, moving about—men who have thus never gone forth from this the native home of all sensible life, are veritable animals when there is question of understanding the high things of God. Their interior being is like a mountain of iron, in which no gleam of light ever shines. When outward things and images and forms are gone, they no longer know and feel anything. They are, indeed, at home; but for that very reason they do not experience this wonderful resignation. Therefore did Christ say: "If any man come to Me and hate not his father, and mother, and wife, and children, and brethren, and sisters, yea, and his own life also, he cannot be My disciple" (*Luke* 14, 26).

We have so far spoken of the first and last births, and how by the last we learn a lesson about the first. And now we shall instruct you about the second birth, in which this night the Son of God is born of His mother and becomes our Brother. In eternity He was born a Son without a mother, and in time He was born a Son without a father. Now, Saint Augustine tells us: "Mary is much more blessed because God was born spiritually in her soul than because He was born her fleshly Son." Now, whosoever would experience this spiritual and blessed birth in his soul, as Mary did in her soul, should consider the qualities of Mary, that mother of God both fleshly and spiritual. She was a virgin, all chaste and pure, and yet she was retired and separated from all things, and so the angel found her. It is thus that one must be who would bring forth God in his soul. That soul must be chaste and pure. If it has strayed away from purity, then must it come back and be made pure again; for the meaning of virginity in this teaching is to be outward unfruitful and inwardly very fruitful. And this virgin soul must close its outward senses, having little external occupation, for from such it can have little fruit. Mary thought of nothing else but of Divine things. Inwardly the soul must have much fruit; the beauty of the King's daughter is all within. Hence must this virgin soul live in detachment in all its habits, senses, behaviour, in all its speech. Thus will it bear many and great fruits, namely, God's Son, God's Word, who is all in all and contains all things in Himself.

Mary was a wedded virgin, and so must the soul be wedded, as St. Paul teaches. Thou must sink thy fickle will deep into the Divine will, which is immovably steadfast, so that thy feebleness may be strengthened. Mary lived retired, and so must the soul espoused to God be in retirement, if it will experience the interior regeneration. But not alone from those wanderings after temporal things which appear to be faulty, but even from the sensible devotion attached to the practice of virtue must the soul refrain. It must establish rest and stillness as an enclosure in which to dwell, hiding from and cutting off nature, and the senses guarding quiet and interior peace, rest, and repose. It is of this state of the soul that we shall sing next Sunday in the introit of the mass: "While all things were in quiet silence, and the night was in the midst of her course, Thine Almighty Word, O Lord, came down from Heaven, out of Thy royal throne" (*Wisdom* 18, 14–15). That was the Eternal Word going forth from the Father's heart. It is amid this silence, when all things are hushed in even eternal silence, that in very truth we hear this Word; for when God would speak thou must be silent. When God would enter in, all things must go out. When our Lord entered Egypt, all the idols in the land fell down. However good or holy anything may seem, if it hinders the actual and immediate Divine generation in thee it is an idol. Our Lord tells us that He has come bringing a sword, cutting off all that clings to men, even mother, brother, sister; for whatever is intimately joined to thee without God is thy enemy, forming, as it does, a multitude of imaginations covering and hiding the Divine Word.

Although this tranquillity may not as yet wholly possess thee, nor last all the time within thee, yet thou shouldst so constantly cultivate interior silence as a means of experiencing the Divine birth that it shall finally become a spiritual habit. What is easy to a well-practised man may seem impossible to an unpractised one, for practice makes perfect. May God grant us all the grace of inner stillness, and thereby the birth of His Divine Word in our souls. Amen.

Blessed John Tauler

WHAT IS ETERNITY?

For if eternity and time be well considered, time never to be extant without motion, and eternity to admit no change, who would not see that time could not have being before some movable thing were created; whose motion and successive alteration (necessarily following one part another) the time might run by? Seeing, therefore, that God, whose eternity alters not, created the world and time, how can He be said to have created the world in time, unless you will say there was something created before the world, whose course time will follow? And if the holy and most true Scriptures say that "In the beginning, God created heaven and earth," to wit, that there was nothing before then, because this was the beginning, which the other should have been if aught had been made before, then verily the world was made from time, and not in time, for that which is made in time is made both before some time and after some. Before it is time past, after it is time to come: but no time passed before the world, because no creature was made by whose course it might pass. But it was made with the time if motion be time's condition, as that order of the first six or seven days went, wherein it were counted morning and evening until the Lord fulfilled all the work upon the sixth day, and commended the seventh to us in the mystery of sanctification. Of what fashion those days were it is either exceeding hard, or altogether impossible, to think, much more to speak.

Saint Augustine

IN PARADISUM DEDUCANT TE ANGELI

FUNERAL SERVICE

May the Angels lead thee into paradise,
may the martyrs receive thee at thy coming
and take thee to Jerusalem, the holy city.
May the choirs of the angels receive thee
and mayest thou with the once poor Lazarus
have rest everlasting.

Roman Ritual

The Lord is my shepherd; I shall not want.
He maketh me to lie down in green pastures;
He leadeth me beside the still waters.
He restoreth my soul;
He guideth me in straight paths for His name's sake.
Yea, though I walk through the valley of the shadow of
　　　death,
I will fear no evil,
For thou art with me;
Thy rod and thy staff, they comfort me.
Thou preparest a table before me in the presence of mine
　　　enemies;
Thou hast anointed my head with oil; my cup runneth
　　　over.
Surely goodness and mercy shall follow me all the days of
　　　my life;
And I shall dwell in the house of the Lord for ever.

Psalm 23

And a great wall was raised high all round it, with twelve gates, and twelve angels at the gates, and the names of the twelve tribes of Israel carved on the lintels.

Apocalypse 21, 12

And the twelve gates were twelve single pearls, one pearl for each gate; and the street of the city was of pure gold, that seemed like transparent glass. I saw no temple in it; its temple is the Lord God Almighty, its temple is the Lamb. Nor had the city any need of sun or moon to show in it; the glory of God shone there, and the Lamb gave it light. The nations will live and move in its radiance; the kings of the earth will bring it their tribute of praise and honour. All day the gates will never be shut (there will be no night there).

Apocalypse 21, 21–25

There will be no more night, no more need of light from lamp or sun; the Lord God will shed his light on them, and they will reign for ever and ever.

Apocalypse 22, 5

I, Jesus, have sent my angel to give you the assurance of this in your churches; I, the root, I, the offspring of David's race, I, the bright star that brings in the day. The Spirit and my bride bid me come; let everyone who hears this read out say, Come. Come, you who are thirsty, take, you who will, the water of life; it is my free gift.

And he who gives this warning says, Indeed, I am coming soon. Be it so, then; come, Lord Jesus.

Apocalypse 22, 16–17, 20

THE EPISTLE OF THE ASSUMPTION

In all things I have sought rest,
and I shall abide in the inheritance of the Lord.

Then the Creator of all things directed me
and spoke to me;
and He who made me rested in my house,
and He said to me:
Abide in Jacob and be an heir in Israel,
and take root among my chosen ones.
And so I am established in Sion
and in the holy city I have also found my rest,
and in Jerusalem my strength.
And I have taken root in an honourable people,
and the portion of God is
His inheritance to me,
and my abode is in the company
of all the saints.
I have been exalted as a cedar in Libanus
and as a cypress on Mount Sion
I have been exalted as a palm tree in Cades
and as a rose garden planted in Jericho.
I have been exalted as a splendid
olive in an open field,
and I have been exalted as a plane tree
by the water ways along the city streets.
I have breathed forth fragrance as of
balsam and cinnamon;
I have exhaled the sweetness of the
choicest myrrh.

Ecclesiasticus 24, 11–13, 15–20

THE CITY OF GOD

But that which is the house of God is also a city. For
the house of God is the people of God; for the house of
God is the temple of God. And what doth the Apostle say?
The temple of God is holy, which are ye. But all the faithful who are the house of God are not only those who now
exist, but those also who have been before us and have
already slept, and those who are to come after us, untc

the world's end. Innumerable hosts of the faithful gathered into one body, but counted by the Lord of whom the Apostle said, The Lord knoweth them that are His; those grains which as yet groan among the chaff, which will constitute one mass, when the floor shall in the end have been winnowed; the whole number of faithful Saints, destined to be changed from the human state that they may become equal with the Angels of God; themselves, joined unto the Angels, who are no longer pilgrims, all make together one house of God, and one city.

Saint Augustine

IS THIS THE JOY?

My God and my Lord, my hope and the joy of my heart, speak unto my soul and tell me whether this is the joy of which Thou tellest us through Thy Son: Ask and ye shall receive, that your joy may be full. For I have found a joy that is full and more than full. For when heart, and mind, and soul, and all the man are full of that joy, joy beyond measure will still remain. Hence, not all of that joy shall enter into those who rejoice; but they who rejoice shall wholly enter into that joy.

Show me, O Lord, show Thy servant in his heart whether this is the joy into which Thy servants shall enter who shall enter into the joy of their Lord. But that joy, surely, with which Thy chosen ones shall rejoice, eye hath not seen nor ear heard, neither has it entered into the heart of man in this life, how far they shall know Thee, and how much they shall love Thee in that life.

I pray, O God, to know Thee, to love Thee, that I may rejoice in Thee.

Saint Anselm of Canterbury

LIKE THE BURSTING OF A DYKE

When a soul has been long in sorrow . . . God establishes it in peace . . . This peace comes like a river whose course flowed through one country and then was turned aside into another, as if by the bursting of a dyke. Upon entering, this peace produces what is not proper to it, that is to say very great vehemencies, and it only belongs to the peace of God to do this. It alone can march in such trappings, like the noise of the sea which comes not to ravage the earth but to fill the breadth of the bed that God has given to it. This sea comes as though untamed and with roarings, even though it is tranquil: the abundance of the waters alone makes this noise, and not their fury. . . . The sea in its plenitude comes to visit the earth and to kiss the shores given it by God for its bournes. This sea comes in majesty and in magnificence. So also peace comes into the soul, when the grandeur of peace comes to visit it after anguish, without there being even a breath of wind to make thereon a ripple. This divine peace, which brings with it God's goods and the riches of His Kingdom, also has its forerunners, the halcyons and birds which mark its coming: such are the visits of the angels which precede it. It comes like an element from the other life, with a sound of celestial harmony, and with such strictness that the soul itself thereby is quite overcast, not by opposition to its good, but by abundance. This abundance does no violence except against the obstacles to its good, and all animals that are not peaceful flee before the approach of this peace, and with it come all the good things promised to Jerusalem . . . cassia, amber, and other rarities upon its shores. Thus this divine peace comes with abundance and richness of good things and the precious riches of grace.

Father J. J. Surin

GIVE GOD MORE THAN THE DREGS OF LIFE

God is always ready to inspire strength and divine mercy to the sinner the instant he returns, even though he may have passed a lifetime in abominations and sacrilege. There is serious danger . . . in putting off repentance to the end of life, in giving God but the dregs . . . Nevertheless, He is so good as to receive us at whatever moment we turn to Him. I believe that the demerits of a man must be of the utmost to ensure his condemnation—of him who was created in His image and to enjoy His glory . . . we may have the best possible hopes of salvation in that it is the aim which God has set before Himself.

Yves of Paris

For all the long years of this present life disappear when you have regard to the eternity of the future glory: and all our sorrows vanish away in the contemplation of that vast bliss, and like smoke melt away and come to nothing, and like ashes are no more seen.

Cassian

SAINT FRANCIS ON PERFECT JOY

When as Saint Francis was going one day from Perugia to Saint Mary of the Angels with Brother Leo in the springtide, and the very bitter cold grievously tormented him, he called to Brother Leo that was going on before and said thus: "Brother Leo, though the Brothers Minor throughout all the world were great examples of sanctity and true edifying, nathless write it down and take heed diligently that not therein is perfect joy." And going on little further, Saint Francis called a second time: "O Leo, albeit the Brother Minor should give sight make straight the crooked, cast out devils, to hear, the lame to walk, the dumb to

speak, and (greater still) should raise them that have
been dead a four days' space, write that not therein is
perfect joy." And going on a little, he cried aloud: "O
Brother Leo, if the Brother Minor should know all tongues
and all sciences and all the Scriptures, so that he could
prophesy and reveal not only things to come but also the
secrets of consciences and souls, write that not therein is
perfect joy." Going on yet a little further, Saint Francis
called aloud once more: "O Brother Leo, thou little sheep
of God, albeit the Brother Minor should speak with the
tongue of angels, and know the courses of the stars and
the virtues of herbs; and though all the treasures of the
earth were revealed unto him and he understood the virtues of birds, and of fishes, and of all animals, and of men,
and of trees, and of stones, and of roots, and of waters,
write that not therein is perfect joy." And going on a little
further, Saint Francis cried aloud: "O Brother Leo, albeit
the Brother Minor could preach so well as to turn all the
infidels to the faith of Christ, write that not therein is perfect joy." And this manner of speech continuing for full
two miles, Brother Leo with much marvel besought him,
saying: "Father, I pray thee in the name of God that thou
tell me wherein is perfect joy." And Saint Francis thus
made answer: "When we come to Saint Mary of the Angels, all soaked as we are with rain and numbed with cold
and besmirched with mud and tormented with hunger,
and knock at the door; and the porter comes in anger and
says: 'Who are ye?' and we say: 'We be two of your
brethren'; and he says, 'Ye be no true men; nay, ye be
two rogues that gad about deceiving the world and robbing the alms of the poor; get ye gone'; and thereat he
shuts to the door and makes us stand without in the snow
and the rain, cold and a-hungered, till nightfall; if there-
withal we patiently endure such wrong and such cruelty
and such rebuffs without being disquieted and without
murmuring against him; and with humbleness and charit·
bethink us that this porter knows us full well and that G
makes him to speak against us; O Brother Leo, write

herein is perfect joy. And if we be instant in knocking and he come out full of wrath and drive us away as importunate knaves, with insults and buffetings, saying: 'Get ye gone hence, vilest of thieves, begone to the alms-house, for here ye shall find nor food nor lodging'; if we suffer this with patience and with gladness and with love, O Brother Leo, write that herein is perfect joy. And if we, still constrained by hunger, cold and night, knock yet again and shout and with much weeping pray him for the love of God that he will but open and let us in; and he yet more enraged should say: 'These be importunate knaves, I will pay them well as they deserve,' and should rush out with a knotty stick and taking us by the hood, throw us upon the ground and send us rolling in the snow and beat us with all the knots of that stick: if with patience and with gladness we suffer all these things, thinking on the pains of the blessed Christ, the which we ought to suffer for the love of Him: O Brother Leo, write that here and herein is perfect joy: then hear the conclusion of the whole matter, Brother Leo: Above all graces and gifts of the Holy Spirit, that Christ granteth to His beloved, is to overcome oneself, and willingly for the love of Christ endure pains and insults and shame and want: inasmuch as in all other gifts of God we may not glory, since they are not ours but God's; whence saith the Apostle: What hast thou that thou hast not received of God? And if thou hast received it of Him, wherefore boastest thou thyself as if thou hadst it of thyself? But in the cross of tribulation and affliction we may boast, since this is ours; and therefore saith the Apostle, I would not that I should glory save in the cross of our Lord Jesus Christ."

Fioretti

THE FACE OF GOD

vellous is Thy face, which a young
to imagine it, would conceive as a

youth's; a full-grown man, as manly; an aged man, as an aged man's! Who could imagine this sole pattern, most true and most adequate, of all faces—of all even as of each —this pattern so very perfectly of each as if it were of none other? He would have need to go beyond all forms of faces that may be formed, and all figures. And how could he imagine a face when he must go beyond all faces, and all likenesses and figures of all faces, and all concepts which can be formed of a face, and all colour, adornment, and beauty of all faces? Wherefore he that goeth forward to behold Thy face, so long as he formeth any concept thereof, is far from Thy face. For all concept of a face falleth short, Lord, of Thy face, and all beauty which can be conceived is less than the beauty of Thy face; every face hath beauty, yet none is beauty's self, but Thy face, Lord, hath beauty and this having is being. 'Tis therefore Absolute Beauty itself, which is the form that giveth being to every beautiful form. O face exceeding comely, whose beauty all things to whom it is granted to behold it, suffice not to admire!

In all faces is seen the Face of faces, veiled, and in a riddle; howbeit, unveiled it is not seen, until above all faces a man enter into a certain secret and mystic silence where there is no knowledge or concept of a face. This mist, cloud, darkness, or ignorance into which he that seeketh Thy face entereth when he goeth beyond all knowledge or concept is the state below which Thy face cannot be found except veiled; but that very darkness revealeth Thy face to be there, beyond all veils. 'Tis as when our eye seeketh to look on the light of the sun which is its face; first it beholdeth it veiled in the stars, and in colours and in all things that share its light. But then it striveth to behold the light unveiled, or goeth beyond all visible light, because all this is less than that which it seeketh. A man seeking to see a light beyond his seeing knoweth that, so long as he seeth aught, it is not that which he seeketh. Wherefore it behoveth him to go beyond all visible light. For him, then, who must go beyond all light, the place he entereth must needs lack visible light, and is thus, so to speak, darkness to the eye. And while he is in that darkness which is a mist, if he there knows himself to be in a mist, he knoweth that he hath drawn nigh the face of the sun; for that mist in his eye proceedeth from the exceeding bright shining of the sun. Wherefore, the denser he knoweth the mist to be, by so much the more truly doth he attain in the mist unto the light invisible. I perceive that 'tis thus and not otherwise, Lord, that the light inaccessible, the beauty and radiance of Thy face, may, unveiled, be approached.

Nicholas of Cusa

ACKNOWLEDGMENTS

My personal indebtedness in connection with this book is immense: had it not been for my ordinary, Mgr. Gerald Shaughnessy, Bishop of Seattle, who granted me a long furlough, I should never have been able to collect and organize these texts. My gracious host, Father George B. Ford, pastor of Corpus Christi Church in New York and Catholic Students' councilor of Columbia University, his friendly assistants and his household were patient, helpful and kind through ten pleasant and inspiring months in their model parish. Without them this book would never have materialized. I am also deeply indebted to the kindness of the librarians and their staffs at Columbia University, Manhattanville College, the Public Library of New York, and Union Theological Seminary.

I wish to express my thanks to Mr. Robert O'Donnell, who helped me in finding the texts in the best available translations, or in their original editions, and to Mr. John Coleman, who took over much of the burden of editorial work, revision of translations, etc.

A considerable part of this book contains new translations. Most of them were done by Carol North Valhope, who rendered into English prose and poetry by Angelus Silesius, Marguerite Teilhard de Chardin, St. Hildegarde of Bingen, St. Francis of Assisi, Suso, Mechtild of Magdeburg, Heinrich of Lauffenberg, Anonymous (p. 118), Anna of Munzingen, Meister Eckhart (p. 129 to p. 142), Pascal, The Book of the Poor in Spirit, Fénelon, St. Frances of

Rome, Blessed Angela of Foligno, Anna Katharina Emmerich, Father Léonce de Grandmaison, St. Maria Maddalena de' Pazzi, Gerlach Peters.—To Sister Madeleva, C.S.C., I am greatly indebted for translations from the Roman Breviary, the Monastic Breviary, the Roman Missal, Roman Pontifical, and Roman Ritual.—Dom Ansgar Nelson, O.S.B., kindly contributed translations from St. Gregory of Nyssa and Symeon the Younger.—The translations from St. Thomas Aquinas, Charles Péguy, of Pascal's Mémorial, and a piece by St. Teresa of Avila (p. 426) were done by John Coleman.

An excerpt from *The Life of St. Rose of Lima* was quoted in the translation by Marian Storm. The "Dies Irae" by Thomas a Celano was quoted in the translation by James Macmaster Codman. The poem on page 270 was translated by Father John La Farge, S.J. The poems on pages 176, 248, 252, 445 were translated by Helen Waddell.

To Joseph Bernhart's excellent work, *Der Stumme Jubel,* Anton Pustet, Salzburg, I owe the basic idea of this collection, which is an adaptation and variation of that book. For various other suggestions, I am indebted to Mr. Wystan H. Auden, Father Benedict Ehmann, Dom Richard Flower, O.S.B., Father John La Farge, S.J., Father Albert Le Roy, S.J., Mr. and Mrs. Jacques Maritain, Mrs. Elizabeth Mayer, Sister Mary of the Compassion, O.P.

The editor and Messrs. Burns Oates wish to express their gratitude to the publishers who have kindly given reprint permissions, as listed below in alphabetical order. Every effort has been made to determine the copyright owners, but circumstances at present have made communication not only difficult, but in some cases impossible. We offer our apologies, therefore, to those whose rights may appear to have been overlooked.

For quotations from:
The Whole Christ by E. Mersch, translated by J. R. Kelly, to the Bruce Publishing Co., Wisconsin.

St. John of the Cross, the Rede Lecture by E. Allison Peers, to the Cambridge University Press.

Grey Eminence by Aldous Huxley, to Chatto & Windus.

Liturgies Eastern and Western, edited by F. E. Brightman, to the Clarendon Press.

St. Catherine of Genoa, as related by Jean de Menasce, to *The Commonweal,* New York.

Medieval Latin Lyrics and *The Desert Fathers* by Helen Waddell; also *Western Mysticism* by Cuthbert Butler, O.S.B., to Constable.

Plotinus, translated by Stephen Luckenna and B. S. Page, to Sir Ernest Debenham, Bart.

St. Catherine of Siena, translated by Vida Dutton Scudder; *The Adornment of Spiritual Marriage* by Ruysbroeck, translated by Dom C. A. Wynschenk, edited by Evelyn Underhill; *The Vision of God* by Nicholas of Cusa, translated by Emma Gurney Salter; *The Divine Comedy* by Dante, translated by Cary; *City of God* by St. Augustine, translated by John Healey; *The Life of St. Francis* by St. Bonaventure, with an introduction by Thomas Okey, to Dent.

The Angelic Doctor; The Life and Thought of St. Thomas Aquinas, to the Dial Press, New York.

Lucie Christine's Spiritual Journal, edited by A. Poulain, to B. Herder Book Co., St. Louis, Missouri.

The Little Flowers of St. Francis, translated by the Franciscan Fathers and revised by Thomas Okey, to Hollis & Carter.

The Nun's Rule by Bishop Richard Poowe, to Kegan Paul.

Rorate Coeli, translated by Dom Godfrey Diekman, O.S.B., in the November 1941 issue of *Orate Frates,* to The Liturgical Press, Collegeville, Minnesota.

The Westminster Version of the Old Testament; We Have Been Friends Together by Raissa Maritain; and *Newman Synthesis,* edited by E. Przywara, to Longmans Green.

Fruit Gathering by Rabindranath Tagore; *Theologia Germanica,* edited by Dr. Pfeiffer, translated by Susanna

Winkworth; and *The Apostolic Fathers*, edited by J. B. Lightfoot, to Macmillan.

Letters and Instructions of St. Ignatius, to Manresa Press.

Revelations of Divine Love, by Juliana of Norwich, edited by Grace Warrack, to Methuen.

Spiritual Conferences of St. Francis de Sales, translated from the Annecy text of 1895 under the supervision of Abbot Gasquet and the late Canon Mackey; and *The Dialogue of St. Catherine of Siena*, translated by Algar Thorold, to the Newman Bookshop, Baltimore, Maryland.

John Donne, edited by John Hayward, to the Nonesuch Press.

Proslogium, Monologium of St. Anselm of Canterbury, translated from the Latin by Sidney Norton Deane, to the Open Court Publishing Co., Chicago, Illinois.

The Notebooks and Papers of Gerard Manley Hopkins; Poems of Gerard Manley Hopkins; and *Cardinal Newman* quoted from *The Oxford Book of Christian Verse*, to the Oxford University Press.

Sermons and Conferences by John Tauler, translated by Walter Elliott, to The Paulist Fathers, New York.

Introduction to a Devout Life by St. Francis de Sales, translated from the French, to Frederick Pustet, New York.

The Works of Plato, selected and edited by Irwin Edman, translated by B. Jowett, to Random House, New York.

True Life by Don Luigi Sturzo, to St. Anthony's Guild, Paterson, New Jersey.

The Westminster Version of the Psalter, translated by C. Lattey, S.J., to Sands.

Confessions of St. Augustine, translated by F. J. Sheed, and *Prayer and Intelligence* by J. & R. Maritain, translated by Algar Thorold, to Sheed & Ward.

Studies of the Spanish Mystics by E. Allison Peers; *Fifty Spiritual Homilies of St. Macarius the Egyptian*, edited by A. J. Mason; *Book of the Lover and the Beloved* by Ramon Lull, translated by E. Allison Peers; *Lit-*

erary History of Religious Thought in France by Henri Bremond; *On the Divine Names and the Mystical Theology* by Dionysius the Areopagite, translated by C. E. Rolt, to The Society for Promoting Christian Knowledge and The Sheldon Press.

On the Love of God by St. Bernard of Clairvaux, translated by T. L. Connolly, to the Spiritual Book Associates, New York.

The Interior Castle, and *The Way of Perfection* by St. Teresa of Avila, translated by the Benedictines of Stanbrook, revised by Dom Benedict Zimmerman, to Stanbrook Abbey.

Meister Eckhart by Franz Pfeiffer, translated by C. de B. Evans, to John M. Watkins.

INDEX OF AUTHORS AND SOURCES